AMERICAN ACCENT TRAINING: GRAMMAR

Ann Cook

BARRON'S

Dedication
This book is dedicated to my son and my brother.

Special thanks to Benjamin Ferguson, Bob Freud, Somluck Chumpiew,
Dr. Masaki O. Abe, Vasilika Kostofsky, and Voice TraxWest.com for the audio.

All inquiries should be addressed to:
Barron's Educational Series, Inc.
250 Wireless Boulevard
Hauppauge, NY 11788
www.barronseduc.com

ISBN-13: 978-0-7641-4288-8 (book only)
ISBN-10: 0-7641-4288-7 (book only)
ISBN-13: 978-0-7641-9651-5 (book and 2 CD set)
ISBN-10: 0-7641-9651-0 (book and 2 CD set)

Library of Congress Control Number: 2009927294

Printed in the United States of America
9 8 7 6 5 4 3

Table of Contents

Overview   **vi**
  What Is Grammar?   vii
    Simplified Terminology   viii
  Chapter Structure   viii
  Visual Grammar   x
  The Verb Map   xii
    Integrating Grammar and Speech   xiii
    Vowel Chart   xiii
    Sample Curriculum   xiv
  Tests   xv
    Where Do I Start?   xv
    Consonant Chart   xxiii
    Telephone Tutoring   xxiv

Chapter 1: Simple Nouns and Verbs   **1**
  Dictation   1
  Story   1
    Word Order and Story Order   2
    Intonation and Phrasing 3
  Pronunciation æ ä r th   3
  Word Connections   4
  Nouns Singular/Plural   7
  Pronunciation S / Z in Plurals   8
    A or The   9
    This / That / These / Those   9
  Phrasing   10
    Questions (Who / What)   11
    Pronouns   12
      Subject   12
      Object   13
    It or One   14
      Possessive   16
  Verbs Simple Present / Verb to Be   18
    Contractions   19
    Negatives   20
    Questions Y/N Subject ↻ 21
    Question Tags ↻   22
    Time Words   23
  Test   25
  Essay   27

Chapter 2: Modified Nouns and Main Verbs   **28**
  Dictation   28
  Story "The Incident in Venice"   28
    Intonation Staircase   29
    High Frequency Words   29
  Nouns and Pronouns   30
    Descriptions   30
    Compound Nouns   31

  Pronoun Review   32
  Prepositions of Location   33
  There Is / There Are   34
  Basic Conjunctions   35
  Verbs Simple Present / Main Verb   36
    Emphatic   40
    Can   41
    Infinitives (Have to Do, Need to Do)   41
    Negatives   42
    Contractions   43
    Questions Y/N ↻   43
    Question Tags ↻   46
    Imperatives (Go! Don't Go! Let's Go!)   48
  Test   49
  Essay   51

Chapter 3: Comparisons and the Past   **52**
  Dictation   52
  Story "Max's Diet"   52
  Accent Squeezed Out Syllables   53
  Nouns Singular and Plural   53
    A or The   54
    Comparisons   55
    Prepositions of Direction   58
  Verbs Simple Past   60
    Emphatic   62
    Negatives   62
    Negative Contractions   63
    Making Yes / No Questions About the Subject   64
    Question Tags ↻   66
    Middle "I" Pronunciation   68
    Get (phrasal verb)   68
    Time Words / Adverbs   70
  Test   71
  Essay   73

Chapter 4: Noun Countability and Continuous Verb Forms   **74**
  Dictation   74
  Story "The Windshield Incident" 74
    Pronunciation: Reduced Vowels   75
  Nouns Countable/Uncountable   76
    Much / Many   78
    Prepositions of Time   78
    Prepositions of Manner   79
    Jack and the Beanstalk (Modifiers)   79
  Accent Noun / Verb Intonation   80
    Reading Comprehension   81
  Pronunciation Th   82

Table of Contents

Accent Word Stress and Meaning 82
Verbs Continuous (Present / Past) 83
  Negative Contractions 85
  Questions 85
  Get with the Continuous (phrasal verb) 88
  Questions What / Who ↻ **Subject** 89
  Questions Y/N ↻ 90
  Questions 5 W ↻ **Object** 91
  How + Adjective ↻ 92
  How + Adverb + Adjective ↻ 92
Test 93
Essay 95

Chapter 5: Future Tense Comparisons and Modifiers 96
  Dictation 96
  Story "The Motorcycle Accident" 96
  Nouns Descriptions and Compounds 97
    Intonation 97
    Word Order 98
    More Conjunctions 100
    How Much / How Many / How Often ↻ 101
    Both / Each / Either / Too / Neither 104
    Forms of Use 105
    Countable / Uncountable 106
    Eureka (Modifiers / Articles) 108
  Verbs Simple Future (2 forms) 110
    Negatives 110
    Negative Contractions 111
    Two Futures (Will / Going to) 111
    Future Unreal Duo (If) 114
    Grammar in a Nutshell 115
    Do / Make 118
    Stand (phrasal verb) 119
  Test 121
  Essay 123

Midterm Exam 124

Chapter 6: Indirect Speech and the Unreal Duo 128
  Dictation 129
  Story "The Italian Incidents" 129
  Nouns 130
    Intro Phrases 130
    Noun Phrases (Joined with That) 130
    Noun Phrases (Indirect Speech) ↻ 131
    Noun Phrases (Indirect Questions) ↻ 132
    Question Review 134
    So / Such 135
  Verbs Present **Unreal** Duo (If) 135
    Hope and Wish 138
    Opinion Words (Probability) 139
    Opinion Words (Obligation) 140
    Three Verb Forms 141

Say / Tell / Speak / Talk 142
Verbs of Perception 143
  Look / See / Watch 143
  Hear / Listen 143
  Look / Appear / Seem / Feel 144
Take / Have 145
Take (phrasal verb) 145
Test 147
Essay 149

Chapter 7: Reverse Modifiers and Opinion Words 150
  Dictation 150
  Story "The Boy Who Cried Wolf" 150
  Pronunciation (What / But / That) 151
  Nouns Reverse Modifiers (That / Who) 152
    Compacting Sentences (That / Who) 154
    How Does It Work? 156
    5 Ws and How Review 157
    Some or Any 158
    Time Words 159
      During / While 160
      By / Until 160
      For / Since 161
      Ago / Before / In / After / Later 161
      Yet / Already / Still / Anymore 162
  Verbs Present **Real** Duo 163
    The V Sound 166
    There Is or It Has 166
    There Is or It Is 167
    Opinion Words with There 167
    Verb Review 169
    Present to Past Tense 170
    Tags 171
    Turn (phrasal verb) 172
  Test 173
  Essay 176

Chapter 8: Complex Intonation, the Past Unreal Duo, and the Causative 177
  Dictation 177
  Story "The Flower Incident" 177
  Nouns 178
    Common Courtesy 178
  Accent Empathy 180
  Pronunciation L & R 180
  Accent 2- to 5-Word Intonation 183
    How + Adjectives 186
    Adjective to Verbs (–en) 187
    Prepositions 189
  Verbs Past **Unreal** Duo 195
    Causative 198
  Test 201
  Essay 203

Chapter 9: Comprehension and Reported Speech 204
- **Dictation** 204
- **Story** "The Bodyguard Incident" 204
- **Nouns** Comprehension Exercises 205
  - Listening Comprehension 205
- Reading Comprehension 207
- Gin-Soaked Raisins 209
- **Verbs** Reported and Indirect Speech 212
  - Past **Unreal** Duo 213
  - Three Theres / Four 2s / Four Hads / Four Woulds / Seven Bes 214
  - Grammar in a Bigger Nutshell 218
  - Give 220
- **Test** 221
- **Essay** 223

Chapter 10: Comprehension and the Passive Voice 224
- **Dictation** 224
- **Story** "The Army Incident" 225
- **Accent** Nasal Consonants 225
  - The Held T 226

Nouns 227
- Only 227
- Doubt / Question 228
- Prefixes and Suffixes 229
Verbs Passive 232
- Six Useful Verbs 235
- Past Duo 235
- Future Real Duo 237
- Verb Review 238
Test 240
Essay 242
Outline Format 242
Writing Structure Checklist 243
Technical Editing Checklist 244

Final Exam 245

Answer Key 251

Grammar Glossary 279

Index 284

Overview CD 1 Track 1

Welcome to *American Accent Training: Grammar*. This book and CD set is designed to teach you to speak standard American English. Everything is explained and a complete answer key is provided in the back of the text. At any point, you can call (800) 457-4255 toll-free for support.

"I hate grammar. It's boring." CD 1 Track 2

Studying grammar rules is, for most people, not fun. This method stays as far away from memorization as possible, and lets you jump right into applying and using the techniques in actual speech. After all, in conversation, you're not going to think, "Was that modifier dangling?" or "Hmm, was that subjunctive pluperfect enough?"

"Is this just a grammar book?"

No, this isn't just a grammar book. You will learn vocabulary, sentence types, story order, logic, intonation, word connections, and pronunciation. Your comprehension and listening skills will become sharp and accurate. Your writing will become crisp and detailed, yet concise and to the point. When you apply all the techniques in this book, your writing and speaking will be fluent, logical, and easily understood.

"But I've already studied grammar . . ." CD 1 Track 3

Studying grammar in the traditional way doesn't do much for many students, and that's why we've come up with an entirely new approach. You know how when you're in a new town or in a shopping mall, there is a map on a pedestal with an arrow indicating "You Are Here"? The problem most students have is that they are literally lost in the language. They know some of the details, but they don't really know how the puzzle pieces fit together. In other words, they lack a good understanding of the big picture of English. This book provides a visual map, so you always know right where you are.

"English is too hard."

English has about half a million words, but nobody uses all of them. The average educated person only uses about 2,500 high-frequency words, most of which you already know. By starting with the basic structures presented here, along with the high-frequency vocabulary, you will quickly learn how to make simple, 100% accurate sentences. By gradually building on the perfect foundation with different vocabulary, you will soon be able to express yourself easily.

"I can't understand when Americans talk to me." CD 1 Track 4

Although this is a grammar book, it takes a singularly auditory approach. The exercises are also on the CDs, so you will learn to hear the sounds, rhythms, patterns, structures, and vocabulary of spoken American English.

"How long will this take?"

The amazing thing about this approach is, because you will quickly understand where you are in the language-learning process—*what you already know and what areas you still need to study*—you will be able to fill in the gaps in just a month or two.

"How do I know what to do?"

Clear instructions are given for each lesson. Each exercise is reviewed from seven different perspectives: vocabulary, grammar, word order, story order, intonation, word connections, and pronunciation. This is essentially the way you learned your first language as a child.

"Where am I now?"

It's natural to wonder where you are in something as big as a language, especially when it's your second language. To help with that, we use the simple icons ◀ ● ▶ to indicate where you are on the language map. (See page x.)

The structure of the chapters themselves also serves to orient you to what you already know, what there is to learn, and how the puzzle pieces fit together.

What Is Grammar? CD 1 Track 5

| American Logic |
| Story Order |
| Sentences |
| Words |
| ABCs |

Grammar is a combination of the eight parts of speech: *nouns, pronouns, adjectives, verbs, adverbs, prepositions, conjunctions*, and *interjections*. Think of these eight parts as the building blocks that you will use to construct your sentences.

We start out with a very simple three-block foundation (noun-verb-noun), and, bit by bit, you add blocks until you have a solid, well-constructed sentence. Our goal is clear, direct speech, not flowery language.

The starting point—the first two building blocks—are nouns and verbs. It's important to realize how many ways these two building blocks can be used.

How do we fit all the pieces together? The key to English grammar is the **nine-grid**. It is a synopsis of the most basic structures. Later, you will learn different structures, but if you master this form, you will always be able to communicate clearly and logically, both in speech and in writing.

Every Hollywood Movie!

	Noun	Verb	Noun
Beginning	Boy	meets	girl.
Middle	Boy	loses	girl.
End	Boy	gets	girl.

Dictation Placement Test CD 1 Track 6

Write down the following recording as accurately as possible on p. xxi. When you are finished, take the grammar placement tests and complete the initial writing sample.

Simplified Terminology

This book presents grammar and accent from a simplified perspective. For instance, you may know that **Bob sees Betty** is an SVO (Subject-Verb-Object) sentence, and that **Bob is late** is SVC (Subject-Linking Verb-Complement). However, our goal is not to create grammarians, but rather to get you to understand the basic structures in a simplified manner. To this end, both sentences fit in the nine-grid in the same way.

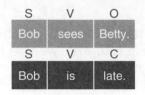

In the same vein, terms such as **intonation, pitch, pitch change, stress, the staircase, up and down, inflection, strong words, emphasis**, and **peaks and valleys** are all used to indicate that the speaker is highlighting one or two words in a sentence.

Chapter Structure

Each chapter has six sections.

The **Dictations** start out easy and get progressively more difficult. They are tied in to the grammar topic of each chapter. For example, the first dictation only uses the simple present tense of the verb **to be**, whereas the later ones use all of the structures presented up to that point. The dictations intentionally use contractions so that they resemble standard, colloquial speech. The audio is on the CDs.

The **Story** progresses from the simple nine-grid of the classic Hollywood movie plot to a complete story with various verb tenses and a wide range of sentence structures. It is about a quirky Italian bodybuilder named Max and recounts his life in California.

In each chapter, the **Nouns** section addresses nouns and noun-related concepts, such as *plurals, pronouns, prepositions, conjunctions, comparatives, superlatives, countable/ uncountable, articles, adjectives, compound nouns, word order*, and *reverse adjectives* (traditionally known as relative clauses).

One Noun, Many Uses

After you think about what a noun can do, you should turn your attention to *actions* (verbs).

The **Verbs** section covers all of the *tenses*, as well as *contractions, negatives, questions, adverbs, tag endings, phrasal verbs, main verbs, linking verbs,* and *verbs of perception,* as well as verbs that typically cause difficulty such as *do/make, take/have, get,* and so on. A visual verb map shows you where you are and what you need to learn (see page xii).

One Verb, Many Uses

In addition to getting as much speaking practice as possible, it's important for you **to learn to write** and **to write to learn**. At the end of each chapter are the **Test** and **Essay** sections. By taking the time to review what you have learned and putting your thoughts down on paper, you will assimilate the grammatical concepts and vocabulary into your writing.

Student's Before/After Writing Sample

The following is a writing sample from a student before he began using this book. The second sample represents his progress after three months of study.

Initial Writing Sample

I lives in San Luis Obispo . This isn't a big town but it so beatiful . It have alot of moutains,hills . We can hiking to the top for see over this town.Here not far from the beach it about 15 minutes drive to beach. So that it have many tourist visit here.In down town we have 2 book stores,fashion stores and restaurants. This town have 3 thai restaurants.

I like thai food restaurant more than another one.It address in down town and test is so delicious.Here we have down town market every thusday.This market have fresh fruit from farmmer dilect to customer.So I think here is a good choise if you wanted to take vacation,I would be your guide.

Three Months Later

Last weekend Steve and I did many things. At first we thought Steve would go to work, but it was raining, so he couldn't go. Saturday morning we went to the donut shop. After we got home we played the puzzle untill afternoon then we went to the beach. In the evening after dinner time we went to the gym. I worked out with the cardiomachine a little bit then I went to the pool, the hot tub and also the sauna. I was reading " a little princess" while I sat in the sauna room. Sunday morning we went to the donut shop again. Actually Steve like to have some sweet in the morning everyday, but we know it isn't good for his health, so he try to have it only the weekend. We were watching TV while we had donuts. Every sunday we have to clean the fish tank. We have 3 gold fish. All of them have a different color. One's gold another one's black and the last one's mix 2 color together (the gold and the back). There aren't different only the color but also diferrent in the charcter too. They are my good friend. They have been eating all the time, it made a lot of poo, so that their house need to be cleaned every week. After took care of our fish, we played the Video-games he's always win me. I had been practicing many times before I played with him, but I never won him. If I won, I would be happy. I believe if I keep go on practicing, I will win in one day.

Visual Grammar

The idea of a visual grammar is a very important aspect of our language-learning approach. The verb map that you'll see throughout this book is similar to the shopping mall map with a large **You Are Here** arrow.

When you start, you will be using the **simple present tense**. You will learn where the verb belongs in a simple sentence, how to conjugate verbs, and what supporting words go with a particular tense.

Throughout this book, the three symbols are ◀ **past**, ● **present**, ▶ **future**. Whenever you see the dot ●, you will know that you are dealing with some aspect of "now." The two triangles ◀▶ point in the relevant time direction.

Look at the chart below. If this were all you knew—but you used it perfectly every time —you would have a good start in English.

Simple Tenses Are Simple

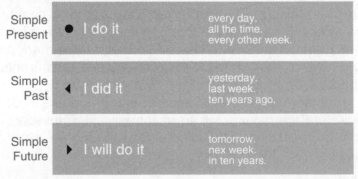

Simple Present	● I do it	every day. all the time. every other week.
Simple Past	◀ I did it	yesterday. last week. ten years ago.
Simple Future	▶ I will do it	tomorrow. nex week. in ten years.

Time relationships are very important in English. We are very interested in the sequence of events, as well as the dependence of one event on another.

After you work through the various aspects of the **simple** tenses, you will go on to the **duo** tenses. The main thing to remember is that there are always two related events with the duo tenses. The symbols are **present duo ◀●**, **past duo ◀◀**, and **future duo ▶▶**.

Notice that the present duo has both a past and a present symbol. This is because you are pulling the past up into the present time. Even if you don't mention the present, it is there. This is a difference between **I didn't do it** and **I haven't done it**. In the first example, the event is over. In the second example, however, there is a strong element of the present, as—even now—you may still do it.

Duo Tenses Are In **Pairs**

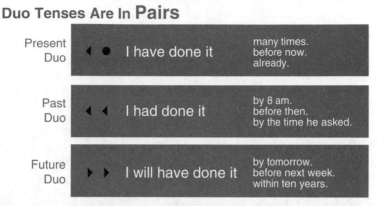

These are traditionally referred to as the perfect tenses.

Once you have a strong understanding of the difference between the **simple** and the **duo** tenses, you are ready to work on the **unreal duos**. You'll notice a black-to-white symbol change to reflect this unreal status. These tenses are called "contrary to fact" because they don't actually happen.

Duo Tenses Can Be **Unreal**

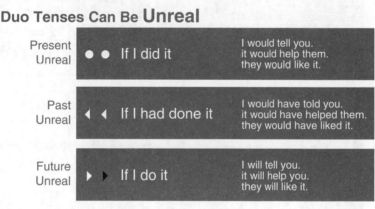

These are traditionally referred to as the subjunctive conditional, and they are sometimes considered a mood or mode rather than a tense.

Now, let's pull the three elements together into a verb map. This is a map of statements.

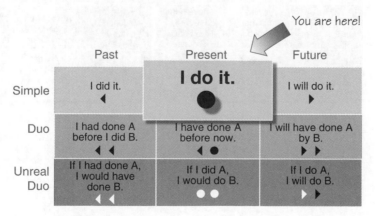

The Verb Map

When you have completed this book, you will be familiar with all of the components below. The **T formation** in each box indicates the more commonly used verb tenses.

Active

	Past	Present	Future
Simple	I did it. ◀	I do it. ●	I'll do it. ▶
Real Duo	I'd done A before I did B. ◀ ◀	I've done it. ◀ ●	I'll have done A before I do B. ▶ ▶
Unreal Duo	If I had done A, I would've done B. ◀ ◀	If I did A, I'd do B. ◀ ○	If I do A, I'll do B. ▷ ▶

To Be

	Past	Present	Future
Simple	I was there. ◀	I am there. ●	I'll be there. ▶
Real Duo	I had been there .... ◀ ◀	I've been here for an hour. ◀ ●	I will've been here for an hour .... ▶ ▶
Unreal Duo	If I had been there .... ◀ ◀	If I were there.... ◀ ○	If I'm there... ▷ ▶

Negative

	Past	Present	Future
Simple	I didn't do it.	I don't do it.	I won't do it.
Real Duo	I hadn't done A until I did B.	I haven't ever done it.	I won't have been doing A before I do B.
Unreal Duo	If I hadn't done A, I wouldn't have done B.	If I didn't do A, I wouldn't do B.	If I don't do A, I won't do B.

Continuous

	Past	Present	Future
Simple	I was doing it.	I am doing it.	I will be doing it.
Real Duo	I had been doing A before I did B.	I've been doing A for a long time.	I'll have been doing A for a while when I start B.
Unreal Duo	If I had been doing A, I would've been doing B.	If I were doing A, I'd be doing B.	If I'm doing A, I'm doing B.

Questions

	Past	Present	Future
Simple	Did I do it?	Do I do it?	Will I do it?
Real Duo	Have I done A before I did B?	Have I done it before?	Will I have done A before I do B?
Unreal Duo	If I had done A, would I have done B?	If I did A, would I do B?	If I do A, will I do B?

Modals

	Past	Present	Future
Simple	I had to do it.	I have to do it.	I'll have to do it.
Real Duo	I'd had to do A before I had to do B.	I've had to do A many times.	I'll have had to do A before I have to do B.
Unreal Duo	If I'd had to do A, I would've had to do B.	If I had to do A, I'd have to do B.	If I have to do A, I'll have to do B.

Causative

	Past	Present	Future
Simple	I had it done.	I have it done.	I'll have it done.
Real Duo	I'd had A done before I had B done.	I've had A done many times.	I'll have had A done by the time I have B done.
Unreal Duo	If I'd had A done, I would've had B done.	If I had A done, I'd have B done.	If I have A done, I'll have B done.

Passive

	Past	Present	Future
Simple	It was done.	It is done.	It will be done.
Real Duo	A had been done before B was done.	A has been done many times.	A will be done before B is done.
Unreal Duo	If A had been done, B would've been done.	If A were done, B would be done.	If A is done, B will be done.

Integrating Grammar and Speech

Traditionally, written and spoken English are taught separately. This has the unfortunate consequence that students internalize the grammar with their own accents. They are then faced with the need to go back and try to reconfigure their presentation. With this method, you learn the same way you did with your first language. The words and structure are introduced at the same time as the sounds and rhythms. The goal is to master the foundations in all aspects and then build up to the higher levels. If you only learn grammar, there are times that your accent will make it seem like you haven't mastered the basics. For instance, native Chinese speakers sometimes drop the final consonants in speech, so it seems like they don't conjugate well. Once they are taught to link the words together, they come across with both the correct grammar and the standard accent.

It's also vital to understand how intonation plays a part in grammar. For example, when you have a **description**, the second word is stressed (cold **milk**), but when you have a compound, you need to stress the first part of the word (**milk**man). Adding a suffix like **-y** can give you an adjective (milk**y**), and adding **to** will often create a verb from a noun (**to** milk).

In the later chapters, you'll find exercises to help you develop advanced comprehension skills. These exercises will ask you to supply missing information, select an appropriate response, identify if a statement is true or false, identify the gist of a statement, recognize specific facts, and draw logical conclusions.

Vowel Chart

Consonant Chart on p. xxiii.

There are only five characters that are different from the standard English alphabet: æ, ä, ə, ε, and ü.

Tense Vowels

Symbol	Sound	Spelling	Example
ā	εi	take	[tāk]
ē	ee	eat	[ēt]
ī	äi	ice	[īs]
ō	ou	hope	[hōp]
ū	ooh	smooth	[smūth]
ä	ah	caught	[kät]
æ	ä + eh	cat	[kæt]
æo	æ + o	down	[dæon]
oi	oh + ee	boy	[boi]

Lax Vowels

Symbol	Sound	Spelling	Example
ε	eh	get	[gεt]
i	ih	it	[it]
ü	ih+uh	took	[tük]
ə	uh	sun	[sən]
Semi-Vowels			
r	er	her	[hr]
l	ᵊl	dull	[dəᵊl]
w	wᵊ	quick	[kwik]
y	yᵊ	onion	[ənyᵊn]

SAMPLE CURRICULUM: 4-hour classes / Total 80 hours

Week 1: Chapter 1		Week 2: Chapter 2	
Testing Grammar Placement Dictation Writing Sample **Chapter 1** Dictation **Story** 1-2 to 1-19 **Nouns** 1-20 to 1-28	**Questions** 1-29 **Pronouns** 1-30 to 1-41 **Present Tense** 1-42 to 1-53 **Time Words** 1-54 to 1-57 **Test & Essay**	**Dictation** **Story** 2-2 to 2-3 **High Frequency Words** 2-4 **Nouns** 2-5 to 2-13 **Prepositions of Location** 2-14 **There is / are** 2-15 **Conjunctions** 2-16	**Present Tense** 2-17 to 2-27 **Negatives** 2-28 **Contractions** 2-29 **Questions** 2-30 to 2-33 **Tags** 2-34 to 2-36 **Verb Grid** 2-37 **Commands** 2-38 **Test & Essay**
Week 3: Chapter 3		Week 4: Chapter 4	
Dictation **Story** 3-2 **Syllables** 3-3 **Nouns Countable / Uncountable** 3-4 to 3-5 **Comparatives** 3-6 to 3-8 **Prepositions of Direction** 3-9 to 3-11	**Past Tense** 3-12 to 3-24 **Middle I** 3-25 **Get** 3-26 **Time Words** 3-27 **Test & Essay**	**Dictation** **Story** 4-2 to 4-3 **Reduced Vowels** 4-4 **Countable Nouns** 4-5 to 4-8 **Prepositions of Time & Manner** 4-5 to 4-8 **Modifiers** 4-11 to 4-12 **Intonation** 4-13 **Reading Comp** 4-14	**Tee Aitch** 4-15 to 4-16 **Intonation** 4-17 **Verbs: Continuous** 4-18 to 4-23 **Get** 4-24 to 4-25 **Questions** 4-26 to 4-33 **Test & Essay**
Week 5: Chapter 5		Week 6: Chapter 6	
Dictation **Story** 5-2 **Intonation** 5-3 to 5-4 **Word Order** 5-5 to 5-6 **Conjunctions** 5-9 to 5-11 **Countable Nouns** 5-9 to 5-11 **How** 5-12 to 5-13 **Two** 5-14 to 5-16	**Use** 5-17 to 5-18 **Countable Nouns** 5-19 to 5-23 **Future Tense** 5-24 to 5-36 **Grammar in a Nutshell** 5-37 to 5-42 **Do / Make** 5-43 **Stand** 5-44 **Test & Essay**	**Dictation** **Story** 6-2 **Joiners** 6-3 **Indirect Speech** 6-4 to 6-7 **Question Review** **So / Such** 6-8 **Verbs: Present Unreal** 6-9 to 6-12	**Opinion Words** 6-13 to 6-14 **Do / To Do / Doing** 6-15 **Say, Tell, Speak, Talk** 6-16 to 6-17 **Verbs of Perception** 6-18 to 6-22 **Take** 6-23 to 6-24 **Test & Essay**
Week 7: Chapter 7		Week 8: Chapter 8	
Dictation **Story** 7-2 **Linking** 7-3 to 7-4 **Reverse Adjectives** 7-5 to 7-9 **How** 7-10 to 7-12 **Some / Any** 7-13 **Time** 7-14 to 7-20	**Present Duo** 7-21 to 7-24 **P B F V W** 7-25 **There / It** 7-26 to 7-27 **Verb Review** 7-28 to 7-30 **Turn** 7-31 **Test & Essay**	**Dictation** **Story** 8-2 **Common Courtesy Intonation** 8-3 **L & R** 8-4 to 8-7 **Complex Intonation** 8-8 to 8-16 **How Questions** 8-17	**Noun / Verbs** 8-18 **Prepositions** 8-19 to 8-25 **Unreal Duo** 8-26 to 8-28 **Causative** 8-29 to 8-31 **Test & Essay**
Week 9: Chapter 9		Week 10: Chapter 10	
Dictation **Story** 9-2 **Listening Comp** 9-3 to 9-14 **Review**	**Reported Speech** 9-16 **Past Unreal Duo** 9-17 **Verb Review** 9-18 **There / Had / Be** 9-19 to 9-23 **Nutshell** 9-24 **Give** 9-25 **Test & Essay**	**Dictation** **Story** 10-2 **Nasals** 10-3 to 10-5 **Word Order** 10-6 & 10-7 **Doubt / Question** 10-8 **Prefixes** 10-9 **Comprehension** 10-10	**Synonyms** **Passive** 10-11 to 10-13 **Useful Verbs** 10-14 **Past & Future Duo** 10-15 to 10-19 Verb Review 10-20 **Test & Essay**

Tests

You'll find three types of **Tests** in this book:

1. Comprehensive grammar **placement** tests (basic and advanced)
2. **Mastery** tests at the end of each chapter
3. A **mid-term** and a comprehensive **final**

Even if you are advanced, you should go through the entire program to make sure everything is in place and in the proper order. Of course, advanced students can go through more quickly, as long as they get 100% on each of the chapter tests.

"Where do I start?"

It's important to determine your level, so the first step is to take the four placement tests:

∻ Basic Grammar
∻ Advanced Grammar
∻ Dictation
∻ Writing Sample

TEST

Below are two grammar placement tests. Each one should only take about 15 minutes. The Answer Key is on page 251.

Placement Test: Basic Grammar

1. Circle the correct answer.
    a.   I **is / am / are** a student.
    b.   They **is / am / are** at a party.
    c.   She **is / am / are** out of the office.
2. Change the sentence to the plural.
    a.   This test is easy. _____
    b.   The tree is tall. _____
3. Change the positive statement to a negative.
    a.   Shelly is in Europe. _____
4. Change the statement to a question.
    a.   Your brother is in college. _____
5. Fill in where the **blue text** should appear in the sentence.
    a.   _____ I _____ am _____ late _____. **(always)**
    b.   _____ I _____ am _____ late _____. **(every day)**
6. Circle the correct answer.
    a.   The zookeeper **feed / feeds** the animals.
    b.   Joe and Ellie **tell / tells** funny jokes.
7. Replace both nouns with pronouns.
    a.   **Edgar** reads a **book**. _____
    b.   The **boys** fly the **kite**. _____
    c.   **Moira** plans her **classes**. _____
8. Fill in the most appropriate word.
    a.   The ring is _____ her finger.
    b.   He is sitting _____ a chair.
    c.   They are working _____ an office.
    d.   The subway is _____ ground.

9. Circle the most appropriate connecting word. Use each word only once.
   a. They speak French **and / but / so** Italian.
   b. We eat the cheese, **and / but / so** not the crackers.
   c. It is late, **and / but / so** we are in a hurry.

10. Change the positive statement to a negative.
   a. Lou knows Ed. _____
   b. The cars go fast. _____

11. Change the statement to a question.
   a. It rains every day. _____
   b. You like it. _____

12. Circle the correct answer.
   a. That plan is **bad / worse / the worst** of all.

13. Fill in the most appropriate direction word.
   a. The boys jump _____ the pool.
   b. The cat runs _____ from the dog.

14. Convert to the past.
   Example: I **watch** TV. I **watched** TV.
   a. They think about it. _____
   b. We see him at the gym. _____
   c. We have enough time. _____

15. Change the positive statement to a negative.
   a. Morgan heard a noise. _____

16. Change the statement to a question.
   a. James drove to New York. _____
   b. Andrea and Sarah walked to work. _____

17. Fill in where the **blue text** should appear in the sentence.
   a. _____ James _____ drove
      _____ to New York. (**frequently**)

18. Fill in the proper tag ending.
   a. He was funny, _____?
   b. I am here, _____?

19. Indicate the proper tag ending.
   a. They thought about it, _____?
   b. She didn't say it, _____?

20. Circle the correct answer.
   a. There was **a / some** water on the floor.
   b. He took **a / some** bath last night.

21. Circle the correct answer.
   a. What **a / the** surprise!
   b. It's **a / the** only way we can do it.

22. Circle the correct answer.
   a. They poured **a / —** water on the plants.
   b. Did you bring **a / —** water bottle?

23. Circle the correct answer.
   a. Did you have **much / many** trouble?
   b. Did you have **much / many** problems?

24. Circle the correct answer.
   a. He **sleeps / is sleeping** right now.
   b. They **work / are working** hard every day.

25. Change the statement to a question.
   a. The store is being remodeled. _____

26. Circle the correct answer.
    a. What time do you get **down / up / to** in the morning?
    b. Stop the bus! I need to get **down / off**!
27. Change the statement to the future.
    a. Charlie went to France. _____
    b. Marcus did not order shoes from Italy. _____
    c. Did Larry fix my computer? _____
28. Change the positive statement to a negative.
    a. Timmy will answer your questions. _____
29. Change the statement to a question. Do not use pronouns or contractions.
    a. The cell phone will need to be charged. _____
30. Circle the correct answer.
    a. Could you **do / make** me a favor, please?
    b. Try not to **do / make** any more mistakes.
    c. We need to **do / make** a final decision.
31. Circle the correct answer.
    a. What are you **saying / telling / talking** about?
    b. Bonnie **said / told / talked** the truth.
32. Fill in the proper word.
    a. What does ASAP stand _____?
    b. What letter does your first name start _____?

Placement Test: Advanced Grammar

1. Respond using **We don't know**.
    a. Do you know who did it? _____
    b. Do you know who makes them? _____
    c. Do you know who will take care of it? _____
2. Convert from a statement to a question.
    a. He did it.   What _____
    b. They will buy that.   What _____
    c. He did it there.   Where _____
    d. He did it then.   When _____
    e. He did it quickly.   How _____
    f. She paints beautifully. How _____
3. Respond using **I'm not sure if**.
    a. Did he do it? _____
    b. Do we need one? _____
4. Convert to a reported statement using **I thought that**.
    a. He does it. _____
    b. She will buy one. _____
    c. We are trying our hardest. _____
5. Circle the correct answer.
    a. It's 20 degrees out! You **will be / must be** freezing!
    b. He has a slight fever. He **will be / may be** getting sick.
    c. There's a slight possibility that he **will be / could be** telling the truth this time.
    d. I am required to do this tonight. It **will be / has to be** finished tonight.
    e. **May / Will** I sit here? Do I have your permission?
    f. He is very strong. He **can / may** lift 300 pounds.
    g. I have a cold. I **should / will be** go to bed early tonight.

h. I hope **to see / seeing / see** you later.
i. How can we avoid **to go / going / go** to that meeting?
j. Did he **to manage / managing / manage** to figure it out?
k. She promised **to give / giving / give** it careful consideration.
l. The landlord asked the tenant **to keep / keeping / keep** the noise down.
m. Do you plan on **to go / going / go** on the field trip?
n. They refused **to tell / telling / tell** us what happened.
o. Everyone insisted on **to leave / leaving / leave** early.
p. Did anyone see him **to take / take / taking** the folder?
q. You have to let him **to try / trying / try**.
r. I didn't **look / see** him at work today.
s. Could you **look / see** at this proposal, please?
t. Can you **hear / listen** the birds singing?
u. We need to **hear / listen** carefully in order to understand everything.
v. He's the person **who / whose / that / what** wrote the report.
w. That's the idea **who / whose / that / what** changed everyone's way of thinking.
x. I'm not sure **who / whose / that / what** idea that was.
y. This thing is not **who / whose / that / what** I wanted!
z. I hope it **will / is / was / were** work out.
aa. I wish it **will / is / was / were** possible.
bb. If there **is / were / had been** time right now, we would take care of it.
cc. If there **is / were / had been** time tomorrow, we will take care of it.
dd. If there **is / were / had been** time yesterday, we would have taken care of it.
ee. You **should be / should have been** there yesterday.
ff. When I was young, I **could dance / could have danced** really well.
gg. I'm sorry you had to walk. You **could call / could have called** me.

6. Fill in the proper tag ending.
   a. We have to finish quickly, _____?
   b. They had to redo it, _____?
   c. She has been there before, _____?
   d. They had never acted like that before, _____?
   e. The school will be closed Thursday, _____?
   f. She has good grades, _____?
   g. He had better think about it, _____?
   h. They'd rather play, _____?

7. Select the proper answer.
   a. He enlisted in the army two years **for / ago / in**.
   b. He's been in the army **for / ago / in** two years now.
   c. He'll be getting out **for / ago / in** a couple of days.
   d. They thought it over **during / while** the meeting.
   e. We chatted amiably **during / while** the intermission.
   f. **During / While** you're up, could you get me a glass of water?
   g. What do you do **during / while** the day?
   h. It's not safe to talk on the phone **during / while** driving.
   i. We plan on working **by / until** 10:00.
   j. We need to start **by / until** 7:00.
   k. They have worked here **for / since** ten years.
   l. They have been here **for / since** 2001.
   m. Let me call you back **in / after** a couple of minutes, OK?
   n. He had to take another call, but called me back **in / after** a few minutes.

o. Have you finished **yet / already / still / any more**?

p. They have **yet / already / still / any more** finished.

q. The others are **yet / already / still / any more** working on it.

r. We don't want to do this **yet / already / still / any more**.

8. Fill in the blank using the proper form of **to / for / of / about / on / with / from**.

a. Did they have a good reason _____ their actions?

b. Have you decided _____ a strategy?

c. I hope you don't object _____ this schedule change.

d. The new employee really reminds me _____ my cousin.

e. They insisted _____ doing it a particular way.

f. We just don't have time to deal _____ this right now!

g. Did you happen _____ find out who will be there?

h. Many people prefer _____ skip breakfast.

9. Convert to the present real duo.

Example: I **watch** TV. I **have watched** TV.

a. They do the dishes. _____

b. Things fall in earthquakes. _____

c. The situation gets better. _____

d. The competitors bring their own gear. _____.

e. Everyone saw that movie. _____

f. The students learned the lessons. _____

g. The CEO was thinking about it. _____

h. Many people forgot the answer. _____

10. Circle the correct answer.

a. He **thought / has thought** about it many times before today.

b. Jennie **bought / has bought** it two years ago.

c. I **never saw / have never seen** such a thing in my life.

d. Do you think he **did / has done** his homework yet?

e. I think he **already went / has already gone** home.

f. He **thinks / has thought** about it for years.

g. We **need / have needed** to start studying for quite some time now.

h. Jennie **lived / has lived** there in 1968.

i. Jennie **lived / has lived** there since 1968.

11. Fill in where the **blue text** should appear in the sentence.

a. _____they_____do_____it_____. **perfectly**

b. _____they_____do_____it_____. **usually**

c. _____they_____do_____it_____. **here**

d. _____they_____do_____it_____. **at night**

e. _____they_____do_____it_____. **definitely**

12. Circle the correct answer.

a. The boy wanted to buy the toy, but his mother wouldn't **let / make** him.

b. My coworker needed the day off, but our boss wouldn't **let / allow** him to leave.

c. Our schedule didn't **let / permit** us to take unplanned vacations.

d. I **let / had / made** my hair cut yesterday.

e. We're trying to **make / get** him change his mind.

f. It's hard to **make / get** him to change in any way, shape or form.

g. That man **looks / sees** just like George Clooney!

h. I love that song; it **sounds / hears** like Liza Minelli.

i. This is so soft, it **touches / feels** like silk.

13. Convert to an active statement. Do not use contractions or pronouns.
    Example: It was chosen by Edward. Edward chose it.
    a. The pyramids were built by the ancient Egyptians. _____
    b. Our friends were stunned by the accusation. _____
    c. The colors were selected by the design committee. _____
    d. Your ideas will be presented by a professional speaker. _____
    _____

14. Circle the correct answer.
    a. Our friends **are / have always been** very supportive throughout the years.
    b. The press **has reported / had reported** on the story before that article, but this time they gave more details.
    c. I hope we **have thought this through / will have really thought this through** before we finalize the decision.
    d. If they had been more thorough, they **wouldn't miss / wouldn't have missed** that report.
    e. If our campaign is successful, we **would all be promoted / will all be promoted**.
    f. If Lewis were in charge, we **will / would have** more fun at the office.
    g. I **would definitely take / will definitely take** care of that tomorrow.
    h. If you **let / had let** me borrow it, I'll be sure to return it by tomorrow.
    i. If it weren't raining, **we'd walk / we'll walk**.
    j. If it hadn't been raining last week, **we would've walked / we will've walked**.

Placement Test: Dictation

There is a 30-second audio clip on the CD, Track 6. Write down what you hear. The time limit is seven minutes.

_____

_____

_____

_____

_____

_____

_____

_____

_____

_____

ESSAY

Placement Test: Writing Sample

Now, let's establish your writing level.
Write a short essay about yourself.

_____

_____

_____

_____

_____

_____

_____

_____

_____

_____

_____

_____

_____

_____

_____

_____

_____

_____

_____

_____

The **Vowel Chart** on page xiii covers the vowels and diphthongs. Here, you can see the consonants and blends.

Consonant Chart

Unvoiced	Voiced
p	b
t	d
f	v
k	g
s	z
ch	j
sh	zh
th	th
h	
	l
	r
	m
	n
	ng
	y
	w

The columns are labeled un*voiced* and *voiced*. What does that mean?

Put your thumb and index fingers on your throat and buzz like a bee, zzzzzzzzzzz. You will feel a vibration from your throat in your fingers.

If you whisper that same sound, or hiss like a snake, you end up with sssssssssssss. You will feel that your fingers don't vibrate.

This means that Z is a voiced sound and S is unvoiced.

Telephone Tutoring

Preliminary Diagnostic Analysis

The preliminary diagnostic is part of a comprehensive analysis to determine your language skills in grammar, vocabulary, writing, comprehension, accent, and pronunciation. If you are studying this book on your own, please contact us toll-free at **(800) 457-4255** or **AmericanAccent.com** for a referral to a qualified telephone analyst. The analysis is designed to let you know where your English is standard and non-standard.

Read the following groups of words out loud.

1. all, long, caught	5. ice, I'll, sky	9. come, front, indicate	13. out, house, round
2. cat, matter, laugh	6. it, milk, sin	10. smooth, too, shoe	14. boy, oil, toy
3. take, say, fail	7. eat, me, seen	11. took, full, would	
4. get, egg, any	8. work, girl, bird	12. told, so, roll	

A	B	C	D	E	F
1. pin	1. bin	1. wrapping	1. grabbing	1. rip	1. rib
2. fat	2. vat	2. refers	2. reverse	2. half	2. have
3. sip	3. zip	3. doses	3. dozes	3. face	3. phase
4. she	4. den	4. you should	4. usual	4. bash	4. beige
5. ten	5. joke	5. petal	5. peddle	5. not	5. nod
6. choke	6. that	6. etcher	6. edger	6. etch	6. edge
7. think	7. gold	7. with her	7. wither	7. bath	7. bathe
8. cold	8. rip	8. locking	8. logging	8. lack	8. lag
9. yes	9. brain	9. mayor	9. correction	9. day	9. car
10. would	10. me	10. coward	10. prayed	10. how	10. temper
11. his	11. knee	11. reheat	11. dimmer	11. call	11. them
12. lip		12. collection	12. dinner	12. temple	12. then
13. plain		13. played	13. ringing		13. thing

1. Get a better water heater.		1. Try it again.	
2. Gedda bedder wader heeder.		2. Put it on.	
3. Italian	Italy	3. It's not a bus.	
4. attack	attic		
5. atomic	atom	1. Tryida **gen**.	
6. photography	photograph	2. Pudi**dan**.	
7. let	led	3. Its nada bus.	

Chapter 1: Simple Nouns and Verbs

In this chapter, you will learn singular and plural nouns using the present tense of the verb **to be**, pronouns, contractions, negatives, questions, time words, word order and story order, and the basics of intonation and pronunciation.

 **DICTATION**

Let's find out exactly what you hear at this point. There are five sentences on the CD. Listen to each one several times and write what you hear. Even if you are more advanced, this is a good exercise to establish a benchmark for your current level.

Exercise 1-1: Dictation	CD 1 Track 7

Listen to the audio and write the exact transcription in the spaces below. When you're done, check the Answer Key, beginning on page 251.

1. _____

2. _____

3. _____

4. _____

5. _____

Now that you have taken the grammar placement tests on page xv and completed the initial dictation and essay on pages xxi–xxii, you are ready to start with a simple story.

STORY

Our story starts in a very basic way. We will use just nine words to tell the entire story. This nine-grid is the most basic structure in English.

Each sentence has three parts — noun, verb, noun.

Each story has three parts — introduction, body, conclusion.

Later, you will learn different structures, but if you master this form, you will always be able to communicate clearly, both in speech and in writing.

One of the most important things to do when listening to a story is to ask questions. Memorize these forms:

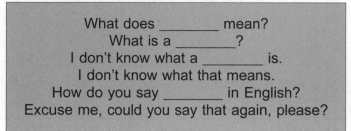

What does _____ mean?
What is a _____?
I don't know what a _____ is.
I don't know what that means.
How do you say _____ in English?
Excuse me, could you say that again, please?

Exercise 1-2: Telling a Story — Introduction   CD 1 Track 8

Listen to the audio and repeat the basic nine-word story five times out loud.

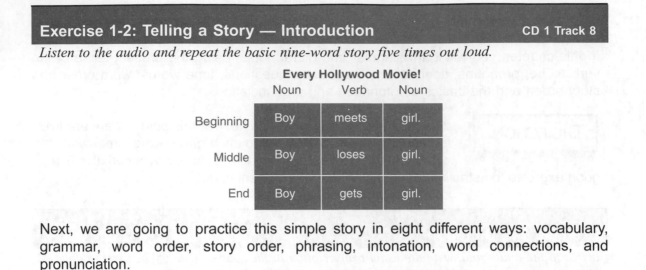

Every Hollywood Movie!

	Noun	Verb	Noun
Beginning	Boy	meets	girl.
Middle	Boy	loses	girl.
End	Boy	gets	girl.

Next, we are going to practice this simple story in eight different ways: vocabulary, grammar, word order, story order, phrasing, intonation, word connections, and pronunciation.

It's important to ask questions in order to learn new vocabulary. What does **meet** mean? What's a **boy**?

Exercise 1-3: Telling a Story — Vocabulary

Look up and learn the following words.

boy, **girl**, **meets**, **loses**, **gets**

Exercise 1-4: Telling a Story — Grammar

Memorize the parts of speech.

Boy and **girl** are *nouns*; **meets**, **loses**, and **gets** are *verbs*.

Exercise 1-5: Telling a Story — Word Order   CD 1 Track 9

Listen to the audio and repeat the story five times out loud, focusing on word order.

The *word order* starts with the *subject* (**boy**), ends with the *object* (**girl**), and is linked with the *verb* (**meets, loses, gets**).

Every Hollywood Movie!

	Noun	Verb	Noun
Beginning	Boy	meets	girl.
Middle	Boy	loses	girl.
End	Boy	gets	girl.

Exercise 1-6: Telling a Story — Story Order   CD 1 Track 10

Listen to the audio and repeat the story five times out loud, focusing on story order.

The story order *starts* with the meeting, *changes* in the middle with the loss, and *ends up* with the happy couple.

	Subject	Verb	Object
Intro	Boy	meets	girl.
Body	Boy	loses	girl.
Conclusion	Boy	gets	girl.

When you have a noun-verb-noun sentence, the nouns are stronger than the rest of the words. There is more emphasis on the words **boy** and **girl**. In the second sentence, you have already been introduced to the boy and the girl, so you need to indicate the *contrast* by stressing the verb. Use the staircase intonation for this.

Exercise 1-7: Intonation CD 1 Track 11

Listen to the audio and repeat out loud five times. Focus on correct intonation.

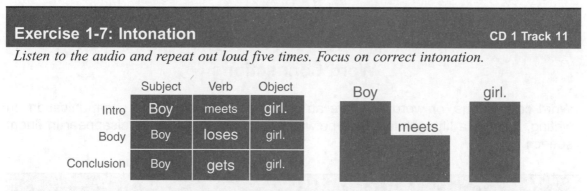

	Subject	Verb	Object
Intro	Boy	meets	girl.
Body	Boy	loses	girl.
Conclusion	Boy	gets	girl.

Notice the arrows to the right of the box in Exercise 1-8. These indicate the tone of your voice, so you can tell that the first two sentences are not the end of the story.

Exercise 1-8: Phrasing CD 1 Track 12

Listen carefully to the audio and repeat out loud five times. Notice the arrows indicating the phrasing.

Boy	meets	girl.
Boy	loses	girl.
Boy	gets	girl.

Exercise 1-9: Pronunciation Intro CD 1 Track 13

ACCENT

Listen to the audio and repeat the sounds out loud five times. These five sounds will be used every time you speak.

æ	ä	ə	r	th
cat	caught	cut	car	the
bat	bought	but	water	this
hat	want	what	her	these
last	lost	lump	real	then
sat	saw	such	roar	they
that	thought	thus	rather	there

Exercise 1-10: Pronunciation   CD 1 Track 14

Listen to the audio and repeat out loud five times. Focus on the pronunciation.

Boy	meets	grrrl.
Boy	luz'z	grrrl.
Boy	gets	grrrl.

The three pronunciation points are **meets**, **loses**, and **girl**. Make a clear ee sound in **meets**, so it doesn't sound like **mitts**. The two S's in **loses** have a Z sound. The R should be a clear, throaty sound.

Note: In this book, you will see three symbols used interchangeably— *, ', ə. This is a soft vowel sound that you can almost skip over—poss*ble, poss'ble, possəble.

Word Connections

Word connections, or word flow, are an important aspect of clear communication. In writing, there is a little white space between each word, but these disappear in fluent speech.

Exercise 1-11: Word Connections   CD 1 Track 15

Listen to the audio and repeat the text on the right out loud five times. Focus on letting the words run together. Yes, it looks strange, but trust the phonetics!

Looks like ...			Sounds like ...		
Bob	opens	an **envelope**.	**Bää**	bopən	zə **nänvəlop**.
Bob	**drops**	the envelope.	Bääb	**dräps**	thee[(y)]envəlop.
Bob	gets	**angry**.	Bääb	gets	**sængry**.

Here is a quick overview of the main rules of word connections.

Final Consonant + Initial Vowel	**Jum**p **o**ver sounds like jum **p**over.
T + Y = Ch D + Y = J	Di**d y**ou pu**t y**our **car away?** Di**d ju** pu**ch**er **car away?**
Y & W Connectors Between Vowels	**He opens** > he[(y)]**opens** **Go away** > go[(w)]**away**

Once you are fully comfortable with the basic nine-grid and can imitate it perfectly, you are ready to go on to two classic stories: *Goldilocks and the Three Bears* and *Sleeping Beauty*.

Exercise 1-12: "Goldilocks" — Intonation and Phrasing   CD 1 Track 16

Listen to the audio and repeat the story. Notice the intonation of new information and phrasing.

	Noun	Verb	Noun	
Beginning	Girl	finds	house.	↗
Middle	Girl	eats	food.	↗
End	Bears	chase	girl.	↘

Exercise 1-13: "Goldilocks" — Pronunciation and Linking CD 1 Track 17

Listen to the audio and repeat the story. Focus on the pronunciation and linking the words.

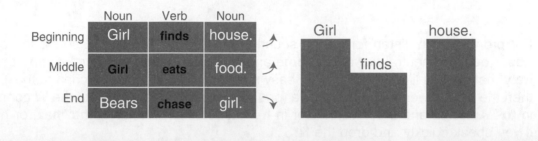

	Noun	Verb	Noun	
Beginning	Girl	**finds**	house.	↗
Middle	**Girl**	**eats**	food.	↗
End	Bears	**chase**	girl.	↘

Girl finds house.

Exercise 1-14: "Sleeping Beauty" — Intonation and Phrasing CD 1 Track 18

Listen to the audio and repeat the story. Notice the intonation of new information and phrasing.

	Subject	Verb	Object	
Introduction	Witch	enchants	girl.	↗
Body	Prince	wakes	girl.	↗
Conclusion	Girl	marries	prince.	↘

Exercise 1-15: "Sleeping Beauty" — Pronunciation and Linking CD 1 Track 19

Listen to the audio and repeat the story. Focus on the pronunciation and linking the words.

Wit	chenchants	grrrl.
Prints	wakes	grrrl.
Grrrl	merreez	prints.

Exercise 1-16: Your Own Story

*Using the nine-grid, write a short story with a **beginning**, **middle**, and **end**, also known as an **introduction**, **body**, and **conclusion**.*

	Noun	**Verb**	**Noun**
Introduction			
Body			
Conclusion			

Exercise 1-17: "Let's Meet Max" — Intonation   CD 1 Track 20

Listen to the audio and repeat the story, focusing on intonation.

Max	comes	to America.
He	has	fun.
He	goes back	to Italy.

For pronunciation, listen for the ae sound in **Max**, **back**; the final Z sound in **comes**, **has**, **goes**; the neutral vowels in **come** and **America** (kəm and əmerəkə); and the T in **Italy** that sounds like a D (idəly). An easy rule to remember is if you change the T to D, then the next vowel will be the schwa (or ə). For word connections, put the W connector in **to⁽ʷ⁾America** and the Y connector in **he has**. This can either be **he⁽ʸ⁾haz**, or **he⁽ʸ⁾az** if you speak quickly and drop the H.

Exercise 1-18: "Let's Meet Max" — Pronunciation and Linking   CD 1 Track 21

*Listen to the audio and repeat the story, focusing on pronunciation and word connections. Notice that the H in **has** is dropped.*

Mæx	kəmz	to⁽ʷ⁾ əmerəkə.
Hee	⁽ʸ⁾æz	fən.
Hee	goz bæk	tə idəly.

Exercise 1-19: Your Own Stories

Using the nine-grid, write two short stories with a beginning, middle, and end. You can start adding simple words to complete the sentences.

	Noun	Verb	Noun
Beginning			
Middle			
End			

	Subject	Verb	Object
Introduction			
Body			
Conclusion			

| NOUNS | This section tells about *nouns* and how to change them to *pronouns*. A noun is a person, place, or thing. Nouns can usually be represented with a picture. In the nine-grid story, the first and |

last word of the first sentence is a noun. You will also work with the basic modifiers (*a, the, this, that, these, those, some, many, most, all, my, your, his, her, our*, numbers, etc.).

Nouns Are Things

A Person   **A Place**   **A Thing**

A or *An*

Exercise 1-20: *A* or *An*

*Use **a** or **an** for general words or for introducing a noun. **An** is used before a vowel. When you're done, check the Answer Key.*

This is _____ bike.   This is **a** bike.

This is _____ apple.   This is **an** apple.

1. Here is _____ car.
2. There is _____ egg.
3. _____ dog is _____ animal
4. Sam is _____ honest man.
5. It is _____ nice day today.

Plural Rule: Add an S

The nice thing about English is that, generally, you just add an S to indicate that there is more than one thing. These are called *plurals*.

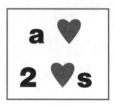

There are a few exceptions to the –**s** rule.

Common Irregular Plurals			
Singular	**Plural**	**Singular**	**Plural**
man	men	foot	feet
woman	women	tooth	teeth
child	children	mouse	mice
person	people	knife	knives

Woman is pronounced **wüm'n** and **women** is **wimmen**.

däk   däks   dä   dä
                        ägg   äggz

dock   docks   dog   dogs

Pronunciation of the Final S

The final S sounds like a Z. **Dogs** sounds like **dogz**.

Even if you put a Z at the end of a word that ends in a T, K, P, or F, it will still sound like the proper S sound: **eatz**, **lookz**, **popz**, **laughz**.

If the word ends in S, SS, SH, ZH, CH, X, Z, J, or O, add **-es**. It will sound like əz.

If the word ends in Y, the Y changes to I, and you add **-es** (**party/parties**).

Note: This does not apply for **-ey**, or **-ay**, or **-oy** words, such as **key**, **play**, or **toy**.

z	əz
reads	buses
sags	misses
rubs	sauces
saves	roses
rows	buzzes
calls	dishes
hums	watches
sins	boxes
sings	judges
	garages

All final vowels are followed by the Z sound:

sees = seez

New or General Things

A and **one** are similar, but **a** is much more commonly used. **One** is very specific and is used with other numbers: one book, two books. The plural of **a** or **one** is **some**. **Some** is one of several common words that can be added before the plural noun: **some** things, **all** things, **two** things, **many** things. Let's look at some of them.

Exercise 1-21: A Thing, Two Things — CD 1 Track 22

Listen to the audio and repeat the phrases.

Singular	Plural
a dog	some dogs
one dog	three dogs
a book	some books
a hat	some hats
a dish	all dishes
one watch	two watches
one car	three cars
a person	some people

Exercise 1-22: A Thing, Two Things — Intonation / Pronunciation — CD 1 Track 23

Listen to the audio and repeat the phrases, stressing the nouns and focusing on the pronunciation.

Singular		Plural	
a dog	ə **däg**	some dogs	səm **dägz**
one dog	wən **däg**	three dogs	three **dägz**
a book	ə **bük**	some books	səm **büks**
a hat	ə **hæt**	some hats	səm **hæts**
a dish	ə **d'sh**	all dishes	äll **d'shez**
one watch	wən **wätch**	two watches	too **wätchez**
one car	wən **cär**	three cars	three **cärz**
a person	ə **prsən**	some people	səm **peepəl**

8

Exercise 1-23: A Thing, Two Things — Plurals   CD 1 Track 24

Make these plural by adding a final S in the spaces. Some sound like S, some sound like Z.

		Pronunciation				Pronunciation
1. a chair	two chair**s**	too chairz	6. a pill	two pill__		too pillz
2. an egg	two egg__	too⁽ʷ⁾eggz	7. a lamp	two lamp__		too læmps
3. a day	two day__	too dayz	8. a hair	two hair__		too hehrz
4. a week	two week__	too weeks	9. a letter	two letter__		too ledderz
5. a desk	two desk__	too desks	10. a pencil	two pencil__		too pens'lz

Rule: No Naked Nouns

You almost always need a word before the noun in English, such as *a book, my book, this book*. If someone says, *I want book* or *Book is good*, he sounds like a caveman. This is the No-Naked-Nouns Rule. Remember, the first time use **a**, the second time use **the**. Both sound like ə.

Already Known Things

You can use **the** with both singular and plural nouns. Remember to add **–s** to the plural noun.

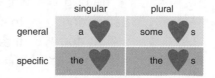

	singular	plural
general	a ♥	some ♥ s
specific	the ♥	the ♥ s

A and *The*

Exercise 1-24: *A* or *The*

*Use **the** for specific or unique words, or when the noun has already been introduced. When you're done, check the Answer Key.*

1. ____ sun is bright.
2. He is ____ doctor.
3. Where is ____ kitchen?
4. It is ____ falling star.
5. There is ____ mistake here.
6. ____ car is expensive.
7. Where is ____ bathroom?
8. Is this ____ mistake?
9. He is ____ president.
10. She is ____ child.

This and *That*

This and **these** are close by you, and **that** and **those** are farther from you.

This and **that** are singular, and **these** and **those** are plural.

	near	far
singular	this	that
plural	these	those

Exercise 1-25: This Thing, These Things
CD 1 Track 25

Listen to the audio and repeat the phrases.

Singular	Plural
the **dog**	the **dogs**
this **dog**	these **dogs**
that **dog**	those **dogs**
the **book**	the **books**
the **hat**	the **hats**
the **dish**	the **dishes**
this **watch**	these **watches**
that **car**	those **cars**

Exercise 1-26: This Thing, These Things — Pronunciation
CD 1 Track 26

ACCENT

*Listen to the audio and repeat the phrases, stressing the nouns and focusing on the pronunciation, particularly the beginning **Th** sound. Make sure the tip of the tongue is pressed against the back of your top teeth.*

Singular		Plural	
the dog	thə **däg**	the dogs	thə **dägz**
this dog	th's **däg**	these dogs	theez **dägz**
that dog	thæt **däg**	those dogs	thoz **dägz**
the book	thə **bük**	the books	thə **büks**
the hat	thə **hæt**	the hats	thə **hæts**
the dish	thə **d'sh**	the dishes	thə **d'shəz**
this watch	th's **wätch**	these watches	theez **wätchəz**
that car	thæt **cär**	those cars	thoz **cärz**

Exercise 1-27: Here or There

*Fill in the blank with **this**, **that**, **these**, **those**. Then check the Answer Key.*

1. *This* car is near me.
2. ___ car is over there.
3. ___ cars are near me.
4. ___ cars are over there.
5. ___ dogs are close to us.
6. ___ books are near you.
7. ___ books are far from you.
8. ___ shoes are near you.
9. ___ shoes are far from you.
10. ___ dog is not close to us.

Phrasing

As you know, phrasing gives you important information. When you use a rising tone at the end of a sentence, you are asking a question. When you use a falling tone, you are making a statement.

Exercise 1-28: Asking Questions CD 1 Track 27

Listen to the audio and notice how a statement sounds different from a question. Notice the arrows.

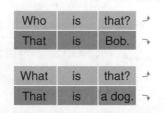

| Who | is | that? | ⌐ |
| That | is | Bob. | ⌐ |

| What | is | that? | ⌐ |
| That | is | a dog. | ⌐ |

Exercise 1-29: Asking Questions

Put a check mark by the correct answer to each question. Then check the Answer Key.

1. Who is that? ⌐
   - ☐ This is Ed.
   - ☐ These are Ed.
   - ■ That is Ed. ⌐
   - ☐ Those are Ed.

2. What is this?
   - ☐ This is a garden.
   - ☐ These are gardens.
   - ☐ That is garden.
   - ☐ Those are gardens.

3. What are those?
   - ☐ This is a paper clip.
   - ☐ These are paper clips.
   - ☐ That is a paper clip.
   - ☐ Those are paper clips.

4. Who are they?
   - ☐ This person is a man.
   - ☐ These people are men.
   - ☐ That person is a man.
   - ☐ Those people are men.

5. What is that?
   - ☐ This is a donut.
   - ☐ These are donuts.
   - ☐ That is a donut.
   - ☐ Those are donuts.

6. What are these?
   - ☐ This is a coffee cup.
   - ☐ These are coffee cups.
   - ☐ That is a coffee cup.
   - ☐ Those are coffee cups.

7. Who is this?
   - ☐ This is my friend.
   - ☐ These are my friends.
   - ☐ That is my friend.
   - ☐ Those are my friends.

8. What is this thing?
   - ☐ This is a teapot.
   - ☐ These are teapots.
   - ☐ That is a teapot.
   - ☐ Those are teapots.

9. Who are these people?
   - ☐ This is a cowboy.
   - ☐ These are cowboys.
   - ☐ That is a cowboy.
   - ☐ Those are cowboys.

10. Who are those people?
    - ☐ This is a teacher.
    - ☐ These are teachers.
    - ☐ That is a teacher.
    - ☐ Those are teachers.

The first time you mention something, use a *noun*. Then, once the topic is known, replace it with a *pronoun*.

Nouns at the beginning of the sentence are called *subject* nouns. After the verb, they are called *object* nouns. Object pronouns are slightly different from subject pronouns.

Exercise 1-30: Replacing Nouns at the Beginning of a Sentence CD 1 Track 28

*Listen to the audio and notice the word order. The **pronoun** is not stressed.*

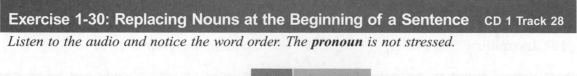

| noun | Tom | is a doctor. |
| pronoun | He | is very kind. |

Pronouns at the beginning of a sentence:

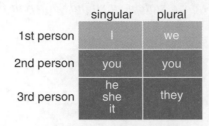

	singular	plural
1st person	I	we
2nd person	you	you
3rd person	he she it	they

Exercise 1-31: Replacing Subject Nouns with Pronouns

Fill in the blank with the proper pronoun: **I**, *you,* **he**, *she*, *it*, *we*, *they. Note that the boldface words are stressed. When you're done, check the Answer Key.*

Nouns	Pronouns	
My father	**He**	is in the car.
1. Ben and **Bill**		are at the **library**.
2. **Jenny**		is reading a **book**.
3. Bill and **Mark**		are planning a **party**.
4. Betty and **Jan**		are **tourists**.
5. My **friends** and I		are at **home**.
6. Those **cars**		are too **expensive**.
7. You and your **cousins**		are in **France**.
8. This **cheese**		is **delicious**.
9. Our **city**		is **crowded**. (many people)
10. **Jasmine**		is not at **home**.

Exercise 1-32: Replacing Subject Nouns with Pronouns — Pronunciation
CD 1 Track 29

ACCENT

*Listen to the audio and repeat five times. This is how Exercise 1-31 should sound. Focus on the intonation, word connections, and pronunciation. Remember that ə is pronounced **uh**.*

Nouns	Pronouns
1. Benen **Bill**er ət thə **librery**.	Therət thə **librery**.
2. **Jenny**iz reading ə **bük**.	Sheez reading ə **bük**.
3. Billen **Mark**er plænning ə **pardy**.	Ther plænning ə **pardy**.
4. Beddyan **Jænn**er **turists**.	Ther **turists**.
5. My **friend** zanäi arət **home**.	Wirət **home**.
6. Thoz **cärz**er too⁽ʷ⁾**eksspensive**.	Ther too⁽ʷ⁾**eksspensive**.
7. Youan yer **cuzin** zerin **Frænce**.	Yerin **Frænce**.
8. This **cheez**iz dəlish**əs**.	Its dəlish**əs**.
9. Ar **cidy** iz **crowded**.	Its **crowded**.
10. **Jæzmin**iz nädət **home**.	Sheez nädət **home**.

Exercise 1-33: Replacing Nouns at the End of a Sentence   CD 1 Track 30

Listen to the audio and notice the unstressed pronoun.

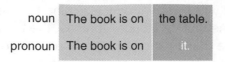

Pronouns at the **end** of a sentence:

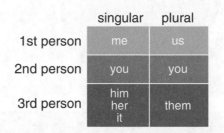

	singular	plural
1st person	me	us
2nd person	you	you
3rd person	him her it	them

Exercise 1-34: Replacing Object Nouns with Pronouns

Fill in the blank with the proper pronoun: **me, you, him, her, it, us, them**. *The boldface words are stressed. Then check the Answer Key.*

	Noun	**Pronoun**
The doctor is in	her office.	it
1. The **news**papers are on	the **table**.	
2. The women's **shoes** are on	their **feet**.	
3. This **package** is for	Mr. **Jones**.	
4. That **letter** is for	my **mom**.	
5. **Joe** is sitting next to	Mr. and Mrs. **Wilson**.	
6. Sam is **reading** to	my **sister** and me.	
7. The **call** is for	you and your **friends**.	
8. This **story** is about	you and **me**.	
9. My **car** is in	the **garage**.	
10. Her **brothers** are in	**school**.	

Exercise 1-35: Replacing Object Nouns with Pronouns — Pronunciation

CD 1 Track 31

ACCENT

*Listen to the audio and repeat five times. Notice how the stress changes from the object noun to the verb. Notice that the **h** of **him** and **her**, and the **th** of **them** can be dropped.*

Nouns
1. thə **nooz** paperzrän thə **table**.
2. thə wimmenz **shooz**erän ther **feet**.
3. th's **pæk**əjiz fr mister **jonz**.
4. that **ledd**eriz fr my **mäm**.
5. **joz** sidding neks t' misteran miss'z **wils**'n.
6. **sæm**iz reeding to my **sis**terən me.
7. the **cäll**iz fr you⁽ʷ⁾an yer **frenz**.
8. th's **story**izə bout you⁽ʷ⁾and **me**.
9. my **cär**zin thə gə**raj** (or gərazh or groj).
10. her **brə**ther zerin **skool**.

Pronouns
1. thə **nooz** paper ze**rän**it.
2. thə wimmenz shoozerän em.
3. th's **pæk**əjiz fr **him**.
4. that **ledd**erz fer **her**.
5. heez sidding **neks** too⁽ʷ⁾m.
6. sæmiz **reed**ing d⁽ʷ⁾s.
7. thə **cäll**iz fer **you**. (you guys)
8. th's **story**izə bow dəs.
9. my **cär**zin it.
10. her **brə**ther ze**rin**it.

Earlier, we discussed that when you introduce a thing for the first time, you need to say "a thing." After you have mentioned it once, you say "the thing." There is another pattern to follow when you replace these words with pronouns. **A thing** turns into **one**, and **the thing** turns into **it**.

noun	subject pronoun	object pronoun	possessive modifier	possessive pronoun
Tom Mary the book the books a book	I you he she it we they	me you him her it us them one	my your his her its our their	mine yours his hers its ours theirs

Exercise 1-36: Replacing Nouns with Pronouns — *It* or *One*

*Fill in the blank with the proper pronoun, **it** or **one**. The boldface words are stressed. Then check the Answer Key.*

A

| The man is near a store. |
| The man is near one. |

The

| The man is near the door. |
| The man is near it. |

Pronouns

Your friend is on — an airplane. one

1. My **brother** is on — the **phone**.
2. **George** is near — a **window**.
3. **Joe** is far from — his **hotel**.
4. I am in a good — **mood**.
5. This is a very expensive — **present**.
6. Joe's brother and I are so happy to see — **your family**.
7. All of the **kids** are still in — the **pool**.
8. **Everyone** is talking about — his **idea**.
9. The **puppies** are in — a **pile**.
10. I have another — **problem**.

the first time	a	noun
the next time	the	noun

Exercise 1-37: Replacing Nouns with Pronouns — Pronunciation   CD 1 Track 32

ACCENT

Focus on the intonation, word connections, and pronunciation. Notice how the stress moves off the noun.

Nouns
1. My **brəther** izän thə **phone**.
2. **Jorj**iz nir ə **window**.
3. **Joz** fär frəm thə hotel.
4. I minnə güd **mood**.
5. Thisizə very expensive **prezənt**.
6. Joz brəthr anai ər so hæppy t' see yer **family**!

Pronouns
My **brəther zän**it.
Jorjiz **nir** wən.
Joz fär frəmit.
I minnə **güd**wən.
Thisizə very **expensive** wən.
Joz brəthr anai ər so hæppy t' **see**(y)em!

14

7. Alləv thə **kid**zer stillin thə **pool**.   Alləv thə kidzer still**lin**it.
8. **Every**wəniz tähking əbow dhiz **ideə**.   Everywəniz **tähk**ing əbow dit.
9. Thə **pəppee**zerin ə **pile**.   Thə pəppeezer**in** wən.
10. I hævə nəther **präblem**.   I hævə **nəther** wən.

Exercise 1-38: Replacing the Nouns

Rewrite each sentence, replacing all nouns with pronouns. The intonation is marked for you in bold. The stress moves to the verb in the new pronoun sentences. When you're done, check the Answer Key.

My sister is reading a book.   **She** is reading **one**.

1. Ben and **Bill** are in the **pool**.
2. **Frank** is watching **TV**.
3. **Debbie** is near the **door**.
4. The **bags** are on the **table**.
5. **Jim** is holding a **pen**.
6. **Sam** is in a good **mood**.
7. The **dogs** are in the **house**.
8. My **family** is in the **car**.
9. My **brother** and I are good **friends**.
10. You and your **cousins** are on a **break**.
11. His **wallet** is in his back **pocket**.
12. The **car** keys are in his **hand**.
13. His **pen** is on the **floor**.
14. The **cars** are in a different **garage**.
15. Their **clothes** are in the **closet**.

Exercise 1-39: Replacing the Nouns — Pronunciation   CD 1 Track 33

ACCENT   *Listen and repeat.*

My **sisterz** reeding ə **bük**.   Sheez **reed**ing one.

1. Ben'n **Bill**er in thə **pool**.   Ther **in**nit.
2. **Frænk**s wätching **TV**.   Heez **wä**tching it.
3. **Debbee**z nir thə **door**.   Sheez **nir**it.
4. Thə **bæg**zer än thə **tay-bəl**.   Ther **än**nit.
5. **J'm**z holding ə **pen**.   Heez **holding** one.
6. **Sæm**zinə a güd **mood**.   Hee**zin** one.
7. The **däg**zerin thə **house**.   Ther **in**nit.
8. My **fæm**lee zin thə **cär**.   Ther **in**nit.
9. My **brother** an aiyer güd **frenz**.   Wir **güd** wənz.
10. Yoo^(w)ən yer **cəzin**zer ännə brayk.   Yrr **än** wun.
11. His **wället**siniz bæck **päckət**.   Its **in**nit.
12. Thə **cär** keezeriniz **hænd**.   Ther **in**nit.
13. Hiz **pen**zän thə **flor**.   Its **än**nit.
14. Thə **cär**zerinə different **gəräzh**.   Therinə **diff**rent one.
15. Ther **cloz**erin thə **cläzet**.   Ther **in**nit.

Possessive Pronouns

We have looked at *subject* and *object* pronouns. These are words that replace the nouns at the *beginning* and the *end* of a sentence. Now, we will look at possessives. Possessives indicate that you own something, or that something belongs to a person. Let's start with the modifiers. They are the same at the beginning or the end of a sentence.

noun	subject pronoun	object pronoun	possessive modifier	possessive pronoun
	I	me	my	mine
	you	you	your	yours
Tom	he	him	his	his
Mary	she	her	her	hers
the book	it	it	its	its
	we	us	our	ours
the books	they	them	their	theirs

Exercise 1-40: Possessive Modifiers

Fill in the blank with the appropriate possessive modifier. Then check the Answer Key.

My sister is reading _____ book.

1. Ben and **Bill** are in _____ **pool**.
2. **Frank** is watching _____ **TV**.
3. **Debbie** is near _____ front **door**.
4. _____ **keys** are in her **hand**.
5. **Jim** is holding _____ **pen**.
6. **Sam** is in _____ **room**.
7. _____ **dogs** are in Joe's **house**.
8. My **family** is in _____ **car**.
9. My **brother** and I are on _____ **way**.
10. You and your **wife** are on _____ **boat**.
11. His **wallet** is in _____ back **pocket**.
12. My **car** keys are in _____ **hand**.
13. _____ **pen** is on her **desk**.
14. The **car** is in _____ usual **place**.
15. Their **clothes** are in _____ **closet**.

She is reading her book.

Exercise 1-41: Possessive Pronouns

Fill in the blank with the appropriate possessive pronoun. Then check the Answer Key.

My sister is reading her book.

1. That's their **pool**.
2. It's his **TV**.
3. It's her front **door**.
4. They're her **keys**.
5. It's his **pen**.
6. It's his **room**.
7. They're Joe's **dogs**.
8. It's our **car**.

It's hers.

It's _____.
It's _____.
It's _____.
They're _____.
It's _____.
It's _____.
They're _____.
It's _____.

9. It's our **way**.	It's _____.
10. That's their **boat**.	It's _____.
11. That's his **wallet**.	It's _____.
12. This is my **car**.	It's _____.
13. They're her **pen** and her **desks**.	They're _____.
14. It's the robot's **schedule**.	It's its. **Grammatical but not used.***
15. That's our **closet**.	It's _____.

*To use **its** you need a noun sentence, such as *I am not sure of its use*. Note the apostrophe in the contraction **it's** and the lack of one with the possessive pronoun **its**.

Let's go back to the basic grid pattern, but this time, we'll focus on the *verbs* rather than the nouns. On the chart, the time is indicated with words and symbols: **Past ◀**, **Present ●**, **Future ▶**. The name of the verb type is indicated on the left.

Simple refers to verbs that are completed in a single action. **Duo** is when an action or situation is linked to a moment in the past. You always need two events for a duo. The symbols for the duo are **Past ◀◀**, **Present ◀●**, **Future ▶▶**. (These are traditionally called the perfect tenses.) The **Unreal Duo** also requires two events. The symbols for the unreal duo are **Past ◁◁**, **Present ◁○**, **Future ▷▶**. However, the key is that they don't actually happen because they are contrary to fact (traditionally called the subjunctive conditional). These will be covered in detail in subsequent chapters.

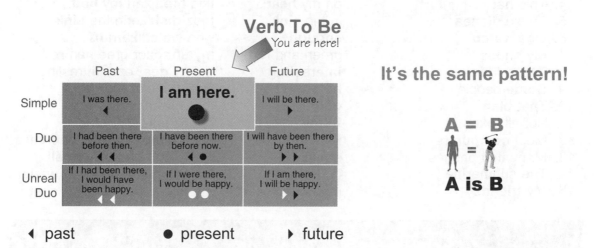

◀ past   ● present   ▶ future

The verb **to be** is the same as an equal sign. **Tom = golfer**.

The emphasis goes on the *nouns*. When there are pronouns instead of nouns, the stress falls on the *verb*. The audio tells where the stress goes: **Tom** is a **golfer**. He **is** one. Notice the pronunciation.

Nouns and pronouns are both important, but pronouns are much more common. It's important for you to understand these patterns, so that you can understand the subject–verb–object (SVO) structure.

Let's look at the different grammatical persons and see how the verb changes. This is called *conjugating*. You only need three words: **is**, **am**, **are**.

Exercise 1-42: The Simple Present — Now | CD 1 Track 34

Listen to the audio and repeat until you have mastered the sounds and rhythms.

	Singular	Plural
1st person **Me!**	I am here.	We are here. You and I are here.
2nd person **You!**	You are here.	You (all) are here.
3rd person **Other People**	He is here. She is here. It is here.	They are here.

Exercise 1-43: The Verb *To Be* — *Is* or *Are* | CD 1 Track 35

ACCENT

*These sentences follow the subject–verb–object structure. Fill in the blanks with **is** or **are**. Then, listen to the audio and pay close attention to the intonation. Check your work using the Answer Key.*

His hands	**are**	small.	hiz hænzer smäll.
1. **Tom**		a **golfer**.	tämizə gälfr.
2. The **car**		new.	thə cäriz new.
3. The **kids**		at **school**.	thə kidzerat skool.
4. This **hat**		on my **head**.	this hædizän my hed.
5. Those **dishes**		in the **sink**.	thoz dish'zerin the sink.
6. One **watch**		enough.	wən wätchiza nuff.
7. My **shoes**		green and **red**.	my shoozer gree nän red.
8. Those **ideas**		**interesting**.	tho zy dee⁽ʸ⁾əzer intresting.
9. **Some** people		helpful.	səm peepler helpfəl.
10. That **plan**		good.	that plæniz güd.
11. Not all **jokes**		funny.	nädäll jokser funny.
12. Most **computers**		PCs.	most c'mpyoodrzer pee ceez.
13. Many **cell** phones		small.	meny cell phonzer smäll.
14. The sub**marine**		under**water**.	the səbməree nizənder wäder.
15. My **friends**		in the back **seat**.	my frenzerin the bæck seet.

Exercise 1-44: The Verb *To Be* — *Am, Is, Are* | CD 1 Track 36

*Here, fill in the blanks with **am, is,** or **are**. Then, listen to the audio and pay close attention to the intonation. Check your work using the Answer Key.*

I	**am**	here.
1. He		a **student**.
2. You		nice.
3. Bob and **Betty**		late.
4. This **student**		ready.
5. Your **brother**		there.
6. I		tired.
7. This **dancer**		good.
8. My **brothers**		hard **workers**.
9. **Businessmen**		busy.
10. Your **sister**		a **cook**.

Now that you have a good understanding of the basic grid order, we're going to shorten some of the words, add a word, and change the word order. This will give us *contractions*, *negatives*, and *questions*.

After completing this section, you will be able to make statements (positive and negative) and ask questions. You will have a very strong foundation in English. From here on, you will just need to add more vocabulary to these patterns.

Contractions, Negatives, and Questions Are Closely Related

In the top rows of the following charts, you will see the same sentence three times. Below each one you will see three changes.

1. **Contraction**   The apostrophe replaces the letter i in the word **is**.
2. **Negative**   The word **not** is added.
3. **Question**   The first two words are reversed.

Exercise 1-45: Contractions, Negatives, and Questions   CD 1 Track 37

Listen to the audio and repeat until you have mastered the sounds, rhythms, and concepts.

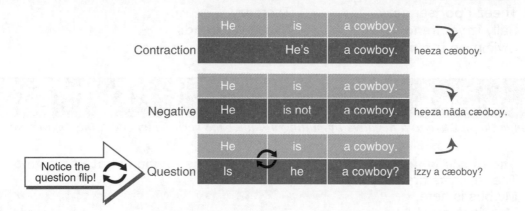

In the contracted form, you can see that the apostrophe replaces the first letter of the verb.

Full Form	Contraction		Full Form	Contraction
I am	I'm		We are	We're
You are	You're		You are	You're
He is She is It is	He's She's It's		They are	They're

Exercise 1-46: Contractions

Change the nouns to pronouns and put in the verb contraction. Then check the Answer Key.

The movie **is** interesting.   It**'s** interesting.

1. The **teachers** are **happy**.
2. My **bus** is here.
3. The **dogs** are **dirty**.

4. My **hair** is **wet**.
5. The **boys** are **late**.
6. The **clock** is **fast**.
7. **Tom** is **French**.
8. These **reports** are **easy**.
9. **Sally** is your **friend**.
10. **Swimming** is **fun**.

Exercise 1-47: Contractions — Intonation and Pronunciation   CD 1 Track 38

ACCENT

Listen to the audio and repeat five times, focusing on intonation and pronunciation.

1. The **teechrz**er **hæppy**.   Ther **hæppy**.
2. My **bə**siz hir.   Its **hir**.
3. Thə **dägz**er **dirdy**.   Ther **dirdy**.
4. My **hair**z **wet**.   Its **wet**.
5. The **boyz**er **late**.   Ther **late**.
6. The **cläcks fæst**.   Its **fæst**.
7. **Tämz French**.   Heez **French**.
8. Theez r'**port**ser **ee**zy.   Ther**eezy**.
9. Sally iz yer **frend**.   Sheez yer **frend**.
10. Swimming iz **fən**.   Its **fən**.

Exercise 1-48: Negatives

*Change the positive to a negative by putting **not** after the verb. Then check the Answer Key.*

The movie is interesting.   **The movie is not interesting.**
1. The teachers are happy.
2. My bus is here.
3. The dogs are dirty.
4. My hair is wet.
5. You are silly.
6. The clock is fast.
7. Tom is French.
8. These reports are easy.
9. I am your friend.
10. This is fun.

There are two ways to make negative contractions. One way is to replace the o in **not** with an apostrophe. The other way is to replace the first letter of **is** or **are** with an apostrophe. The meaning does not change between the two forms. One example of each contraction is highlighted.

Full Form	A	B
You are not	You aren't	You're not
We are not	We aren't	We're not
They are not	They aren't	They're not
He is not	He isn't	He's not
She is not	She isn't	She's not
It is not	It isn't	It's not

Exercise 1-49: Negative Contractions

Change the positive to a negative contraction. Change all nouns to pronouns. Then check the Answer Key.

The movie is interesting.	**It is not** interesting.	**It isn't** interesting.
1. The teachers are happy.		
2. My bus is here.		
3. The dogs are dirty.		
4. My hair is wet.		
5. You are silly.		
6. The clock is fast.		
7. Tom is French.		
8. These reports are easy.		
9. I am your friend.		
10. This is fun.		

Rule: The Question Flip ↻

As mentioned, you can ask a question by flipping the subject and the verb.

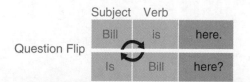

Exercise 1-50: Questions ↻

Change the statements to questions, using the question flip. Move the verb to the front. Then check the Answer Key.

The movie is interesting.	**Is the movie** interesting?
1. The teachers are happy.	
2. My bus is here.	
3. The dogs are dirty.	
4. My hair is wet.	
5. You are silly.	
6. The clock is fast.	
7. Tom is French.	
8. These reports are easy.	
9. I am your friend.	
10. This is fun.	

Exercise 1-51: Questions with Pronouns ↻

Change the statements to questions and the nouns to pronouns. Then check the Answer Key.

The movie is interesting.	**Is it** interesting?
1. The teachers are happy.	
2. My bus is here.	
3. The dogs are dirty.	
4. My hair is wet.	

  5. You are silly.
  6. The clock is fast.
  7. Tom is French.
  8. These reports are easy.
  9. I am a student.
10. This is fun.

Now let's talk about **tag questions**, which are used to confirm or verify. They are common in spoken English, but you don't see them as much in writing.

Note: The tag for **I am** is irregular. It is: **aren't I?**

Exercise 1-52: Making a Tag Question ⟳

*Reverse the order and the polarity to form a tag question. If the verb is positive, the tag is negative. If the verb is negative, the tag is positive. Use the **question flip** to create the tag ending. When you're done, check the Answer Key.*

+ − **Sam is** lazy,   **isn't he?** ⟳
− + **Sam isn't** lazy,   **is he?** ⟳
  1. The teachers are happy,
  2. My bus isn't here,
  3. The dogs are dirty,
  4. My hair is wet,
  5. You are silly,
  6. The clock is fast,
  7. Tom is French,
  8. These reports aren't easy,
  9. I am your friend,
10. This is fun,

Exercise 1-53: Contractions, Negatives, and Questions ⟳

*Complete the grid using the verb **to be**. Then check the Answer Key.*

	Statement	Negative	Question ⟳
I			Am I here?
You			
He		He isn't here.	
She			
It			
We			
They	They are here.		

Time Words: Mid and End Position

Some time words come in the middle of the sentence and some come at the end. Let's start with the ones in the middle.

Exercise 1-54: Time Words, Mid (Before the Adjective)   CD 1 Track 39

Listen to the audio and repeat until you have mastered the sounds and concepts.

		◀ Mid ▶	Adjective
1.	I'm	always	**late**.
2.	You're	almost always	**tired**.
3.	Bob and **Betty** are	generally	**confused**.
4.	He's	usually	**ready**.
5.	It's not	often	**sunny**.
↻ 6.	Are they	frequently	**hungry**?
7.	She's	sometimes	on **time**.
8.	We're	hardly ever	**worried**.
9.	You are	almost never	**satisfied**.
10.	Some people are	never	**focused**.

Exercise 1-55: Time Words, End (After the Adjective)   CD 1 Track 40

Listen to the audio and repeat until you have mastered the sounds and concepts. Notice that the ending time words all have a noun.

		Adjective	◀ End
1.	I'm	late	every **day**.
2.	You're	tired	all the **time**.
3.	Bob and **Betty** are	confused	on a daily **basis**.
4.	He's	ready	every **time**.
5.	It's not	sunny	all **day**.
↻ 6.	Are they	hungry	once a **week**?
7.	She's	on time	every **Monday**.
8.	We're	worried	twice a **day**.
9.	You are	satisfied	every **morning**.
10.	**Some** people are	focused	almost every **day**.

Exercise 1-56: Time Words, Mid — Pronunciation   CD 1 Track 41

Listen to the audio and repeat until you have mastered the sounds and concepts.

	Grammar and Spelling	Pronunciation and Intonation
1.	I'm always **late**.	äimäweez **lay**-eet.
2.	You're always **tired**.	yeräweez **täi**-yrrd.
3.	Bob and **Betty** are generally **confused**.	bäb'n **bed**dyer gen-rəlly c'n**fyu**zd.
4.	He's usually **ready**.	heez yuzhlly **reddy**.
5.	It's not often **sunny**.	its nädäffen **sənny**.

6. Are they frequently **hungry**?   är they freekwently **həngry**?
7. She's sometimes on **time**.   sheez səmtimzän **ty**-eem.
8. We're hardly ever **worried**.   wir härdly ever **wrr**-eed.
9. You are almost never **satisfied**.   yer ähmost never **sædəsfyd**.
10. **Some** people are never **focused**.   səm peepler never **foucəst**.

Exercise 1-57: Time Words, End — Pronunciation   CD 1 Track 42

Listen to the audio and repeat until you have mastered the sounds and concepts.

Grammar and Spelling	Pronunciation and Intonation
1. I'm **late** every **day**.	äim **lay** devery **day**.
2. You're **tired** all the **time**.	yer **täi**-yrrdäll the ty-**eem**.
3. Bob and **Betty** are confused every **time**.	bäb'n **bed**dyer c'nfyuzd evry **ty**-eem.
4. He's **ready** once a **week**.	heez **reddy** wəntsə **week**.
5. It's not **sunny** all **day**.	itsnäts**ənny** äll **day**.
6. Are they hungry on a daily **basis**?	är they **həngry** änə day-lee **bay**-səs?
7. She's on **time** every **Monday**.	sheezän ty mevry **mən**day.
8. We're **worried** twice a **day**.	wir **wrr**-reed twy sə **day**.
9. You are **satisfied** every **morning**.	yer **sædəsfyd** evry **morn**ing.
10. **Some** people are **focused** almost every **day**.	səm peepler **focəst** ähmost evry **day**.

Before you take the Chapter 1 test, let's quickly review the verb map. You have learned a lot in a short time, and you can now see clearly where you are on the map. You have mastered the verb **to be** in the *simple present tense*.

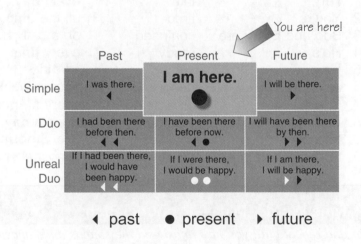

◀ past   ● present   ▶ future

Let's review everything you have learned in Chapter 1, including singular and plural nouns, pronouns, the present tense of the verb **to be**, time words, and word order. Make sure you get 100% on the test before going on to the next chapter. The Answer Key is on page 251.

To test your grammar and accent skills at this point or later, call toll-free (800) 457-4255.

Part 1: Fill in the proper pronoun for the blue words.

1. **The boy** is a student.
2. **That woman** is my friend.
3. **My parents** are very helpful.

Part 2: Replace all nouns with pronouns.

1. Bob and Bill are in the kitchen.
2. Sue and Jill are in a car.

*Part 3: Fill in the proper verb: **is, am, are**.*

1. I   *am*   a student.
2. You   my friend.
3. We   having a good time.
4. They   at a party.
5. She   out of the office.
6. He   on his way.
7. It   raining hard.
8. I   in my pajamas. (in my PJs)
9. It   not in this room.
10. They   playing outside.

Part 4: Change the sentence to the plural.

1. This test is easy.
2. There is a book.
3. That man is hungry.
4. The tree is tall.
5. My sister is a nurse.

Part 5: Put in the verb contraction.

1. It is a good idea.
2. That is old.
3. We are here.
4. You are there.
5. I am in class.
6. She is late.
7. He is funny.

Part 6: *Change the positive statement to a negative. Do **not** use contractions or pronouns.*

1. Shelly is in Europe.
2. Paul and Larry are here.
3. The girls are tired.

Part 7: *Change the positive statement to a negative. **Use** contractions and pronouns.*

1. The boys are outside.
2. Charlie is happy.
3. My eyes are closed.

Part 8: *Change the statement to a question. Do **not** use pronouns.* ↻

1. Your brother is in college.
2. His bike is in the shop.
3. My watch is fast.

Part 9: *Change the statement to a question. Change the nouns to pronouns.* ↻

1. The car is in the garage.
2. Her son is in the pool.
3. My watch is in a box.

Part 10: *Indicate where the blue words should go.*

1. He		is		rude		**never**
2. I		am		late		**every day**
3. We		are		confused		**often**
4. She		is		sleepy		**in the morning.**
5. You		are		right		**usually**

Part 11: *Underline the words that should be stressed.*

1. Bob is my friend.
2. The boys are in the car.
3. The teacher is in the room.
4. The students are happy.
5. The dogs are in the yard.

Part 12: *Identify the sound in each of the following words.*

1. plan ☐ æ ☐ ä ☐ ə
2. does ☐ æ ☐ ä ☐ ə
3. lot ☐ æ ☐ ä ☐ ə

Using what you have learned, write a five-sentence essay about your favorite subject in school. You can also write about yourself.

You can handwrite your paragraph below or e-mail it to para@grammar.bz. These paragraphs are not graded or reviewed, but simply by writing them, your English will improve. You can also request feedback and training at (800) 457-4255.

				Student Paragraph					
Send	Chat	Attach	Address	Fonts	Colors	Save As Draft		Photo Browser	Show Stationery

To: para@grammar.bz

Cc:

Bcc:

Subject: My favorite Subject in School

Signature: Corporate ⬍

My name is _____

My Favorite subject in school   is   _____
_____   Verb   Noun
Noun

_____   It   is   _____ .
                        Noun or Adjective

_____   It   is   not   _____ .
                        Noun or Adjective

_____   I   am   _____ .
                        Adjective/Noun

_____   This   is   _____ , isn't it!
                        Adjective

Chapter 2: Modified Nouns and Main Verbs

This chapter covers nouns, pronouns, prepositions of location, conjunctions, time words, and the present tense of main verbs and helping verbs.

| DICTATION | Listen carefully to the dictation and write the five sentences. Use standard spelling and make a note of important sounds, such as **æ**, **ä**, and **ə**. |

Exercise 2-1: Dictation — CD 1 Track 43

Listen to the audio and write the exact transcription in the spaces below. Then check the Answer Key.

1. _____

2. _____

3. _____

4. _____

5. _____

| STORY | This is a continuation of the story about Max. In Chapter 1, we worked with the nine-grid for stories, using only the verb **to be** in the present tense (*is, am, are*). |

Max

Here, we are going to use the same format, but we add simple intro words such as **suddenly** and **fortunately**. We also use *main verbs* in addition to the verb **to be**. This is still in the present tense.

Exercise 2-2: "The Incident in Venice" — CD 1 Track 44

*Listen to the audio and repeat out loud five times. Focus on the intonation. The verbs are blue. Look up new vocabulary in the back of the book and write the definition above the word. Notice that each sentence has a **subject** in the beginning, a **verb** in the middle, and an **object** at the end.*

I'm a **body**builder. **One** day, I'm in Gold's **Gym** in Venice, **California**. After **training**, I go to the **parking** lot. **Suddenly**, I hear three **gun**shots. There are three **guys**. **One** of them has a **gun**. He shoots a man! I think that they're in a **gang**. It's really **dangerous**. I go **home**. **Fortunately**, I'm not **hurt**. My **girl**friend, **Eve**, is **careful**, but she's **used** to living in **Venice**.

Exercise 2-3: "The Incident in Venice" — Pronunciation   CD 1 Track 45

Listen to the audio and repeat out loud five times. Focus on the pronunciation and the word connections.

ACCENT

Imə **bä**dybilder. **One** day, aimin Goldz **Gym** in Venəs, Cælə**for**nyə. æfter training, I go t' thə **pärking** lät. **Suddənly**, I hir three **gən**shots. Therər three **guyz**. **Wən**əvəm hazə **gən**. He **shoots** a mæn! I **think** thət thehr inə **gæng**. It's rilly **danjerəs**. I go **home**. **Forch**ənətly, I'm nät **hrrt**. My **girl**friend, **Eve**, iz **care**fəl, bət sheez **ustə** living in **Venəs**.

An important part of telling a story is how well you reduce the high-frequency words. *The reduced sounds are the unstressed vowels. These lose their original pronunciation and sound like a schwa (ə).* Look at the story above, and notice all the schwa (ə) symbols. There are a couple dozen in just this short story!

If you count all the words an American uses in a day, the number one word is **the** (thə). Make sure you have a clear, popping TH and a very reduced schwa, **uh** (ə).

Exercise 2-4: Top 30 High-Frequency Words and Sounds   CD 1 Track 46

Listen to the audio and repeat out loud five times. The high-frequency words are in blue. They are shown in context to help you pronounce them naturally.

1–5

the **car**	**one** of us	on and **on**	once a **week**	We plan to **go.**
thə car	wənəvəs	änənän	wəntsə week	We plan də go.

6–10

in it	Is he?	You **know?**	that I **said**	**Get** it!
innit	Izzy?	Y' know?	the dai sed	Geddit!

11–15

He says O**K**.	How was it?	It's for **you.**	I'm on it.	What are they **doing?**
hee sezoh K	How wəzzit?	its fr **you**	aim**ä**nit	whadder they doing?

16–20

as **big** as	with us	my **only**	They **like** it.	**Bob** and I
əz bigəz	withus	myonly	they ly kit	**bä**ban I

21–25

this time	There it is.	This or that?	She's here.	Can I have one?
this ty-eem	theridiz	thiser that?	sheez here.	Knai haev w'n?

26–30

Did he do it?	We are here.	Let's get it.	How?	That's not it.
diddee do(w)it?	Wir here.	lets geddit.	hæow?	That's nadit.

 NOUNS

In Chapter 1, we learned that nouns are people, places, and things. We also learned that pronouns replace nouns (Joe = he).

We are going to start adding information to nouns. This added information is called a **modifier**.

Then, we're going to work with **prepositions** to tell us where the noun is, and with **conjunctions** to link nouns and sentences together.

Describing Nouns

Now that we know what nouns are, we're going to start dressing them up a bit. If you say, **He has a car**, this leaves out a lot of information. You need to describe the noun: a new car, an old car, a black car, a red car, a big car, a small car, some cars, ten cars.

Let's talk about the **intonation** of nouns for a moment. When you introduce new information, you need to stress the noun: It's a new **car**.

Exercise 2-5: New Information   CD 1 Track 47

Listen and repeat five times, focusing on the intonation.

1. He has a blue **pen**.
2. She seems like a nice **person**.
3. You take long **walks**.
4. I like my red **coat**.
5. She plays two **instruments**.

You can also use contrast by stressing the modifier: It's a **new** car, not an **old** one.

Exercise 2-6: New Information and Contrast   CD 1 Track 48

Listen and repeat five times, focusing on the intonation.

New Information	Contrast
1. He has a blue **pen**.	He has a **blue** pen, not a **black** one.
2. She seems like a nice **person**.	She **seems** like a nice person, but she is **not**.
3. You take long **walks**.	You take **long** walks, not **short** ones.
4. I like my red **coat**.	I **like** my **red** coat, but I **love** my **blue** one.
5. She plays two **instruments**.	She plays **two** instruments, not **three**.

In Max's story, you may have noticed words like **bodybuilder**, **girlfriend**, and **parking lot**. Two nouns are stuck together to form a new word, with a new meaning. This is called a compound noun. The stress goes on the first noun: **body**builder, **girl**friend, **parking** lot.

Exercise 2-7: Descriptions   CD 1 Track 49

Listen and repeat five times, placing the emphasis on the second word.

1. It's a metal **clip**.
2. It's a good **book**.
3. It's a plastic **cup**.
4. He's a little **boy**.
5. It's a rusty **can**.
6. It's a thick **book**.
7. It's fresh **sauce**.
8. It's a bronze **pot**.
9. It's a paper **plane**.
10. It's an expensive **grater**.

Exercise 2-8: Compound Nouns   CD 1 Track 50

Listen and repeat five times, placing the emphasis on the first word.

1. It's a **paper** clip.
2. It's a **book**shelf.
3. It's a **coffee** cup.
4. He's a **cow**boy.
5. It's a **trash**can.
6. It's a **note**book.
7. It's **hot** sauce.
8. It's a **tea**pot.
9. It's an **air**plane.
10. It's a **cheese** grater.

Exercise 2-9: Contrasting Descriptions — Compound Nouns   CD 1 Track 51

Listen and repeat five times, focusing on the intonation.

Descriptions	**Compounds**
1. It's a metal **clip**.	It's a **paper** clip.
2. It's a good **book**.	It's a **book**shelf.
3. It's a plastic **cup**.	It's a **coffee** cup.
4. He's a little **boy**.	He's a **cow**boy.
5. It's a rusty **can**.	It's a **trash**can.
6. It's a thick **book**.	It's a **note**book.
7. It's fresh **sauce**.	It's **hot** sauce.
8. It's a bronze **pot**.	It's a **tea**pot.
9. It's a paper **plane**.	It's an **air**plane.
10. It's an expensive **grater**.	It's a **cheese** grater.

Exercise 2-10: Max Revisited   CD 1 Track 52

Listen and repeat five times, focusing on the difference between descriptions and compounds.

I'm a **bodybuilder**. One day, I'm in Gold's **Gym** in Venice, **California**. After **training**, I go to the **parking** lot. Suddenly, I hear three **gun**shots. There are three **guys**. One of them has a gun. He shoots a man! I think that they're in a gang. It's really **dangerous**. I go home. Fortunately, I'm not hurt. My **girl**friend, Eve, is careful, but she's used to living in Venice.

Let's do a quick review of nouns and pronouns. With **he** / **she** / **it** add –s to the end of the main verb.

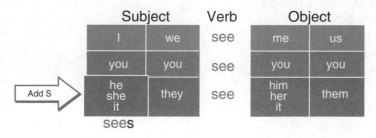

31

Exercise 2-11: Noun and Pronoun Review

Let's do a quick pronoun review. Notice the compound nouns and descriptions. Fill in the blanks with the appropriate pronoun. The emphasis is on the noun in the first set and on the verb in the second set. When you're done, check the Answer Key.

Nouns		Nouns	Pronouns		Pronouns
The **boy**	eats	an **apple**.	He	eats	one.
1. **Susie**	studies	**French**.		studies	
2. The **employees**	need	long **breaks**.		need	
3. **Students**	ask	hard **questions**.		ask	
4. The **child**	breaks	his favorite **toy**.		breaks	
5. Your **parents**	make	a **phone** call.		make	
6. The **CEO**	forgets	his latest **plan**.		forgets	
7. **Commuters**	take	the **bullet** train.		take	
8. My **sister**	wants	a new **car**.		wants	
9. Your **mom**	likes to cook	**pan**cakes.		likes to **cook**	
10. **The dogs**	need	warm **baths**.		need	

Exercise 2-12: Noun and Pronoun Review — Pronunciation   CD 1 Track 53

ACCENT

Now, let's see how that sounds. Listen to the audio and repeat five times.

Nouns	Pronouns
1. **Suzee** stədeez **French**.	She **stədee** zit.
2. Thee⁽ʸ⁾**employeez** need **breaks**.	They **need**'m.
3. **Students** æsk **kwesj'nz.**	They **æsk**'m.
4. The **child** breaks hiz **toy**.	He **break** sit.
5. Your **perents** may kə **phone** call.	They **may** kwən.
6. The **CEO** frgets hiz **plæn**.	He frget sit.
7. **Cəmmyuderz** take **trains**.	They **take**'m.
8. My **s'strr** wantsə new **car**.	She **wänts** wən.
9. Yrrrr **mäm** likes t' cook **pæn**cakes.	She likes to **cook**'m.
10. The **dägz** need wōrm **bæthz**.	They need wōrm wənz.

Exercise 2-13: Replacing Nouns

Rewrite each sentence, replacing all nouns with pronouns. The stress moves from the nouns to the verbs. Check the Answer Key when you're done.

Edward likes his **classes**.   He **likes** them.
1. Joe and **Frank** saw a **movie**.
2. **Tammy** plays **tennis**.
3. **Mary** and I took a **trip**.
4. **Dave** married **Susie**.
5. Our **friends** gave the **book** to **Ed** and me.

Things and Locations

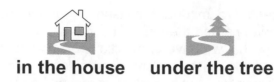

in the house   under the tree

Prepositions tell you the **location** of a thing. Location includes **places**, **people**, and **time**.

The classic definition is

"What a plane can do to a cloud."

In a cloud, *by* a cloud, *near* a cloud, etc.

The ✈ is
in a cloud.

on a cloud.
over a cloud.
above a cloud.
behind a cloud.
after a cloud.
from a cloud.
for a cloud.
of a cloud.
to a cloud.
in a cloud
by a cloud.
near a cloud.
next to a cloud.
beside a cloud.
in front of a cloud.
before a cloud.
under a cloud.
below a cloud.
underneath a cloud.

This explains where a plane can be in relation to a cloud. Of course, it can be much more than just **in** a cloud.

For locations, you can use a single word (*above*) or a phrase (*on top of*).

The **be-** words (*below*, *behind*, *before*, *beside*, *beneath*) are stressed on the second syllable and the first syllable is shortened (b'**low**, b'**hind**, b'**fore**, b'**side**, b'**neath**).

Exercise 2-14: Prepositions of Location

Circle the appropriate location word. Then check the Answer Key.

1.	The little **boy** hides	on / under / over	the **table**.
2.	My **sister** jumped	over / of / after	the **bush**.
3.	I **always** go	after / beyond / through	the **tunnel**.
4.	My **dog** is always	for / beside / to	me.
5.	**Look**	before / behind / after	the **couch**.
6.	It is	underneath / for / behind	the **super**market.
7.	I always sit	for / next to / under	the **door**.
8.	I put it	under / to / for	the **door**mat.
↻ 9.	Is it	for / over / on	the **table**?
10.	She gets **letters**	in / above / from	her **sister**.
11.	I **put** that	on / after / in	a **box**.
12.	You say that	under / in front of / from	them this time.
13.	I have a **scar**	in / on	my **knee**.
14.	You are	on / in / by	a good **mood**.
↻ 15.	Is the little **box**	above / under / to	the **couch**?
16.	He is looking	below / for / behind	her.
17.	She only uses **English**	in / at / by	**class**.
18.	I am working	in / at / by	**home** today.
19.	The students live	in / at / by / on	the second **floor**.
20.	We live	in / at / on	**New** York.

33

There Is / There Are

As you have seen, patterns are important. Instead of learning thousands of words, you can learn a couple of patterns and then just mix and match. Let's go back to the verb **to be** for a moment. Now that we have prepositions of location, we can use **there** and the verb **to be** to indicate the existence and general location of things, as in **there is** and **there are**. Notice that, instead of individual words, we're now linking phrases. Look at the chart below. In the first column, we have **there + is / are**. In the noun column, we add modifiers. The last column is for the location. Learn the various phrases and then link them together in order: A-B-C.

	A verb	B noun	C location
There	is	a book	on the table.
	isn't	two lamps	in the den.
	are	a picture	on the wall.
	aren't	some pens	in the desk.
		no food	in the refrigerator.
		a few kids	at school.
		few kids	in the gym right now.
		too many cars	in the garage.
		six bottles	under the table.
		any food	in the sink.
		much sun	in the afternoon.
		many people	in the park.
		a couple of	at the beach.

This exercise lets you start combining *phrases*, rather than single *words*.

Exercise 2-15: *There Is* vs. *There Are*   CD 1 Track 54

Listen to the audio and pay close attention to the intonation.

A	B What / Who	C Where	Pronunciation
There is	a **fly**	in my **soup**!	therzə **fly**in my **soop**. (*not therizə*)
There is	a **credit** card	in my **wallet**.	therzə **credit** card in my **wäll**et.
There are	**cars**	in the **garage**.	therer **cär**zin the gə**raj**.
There is	not enough **room**	in my **house**.	therz nädə nəff **room**in my **house**.
There are	some **people**	at my **door**.	therer s'm **pee**pəlat my **dore**.
↻ Are there	many **students**	at this **school**?	är ther meny **stud**entsat this **skool**?
There are	a couple of **dogs**	over there.	thererə couplə **däg** zover there.
There are	very many **words**	**here**.	therer very meny **wrrd**z **hir**.
There are	not many **people**	at the **party**.	therer nät meny **pee**pəlat thə **pär**dy.
There are	too many **cooks**	in the **kitchen**!	therer too meny **cük**sin thə **kit**chen.
↻ Is there	a good **restaurant**	near my **house**?	iz therə güd **res**tränt nir my **house**?
There are	a few **zebras**	in **California**.	ther arə few **ze**brəzin cælə **for**nyə.
There are	few **zebras**	in **Alaska**.	therer few **ze**brazinə **læs**kə.

Note: a few = some / few = not many

Linking Words, Phrases, and Sentences

Let's use **conjunctions** to link nouns, phrases, and sentences together.

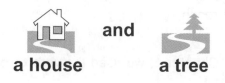

a house   and   **a tree**

The five primary conjunctions are **and**, **but**, **so**, **or**, and **because**.

And is the same as a *plus sign*.

$A + B = C$
Bob and Betty are friends.

But indicates the *opposite* situation.

A, but not B
Joe likes to drive, but not to fly.

So means *for that reason*.

A, so B
It's cold, so we put on a sweater.

Or indicates a *choice*.

A or B
Apples or oranges

Because indicates a *reason*.

A because B
He cries because he is sad.

It can sound childish to use short sentences. As your language skills develop, you will use conjunctions to take many short thoughts and create a single, longer sentence. Notice how the following goes from five sentences to just one. (**Oranges** is pronounced **ornj'z**.)

Ed bought some apples. He bought some pears.
He bought some oranges. He did not buy any bananas.
He did not buy any grapes.

Ed bought apples, pears, **and** oranges,
but **no** bananas **or** grapes.

You are listing several items, so notice the phrasing.

Ed bought apples, ↗ pears, ↗ **and** oranges, ↗
but **no** bananas **or** grapes. ↘

Exercise 2-16: Conjunctions — *And, But, So, Or, Because*

*Fill in the appropriate conjunction, using **and**, **but**, **so**, **or**, and **because**. Then check the Answer Key.*

She knows how to drive,	but	she prefers to ride her bike.
1. We can't swim,		we don't go to the pool.
2. Everyone eats		drinks at weddings.
3. We don't have a map,		we get lost.

4. We get lost   we don't have a map.
5. The workers are tired,   they take a break.
6. We are tired,   we go to work anyway.
7. The tourists go to Italy   France.
8. The tourists go to Italy   not France.
9. They want to speak French,   they go to France.
10. The kids ride bikes   fly kites.

In Chapter 1, we used the verb **to be** and its forms *am, is,* and *are*.

Now, we are going to work with *main verbs* in the present tense. These are action words, such as **run, go,** and **work**. We will also begin using *helping verbs* to make questions, negatives, and the emphatic form.

Main Verb: *Do*

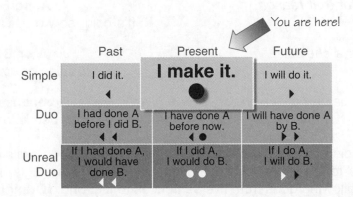

We'll be using the same patterns and pronouns as before. Nouns and pronouns are both important, but pronouns are much more common.

Remember: The stress falls on the *nouns*. When pronouns are used instead of nouns, the stress falls on the *verb*.

Also remember that the letter **O** sounds like **ah**, **S** sounds like **Z**, and the **H** fades away.

Tom	Bob.
sees	
He	him.

Täm	Bäb.
seez	
He	him.

These are the most commonly used *verbs*.

The 16 Most Common Verbs			
to be	to do	to have	to come
to see	to seem	to give	to take
to make	to put	to send	to say
to go	to keep	to get	to let

It's also important to know opposite verb pairs. Make sure that you know the meaning of each set.

Some words have more than one opposite, such as **play / work** and **play / fight**.

Common Verb Opposites			
to ask	to tell	to win	to lose
to bring	to take	to play	to work
to come	to go	to play	to fight
to forget	to remember	to push	to pull
to give	to take	to put	to remove
to get	to give	to put on	to take off
to hope	to wish	to read	to write
to like	to not like	to talk	to listen
to look for	to find	to walk	to ride
to find	to lose	to walk	to drive

Main verbs change from person to person, normally by adding an –s to the third-person form. This is called **conjugating** the verb.

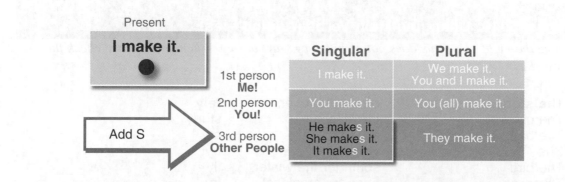

	Singular	Plural
1st person **Me!**	I make it.	We make it. You and I make it.
2nd person **You!**	You make it.	You (all) make it.
3rd person **Other People**	He makes it. She makes it. It makes it.	They make it.

Present **I make it.**

Add S

Exercise 2-17: Changing Main Verbs (Regular)

Circle the proper form. Then read the sentences out loud, stressing the nouns. When you're done, check the Answer Key.

	Lou	**sells**	used **cars**.
1.	**Bob**	speak / speaks	**English**.
2.	**Betty (beddy)**	live in / lives in	**America**.
3.	**People**	need / needs	**money**.
4.	**The book**	seem / seems	**easy**.
5.	**Teachers**	give / gives	**tests**.
6.	**That person**	want / wants	a **car**.
7.	Bob and **Betty**	make / makes	a lot of **mistakes**.
8.	Your **boss**	send / sends	an **e-mail**.
9.	Your **friend**	get / gets	a **job**.
10.	The **class**	take / takes	a **break**.

Just as you saw with plurals in Chapter 1, third-person verbs ending in **O**, **X**, **Z**, **SS**, **SH**, and **CH** add –**es** at the end, instead of just –**s**, to make the plural form.

A little girl came home from school and said, "Mommy, we learned how to make babies today!" The mother was quite surprised and said, "Um, what do you mean?" The little girl replied, "Well, you just drop the Y and add IES!"

Exercise 2-18: Changing Main Verbs (Adding –es)

Add –es to the verb. Then check the Answer Key.

	She	**washes**	her hair every day.	wash
1.	**Elsie**		to the **store**.	go
2.	The **manager**		a lot of **work**.	do
3.	**Joe**		at the **gym**.	box
4.	My **alarm** clock		at 6:00 **am**.	buzz
5.	The **mother**		the **baby**.	kiss
6.	The **boy**		the **ball**.	catch
7.	The **child**		the **swings**.	push

Exercise 2-19: Changing Main Verbs (Adding –ies)

Change the –y to –ies. This does not include –oy, –ay, or –ey. When you're done check the Answer Key.

	The student	**relies**	on the teacher.	rely
1.	The class		the lessons.	study
2.	The baby		all night.	cry
3.	She		very hard.	try
4.	The bird		south for the winter.	fly
5.	The cook		eggs for breakfast.	fry
6.	He		doing it.	deny

Exercise 2-20: Changing Main Verbs (*Go*)

*Complete the sentence, using either **go** or **goes**. Then check the Answer Key.*

1.	He		to the movies.
2.	I		up the stairs.
3.	We		to the mall and shop.
4.	She		out with her boyfriend.
5.	They		hiking.

Exercise 2-21: Changing Main Verbs (*Do*)

*Complete the sentence, using either **do** or **does**. Then check the Answer Key.*

1.	You		not care about good **grades**.
2.	We		enjoy that **restaurant**.
3.	She		dance really **well**.
4.	It		make a **difference**.
5.	I		need to **help** him.

Exercise 2-22: Changing Main Verbs (*Have*)

*Complete the sentence, using either **have** or **has**. Then check the Answer Key.*

1. She _____ a long **name**.
2. You _____ the best **ideas**!
3. We _____ an excellent **plan**.
4. They _____ a **really** nice **house**.
5. It _____ four **doors**.

> There is an ancient invention that allows people to see through walls.
>
> It's called a "window."

Changing and Unchanging Verbs

These next five pages are very important. Do not go further until you understand them perfectly. You will use these concepts every time you speak English.

Main verbs tell the action. Every sentence has a main verb (or the verb **to be**). The main verb has two forms: the *changing* form (**see** / **sees**) and the *unchanging* form (**see**).

The unchanging form is the action part of the main verb: **see**, **do, go, make**. This is also called the *simple* form. You cannot add –s to the simple form.

Helping verbs are a *changing* form. They always go together with the *simple* form of the main verb. The helping verb takes over the job of the main verb.

Let's add a *helping* verb to make a regular statement *emphatic*. This shows a stronger opinion. In a regular statement, you skip over the spot for the *helping verb*.

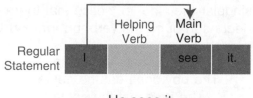

He sees it.
He **does** see it!

With **he / she / it**, the helping verb changes from **do** to **does**. The main verb stays in the simple form. The emphatic form is not high frequency, but it will help you make negative statements and questions.

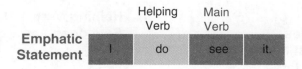

Exercise 2-23: Adding *Do* for Emphasis (I, You, We, They)

*Add **do** to make the statement stronger. Use the unchanging form of the main verb. Then check the Answer Key.*

Main Verb
The boys **eat** apples.
1. The **kids** play at the **park**.
2. The **dogs** get **dirty**.
3. You **forget** many **things**.
4. These re**ports** need **work**.
5. I **work** too **hard**.

Helping Verb + Unchanging Form
The boys **do eat** apples!

The *simple* unchanging form stays the same. The *helping verb* changes for **he / she / it**.

Exercise 2-24: Adding *Does* for Emphasis (He / She / It)

*Add **does** to make the statement stronger. Use the unchanging form of the main verb (simple form). Then check the Answer Key.*

Main Verb
The boy **eats** apples.
1. My **bus** comes **late**.
2. My **boss** needs this **done**.
3. The **clock** costs a **lot**.
4. **Tom** makes **mistakes**.
5. The **car** runs **well**.

Helping Verb + Unchanging Form
The boy **does eat** apples.

The One-S Rule

With the third person singular (he, she, it), notice that there is only one S at a time, either on the subject noun or on the verb, but **not on both**.

The boy eat**s** the apple.
The boy doe**s** eat the apple.
The boy**s** eat the apple.
The boy**s** do eat the apple.

Exercise 2-25: Adding *Do* or *Does* for Emphasis

*Add **do** or **does** to make the statement stronger. Use the simple unchanging form for the main verb. Then check the Answer Key.*

Main Verb
Sam **eats** apples.
1. The **kids** play at the **park**.
2. My **bus** comes **late**.
3. The **dogs** get **dirty**.

Helping Verb + Unchanging Form
Sam **does eat** apples.

4. My **boss** needs this **done**.
5. You **forget** many **things**.
6. The **clock** costs a **lot**.
7. **Tom** makes **mistakes**.
8. These re**ports** need **work**.
9. I **work** too **hard**.
10. The **car** runs **well**.

Exercise 2-26: Adding *Can*

*Add **can** to indicate ability. Use the unchanging form for the main verb. Then check the Answer Key.*

Main Verb	Can + Simple Form
Sam **eats** apples.	Sam **can eat** apples.

1. The **kids** play at the **park**.
2. My **bus** comes **late**.
3. The **dogs** get **dirty**.
4. My **boss** gets things **done**.
5. You **forget** many **things**.
6. The **clock** costs a **lot**.
7. **Tom** makes **mistakes**.
8. These **reports** change **every day**.
9. I **work** too **hard**.
10. The **car** runs **well**.

Positive	Negative	Extra Positive	Extra Negative
I can **do** it.	I can't **do** it.	I **can** do it.	I **can't** do it.
I c'n do it.	I cæn't do it.	I cææn do it.	I cæn't do it.

6 Verbs + Infinitive	
want to do	**like** to do
have to do	**hope** to do
need to do	**try** to do

The infinitive is **to** + *simple form*, such as **to be**, **to do**, or **to go**. It is used like a noun. You can say **I eat pizza**, **I want pizza**, or **I want to eat pizza**.

Exercise 2-27: Adding a Verb + To

Add one of the six verbs in the box above to each sentence. Use the unchanging form for the main verb. Notice that the meanings are more positive with these words. When you're done, check the Answer Key.

Main Verbs	Verb + To + Simple Form
Sam **eats** apples.	Sam **likes to eat** apples.

1. The **kids** play at the **park**.
2. My **friend** comes **early**.
3. The **dogs** get **a bone**.
4. My **boss** has this **done**.

5. You **remember** many **things**.
6. The **girl** dances a **lot**.
7. **Tom** makes **money**.
8. These **guys** find **work**.
9. I **work hard**.
10. **Sam** runs **fast**.

Negatives

Negatives follow the same pattern as the emphatic form. The remaining spot is filled with **not**. It goes between the helping verb and the unchanging form of the main verb. As usual, the helping verb **do** changes to **does** with **he**, **she**, and **it**. The negative of **can** is **cannot**.

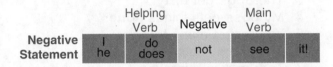

Exercise 2-28: Adding *Not*

*Add **not** between the helping verb and the main verb. Use the unchanging form of the main verb. Then check the Answer Key.*

Sam does eat apples.   **Sam does not eat apples.**

1. The kids **do** play at the park.
2. My bus **does** come late.
3. The dogs can get **dirty**.
4. My boss **does** need this done.
5. You **do** forget many things.
6. The clock **does** cost a lot.
7. **Tom** can make mis**takes**.
8. These reports **do** need work.
9. I **do** work too hard.
10. The **car** can run **well**.
11. My sister **does** want to help him.
12. I **do** have to study.
13. We **do** need to practice.
14. They **do** like to dance together.
15. He **does** want to take the test.

Contractions

Full Form	Contraction
I do not do it.	I don't do it.
You do not do it.	You don't do it.
He does not do it. She does not do it. It does not do it.	He doesn't do it. She doesn't do it. It doesn't do it.

Full Form	Contraction
We do not do it.	We don't do it.
You do not do it.	You don't do it.
They do not do it.	They don't do it.

Exercise 2-29: Changing to a Contraction

*Replace the o in **not** with an apostrophe. Make it into a single word. Then check the Answer Key.*

Sam **does not** eat apples.   Sam does**n't** eat apples.

1. The **kids** do not play at the **park**.
2. My **bus** does not come **late**.
3. The **dogs** do not get **dirty**.
4. My **boss** does not need this **done**.
5. You do not for**get** many **things**.
6. The **clock** does not **cost** a lot.
7. **Tom** does not make **mistakes**.
8. These re**ports** do not need **work**.
9. I do not **work** too hard.
10. The **car** does not **run** well.
11. My **sister** does not want to **help** him.
12. I do not have to **study**.
13. We do not need to **practice**.
14. They do not like to **dance** together.
15. He does not want to take the **test**.

Questions

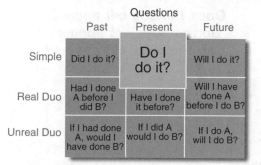

	Past	Present	Future
Simple	Did I do it?	Do I do it?	Will I do it?
Real Duo	Had I done A before I did B?	Have I done it before?	Will I have done A before I do B?
Unreal Duo	If I had done A, would I have done B?	If I did A would I do B?	If I do A, will I do B?

Let's work with questions now. You will be using the same helping verbs, **do** and **does**, but they will change position with the subject. This is called the *Question Flip*.

As usual, you will use the unchanging form of the main verb (called the *simple form*).

Rule: The Question Flip ↻ + Simple Unchanging Form

To make a question from an emphatic statement, you just need to flip the first two words.

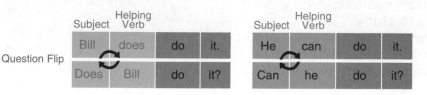

Exercise 2-30: Making a Question from an Emphatic Statement ↻

*Reverse the noun and the helping verb to form a question. Use the **unchanging** form of the main verb (simple form). Then check the Answer Key.*

Sam and Ed **do** eat apples.	**Do** Sam and Ed eat apples?
Sam **does** eat apples.	**Does** Sam eat apples?
Betty **can** play the piano.	**Can** Betty play the piano?

1. The kids **do** play at the park!
2. My bus **does** come late!
3. The dogs **can** get dirty!
4. My boss **does** need this done!
5. You **do** forget many things!
6. The clock **does** cost a lot!
7. Tom **can** make mistakes!
8. These reports **do** need work!
9. I **do** work too hard!
10. The car **does** run well!
11. My sister **can** help him!
12. I **do** have to study!
13. We **do** need to practice!
14. They **do** like to dance together!
15. He **does** hope to pass the test!

The next exercise is very similar to the previous one, but you will start with a regular statement, instead of an emphatic one.

Exercise 2-31: Making a Question from a Regular Statement ↻

*Add **do**, **does**, or **can** to the beginning of each statement to form a question. Use the unchanging form of the main verb. Remember, there is no –s with the simple form. When you're done, check the Answer Key.*

The boy **eats** apples.	**Does** the boy **eat** apples?
The boys **eat** apples.	**Do** the boys **eat** apples?
The boys **can eat** apples.	**Can** the boys **eat** apples?

1. The **kids** play at the **park**.
2. My **bus** comes **late**.
3. The **dogs** can get **dirty**.
4. My **boss** needs this **done**.
5. You **forget** many **things**.
6. The **clock** costs a **lot**.
7. **Tom** can make **mistakes**.
8. These **reports** need **work**.
9. I **work** too **hard**.
10. The **car** runs **well**.
11. My **sister** can **help** him.
12. I have to **study**.
13. We need to **practice**.
14. They like to **dance** together.
15. He **hopes** to pass the **test**.

Exercise 2-32: Making a Question with Pronouns ↻

*Add **do**, **does**, or **can** to the beginning of each statement to form a question. Change the nouns to pronouns. The stress moves to the verb. When you're done, check the Answer Key.*

The **boy** eats apples.
The **boys** eat apples.
The **boys** can eat apples.

1. The kids **play** there.
2. My **bus** comes **late**.
3. The **dogs** can get **dirty**.
4. My **boss** needs this **done**.
5. You **forget** many **things**.
6. The **clock** costs a **lot**.
7. **Tom** can make **mistakes**.
8. These **reports** need **work**.
9. **Bob** works too **hard**.
10. The **car** runs **well**.
11. My **sister** wants to **help** our **friend**.
12. I have to study the **lesson**.
13. We need to practice the **guitar**.
14. The **family** likes to **dance** together.
15. Sam hopes to pass the **test**.

Does he eat them?
Do they eat them?
Can they eat them?

Exercise 2-33: Making a Question with Pronouns — Pronunciation   CD 1 Track 55

ACCENT

Now, let's see how that sounds. Listen to the audio and repeat five times. Notice that the Hs and the THs get dropped. Trust the phonetics. Looks weird, sounds great!

Duzz Sæm eedapplz?
1. Do the kidz **play** there?
2. Duzz my **bɘs** kɘm **late**?
3. C'n the **dägz** get **dirdy**?
4. Duzz my **bäss** need this **dɘn**?
5. Do you **forget** many **things**?
6. Duzz the **cläck cäst** a lät?
7. C'n **Täm** make **mistakes**?
8. Do theez re**ports** need **work**?
9. Duzz **Bäb** work too **hard**?
10. Duzz the **cär** run **well**?
11. C'n my **sister help**im?
12. Dwäi hæf tɘ stɘdy the **lessɘn**?
13. Dwee need tɘ præctice the **guitar**?
14. Duzz thɘ fæmlee like tɘ **dæns** tɘgether?
15. Duzz **Sæm** hope tɘ pæss thɘ **test**?

Duzzy eedem?
Do they **play** there?
Duzzit kɘm **late**?
C'n they get **dirdy**?
Duzzy needit **dɘn**?
D'you fer**ge**dem?
Duzzit **cäst** a lät?
Canny **may** kem?
Do they **need**it?
Duzzy **wrrrrk** too hard?
Duzzit **run** well?
C'n she **help**im?
Dwäi hæf tɘ **stɘdy** it?
Dwee need tɘ **præc**tice it?
D'they like tɘ **dæns** tɘgether?
Duzzy hope tɘ **pæss** it?

Exercise 2-34: Making a Tag Question ↻

*Reverse the order and the polarity to form a tag question. If the verb is positive, the tag is negative. If the verb is negative, the tag is positive. The last five are a review of the verb **to be**. When you're done, check the Answer Key.*

Sam eats **apples,**	**doesn't he?**	duzzanee
1. The **kids** don't play at the **park,**		doo they
2. My **bus** comes **late,**		duzzanit
3. The **dogs** can get **dirty,**		cant they
4. My **boss** needs this **done,**		duzzanee
5. You **forget** many **things,**		donchyoo
6. The **clock** costs a **lot,**		duzzanit
7. **Tom** can make **mistakes,**		cantee
8. These **reports** need **work,**		doan they
9. I **work** too **hard,**		doanai
10. The **car** doesn't run **well,**		duzzit
11. **Bob** is **late,**		izzanee
12. Your **mom** isn't **worried,**		iz she
13. The **papers** are **torn,**		arnt they
14. I'm **here,**		ar nai
15. I'm not **here,**		amai

Using the same pattern, change your tone to make an assertion.

Exercise 2-35: Making a Tag Assertion ↻

*Reverse the order and the polarity to form a tag assertion. If the verb is positive, the tag is negative. If the verb is negative, the tag is positive. The last five are a review of the verb **to be**. When you're done, check the Answer Key.*

Sam eats **apples,**	**doesn't** he!	**duzz**anee!
Sam doesn't eat **apples,**	**does** he!	**duzz**ee!
1. The **kids** don't play at the **park,**		**doo** they!
2. My **bus** comes **late,**		**duzz**anit!
3. The **dogs** can get **dirty,**		**cant** they!
4. My **boss** needs this **done,**		**duzz**anee!
5. You **forget** many **things,**		**donch**yoo!
6. The **clock** costs a **lot,**		**duzz**anit!
7. **Tom** can make **mistakes,**		**can**dy!
8. These **reports** need **work,**		**doan** they!
9. I **work** too **hard,**		**doa**nai!
10. The **car** doesn't run **well,**		**duzz**it!
11. **Bob** is **late,**		**izz**anee!
12. Your **mom** isn't **worried,**		iz she!
13. The **papers** are **torn,**		**arnt** they!
14. I'm **here,**		**ar** nai!
15. I'm not **here,**		**am**ai!

Remember: The inflection on a tag question is **up**, **up**. The inflection on a tag assertion is **down**, **down**.

Exercise 2-36: Identifying Intent — CD 1 Track 56

Listen to the audio and identify if each item is a question or an assertion. Put in either a question mark (?) or an exclamation point (!). Then check the Answer Key.

1. I see him, don't I _____
2. They don't like it, do they _____
3. She wasn't there, was she _____
4. Bob had to leave, didn't he _____
5. You need one, don't you _____
6. You like it, don't you _____
7. He doesn't know, does he _____
8. We can work on it, can't we _____
9. They think so, don't they _____
10. It is good, isn't it _____

Exercise 2-37: Contractions, Negatives, and Questions

*Complete the grid for the verb **to do**. Then check the Answer Key.*

	Statement	Negative	Question
I			Do I do it?
You			
He		He doesn't do it.	
She			
It			
We			
They	They do it.		

Commands and Suggestions

Commands are easy in English. All you need is the simple form of either the verb **to be** or the *main verb*. Colloquially, a command can start with **go**. Formal commands use the present tense of the verb **to be**. You can make a suggestion with **let's**. Commands can be either positive or negative.

Positive	**Negative**
Be good!	Don't be bad!
Stop it! Go away!	Don't stop! Don't go!
Go get me a hammer.	Don't go and forget about it!
Let's go!	Let's not do it.
You are to be here by 5:00.	You are never to speak of this again.

Exercise 2-38: Commands

Change the positive commands to the negative. Then check the Answer Key.

Get lost!	**Don't** get lost!
Let's try it again!	Let's **not** try it again!
You are to finish by tomorrow.	You are **not** to finish by tomorrow.
1. Give up!	
2. They are to be informed!	
3. Try again!	
4. Let's think about it!	
5. Bring it back!	

 **TEST** Let's review everything you have learned in Chapter 2, including nouns, main verbs, helping verbs, commands, prepositions of location, conjunctions, and tag endings. Check your work using the Answer Key.

Part 1: Replace all nouns with pronouns.

1. Edgar buys a new yacht.
2. Sam and Charlie fly the kite.
3. Moira plans her classes.
4. The book tells a good story.
5. The dogs bark at the mailman.

Part 2: Select the appropriate preposition, based on the picture.

1. The gray ball is   the table.
2. The red ball is   the table.
3. The plant is   the pot.
4. The plant is   the table.
5. The table is   the gray ball.

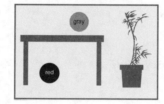

Part 3: Select the appropriate conjunction.

1. They speak French   Italian.
2. We eat the cheese,   not the crackers.
3. It is late,   we are in a hurry.
4. I don't speak French   Italian.
5. He is tired   he works hard.

Part 4: Circle the proper verb form.

1. Susie	speak	speaks	French.
2. Fred and John	eat	eats	dinner.
3. Ella	go to	goes to	school.
4. Edward	like	likes	his classes.
5. The dogs	bark at	barks at	the cat.
6. The zookeeper	feed	feeds	the animals.
7. Our family	have	has	a good time there.
8. Joe and Ellie	tell	tells	funny jokes.
9. The gardener	doesn't speak	don't speak	English.
10. Summer	is	are	hot.

Part 5: Add **do** or **does** for emphasis.

1. They see him every day.
2. He tells the truth.
3. We have fun.

Part 6: Add the helping verb **can**.

1. The boy sees the toys.
2. The girl speaks well.
3. This book is helpful.

Part 7: Make the sentence negative. Do not use pronouns or contractions.

1. Lou knows Ed.
2. It works well.
3. The cars go fast.
4. The well is dry.
5. The boys are in the house.

Part 8: Make the sentence negative using contractions. Do not use pronouns.

1. George works in Las Vegas.
2. Sandy sells seashells.
3. The team members play every day.
4. Big cities are often crowded.
5. It's really hot today.

Part 9: Change the statement to a question. ↻

1. It rains every day.
2. He calls us all of the time.
3. You like it.
4. They are very kind.
5. He is in trouble.

Part 10: Indicate the proper tag ending.

1. He likes it,   ?
2. She is a teacher,   ?
3. They want one,   ?
4. They are here,   ?

Part 11: Identify the story order, by putting 1, 2, and 3 in the boxes in the proper order.

☐ He is happy.
☐ He buys one.
☐ Bob wants a car.

 Using what you have learned, write a paragraph about yourself. Next, write a paragraph about how many keys are on your keychain, and what they are for.

You can handwrite your paragraphs below or e-mail them to **para@grammar.bz** to be stored. These paragraphs are not graded or reviewed, but simply by writing them, your English will improve. Use the SVO format — **Subject-Verb-Object** (or **Noun-Verb-Noun**).

● ○ ○   Student Paragraph

Send   Chat   Attach   Address   Fonts   Colors   Save As Draft   Photo Browser   Show Stationery

To: | para@grammar.bz

Cc: |

Bcc: |

Subject: | About Me

Signature: Corporate ⬍

My name is _____

_____	_____	_____	and but or so because	_____	_____	_____
S	V	O		S	V	O
_____	_____	_____	conjunction	_____	_____	_____
S	V	O		S	V	O
_____	_____	_____	conjunction	_____	_____	_____
S	V	O		S	V	O
_____	_____	_____	conjunction	_____	_____	_____
S	V	O		S	V	O
_____	_____	_____	conjunction	_____	_____	_____
S	V	O		S	V	O

When you have finished, look at **every** noun and make sure it is one of these:

1. Modified with **a**, **the**, **this**, **many**, **my**, etc.
2. Plural
3. A pronoun

Look at every verb and make sure it is one of these:

1. Verb **to be** — is / am / are
2. Main **verb** — he / she / it + S

Chapter 3: Comparisons and the Past

You are now moving toward the end of the beginning level. In this chapter, you will review articles and modifiers, and you will learn comparisons, prepositions of direction, time words, tag endings, and the phrasal verb **get**. With the past tense, you are no longer limited to **now**: You can talk about things that happened **before**, including negatives and questions.

Exercise 3-1: Dictation   CD 1 Track 57

Listen to the audio and write the exact transcription in the spaces below. Then check the Answer Key.

1. _____

2. _____

3. _____

4. _____

5. _____

STORY

Max's Diet

When I **competed**, people were **surprised** by my **diet**. I ate a **lot**. I **needed** to take in **6,000** calories every **day**. The **average** American man eats **2,000** or **2,500** calories every day. Before a big **tournament**, I needed **10,000** calories every day. It was pretty **expensive**. For **example**, for **breakfast**, I had a dozen **eggs**. **Yes**, I ate **12** eggs for **break**fast every **morning**. I had **omelettes**, scrambled **eggs**, **fried** eggs, **hard**-boiled eggs, and **poached** eggs. As a matter of **fact**, I ate them **every** way but **raw**. My doctor checked my **cholesterol** level every **month**. He **also** checked my **liver**. Many **body**builders have **trouble** with their **livers**, but **I** don't. I'm a **miracle** of modern **science**, **aren't** I?

Exercise 3-2: Story Pronunciation   CD 1 Track 58

Listen to the audio and repeat, focusing on intonation and pronunciation.

ACCENT

When I **c'mpeed**əd, peepəl wrr **sprized** by my **diet**. I aydə **lät**. I **need**əd to take in **6,000** cæləreez evry **day**. The **ævrage** əmerəcan **man** eats **two** thouzənd or twenny five **həndrəd** cæləreez evry day. Bəforə big **tərnəmənt**, I needəd **10,000** cæləreez evry day. It wəz priddy **ekss-pens've**. Fregg **zæm**pəl, fər **brekfəst**, I hædə dəzə **neggz**. **Yes**, I[(y)]ate **twel veggz** fər **brek**fəst evry **morning**. I had **ämlettes**, scræmble **deggz**, **fry** deggz, **härd** boil deggz, and **poach** deggz. Aza mæddərə **fæct**, I ay dem **evry** way but **rah**. My **däktr** chekt my **kələsterä**l level evry **mənth**. He **älso** chekt my **liver**. Many **bädy**bildərz hæv **trəbəl** with their **liverz**, bə**däi** don't. I'mə **mirəkəl** əv mädern **science**, **är** nai!

Exercise 3-3: Squeezed Out Syllables

CD 1 Track 59

Listen and repeat.

	Spelling	Pronunciation		Spelling	Pronunciation
1.	aspirin	asprin	11.	family	famlee
2.	average	avr'j	12.	finally	fynlee
3.	basically	basiclee	13.	general	genr'l
4.	business	bizness	14.	history	hisstree
5.	chocolate	choclate	15.	interest	intrest
6.	comfortable	comft'bl	16.	natural	nachrul
7.	conference	confrence	17.	omelette	omlet
8.	corporate	corpr't	18.	probably	problee
9.	different	diffrent	19.	several	sevral
10.	every	evry	20.	separate	seprate

NOUNS

This section covers an important aspect of nouns: how to tell if they are new info or not. It also shows you how to **compare**. Comparison words are another form of modifier. With the superlative, you need a double modifier, such as **the best**, **the only**, **the first**.

In Chapter 2, we looked at prepositions of location. Now, we are going to use prepositions of **direction**, which show movement.

Count Us

We're general.
We're single or multiple.

Single	Multiple
a water drop	**some** water drops
	a couple of water drops
	several water drops
	most water drops
	all water drops
an airplane	**both** airplanes
	three airplanes
	a few airplanes
	a lot of airplanes
a chair	**many** chairs
	so many chairs
	too many chairs
	not many chairs

Exercise 3-4: *A* or *Some*

*Fill in the blank with **a** or **some**. Then check the Answer Key.*

I have _____ bike.　　　　　　　　　**I have a bike.**
I have _____ bikes.　　　　　　　　**I have some bikes.**
1. There are _____ stars in the sky at night.
2. We need _____ details about that.

53

3. There was _____ hurricane in Florida.
4. You put _____ cup of salt in the potatoes!
5. Give me _____ minute to finish.
6. We have _____ things to do!
7. May I have _____ cup of tea, please?
8. He drank _____ glasses of water.
9. She needs _____ more time.
10. Where is _____ public **tel**ephone?

Don't Count Us

We're single or multiple.
But now . . . we're specific, **we're** known.

A and **the** are important signals in front of a noun. They tell you three things about the noun:

Is it **general** or **specific**?
Is it **new** information or **known** information?
It there **one** or **more than one**?

Let's take a look at this sentence with two nouns: The **sun** is a **star**.

We say **the sun** because there is only *one* sun.

We say **a star** because there are *many* stars.

When the word is known and specific, use **the**.

Exercise 3-5: *A* or *The*

*Fill in the blank with **a** or **the**. Then check the Answer Key.*

I have a job.   I have **the** best job in the world.

1. This is _____ best coffee!
2. Wait _____ minute, please.
3. It's _____ long way to Texas from here.
4. It's _____ wrong way to do it. Please do it _____ right way.
5. I have _____ longest name in the **ph**one book.
6. That's _____ great idea!
7. I need _____ new zip drive.
8. I need _____ new zip drive that I bought today.
9. This is _____ only time I need it.
10. Please give me _____ quarter. (korder)
11. Please pass _____ salt.
12. Are you going away next week? No, _____ week after next.
13. My friends live in _____ old house in _____ small town. There is _____ beautiful garden behind _____ house. I would like to have _____ garden like that.
14. I would like to have _____ same garden.
15. I would like to have _____ similar garden.

16. The kids are playing in _____ yard.
17. Cats can see in _____ dark.
18. What's _____ next step?
19. I have to wait _____ year for them to send me _____ documents.
20. _____ first step is to find _____ lawyer.
21. In _____ beginning, we worked on it all of _____ time.
22. Did you listen to _____ news on _____ radio?
23. Does he usually follow _____ rules?
24. *Casablanca* is _____ classic movie.
25. We hope to see them over _____ holidays.
26. Do you know what _____ answer is?
27. They went in one at _____ time. They went in one by one.
28. Do you remember _____ time we were three hours late?
29. Don't forget to lock _____ door on your way out.
30. I have to go to _____ **bath**room. Is there _____ **bath**room in this building?
31. I had _____ good time. It was _____ best time of all.
32. What's that under _____ desk?
33. An office usually has _____ desk.
34. _____ apple _____ day keeps _____ doctor away.
35. It's _____ fast car, but definitely not _____ fastest.

There are two terms for comparing things. These are the *comparative* and the *superlative*. When you have two items, use the comparative. When you have three items or more, use the superlative. With the superlative, you need a double modifier, such as the **first**, the **best**, or the **only**.

The *absolute* is the term for a regular adjective.

Big, **Bigger**, **The Biggest**

This key is big.   This key is bigger.   This key is the biggest.

This key is smaller than that key.   This key is bigger than that key.

This key is as big as that key.
These keys are the same size.
These keys are equally large.

With short words, add –**er** to compare and –**est** for the superlative. If the word ends in –**y**, drop the **Y** and add –**ier** or –**iest**. For example, **pretty** becomes **prettier** / **prettiest**.

When the word ends in a consonant, add –**er** or –**est**. For some words, you may need to double the final consonant—for example, **bigger** / **biggest**, **hotter** / **hottest**, etc.

Short Words

Big	Bigger	Biggest
tall	taller	the tallest
short	shorter	the shortest
smart	smarter	the smartest
hot	hotter	the hottest
cold	colder	the coldest
rich	richer	the richest
hard	harder	the hardest
easy	easier	the easiest
funny	funnier	the funniest
happy	happier	the happiest
pretty	prettier	the prettiest

Absolute Adjective	Comparative (–er)	Superlative (–est)
as _____ as + noun	**_____–er than + noun**	**the _____–est + preposition**
as big as a house	*bigger than a house*	*the biggest in the world*
as _____ as + adjective	**_____–er than + pronoun**	**the _____–est + ever**
as good as new	*bigger than yours*	*the biggest ever*
	_____–er than + time word	**the _____–est + phrase**
	bigger than before	*the biggest I've ever seen*
	_____–er than + phrase	
	bigger than I thought	

These five are irregular, so you need to memorize them. Remember that you need to use **the** with superlatives. With **comparatives**, you need to use **than**.

Absolute	Comparative	Superlative
good	better	the best
bad	worse	the worst
some	more	the most
little	less	the least
far	farther	the farthest
	further	the furthest

Exercise 3-6: Short Comparison Words

Fill in the blank with the appropriate form. Then check the Answer Key.

The sun is	the closest	star.	close / closer / **the closest**
1. This idea is		in the whole world.	good / better / the best
2. Those cars are		than the new ones.	cheap / cheaper / the cheapest
3. An F is		grade on a test.	bad / worse / the worst
4. I needed a long,		shower.	hot / hotter / the hottest
5. Einstein was		than most people.	smart / smarter / the smartest
6. Lola isn't		on her team.	tall / taller / the tallest
7. Alaska isn't very		in the winter.	warm / warmer / the warmest
8. Alaska is much		than Florida.	cold / colder / the coldest
9. This is even		than before.	good / better / the best

10.	Spanish is	_____ than Chinese.	easy / easier / the easiest
11.	He is	_____ man in the world.	old / older / the oldest
12.	I am	_____ to be here.	happy / happier / the happiest
13.	Diamonds are	_____ than glass.	hard / harder / the hardest
14.	My house is as	_____ as your house.	nice / nicer / nicest
15.	This is twice as	_____ as the other one.	big / bigger / the biggest
16.	⟳ Which is	_____ , a fly or a bee?	fast / faster / the fastest
17.	⟳ Which is	_____ , rice, bread, or pasta?	good / better / the best
18.	⟳ Who has	_____ money, Ed or Sam?	some / more / the most
19.	⟳ Who is	_____ , Ed or Sam?	rich / richer / the richest
20.	⟳ Is L.A. or New York	_____ from Bangkok?	far / farther / the farthest

> What five-letter word becomes shorter when you add two letters to it?
>
> **Answer**
> The word is **short**. Add –**er**, and it becomes **shorter**.

With long words, add **more** before the word to compare and **the most** before the word for the superlative.

Long Words

Beautiful	More Beautiful	The Most Beautiful
expensive	more expensive	the most expensive
important	more important	the most important
interesting	more interesting	the most interesting
wonderful	more wonderful	the most wonderful
delicious	more delicious	the most delicious
terrible	more terrible	the most terrible
exciting	more exciting	the most exciting
pathetic	more pathetic	the most pathetic
irritating	more irritating	the most irritating
playful	more playful	the most playful

Exercise 3-7: Long Comparison Words

*Fill in the blank with the appropriate form, including **more** and **the most** where necessary. Then check the Answer Key.*

	He is	**the most intelligent**	one in the class.	intelligent
1.	That is	_____	story I heard today.	interesting
2.	That was	_____	pear!	delicious
3.	That child becomes	_____	every day.	obedient
4.	This is really	_____	for me.	difficult
5.	These shoes are	_____	than we expected.	expensive

57

6. Did you have a		time at the wedding?	wonderful
7. That excuse was		you have ever used.	unusual
8. Were those exercises		than before?	complicated
9. That final detail was		item on our list.	important
10. The seal pup is		animal.	wonderful

Exercise 3-8: Long and Short Comparison Words

Fill in the blank with the appropriate form, including **–er**, **–est**, **more**, *or* **the most**, *where necessary. Then check the Answer Key.*

They have	**better**	**shoes than we do.**	good
She is	**more reliable**	**than the others.**	reliable
1. Peace is		than war.	effective
2. Donuts are		by the dozen.	cheap
3. That situation is		than you realize.	dangerous
4. This is		issue of our time.	important
5. Bill Gates is		than most people.	rich
6. My grammar is		than my pronunciation.	good
7. Snakes are		than spiders.	scary
8. The Mississippi is		river in America.	long
9. 8:00 a.m. is		than 9:00 a.m.	early
10. Is Saturn		planet?	close

Things and Directions

into the house   along the path

In Chapter 2, we saw that prepositions tell you the *location* of a thing—*What a plane can do to a cloud.* Examples are **in** *a cloud*, **by** *a cloud*, **near** *a cloud*, and so on.

Now we're going to work with *direction*. This time, you'll be using prepositions to indicate movement. **To** is the most common preposition in English. It is pronounced **tə** or **də**.

The ✈ goes **through** the cloud.

Exercise 3-9: Prepositions of Direction   CD 1 Track 60

Listen and repeat.

1. The **boy** ran	away from	the **bully**.
2. The **man** jumped	out of	the **window**.
3. The **cat** fell	into	the **box**.
4. My **sister** spoke	to	her **friend**.
5. I was **walking**	toward	the **door**.
6. We **ran**	through	the **tunnel**.

7. They **walked**	up to	the **desk**.
8. It's a **quarter**	past	**five**. (5:15)
9. The **smoke** spread	throughout	the **house**.
10. His **actions** were	beyond	**belief**.
11. The girls were talking	to	the **teacher**.
12. The boys are yelling	at	each **other**.
13. The dog is barking	at	the **mailman**.
14. She threw the ball	to	the **catcher**.
15. She threw the ball	at	the **catcher**.

Common Prepositions

The numbers indicate the Top 10 most common prepositions.

about [10]	at [7]	beyond	into	outside	under
above	away from	by	near	over	underneath
across	before	during	next to	past	until
after	behind	except	of [2]	since	up to
against	below	for [4]	off	through	with [5]
along	beneath	from [9]	on [6]	throughout	within
among	beside	in [3]	onto	to [1] (tə or də)	without
around	between	inside	out [8]	toward	

As you saw in Chapter 2, the infinitive uses **to**, as in **I have to be there**, **He wants to do that**, or **She plans to go there**. This, plus the **to** of *direction*, makes **to** the most commonly used preposition.

With prepositions, you can add a **noun** (*to the store*) or **–ing** (*without taking*). With the infinitive, use the simple form.

Exercise 3-10: *To* as a Preposition
CD 1 Track 61

*Listen and repeat. Remember that **to** is pronounced tə or də.*

1. We plan to **do** it.　　　　　　　　We plændə do⁽ʷ⁾it.
2. Give it to the **clerk**.　　　　　　　G'v't t' the clerk.
3. Everyone wanted to **practice** more.　Evrywən wändəd də præct's more.
4. They hope to **see** you again.　　　　They hope tə see you⁽ʷ⁾əgen.
5. I'm looking forward to **seeing** you again. I'm lüking forw'rd də seeing you⁽ʷ⁾again.
6. She asked me to **help**.　　　　　　She⁽ʸ⁾æskt me də help.
7. Let's go to the **movies**.　　　　　Let's go də the moveez.
8. You don't need to **do** that.　　　　You don't need də do that.
9. A **customer** walked up to the **counter**. ə customer wähkt up tə the counter.
10. Our **dog** likes to bark at the **mailman**. är däg likes tə bärk at the mailman.

You don't need **to** in phrases like He told him, He called him, He paid him.

Exercise 3-11: Top 10 Prepositions
CD 1 Track 62

*Listen and repeat the top ten prepositions of **direction**, **location**, and the **infinitive**.*

1. She went to **school** every **day**.	She went tə **school** every **day**.
2. It was in Chapter **20**.	It wəzin Chæpter **twenny**.
3. It was on page **8**.	It wəzän pay **jate**.
4. Please **come** with me.	Pleez **cəme** with me.
5. My **car's** in front of my **house**.	My **cärz** in front of my **house**.
6. Call me at **5**:00.	**Cäll** me at **5**:00.
7. He **did** it for **us**. He did it **for** us.	He **did**it frəs. He didit **for** əs.
8. Where are you **from**?	Where are you **frəm**?
9. Send it to the **boss**.	Send it tə the **boss**.
10. We hope to **see** him in three **days**.	We hope tə **see** him in three **days**.
11.What do you hope to find **out**?	Wəddə you hope tə find**out**?
12. We can't **work** with him.	We cænt **wrrk** withim.
13. It's the best of **all**.	It's the best ə**väll**.
14. What are you **talking** about?	Wədder you **tähking** əbout?
15. Thank you for under**stand**ing.	Thænk you fr ənder**stænd**ing.
16. They learned to do it them**selves**.	They lrrnd də do⁽ʷ⁾it them**selves**.
17. She ran out of the **house**.	She ræn oudəv the **house**.
18. When do you plan on **telling** them?	When d' you plæn än **telling** 'em?
19. He said it without **thinking**.	He sɛdit without **thinking**.
20. At **first**, we didn't under**stand**.	At **first**, we didn't ənder**stænd**.
21. Let's keep him from finding **out**.	Let's keepim frəm finding **out**.
22. He fell in the **water**.	He fellin the **wäder**.
23. He landed on his **back**.	He landəd äniz **back**.
24. He's about **six** feet **tall**.	Heezə bout **six** feet **tall**.
25. I'm on my **way**.	I män my **way**.

VERBS

In Chapters 1 and 2, we looked at verbs in the present tense:

is, am, are, do, does

Now, we are going to work with the *past*. In addition to **was** and **were** for the verb **to be** we will learn about main verbs in the past. The pattern and intonation stay the same as the present tense, but the verb changes.

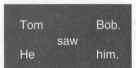

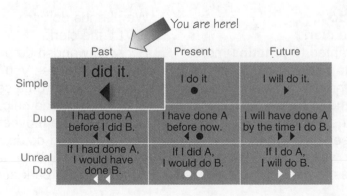

The past tense follows the same patterns as the present tense. For example, alone, the main verb **to do** changes to **did** in the past: **I did it**. When you have a helping verb, you must also use the unchanging form of the main verb: **I did do it**. The word **not** falls in the same position between the helping verb and the main verb: **I did not do it**. Questions have the same subject/verb flip: **Did I do it?**

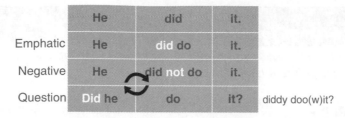

	He	did	it.
Emphatic	He	**did** do	it.
Negative	He	did **not** do	it.
Question	**Did** he	do	it?	diddy doo(w)it?

Good news! For questions, and negative and emphatic statements, the past tense of **do** only uses one form, **did**. There is no conjugating.

There are about 50 irregular verbs, however, and you just have to learn them.

Verb Form

For regular verbs, add –**ed** to make the past tense.
If the verb ends in **y**, change it to –**ied** (study > studied).

Regular Verbs

Infinitive	Past	Pronunciation
to work	work**ed**	wrrkt
to jump	jump**ed**	jumpt
to pull	pull**ed**	pulld
to need	need**ed**	needed
to pin	pinn**ed**	pind
to change	chang**ed**	chanjd
to study	stud**ied**	studeed

Pronunciation

Notice that when the final consonant is *unvoiced* (P, K, S, SH, CH), the –**ed** ending sounds like a **T**.

hoped / hopt
washed / washt
watched / watcht

When the final consonant is *voiced* (B, G, Z, ZH, J) or a *vowel*, the –**ed** ending sounds like a **D**. For a final T or D, the ending sounds like –~~e~~**d**.

50 Main Irregular Verbs

to be	**was / were**	to know	**knew**
to become	**became**	to leave	**left**
to begin	**began**	to lose	**lost**
to break	**broke**	to make	**made**
to bring	**brought**	to mean	**meant**
to catch	**caught**	to meet	**met**
to choose	**chose**	to put	**put**
to come	**came**	to read	**read**
to do	**did**	to ride	**rode**
to drink	**drank**	to run	**ran**
to drive	**drove**	to say	**said**
to eat	**ate**	to see	**saw**
to fall	**fell**	to sell	**sold**
to feel	**felt**	to send	**sent**
to fight	**fought**	to sit	**sat**
to find	**found**	to speak	**spoke**
to fly	**flew**	to stand	**stood**
to forget	**forgot**	to take	**took**
to give	**gave**	to teach	**taught**
to get	**got**	to tell	**told**
to go	**went**	to think	**thought**
to grow	**grew**	to throw	**threw**
to have	**had**	to understand	**understood**
to hear	**heard**	to win	**won**
to hold	**held**	to write	**wrote**

Pronunciation

äh
saw / caught / brought / taught / lost / thought / got / forgot / fought

ü
took / put / looked
stood / understood

z
was / chose

eh
said = sɛd
meant = mɛnt
read = rɛd

T sounds like D
Italy / Idaly
water / wader
better / bedder

Exercise 3-12: Change to the Past

Change the verb from the present tense to the past tense. (The emphasis stays on the nouns.)
When you're done, check the Answer Key.

Sam eats **apples**.

Sam **ate** apples.

1. The **teachers** write on the **black**board.
2. **Larry** rides his **bike** everywhere.
3. Your **cousin** flies first **class**.
4. The **managers** arrange **meetings**.
5. I give many **presents**.
6. We **think** about it all of the **time**.
7. They throw it **away** every **day**.
8. **Virginia** has long **hair**.
9. **Happy** people have good **luck**.
10. Her **sister** says **hello**.
11. The **kids** want to ride their **bikes**.
12. **Students** try to pass **tests**.
13. **Ed** likes to go to the **gym**.
14. The **class** hopes to have a **party**.
15. **Every**one needs to have more **fun**.

Exercise 3-13: Change to the Emphatic

*Add **did** between the helping verb and the main verb. (The S disappears from the main verb.)*
Then check the Answer Key.

Sam ate **apples**.

Sam **did eat** apples!

1. The teachers wrote on the blackboard.
2. Larry rode his bike everywhere.
3. Your cousin flew first class.
4. The managers arranged meetings.
5. I gave many presents.
6. We thought about it all of the time.
7. They threw it away every day.
8. Virginia had long hair.
9. Happy people had good luck.
10. Her sister said hello.
11. The kids wanted to ride their bikes.
12. The students tried to pass the tests.
13. Ed liked to go to the gym.
14. The class hoped to have a party.
15. Everyone needed to have more fun.

Exercise 3-14: Change to the Negative

*Add **not** between the helping verb and the unchanging form of the main verb. (There's no S on the main verb.) Check the Answer Key when you're done.*

Sam did eat **apples.**   **Sam did not eat apples.**

1. The teachers did write on the blackboard.
2. Larry did ride his bike everywhere.
3. Your cousin did fly first class.
4. The managers did arrange meetings.
5. I did give many presents.
6. We did think about it all of the time.
7. They did throw it away every day.
8. Virginia did have long hair.
9. Happy people did have good luck.
10. Her sister did say hello.
11. The kids did want to ride their bikes.
12. The students did try to pass the tests.
13. Ed did like to go to the gym.
14. The class did hope to have a party.
15. Everyone did need to have more fun.

Exercise 3-15: Change to Negative Contractions

*Change **did not** to a contraction. (There's no S on the main verb.) Check the Answer Key when you're done.*

Sam did not eat **apples.**   **Sam didn't eat apples.**

1. The teachers did not write on the blackboard.
2. Larry did not ride his bike everywhere.
3. Your cousin did not fly first class.
4. The managers did not arrange meetings.
5. I did not give many presents.
6. We did not think about it all of the time.
7. They did not throw it away every day.
8. Virginia did not have long hair.
9. Happy people did not have good luck.
10. Her sister did not say hello.
11. The kids did not want to ride their bikes.
12. Students did not try to pass tests.
13. Ed did not like to go to the gym.
14. The class did not hope to have a party.
15. Everyone did not need to have more fun.

Exercise 3-16: Change the Positive to Negative Contractions

Let's review. Change the positive to a negative contraction, using pronouns. Then check the Answer Key.

Sam ate apples.   **He didn't eat them.**

1. The teachers wrote on the blackboard.
2. Larry rode his bike everywhere.
3. Your cousin flew first class.
4. The managers arranged meetings.
5. I gave many presents.

6. We thought about it all of the time.
7. They threw it away every day.
8. Virginia had long hair.
9. Happy people had good luck.
10. Her sister said hello.
11. The kids wanted to ride their bikes.
12. Students tried to pass tests.
13. Ed liked to go to the gym.
14. The class hoped to have a party.
15. Everyone needed to have more fun.

Exercise 3-17: Change the Emphatic to a Question ↻

Flip the subject and the helping verb. Then check the Answer Key.

Sam did eat **apples.**	**Did Sam** eat apples?
Sam can eat **apples.**	**Can Sam** eat apples?

1. The teachers did write on the blackboard.
2. Larry did ride his bike everywhere.
3. Your cousin can fly first class.
4. The managers did arrange meetings.
5. I can give many presents.
6. We did think about it all of the time.
7. They did throw it away every day.
8. Virginia did have long hair.
9. Happy people can have good luck.
10. Her sister did say hello.
11. The kids did want to ride their bikes.
12. Students did try to pass tests.
13. Ed did like to go to the gym.
14. The class did hope to have a party.
15. Everyone did need to have more fun.

The next exercise is very similar to the previous exercise, but this time, instead of starting with the emphatic form, you will make the question directly from a regular statement.

Exercise 3-18: Change a Regular Statement to a Question ↻

*Add one of the four helping verbs **did**, **didn't**, **could**, or **couldn't** and use the unchanging form of the main verb. Remember that the helping verb shows the past: **He went**. > **Did he go?** You can't say, **Did he went?** Check the Answer Key when you're done.*

Sam ate **apples.**	**Did Sam** eat apples?
Sam ate **apples.**	**Didn't Sam** eat apples?
Sam ate **apples.**	**Could Sam** eat apples?
Sam ate **apples.**	**Couldn't Sam** eat apples?

1. The teachers wrote on the blackboard.
2. Larry rode his bike everywhere.
3. Your cousin flew first class.
4. The managers arranged meetings.

5. I gave many presents.
6. We thought about it all of the time.
7. They threw it away every day.
8. Virginia had long hair.
9. Happy people had good luck.
10. Her sister said hello.
11. The kids wanted to ride their bikes.
12. Students tried to pass tests.
13. Ed liked to go to the gym.
14. The class hoped to have a party.
15. Everyone needed to have more fun.

Exercise 3-19: Change to Pronouns ↻

Replace all nouns with pronouns. Put the stress on the verb. Then check the Answer Key.

Did Sam eat apples?
1. Did the teachers write on the blackboard?
2. Did Larry ride his bike everywhere?
3. Did your cousin fly first class?
4. Can the managers arrange meetings?
5. Did I give many presents?
6. Did Bob think about Betty all of the time?
7. Can Will throw the trash away every day?
8. Did Virginia have long hair?
9. Did happy people have good luck?
10. Can her sister say hello?
11. Did the kids want to ride their bikes?
12. Can the students try to pass tests?
13. Did Ed like to go to the gym?
14. Did the class hope to have a party?
15. Did everyone need to do the dishes?

Did he eat them?

Exercise 3-20: Change a Regular Statement to a Question ↻

*Add an appropriate helping verb to the **unchanging** form of the main verb. Pay attention to the tense. Change nouns to pronouns. The stress goes on the verb. Check the Answer Key when you're done.*

Sam ate apples.
1. The teachers write on the blackboard.
2. Larry rode his bike everywhere.
3. Your **cousin** flies first **class**.
4. The **managers** arranged **meetings**.
5. I gave many **presents**.
6. We **think** about it all of the **time**.
7. They threw it **away** every **day**.

Did he eat them?

8. **Virginia** has long **hair**.
9. **Happy** people had good **luck**.
10. Her **sister** says **hello**.
11. The kids wanted to ride their bikes.
12. Students try to pass tests.
13. Ed liked to go to the gym.
14. The class hopes to have a party.
15. Everyone needed to do the dishes.
16. The **dogs** jumped over the **hedge**. (hej)
17. My **sister** likes **ice** cream.
18. My **brother** wants an **ice** cream cone.
19. **Joe** always loses **patience** with **Will**.
20. The **sailors** got in **trouble** again.
21. The **cook** burned the **meal**.
22. **Soft**ware gets **viruses**.
23. The **senator** dropped out of the **race**.
24. The **kids** fell in the **mud**.
25. **Teachers** give **tests**.
26. The **police** found the **criminals**.
27. The hot **coffee** burned your **mouth**.
28. Your **team** lost the **race**.
29. The **president** forgot to get his **schedule**.
30. My **boss** changed her **mind**.

Exercise 3-21: Change to a Tag Question ♻

Add a tag question to the end of the statement. Check the Answer Key when you're done.

Sam ate **apples**.

1. The teachers wrote on the blackboard,
2. Larry rode his bike everywhere,
3. Your cousin flew first class,
4. The managers arranged meetings,
5. I gave many presents,
6. We thought about it all of the time,
7. They threw it away every day,
8. Virginia had long hair,
9. Happy people had good luck,
10. Her sister said hello,
11. The kids wanted to ride their bikes,
12. Students tried to pass tests,
13. Ed liked to go to the gym,
14. The class hoped to have a party,
15. Everyone needed to do the dishes,

Sam ate apples, didn't he?

Exercise 3-22: Change to a Tag Question — All Verbs ↻

Add a tag question to the end of the statement. Change positive verbs to negative and vice versa. Then check the Answer Key.

1. I drive too fast,
2. You like it,
3. You liked it,
4. You don't like it,
5. You didn't like it,
6. We made some mistakes,
7. They can plan well,
8. She is on the phone,
9. I'm sure,
10. She told the truth,
11. They aren't ready,
12. I'm not sure,
13. There were some problems,
14. There was some trouble,
15. There wasn't any trouble,

Exercise 3-23: Past Tense Review

Fill in the proper past tense form. Check the Answer Key when you're done.

When **Edison** first _____ (**think**) of the **light**bulb, it ____ (**be**) because of a personal **need**. He ____ (**be**) afraid of the **dark**, so he ____ (**want**) to **create** something to deal with the **night**. He ____ (**try**) a **thousand** different **ways** to **do** it, but **none** of them ____ (**work**). **Finally**, as we all **know**, he ____ (**invent**) the electric **light**bulb. **Once**, when he ____ (**be**) **asked** how he ____ (**handle**) the **failure** of his many **attempts**, he ____ (**reply**) that **none** of them ____ (**be**) failures. Each one ____ (**teach**) him **one** more **way not** to make a **light**bulb.

Exercise 3-24: Past Tense — Pronunciation   CD 1 Track 63

Listen to the audio, focusing on past tense pronunciation and intonation.

When **Edəson** frrrrst thähd'v the **light** bəlb, it wəz bəkəzəvə prrrrrsonal **need**. He wəzzə fray dəv the **därk**, so he wän'ed to **create** səmething to deal with the **night**. He try də **thouzənd** diffrent **wayz** to **do** it, but nənəvəm wrrkt. **Fyn-lee**, az we äll **know**, he inven'd thee[(y)]electric **light** bəlb. **Once**, whennee wəzæskt howeee hændld the **fay**-yəl-yr əviz many ə**ttempts**, he rəplyd that nənəvəm wrr fay-yəl-yrz. Each one tädim **one** more **way nät** to make a **light** bəlb.

The letter I in the **unstressed** position is a schwa. The letter T before or after a schwa is a D. S before a schwa sounds like Z.

Exercise 3-25: Middle "I" — Pronunciation   CD 1 Track 64

Listen to the audio and repeat. Read from the blue columns.

ability	abilədy	Florida	Florəda	physical	phyzəcal
accident	aksədent	foreigner	forəner	positive	päzəd'v
activity	activədy	gravity	gravədy	possibility	pässəbilədy
America	əmerəcə	hepatitis	hepətidəs	possible	pässəble
animal	anəmal	identity	idendədy	president	prezədent
article	ardəcle	imitation	imətation	principle	princəple
availability	availabilədy	immigration	imməgration	priority	priorədy
beautiful	byoodəful	invisible	invizəble	qualify	qualəfy
California	Caləfornia	janitor	janədor	quality	qualədy
chemical	cheməcal	Jennifer	Jennəfer	quantity	quandədy
chemistry	cheməstry	liability	liabilədy	resident	rezədent
clarity	clarədy	Maryland	Merəland	security	secyurədy
communication	comyunəcation	medicine	medəs'n	seminar	semənar
confident	cänfədent	majority	majorədy	similar	simələr
critical	cridəcal	maximum	maxəmum	technical	technəcal
difficult	diffəcult	Michigan	Mishəgan	typical	tipəcal
Edison	Edəson	minimum	minəmum	uniform	unəform
engineer	engəneer	minority	minorədy	unity	yunədy
evidence	evədence	modify	mädəfy	university	yunəversədy
facility	facilədy	monitor	mänədor	visitor	vizədor

Get

The word **get** is in the top 20 of high-frequency words. It is used in its basic meaning of **to receive** or **to acquire**, but in combination with other words, it takes on many other meanings. Here are some common combinations.

get up	arise	get back	return from a place
get down	descend	get back	receive again
get on (a bus)	enter	get annoyed	become irritated
get off (a bus)	leave	get along	have good relations
get in (a car)	enter	get confused	become mixed up
get out of (a car)	leave	get worried	become concerned
get away	escape	get ahead	make progress
get tired	become fatigued	get behind	fall behind
get tired of	lose enjoyment of	get in an accident	be in a car crash
get started	begin	get in an argument	have a fight
get used to	become accustomed to	get upset	become sad or angry
get impatient	lose patience	get dressed	put one's clothes on
get done	be finished	get undressed	take one's clothes off
get excited	develop strong feelings	get married	enter in a civil union
get lost	lose one's way	get divorced	break the civil union
get sick	become ill	get rid of something	give or throw away
get better	improve	get even	take revenge
get worse	become less good	get in trouble	have problems

get well	regain health	get together	meet
get somewhere	arrive	get bored	lose interest
get there	arrive somewhere	get by	have the minimum
get fired	lose one's job	get drunk	drink too much alcohol
get hired	become employed	get hungry	need food

Exercise 3-26: *Get*

*Add the proper **get** phrase. Then check the Answer Key.*

1. They don't get ____ any more.	have good relations
2. When did you get ____ from vacation?	return
3. He got ____ because he was always late.	lost his job
4. When I lived in Ohio, I never got ____ to the cold winters.	accustomed to
5. If you don't take care of yourself, you could get ____.	become ill
6. You'd better get ____ from that tree!	descend
7. Hey, would you like to get ____ some time?	meet
8. Don't get mad, get ____!	take revenge
9. Don't get ____ just because you missed one question.	become sad or angry
10. If you want to get ____ in life, you must work hard.	make progress
11. They got very ____ about winning the lottery.	develop strong feelings
12. I tend to get ____ with repetitive tasks.	lose interest
13. Are you getting ____ the bus at the next stop?	leave
14. What a wonderful holiday I have planned to get ____.	escape
15. You married the wrong guy so you need to get ____.	break the civil union
16. It's too early to get ____.	become fatigued
17. Let's get ____ for a cup of coffee.	meet
18. You get ____ so easily!	lose patience
19. Bring a map or you will get ____.	lose one's way
20. We're late because it took you so long to get ____.	put one's clothes on
21. With this promotion I can finally get ____!	make progress
22. You get ____ over the smallest things!	become concerned
23. When are you going to get ____ from Africa?	return
24. Get ____ the car or I'm leaving without you.	enter
25. I get ____ working all day.	lose enjoyment of
26. You need insurance in case you get ____.	be in a car crash
27. You can get ____ in the dressing room.	take one's clothes off
28. My aunt needs to get ____ her extra clothes.	give or throw away
29. Be good or you will get ____!	have problems
30. Study hard and you grades will get ____.	improve
31. I need to get ____ early.	arrive
32. Farmer John gets ____ at 5 a.m. to milk the cows.	arise
33. I get ____ on long drives.	lose interest
34. That boy had better get ____ from that tree!	descend
35. Keep it up if you want to get ____ with me.	have a fight
36. Some people go along to get ____.	have good relations
37. Her boss could not believe that it could get ____.	become less good
38. Let's get ____ with this meeting.	begin
39. If you want to get ____ that sweater, give it to me!	give or throw away
40. I tried to get my money ____, but I couldn't.	receive again
41. Don't get ____ and drive!	drink alcohol
42. He hopes to get ____ for the new job.	become employed
43. Eat lunch before you get too ____ and cranky.	need food

Time Words: End of the Sentence

When we worked with time words in Chapter 1, they came either *before* the adjective (I am **always** late) or *after* the adjective (I am late **every day**.) Now, let's look at time phrases with *main verbs*.

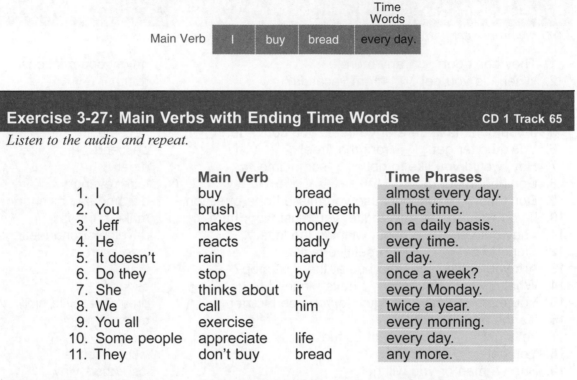

Exercise 3-27: Main Verbs with Ending Time Words   CD 1 Track 65

Listen to the audio and repeat.

	Main Verb		**Time Phrases**
1. I	buy	bread	almost every day.
2. You	brush	your teeth	all the time.
3. Jeff	makes	money	on a daily basis.
4. He	reacts	badly	every time.
5. It doesn't	rain	hard	all day.
6. Do they	stop	by	once a week?
7. She	thinks about	it	every Monday.
8. We	call	him	twice a year.
9. You all	exercise		every morning.
10. Some people	appreciate	life	every day.
11. They	don't buy	bread	any more.

With **to be**, *time words* come in the middle of the sentence after the verb.

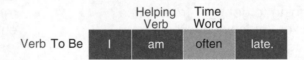

You can see that the time words are in the same position with main verbs, but the helping verb box is empty.

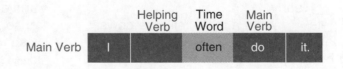

Let's review time words with both the verb **to be** and *main verbs*.

Exercise 3-28: Time Words with the Verb *To Be* and Main Verbs   CD 1 Track 66

Listen to the audio and repeat until you have mastered the sounds and concepts.

1. I am always late.	I always buy bread.
2. You are almost always tired.	You almost always brush your teeth.
3. They are generally confused.	They generally make money.
4. He is usually ready.	He usually reacts badly.
5. It is often sunny.	It often rains hard.

 TEST   Let's review everything you have learned in Chapter 3, including the past tense, negatives, questions, prepositions of direction, the verb **get**, and comparisons. Make sure you get 100% on the test before going on to the next chapter. Check your answers using the Answer Key.

Part 1: *Select the proper form.*

1. That plan is		of all.	good
2. My new apartment is		than my old one.	big
3. Your friend is very		.	nice
4. This blanket is		of all of them.	warm
5. That assignment is		than the others.	interesting

Part 2: *Select the proper word, based on the picture.*

1. The white plane is flying _____ the cloud.
2. The black plane is flying _____ the cloud.

Part 3: *Change the sentences to the past.*

1. Sam lives in Chicago.
2. We think about it.
3. We see him at the gym.
4. You find many good opportunities.
5. I know the answer.
6. She says anything!
7. Charlie does not make mistakes.
8. Does Laura get in trouble?
9. We have enough time.
10. It takes too long!
11. I am hungry.
12. You are right.
13. He is over there.
14. We are not on the committee.
15. She is going to the party.

Part 4: *Change to the negative. Do **not** use pronouns.*

1. Morgan heard the news.
2. Gordon followed the rules.
3. The girl was confused.
4. The boys were late again.

Part 5: *Change to the negative. **Use** contractions and pronouns.*

1. Ed bought a car.
2. The girl went with her father.
3. The woman was on her bike.
4. The men were in the lake.

Part 6: *Change to a question. Do **not** use pronouns.*

1. James drove to New York.
2. Susie is in back.
3. Andrea said hello.
4. Fred and Jim were outside.
5. I like pie.

Part 7: *Rewrite the sentences, with the time and frequency words in the proper place.*

1. Edgar buys groceries.   (all the time)

2. Sam and Charlie fly the kite.   (never)

3. Moira organized her schedule.   (every once in a while)

4. The book tells a good story.   (often)

5. The dogs barked at passers-by.   (all day)

Part 8: *Fill in the proper tag ending.*

1. He was funny,
2. You're coming,
3. They were happy,
4. I am here,
5. It's over,
6. They thought about it,
7. You like it,
8. They tried it,
9. I know him,
10. She didn't say it,

Part 9: *Fill in the blank with either **a**, **some**, or **the**. Use — if no modifier is needed.*

1. We saw _____ good movie last night.
2. It was _____ comedy.
3. That movie was _____ best this year.
4. I ordered _____ popcorn and _____ soda.

*Part 10: Fill in the blank with the appropriate **get** phrase.*

1. We worked so hard that we got really ____. (fatigued)
2. It's hard to get ____ living in another country. (accustomed to)
3. What time did you get ____ last night? (finished)
4. Let's get ____ for coffee next week. (meet)
5. Use a map or you might get ____. (lose your way)

Using what you have learned, write two paragraphs on the following:

1. What is your strongest memory from childhood?
2. What was your first job?

Try joining your sentences with the conjunctions you have studied. After writing each paragraph, check for SVO structure and proper modifiers on each noun.

You can handwrite your paragraphs below or e-mail them to **para@grammar.bz** to be stored. These paragraphs are not graded or reviewed, but simply by writing them, your English will improve.

```
●○○                          Student Paragraph
✈    ○    📎     ▢    Aa    ●    ▢                    📷            ▥
Send  Chat Attach Address Fonts Colors Save As Draft          Photo Browser  Show Stationery

        To:  para@grammar.bz
        Cc:
       Bcc:
    Subject:  Chapter 3
  ☰▼                                    Signature: Corporate ◆
```

My name is _____

S	V	O	and but or so because	S	V	O
S	V	O	conjunction	S	V	O
S	V	O	conjunction	S	V	O
S	V	O	conjunction	S	V	O
S	V	O	conjunction	S	V	O

Chapter 4: Noun Countability and Continuous Verb Forms

DICTATION

In earlier chapters, we learned about nouns and modifiers. Here, we are going to review them, and also look at *countable* and *uncountable* nouns, *prepositions* of time and manner, and the *5 W Words*. For verbs, we will study the continuous form of both the present and past tense (**is doing** and **was doing**), with a review of **get**, **do / doing**, and **have / having**.

Exercise 4-1: Dictation   CD 1 Track 67

Listen to the audio and write the exact transcription in the spaces below. Then check the Answer Key.

1. _____

2. _____

3. _____

4. _____

5. _____

STORY

In this chapter of the story, Max has a wild series of continuing actions. Notice the various –ing forms in the story, including **was doing**, **started doing**, and **kept doing**.

Exercise 4-2: "The Windshield Incident"   CD 1 Track 68

*Listen to the audio and repeat out loud five times. Focus on the intonation. Lincoln Boulevard is a main street in Venice, California. Jeep is a kind of car. The **continuous** has been highlighted in blue.*

The Windshield Incident: Road Rage in Venice

One day, I was driving along in **Venice**. It was a beautiful **day**. I was cruising along Lincoln **Boulevard** in my **Jeep**. **Suddenly**, a **car** cut me **off**. It was very **dangerous**. A young **girl** was driving a **Ford** Mustang **convertible**. I got really **mad** because she was driving so **badly**. I caught **up** to her and cut her **off**. She made a rude **gesture** with her **hand** and drove **away**. I smacked the **wind**shield. It **shattered**. Then I was **really** angry. I drove **fast** and I caught **up** to her again. I started **yell**ing at her. I said that she was a terrible **driver**. She kept **laugh**ing, so I yelled **again**. She looked **over** and **saw** me. Her **eyes** got **big**. She was **scared**. **Remember**, I'm Mr. **World**. I'm 6′4″ and I weigh **300 pounds** (almost 2 meters tall / 136 kilos). She stepped on the **gas**, ran a red **light**, and disappeared in **traffic**. I just kept **driv**ing, but I was **laugh**ing.

Exercise 4-3: Story Pronunciation — CD 1 Track 69

Listen to the audio and repeat out loud five times. Focus on pronunciation and word connections.

One day, I wəz driving aläng in **Venice**. I(t) wəzzə byoodəful **day**. I wəz croozing əläng Ling-k'n **Büləvärd** in my **Jeep**. **Səddenly**, ə **cär** cət me⁽ʸ⁾**äff**. It wəz very **dangerəs**. ə yəng **grrrrrrrəl** wəz drivingə **Ford** Məstæng **c'nvrrdəble**. I gät rilly **mæd** cəz she wəz driving so **bædly**. I cäh **dəp** too⁽ʷ⁾er and cədder **äff**. She maydə rude **jesjer** with her **hænd** and drovə **way**. I smæckt the **wind**shield. It **shædderd**. **Then**, I wəz **rilly** ængry. I drove **fæst** and I cähdəp too⁽ʷ⁾er əgen. I stärdəd **yell**ing ædder. I sed thət she wəzza terrəble **driver**. She kept **læffing**, so I yell dəgen. She lük **dover** and **säh** me. Her **ayz** gät **big**. She wəz **scerd**. **R'member**, I'm Mr. **Wrr-rəld**. I'm six **forrrr** and I way **300** **pæonz**. She step dän thə **gæs**, rænə red **light**, and disəppir din **træffic**. I jəst kept **driving**, bədäi wəz **læffing**.

Exercise 4-4: Reduced Vowels — CD 1 Track 70

We have worked with the most reduced vowel, which is the schwa (ə), but now we're going to look at three others, **ih**, **eh**, and **ü**. These are called *lax vowels* because your mouth is relaxed while you are pronouncing them. When you have a word like list, it's almost like the vowel is gone. You don't want to say least, which would be a tense vowel.

i	eh	ə	ü		ee
big	beg	bug	put		beet
pick	peck	puck	book		peek
chip	check	chuck	could		cheap
ship	shed	shut	should		sheep
whip	wet	what	would		we
lip	let	luck	look		leap
rid	red	run	rook		real

Let's focus on **ü** for a moment. It's what we call the chicken sound. As you know, chickens don't have lips. In order to make an **ooh** sound, you need to round your lips to say **soon** or **choose**. Chickens can only say **bük, bük, bük!** This sound is used in **book**, **took**, **good**, **look**, **could**, **would**, and **should**. These are all very high-frequency words. The secret to saying the following sentence is to put on a wide smile for the entire thing. Do not round your lips. Smile!

The cook took a good look at the cookbook and said,
"By hook or by crook, I should cook!"

Sometimes, people have trouble with the difference between **ah** and **uh**. Let's practice that.

äh	ə
saw	some
dock	duck
chalk	chuck
lost	luck
wrong	rung

How much wood would a woodchuck chuck, if a woodchuck could chuck wood?
How məch wüd wüd ə wüdchəck chəck, if ə wüdchəck cüd chəck wüd?

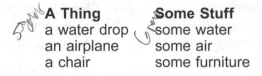

This section covers an important aspect of nouns—if they are *countable* or not. We'll also review plurals and modifiers.

Countable nouns: **one chair / two chairs**
Uncountable nouns: **furniture / some furniture**

Countable and Uncountable Nouns

Let's compare **things** and **stuff**. Things are individual. Stuff is a collection of things. You can count **things**. You can't count **stuff**.

A Thing	**Some Stuff**
a water drop	some water
an airplane	some air
a chair	some furniture

Uncountable Noun Rule

1) Anything that can be sliced, scooped, or poured (separated from a **lump** or a **mass** of stuff). Things like bread, ice cream, and liquids can't be counted: Bread is sliced. Ice cream is scooped. Water is poured. These are all *uncountable* nouns.

2) A collection of items. Furniture is a collection of individual items, such as chairs, couches, dressers, and lamps.

Individual Items	**Collection of Items**
Things	**Stuff**
Add an S	No S
Use an article	No article

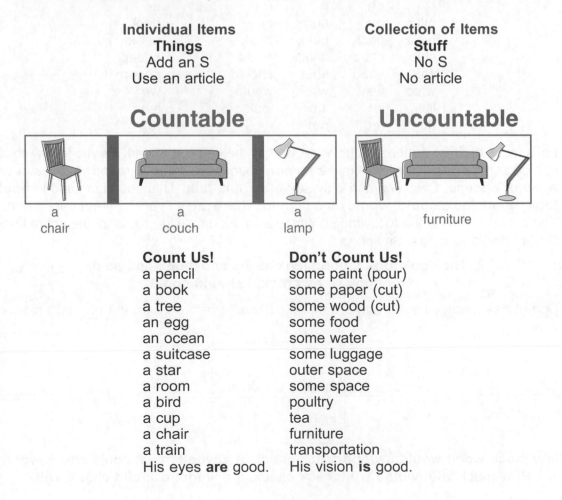

Countable	**Uncountable**
a chair a couch a lamp	furniture

Count Us!	**Don't Count Us!**
a pencil	some paint (pour)
a book	some paper (cut)
a tree	some wood (cut)
an egg	some food
an ocean	some water
a suitcase	some luggage
a star	outer space
a room	some space
a bird	poultry
a cup	tea
a chair	furniture
a train	transportation
His eyes **are** good.	His vision **is** good.

No modifier is needed with uncountable nouns, although you can use **some**. Remember: No naked nouns are allowed, but you may have an invisible **some** or **all**. **Would you like coffee?** and **Would you like some coffee?** have basically the same meaning.

Exercise 4-5: Countable and Uncountable Nouns (*A* / —)

Fill in the blanks with **a** *or* —. *Use the* — *when no words are needed. (***Some*** or* ***all*** *are optional.) Then check the Answer Key.*

I need ___ car.
I need ___ transportation.

I need a car.
I need (some) transportation.

1. ___ sugar is sweet.
2. Our veins are filled with ___ blood.
3. ___ lead is heavy.
4. We put ___ paint on the walls.
5. Sam had ___ sandwich for lunch.
6. Joe brought ___ good food to the party.
7. Those guys are always ready for ___ good time.
8. Museums are filled with ___ art.
9. My cell phone is made of ___ plastic.
10. Let's work on ___ new project!

Exercise 4-6: Countable and Uncountable Nouns (*A* / *An* / *Some* / —)

Fill in the blank with **a, an, some,** *or* —. *Then check the Answer Key.*

Would you like ___ coffee?

1. Could you give me ___ pencil?
2. I need ___ cream for my coffee.
3. The rocket flew into ___ outer space.
4. We need ___ information about it.
5. Buy ___ suitcase for your trip.
6. Here is ___ ice cube for your drink.
7. Do you put ___ ice in ___ tea?
8. I have ___ headache.
9. ___ bottle is made of ___ glass.
10. Would you like ___ glass of ___ water?

Would you like some (a, —) coffee?

When you **limit** an uncountable noun, you can count the **segments**.

Don't Count Us!	Now Count Us!
paint	**a drop of** paint
paper	**a piece of** paper
wood	**a chunk of** wood
food	**a mouthful of** food
cheese	**a slice of** cheese
lead	**a pencil** lead
water	**a splash of** water
luggage / baggage	**a piece of** luggage / baggage
tea / coffee	**a cup of** tea / coffee
furniture	**a set of** furniture

transportation	a means of transportation
communication	a mode of communication

When you want to indicate large quantities, use **much** or **many**. **Much** is used with uncountable nouns (*much time*), and **many** is used with countable nouns (*many times*).

Quick Rule: If you see an **S**, choose **many**.

Exercise 4-7: *Much* or *Many*

*Select **much** or **many**. Then check the Answer Key.*

    I have so ___ to do!

1. I drank too ___ glasses of water.
2. I put too ___ water in the glass.
3. The kids have so ___ to do.
4. The kids have so ___ things to do.
5. There aren't very ___ people in Nome.
6. There isn't very ___ time to work on this.
7. We ordered too ___ furniture for the house.
8. We ordered too ___ chairs for the house.
9. There aren't ___ opportunities.
10. There isn't ___ chance of that!

I have so much to do!

Some old prepositional phrases have been worn down by use and dropped **the**: to bed / to school / to work / to town. Some others have even dropped **to**: home / downtown / back / somewhere.

Exercise 4-8: Phrases with No *The*   CD 1 Track 71

Listen and repeat the following phrases. The intonation is marked for you.

1. He went **home**.
2. We're going to **town**.
3. He went to **bed**.
4. I'm on my way to **work**.
5. They went down**town**.
6. When are you coming **back**?
7. They want to **go** somewhere.
8. When did you **get** there?

Exercise 4-9: Prepositions of Time

Circle the appropriate time preposition. Then check the Answer Key.

1. He visits	in / on	**January**.
2. He visits	in / on	January **10**th.
3. They always call us	in / on	**Sunday**.
4. They always call us	in / on	the **morning**.
5. They always call us	in / on	Sunday **morning**.
6. Let's go skiing	in / on	the winter.
7. I saw him	in / at	night.
8. I saw him	in / at	the evening.
9. Let's leave	on / at	5:00.
10. Let's leave	on / in / at	fifteen minutes.

Exercise 4-10: Prepositions of Manner

Circle the appropriate preposition of manner, which tells you how something was done. Then check the Answer Key.

1. She said it	by / in / with	English.
2. *Hamlet* was written	by / for	Shakespeare.
3. I wrote it	in / by / of	ink.
4. I saw it	in / by / at	the newspaper.
5. They said it	in / by / with	French.
6. They wrote it	by / with / of	hand.
7. He got there	by / with / of	car.
8. He came	on / with / of	foot.
9. I did it	for / of	you.
10. I came here	to / for	learn.
11. The gardener takes care	of / by / with	the yard.

Exercise 4-11: "Jack and the Beanstalk"

*Fill in the blanks with **a**, **an**, **the**, **some**, **any**, or — (if another word isn't necessary). Then check the Answer Key.*

Once upon ___ time, there was ___ poor widow and her son Jack. One day, ___ widow said, "Jack, we don't have ___ food. Take ___ cow to ___ town and sell her so that we can have ___ money for ___ food." Jack said OK and went to ___ town, leading ___ cow behind him. Very soon, he came back all alone. "See what I got for our cow, Mother," he said happily. "I sold her to ___ man for ___ three magic beans." When Jack's mother heard that he traded ___ cow for three beans, she was very angry. "Jack!" she yelled. "Three beans can't keep us from starving!" She threw ___ beans out of ___ window. Jack went to ___ bed.

___ next morning, they saw ___ huge vine. ___ vine rose above ___ house and disappeared into ___ clouds. Jack climbed up ___ vine and soon disappeared into ___ clouds, too. At ___ top of ___ vine, Jack saw ___ huge castle. ___ door was ten times his size. He called out, "Excuse me, do you have ___ food for ___ hungry boy?" ___ door opened, and Jack saw ___ woman who was as tall as ___ tree. She picked him up by his shirt and put him on ___ table. "So, you're hungry? Well, I'll give you ___ bite to eat. But watch out for my husband!" She handed Jack ___ slice of bread as big as ___ mattress, and ___ piece of ___ cheese high enough to sit on. But before Jack could eat, he heard ___ giant-sized footsteps and ___ voice said, "Wife, where's my dinner?" Jack hid out of sight in ___ shadows. Then he heard ___ giant say, "Fee, fie, fo, fum, I smell the blood of an Englishman!" ___ giant didn't want Jack to take ___ goose that laid golden eggs. One thing led to another, and there was ___ huge fight between Jack and ___ giant. Jack grabbed the goose and ran. ___ giant ended up chasing Jack down ___ beanstalk. Fortunately, Jack got to ___ bottom first, grabbed ___ ax, and chopped it down. ___ giant fell to his death and Jack and his mother lived happily ever after with the goose.

Exercise 4-12: "Jack and the Beanstalk" — Pronunciation CD 1 Track 72

Listen to the audio and repeat five times.

ACCENT

Wənsa pənnə **time**, ther wəzzə poor **widow** anner sən **Jæck**. **One** day, the widow **sed**, "**Jæck**, we don't have any **food**. Take the **cow** tə **town** and **sell**er so thət we cən have səm **mə ney** for **food**." Jæck sed **OK** and went tə **town**, **leeding** the cow be**hind**im. **Very** soon, he came **bæck** allə **lone**. "**See** whədai **got** for our **cow**, Məther," he sed **hæppaly**. "I **sold**er to⁽ʷ⁾ə **mæn** fr **three** mægic **beanz**." When Jæck's məther **hrrd** the dee **traded** the cow frr three **beenz**, she wəz very **angry**. "Jack!" she yelld. "Three **beans** cæn't keepəs frəm **starving**!" She **threw** the beans outtə the **window**. **Jæck** went tə **bed**.

The next **morning**, they sah-a hyooj **vine**. The **vine** rozə bəv the **house** and **disə ppird** into the **clouds**. Jack climb dəp the **vine** and soon **disappeared** into the **clouds**, too. At the **tapa** the vine, Jack sah-a huge **cæssəl**. The **door** wəz ten **tymz** hiz **size**. He call **dout**, "Eks-k**yooz** me, do you have any **food** fra həngry **boy**?" The door **opend**, and Jack säh-ə **wümən** who wəzzəz **talləzə tree**. She **pick** diməp by his **shirt** and **püdimän** the **table**. "**So**, yer həngry? **Well**, I'll give you⁽ʷ⁾ə **bite** tə **eat**. Bət **watch**out fr my **həzbənd**!" She **hændəd** Jæckə sly s'v **bread** əz **bigəzə mætt**ress, annə peesə **cheez high** enuf to **sid**dän. But be**fore** Jæck cüd**eat**, he herd **jiant**-sized **füt**steps annə **voice** sed, "**Wife**, wherz my **d'nner**?" **Jæck** hid owddə sight in the **shædowz**. Thenee **herd** the giant **say**, "**Fee**, fie, fo, **fum, I** smell the **bləd** əvə **ninglish**man!" The jiant didn't want Jack tə take the goose thət laid goldən eggz. **One** thing led to⁽ʷ⁾ ənəther, and there wəzza hyooj **fight** b'tween **Jæck** and the **jiant**. Jæck **græbbd** the goos and ræn.The jiant endədəp **chasing** Jæck down the **bean**stalk. **For**chənatly, **Jæck** gät t' the **bäddəm frrrrst**, **grab** dənæx and chäp dit **down**. The jiant fell to⁽ʷ⁾iz **death** and **Jæck** and his **mother** livd **hæppəly** ever **æfter** with the goos.

Exercise 4-13: Noun vs. Verb Intonation CD 1 Track 73

Listen to the audio and repeat five times.

Noun		Verb	
accent	**æc**cent	**ac**cent	**ac**cent
conflict	**cän**flict	con**flict**	c'n**flict**
contract	**cän**tract	con**tract**	c'n**tract**
convert	**cän**vert	con**vert**	c'n**vert**
default	**de**fault	de**fault**	d'**fault**
envelope	**än**velope	en**velop**	en**velop**
insult	**in**sult	in**sult**	in**sult**
perfect	**per**fect	per**fect**	per**fect**
permit	**per**mit	per**mit**	per**mit**
present	**pres**ent	pre**sent**	pr'**zent**
produce	**pro**duce	pro**duce**	pr'**duce**
progress	**prä**gress	pro**gress**	pr'**gress**
project	**prä**ject	pro**ject**	pr'**ject**
subject	**sub**ject	sub**ject**	s'**bject**

Exercise 4-14: Reading Comprehension

Read the following passage and answer the questions. Then check the Answer Key.

Sign Language

Most languages convey **information** with spoken **words**. **Sign** language uses **visual** signals. **Hearing**-impaired people use hand and **arm** gestures, **body** language, and **facial** expressions to convey **meaning**. **Sign** languages develop in deaf **communities**, which can include **interpreters** and **friends** and **families** of **deaf** people, as well as **people** who are **deaf** or hard of **hearing themselves**.

Wherever communities of **deaf** people **exist**, **sign** languages **develop**. In **fact**, their complex **grammars** are very **different** from **spoken** languages. There are **hundreds** of **sign** languages in use around the **world**.

Several sign languages are used in **stage** performances, such as **sign**-language **poetry**. Many of the poetic **mechanisms** available to **signing** poets are **not** available to **speaking** poets.

Like **other** languages, **sign** languages are **different** in **different** countries. In **spite** of this, **hearing**-impaired people from different **countries** seem to under**stand** each other **better** than **hearing** people.

Many people who can **hear also** want to learn to **sign**. For **example, scuba divers use sign language because they can't talk underwater.** Fire**fighters** and **police** officers sometimes sign to each **other** in order to communicate **silently**, while **dog**-trainers can use it to train **dogs**.

Answer the questions based on this text.

Give two synonyms for the word **deaf**.
1. _____ 2. _____

Answer each question with **True** or **False**.
1. Sign language conveys sound patterns.
2. There are sign languages in every community of deaf people.
3. There are almost a hundred different sign languages.
4. The grammar of sign language and spoken language are the same.
5. Sign language is the same in every country.
6. Only deaf people use sign language.

How do most languages convey information?
What does sign language use?

List three reasons why people who can hear might also need to learn sign language.

1. _____

2. _____

3. _____

"Tee Aitch"

ACCENT

Th is a very important sound. After the schwa (ə), it's the highest-frequency sound in English. You will hear it in **the**, **this**, **that**, **these**, **those**, **they**, **them**, **there**, **their**, **they're**, and **then**.

In terms of pronunciation, you need to distinguish between **Th** and **D** for two reasons. The first reason is clarity and comprehension, so **the** doesn't sound like **duh**. The second is because it sounds uneducated to say **Dese are da tings dat we tought about**.

If you ask an American how to pronounce **Th**, you will hear that you put the tip of your tongue between your teeth and blow the air out. This is not accurate when you are using **Th** in actual speech.

The **Th** is actually very similar to the D, but the tongue position is about an inch forward in the mouth. For the D, put the tip of your tongue on the bumps behind your top teeth. Say, da, da, da. Now, press the tip of your tongue against the back of the top teeth, and let the air pop out, **the**.

Exercise 4-15: Tee Aitch Pronunciation: Voiced
CD 1 Track 74

These are the things that we thought about.

Th	D	Th	D
they	day	these	D's
the	duh	though	dough
then	den	those	doze
there	dare	they'll	dale

There are actually two **Th** sounds. One of them is *voiced* (this, that, these, those) and the other is *unvoiced* (thing, think, thank, three, thought).

Exercise 4-16: Tee Aitch Pronunciation: Unvoiced
CD 1 Track 75

I think I need to thank them for three things.

Th	T	Th	T	Th	T
thank	tank	three	tree	thought	taught

Intonation and Meaning

With the same sentence and the same words, you can completely change the meaning by moving the intonation around.

Exercise 4-17: Intonation
CD 1 Track 76

Listen and repeat.

1. **He** didn't say he needed my help. Someone **else** said that.
2. He **didn't** say he needed my help. **That's** not **true**.
3. He didn't **say** he needed my help, but he **indicated** it with his **body** language.
4. He didn't say **he** needed my help. I thought he meant someone **else**.
5. He didn't say he **needed** my help. He just seemed like he **wanted** it.

6. He didn't say he needed **my** help. It seemed like **anyone** could help him.
7. He didn't say he needed my **help**. Maybe he just wanted **advice**.

Note: With acronyms, always stress the final letter: **CD**, **LA**, ASA**P**.

VERBS

Now, you will change verbs in the simple present and the simple past to their continuous forms. The continuous form uses the helping verb **to be** plus a **main verb** and –**ing**.

go > is going / are going
went > was going / were going

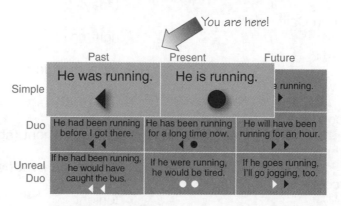

You are here!

	Past	Present	Future
Simple	He was running. ◀	He is running. ●	...e running. ▶
Duo	He had been running before I got there. ◀◀	He has been running for a long time now. ◀●	He will have been running for an hour. ▶▶
Unreal Duo	If he had been running, he would have caught the bus. ◀◀	If he were running, he would be tired. ●●	If he goes running, I'll go jogging, too. ▶▶

There are certain words that go with the continuous, such as **right now**.

I am going to the store right now.

Present	Present Continuous	Past	Past Continuous
I go.	I am going.	I went.	I was going.
You go.	You are going.	You went.	You were going.
He goes.	He is going.	He went.	He was going.
She goes.	She is going.	She went.	She was going.
It goes.	It is going.	It went.	It was going.
We go.	We are going.	We went.	We were going.
They go.	They are going.	They went.	They were going.

The continuous form is used:

1. To indicate that something is taking place right now.
   The kids are playing outside right now.

2. To indicate that something is not permanent.
   He doesn't drink coffee. (permanent situation)
   He isn't drinking coffee these days. (temporary situation)

3. To indicate that something is specific, not general.
   I take a shower every day. (general)
   I'm taking a shower now. (specific)

4. When something continues as compared to something that doesn't continue. You have the ongoing action and then another event.
   He was cleaning his room when the power went out.

Note: Some –ing forms are actually nouns. **I like swimming. Skiing is fun.**

Exercise 4-18: Present Continuous

Rewrite the sentences using the present continuous form. Then check the Answer Key.

I practice a lot.   **I'm practicing** a lot these days.

1. I have **lunch** every day.

   right now

2. Bob gets sick.

   right now

3. It rains in California.

   today

4. It doesn't rain in California.

   right now

5. He works hard.

   for a change

6. She dances well.

   this week

7. He thinks about it.

   at the moment (right now)

8. He doesn't think about it.

   for the moment (for now)

9. She makes cookies.

   tonight

10. They don't drink coffee.

    these days

Exercise 4-19: Past Continuous

Rewrite the sentences using the past continuous form. Then check the Answer Key.

I spoke Italian.   **I was speaking** Italian when they walked in.

1. The teachers wrote on the blackboard.

   when the **bell** rang

2. Larry rode his bike.

   when it started **raining**

3. Your cousin flew first class.

   until he ran out of **money**

4. The managers still arranged the meetings.

   before the **conference**

5. I didn't work hard.

   last **year**, but I am **now**

6. We thought about it.

   before the **situation** changed

7. They threw it away.

   until they realized its **value**

8. Virginia didn't sell her car.

   until she won the **lottery**

9. The candles burned steadily.

   even though it was **windy**

10. Her sister said hello.

    when he rudely **interrupted**

As you learned before, there are two ways to make contractions with pronouns and the verb **to be**. Use them in the next exercise.

Exercise 4-20: Continuous Negative Contractions

Change to a negative contraction. Change all nouns to pronouns. Move the intonation to the verb. Check the Answer Key when you're done.

Sam is speaking Italian.

He isn't speaking it.   **He's not speaking it.**

1. The teachers are writing on the blackboard.

2. Larry is riding his bike.

3. Your cousin is flying first class.

4. The managers are arranging the meetings.

5. I am giving many presents.

6. We are thinking about the play.

7. They are throwing the trash away.

8. Virginia is selling her car.

9. The candles are burning steadily.

10. Her sister was saying hello.

Exercise 4-21: Continuous Questions ↻

Change the statements to questions. Change all nouns to pronouns. Move the stress to the verb. Check the Answer Key when you're done.

Edward's speaking Italian.   **Is he speaking it?** Izzy speekingit?

1. The teachers are writing on the blackboard.

2. Larry and Joe are riding their bikes.

3. Your cousin is flying first class.

4. The managers are arranging the meetings.

5. I am giving many presents.

6. We were thinking about it.

7. Elwin and Martha were throwing the trash away.

8. Virginia was selling her car.

9. The candles are burning steadily.

10. Her sister was saying hello.

Note: The words **writing** and **riding** sound exactly the same.

Contrasting the Simple Present and the Continuous Present

The *simple present* is used for a broader, more general present.
The *continuous present* is more immediate and continuing in the moment.

The **past continuous** can indicate an intention that has changed.

He was going to do it, but he changed his mind.

Exercise 4-22: Simple Present vs. Continuous Present

Listen and repeat.

Simple Present (in general)	Continuous (right now)
I do the **dishes** every day.	I'm doing the **dishes** now.
I have a **book**.	I'm reading a **book** right now.
He has a **head**ache.	He is getting a **head**ache.
We need a **break**.	We're taking a **break** now.
I always take a **taxi** to work.	I'm not taking a **taxi** this morning.
Call me **later**.	Are you **calling** me?
It's already **open**.	Look, it's finally **opening**.
It's too **far**.	He's going too **far** again.
That's a good **idea**.	He's being **good** for a change.
We **always** enjoy your **parties**.	We're enjoying your **party** this evening.
He can spell "**potato**."	He's spelling it **wrong** again.
You always forget to **call**.	Aren't you forgetting to **call**?
We almost **always** play **ball**.	Aren't you ever playing **ball** again?

Exercise 4-23: Simple Present vs. Continuous Present

Fill in the blank with either the simple present or the continuous form. Then check the Answer Key.

She dances well, in general. **She is dancing really well today.**

1. They		to the **gym** every **day**.	go
2. They		to the **gym** right now.	go
3. He		a **hat** on.	have
4. He		a **hat**.	wearing
5. He		**curry** for **lunch** today.	have
6 He		**curry** for lunch every day.	have
7. She		her **boy**friend.	like
8. Elsa		to move to **Texas**.	want
9. You and I		about it very often.	think
10. Everyone else		about it right now.	think
11. I		**hungry**.	be
12. She		**pretty**.	be
13. He		**ridiculous** about the situation.	be
14. The **victim**		admitted to the **hospital** right now.	be
15. ↻ Who		**pan**cakes right now?	make
16. ↻ Why	___ you ___	**pan**cakes every **morning**?	make
17. ↻ Why	___ you ___	**pan**cakes again today?	make
18. ↻	___ you ___	for me?	wait
19. ↻	___ you ___	for me every **day**?	wait
20. **Florida**		a major **heat** wave this **month**.	have
21. **Florida**		**heat** waves every **year**.	have
22. We		a great **time**! (right now)	have
23. They		an awful **time**, so they left **early**.	have
24. She		a **baby** next month.	have
25. She		a **baby** last month.	have
26. He		second **thoughts** about it now.	have
27. Our **friends**		a **party** this **week**end!	have
28. Our **friends**		a party **every** weekend!	have
29. Her **boss**		**angry** because everyone is **late**.	get
30. I		two **aspirin** for my **heart** every day.	take
31. I		two **aspirin** because I just got a **head**ache.	take
32. He		big **cars** all the time.	buy
33. He		a big car to **impress** people.	buy
34. She		that old **house** this **week**end.	sell
35. She		**real** estate for a living.	sell
36. That old **man**		**slowly** because he hurt his **foot**.	walk
37. That old **man**		**slowly** when he goes to the **store**.	walk
38. The **dancer**		so **well**!	dance
39. The **dancer**		in the **ballet** tonight.	dance
40. The **janitor**		really **hard** every **day**!	work
41. The **janitor**		**hard** to get that **floor** clean.	work
42. **So** many **people**		**lunch** right now.	eat
43. **So** many **people**		**lunch** at **noon**.	eat
44. **Laura**		**basket**ball on **Mondays**.	play
45. **Laura**		**basket**ball right now.	play
46. My **son**		a long **letter** to his **father** now.	write
47. My **son**		really **well** for a **six**-year-old.	write
48. The **guard**		that **report** every day.	do
49. The **guard**		that **report** right now.	do
50. The **apple**		n't fall **far** from the **tree**.	do

Get: Review with the Continuous

As we saw in Chapter 3, **get** has many meanings. It's often used in the continuous form. Let's review.

Exercise 4-24: Getting It Right

*Add the proper **get** phrase. Then check the Answer Key.*

We tried to get out of doing it. (escape)
1. They aren't getting ___, so I think they're getting ___. (have good relations; separated)
2. I get ___ to go to work. (arise)
3. The old lady is getting ___ the bus slowly. (enter)
4. My lucky coworker is getting ___ from it all in Hawaii. (escape from)
5. My mom is finally getting ___ to my loud music. (become accustomed to)
6. The **sales** staff is getting ___ about the new **product** line! (develop strong feelings)
7. After **studying** hard, the student's **grades** are getting ___. (improve)
8. We are getting ___ all the extra junk. (throwing away)
9. My coworker is getting ___ from Hawaii soon. (return)
10. The **tiger** is getting ___ because you are throwing **rocks** at him. (become irritated)
11. My **nephew** is getting ___ by all his **math** homework. (become mixed up)
12. I am getting ___ on all my **credit** card payments! (fall behind)
13. Don't tell me you're just getting ___ now?! (put one's clothes on)
14. The Wicked Witch is getting ___ with Snow White. (take revenge)
15. The diplomats are getting ___ to end the fighting. (meet)

Get is also used a great deal with emotions. Oddly, it tends to be used in a negative sense.

Exercise 4-25: Getting Emotional   CD 1 Track 77

Listen to the audio and repeat five times.

1. The **bankers** were getting **worried** about the **loans**.
2. The **kids** were getting really **excited** about the **trip**.
3. We were getting **tired**, so we stopped **working**.
4. She was getting **annoyed** at him.
5. **None** of the **patients** were getting any **better**.
6. The **fourth** graders were getting **bored** in the **assembly**.
7. I was getting really **confused** by his complicated **explanation**.
8. Getting **nervous** is a part of **stage** fright.
9. There's no point in getting up**set**. **That** won't **help**.
10. The **researcher** was getting increasingly **impatient** with the difficult **subject**.
11. **Every**one was getting **frustrated** by the long **delays**.
12. We're still getting **used** to the new **situation**.
13. The **students** were getting **happier** as they got **closer** to finishing their **home**work.
14. His **dad** was getting **madder** by the **minute** when **Joey** didn't make his **curfew**.
15. She was getting **angry** about the lack of **planning**.

Who is it? What is it? ⟳

Up to now, we've learned a certain type of question. You may have noticed that these questions can all be answered **yes** or **no**. Let's replace the subject with **who** or **what**, as we did in Chapter 1.

This is a quick and easy lesson, and you will use it a lot.

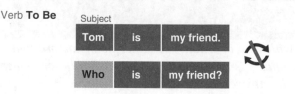

Who and **what** questions about the **subject** don't do the question flip.
The verb is singular (**is** or **was**).

Who?	The **boy** is a student.	**Who** is a student?
	The **kids** are at the park.	**Who** is at the park?
	The **teacher** is gone.	**Who** is gone?
	The **workers** are hungry.	**Who** is hungry?
	My friends are excited.	**Who** is excited?
	Movie stars are exciting.	**Who** is exciting?
	The **students** were reading.	**Who** was reading?
What?	The **sun** is a star.	**What** is a star?
	The **bikes** are in the garage.	**What** is in the garage?
	The **dogs** are gone.	**What** is gone?
	The **painting** is beautiful.	**What** is beautiful?
	The **electrons** are excited.	**What** is excited?
	The **movie** is exciting.	**What** is exciting?
	The **phone** was ringing.	**What** was ringing?
	The **car** is parked outside.	**What** is parked outside?
	The **money** is missing.	**What** is missing?

Exercise 4-26: *Who* and *What* — *To Be* Subject ⟳

*Replace the subject with **who** or **what**. For the word order, remember that there is no question flip. Then check the Answer Key. Remember, the verb becomes singular.*

The babies are crying.	Who is crying?
The cars are on fire.	What is on fire?
1. Our **parents** are **worried**.	
2. That **watch** was **expensive**.	
3. Those **forms** were filled **in**.	
4. The **fire**men were on **duty**.	
5. The **music** is **playing**.	

As usual, after the verb **to be**, we go on to *main verbs*. Again, because **who** and **what** replace the subject, there is no question flip. Use the same word order as you would for a statement.

Main Verbs   Subject

Tom	sees	my friend.

Who	sees	my friend?

Bob likes Betty.	**Who** likes Betty?
Cars go fast.	**What** goes fast?

Exercise 4-27: *Who* and *What* — Main Verbs Subject

*Replace the subject with **who** or **what**. Use either nouns or pronouns in your answer. If you use pronouns, the emphasis is on the verb. For the word order, remember that there is no question flip. Check the Answer Key when you're done.*

The girls wrote the letter.	**Who** wrote it?
The noise scared the children.	**What** scared them?

1. **Janice** told Lou.
2. **The store** closed early.
3. **My parents** left early.
4. **The train** left the station.
5. **The bell** rang loudly.

 or

In Exercises 4-26 and 4-27, where **who** and **what** replace the subject, the question flip is **not** used. These are questions, but they use the **statement** word order.

In Exercises 4-28 and 4-29, we review **yes / no questions**. These do use the question flip.

Exercise 4-28: Yes / No Question Review — *To Be* Subject

Let's do a quick review. Convert each statement to a yes / no question. Then check the Answer Key.

The kids are in the pool.	**Are** the kids in the pool?

1. She is **excited** about the **party**.
2. The **party** is very **exciting**.
3. We weren't **invited**.
4. He isn't **ready** yet.
5. **Bob** is **sick**.

Exercise 4-29: Yes / No Question Review — Main Verbs Subject

Convert each statement to a yes / no question. Then check the Answer Key.

Boris understands.	**Does** Boris understand?

1. They like to **swim**.
2. He can tell you the **answer**.
3. You didn't eat **break**fast.
4. Bob has a **head**ache.
5. Ella doesn't **want** one.

Let's review what we know so far about statements and questions about the *subject*.

Kind	Order	Verb *To Be*	Main Verb
Statement		**He** is there.	**He** likes it.
Who Question	↻	**Who** is there?	**Who** likes it?
What Question	↻	**What** is there?	**What** likes it?
Yes/No Question	↻	**Is he** there?	**Does he** like it?

What **is** it? What **does** it do?

Up to now, we've only been working with questions about the *subject*. Now, let's look at the *object*, using all *5 W* words. You can see that there is a relationship between these words because most of them have similar spellings.

Who? He.
What? That.
Where? There.
When? Then.
Why? Because.

The next step is to take the *object* and replace it with one of the *5 Ws*. Use the question flip. ↻

			Object
Verb **To Be**	He	is	my boss.
	Is	he	my boss?
Who	is	he?	

Izzy my boss? Who izzy?

Exercise 4-30: *5 W* Questions — *To Be* Object ↻

Convert each statement to a question. Then check the Answer Key.

The kids are in the pool.   **Where are the kids?**

1. He is jumping on **the couch**.   What?
2. The book is **on the shelf**.   Where?
3. He was here **at 3:00 p.m.**   When?
4. He was here **at 3:00 p.m.**   What time?
5. He isn't tired **because he doesn't work hard**.   Why?

Now that you understand the format for the verb **to be**, let's take a look at *main verbs*.

He		likes	apples.
Does	he	like	apples?
What	does	he	like?

Duzzy like'm? What duzzy like?

Exercise 4-31: *5 W* Questions — Main Verbs Object ⟳

Convert each statement to a 5 W question. Then check the Answer Key.

The kids like the pool.   **What** do they **like?**
1. She shops at the **mall**.   Where?
2. Janice told **Lou**.   Who?
3. He started work **at 3:00 p.m.**   When?
4. He stopped **because he was tired**.   Why?
5. He wants to move **to another apartment**. Where?

How is it?

Here, **how** tells the *quality* or *condition* of something.

Is it **good**? Is it **bad**? **Old**? **New**?

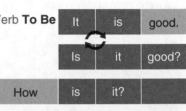

Verb **To Be**	It	is	good.
	Is	it	good?
How	is	it?	

Exercise 4-32: *How* Questions — *To Be* ⟳

*Convert each statement to a **how** question. Change the nouns to pronouns. Then check the Answer Key.*

I am fine.   **How are you?**
1. The boys were **excited**.
2. My sister isn't **happy**.
3. The books were in bad **condition**.
4. The food is **burned**.
5. Our vacation will be too **long**.

How also tells the *degree* of a quality or condition.

Is it **very** good? Is it **really** bad? A **little** old?
Kind of new?

Verb **To Be**	It	is	very	good.
	Is	it	very	good?
How good	is	it?	

Exercise 4-33: *How* Questions — *To Be* ⟳

*Convert each statement to a **how** question. (**How** replaces the adverb.) Change the nouns to pronouns. Check the Answer Key when you're done.*

They are very happy.   **How happy** are they?
1. The boys were really excited.
2. My sister is wonderfully happy.
3. The books were in very bad condition.
4. The food is really burned.
5. Our car is quite old.

TEST

Let's review everything you have learned in Chapter 4. Make sure you get 100% on the test before going on to the next chapter. Check your work using the Answer Key.

*Part 1: Fill in the blank with **a** or **an**.*

1. Would you like _____ after-dinner mint?
2. Would you like _____ mint?
3. I'd like _____ apple, please.
4. He's _____ honest man.
5. It's _____ history book.

*Part 2: Fill in the blank with **a** or **some**.*

1. There was _____ water on the floor.
2. He took _____ bath last night.
3. Please take _____ more time if you need it.
4. We had _____ great time.
5. They put _____ butter on their toast.

*Part 3: Fill in the blank with **a** or **the**.*

1. Would you like _____ bite of my apple?
2. Please pass _____ salt.
3. We had _____ best time!
4. What _____ surprise!
5. It's _____ only way we can do it.

*Part 4: Fill in the blank with **a** or — (if another word isn't needed).*

1. They poured _____ water on the plants.
2. Did you bring _____ water bottle?
3. There is _____ mud on your shoes.
4. Would you like _____ more coffee?
5. Don't rush him. He needs _____ time to finish.

*Part 5: Fill in the blank with the appropriate **preposition** of **time** or **manner**.*

1. Call me ____ Wednesday ____ 3:00.
2. We went to the party ____ meet friends.

*Part 6: Fill in the blank with **much** or **many**.*

1. How _____ did it cost?
2. How _____ of them did you buy?
3. He called so _____ times!
4. Did you have _____ trouble?
5. Did you have _____ problems?

Part 7: *Change from the simple present or past to the appropriate continuous form.*

1. He is silly!
2. They work hard.
3. You chose one.
4. He lost the race.
5. I wrote to him.

Part 8: *Select the simple present or past tense, or the appropriate continuous form.*

1. He		right now.	sleep
2. He		hard every day.	work
3. He		about going out when she called.	think
4. He		in the pool.	be
5. He		admitted to the hospital right now.	be

Part 9: *Change the positive statement to a negative.*

1. Lou knows Ed.
2. The cars go fast.

Part 10: *Change the statement to a question.*

1. It rains every day.
2. It's raining.
3. You like it.
4. You're in charge.

Part 11: *Complete each sentence based on the meaning of the changing intonation.*

1. **My** brother doesn't like dogs,
2. My **brother** doesn't like dogs,
3. My brother **doesn't** like dogs;
4. My brother doesn't **like** dogs,
5. My brother doesn't like **dogs**,

Part 12: *Make a question and change the subject to **who** or **what**.*

1. The basketball players are starting the game now.
2. The boxes fell off the shelf.

Part 13: *Convert each statement to a question.*

1. They are sitting on the floor.   Where
2. We left at noon.   When
3. She looked at the book.   What
4. He laughed because it was funny.   Why

Using what you have learned, write two paragraphs on the following:

1. What type of movie do you like?
2. Are you a *dog person* or a *cat person*?

You can handwrite your paragraphs below or e-mail them to **para@grammar.bz** to be stored. These paragraphs are not graded or reviewed, but simply by writing them, your English will improve.

● ○ ○   Student Paragraph

Send   Chat   Attach   Address   Fonts   Colors   Save As Draft   Photo Browser   Show Stationery

To:	para@grammar.bz
Cc:	
Bcc:	
Subject:	Chapter 4

Signature: Corporate ⬍

My name is _____

Chapter 5: Future Tense
Comparisons and Modifiers

We studied comparisons in Chapter 3. Now, we will look at more comparisons, modifiers, articles, descriptions, compound nouns, word order, and more conjunctions, as well as **how much / how many**.

For verbs, we will work with the real and unreal futures, with both **will** and **going to**. We'll learn some idiomatic expressions with **use**, **do / make**, and **stand**. Look for the "Grammar in a Nutshell" section in this chapter.

Exercise 5-1: Dictation   CD 2 Track 1

Listen to the audio and write in the exact transcription in the spaces below. Then check the Answer Key.

1. _____

2. _____

3. _____

4. _____

5. _____

The Motorcycle Accident: Predicting the Future

    In eight **years**, **three** days after I win Mr. **Europe**, I will be riding a **motor**cycle on a main **street** in Milan, **Italy**. I will be going about **80** miles an **hour**. All of a **sudden**, a **car** will pull in **front** of me. I'll **hit** the car and fly about 10 **yards**. My **leg** will break in three **places**. I will be **in** and out of the **hospital** for seven **months**. The **doctor** will put me in **traction** for the first **month** without a **cast**. After my **leg** is a little better, he will put a **cast** on. He will give me a lot of **antibiotics**. **Every**one will be very **worried** about me. The **news**papers and TV will report **every**thing that **happens**. It will take me **seven** months to **recover**, and it will be a **year** before I **compete** again. I will **still** have a **scar** on my **shin**, and my **right** calf won't be as developed as the **other** one is. I'll be **lucky** to be **alive**, though.

Exercise 5-2: "The Motorcycle Accident" — Pronunciation   CD 2 Track 2

Listen to the audio and repeat, focusing on intonation and pronunciation.

Thə Modercycəl Aksədent

    Innate yirz, **three** day zæafter I win Missder **Yerup**, I'll be ridingə **moder**cycle ännə main **street** in M'lan, **Idəly**. I'll be goingə bout **aye**-dee mile zə **now**er. alləvə **sudden**, a **car'll** püllin **frənna** me. I'll **hit** the car and flyə bout ten **yardz**. My **leg'll** bray kin three **placez**. I'll be(y)inə noudə the **häspidl** fr seven **mənts**. The **däctor'll** put me in **træction** fr the first **mənth** withoudə **cæst**. After my **leg**izə liddle bedder, heel püda **cæst** än. He'll give me ə lät əv **andee-**

96

biodics. **Every**one'll be very **wrrr-reed** about me. The **news**paperz and **TV'll** report **every**thing th't **hæppenz**. Id'll take me **seven** munts tə **rəcover**, and id'll be⁽ʸ⁾ə **yir** b'fore I **compeedə** gen. I'll **still** havə **scär** än my **shin**, and my **right** cæf won bee⁽ʸ⁾əz d'velopt az thee⁽ʸ⁾**əther** one. I'll be **lucky** to be **alive**, tho.

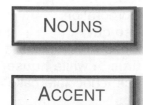

NOUNS

This section shows you how to compare, explains the difference between two types of nouns, and discusses word order and more conjunctions.

ACCENT

We first looked at descriptions and compound nouns in Chapter 2. To review, a description is an adjective and a noun, and the stress goes on the noun. A compound noun is two nouns together, and the stress goes on the first noun. A compound noun is a set phrase, where you have a whole idea in one phrase. It can either be two words, two words with a hyphen, or a single word.

Descriptions	Compounds
a chocolate **cake**	a **pan**cake
a bright **light**	a **light**bulb
a nice **day**	my **birth**day
a new **guitar**	a **guitar** case

Exercise 5-3: Noun Intonation

Circle the word that should be stressed. Then check the Answer Key.

1. a nice time
2. a timeline
3. long hair
4. a haircut
5. a hot dog (food)
6. a big deal
7. a cell phone
8. a good plan
9. a notebook
10. a long walk
11. a big truck
12. a truck stop
13. a hot tub (Jacuzzi)
14. a hot coffee
15. a wedding cake
16. a delicious cake
17. a house key
18. a small key
19. a hairbrush
20. a yellow brush
21. a fried egg
22. an egg yolk
23. a butter knife
24. a sharp knife
25. paper towels
26. clean towels
27. a housekeeper
28. a messy house
29. a baseball
30. an orange ball

Here's an interesting tip: All soups are descriptions and all sauces are compound nouns. Although they may have similar ingredients, they follow different intonation patterns.

Soup	Sauce
tomato **soup**	**tomato** sauce
vegetable **soup**	**hot** sauce
lentil **soup**	**pasta** sauce
split pea **soup**	**barbeque** sauce
chicken noodle **soup**	**white** sauce
minestrone **soup**	**soy** sauce
alphabet **soup**	**Tabasco** sauce

Here is a list of general rules.

	Rules	Examples
Emphasis on the **First Word**	Compound nouns	**potato** chips, a **break**down, the **White** House
	Streets	**Elm** Street
	Co. or Corp.	**Xerox** Corporation
	Nationalities	a **Chinese** guy
	Food nationalities	**French** food
Emphasis on the **Second Word**	Descriptions	a nice **time**, a white **house**
	Adverb + adjective	really **nice**, chocolate **cake**
	Names	Joe **Jones**
	Titles	Assistant **Manager**
	Road names	Fifth **Avenue**
	Place names	Los **Angeles**, Las **Vegas**, New **York**
	Acronyms	ID, IB**M**
	Money	two **dollars**
	Phrasal verbs	to break **down**

Exercise 5-4: Noun Intonation

In each of the blue phrases, underline the word that should be stressed. Then check the Answer Key.

1. They took a **shortcut** down a **dark alley** to the **supermarket**.
2. Are you taking an **airplane** to **Los Angeles**?
3. The **school bus** parked at the **amusement park** for **three hours** in the **hot sun**.
4. The **Vice President** doesn't live at the **White House** in Washington, **D.C.**
5. The **math students** went to a **bookstore** to buy their **textbooks**.
6. Did the **swim team** meet **every day last summer**?
7. There are many **secret recipes** for **junk food**.
8. Her **boyfriend** gave her a **diamond ring** for her **birthday**.
9. The **little dog** gave them a **sad look** from the **front porch** on that **cold day**.
10. There was a **breakdown** in communications, so the system **broke down**.

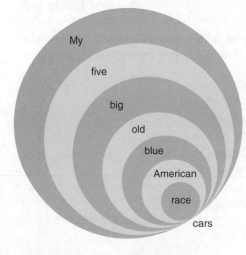

My five big, old, blue American racecars.

Word order follows certain patterns. No matter how big the circle, words like **my**, **your**, and **our** will always be on the outer ring, or at the beginning of the phrase.

Word Order List

1. Owner / Article
2. Number
3. Size
4. Type
5. Color
6. Material
7. Nationality
8. Compound Noun
9. Noun

Stacking Adjectives

Stacking adjectives is an important aspect of communicating in English. Beginning-level students tend to repeat nouns because they are making short sentences. For example: **I have five cars. The cars are red. My cars are American. They are really old. My cars are big. They are racecars.**

This sounds clunky (not smooth) and immature (childish) in both spoken and written English. The goal is to learn how to **stack adjectives**. This will allow you to communicate a large amount of information in just a few words. Americans prefer to use fewer words whenever possible.

To figure out the word order, start with the outside edges. Find either the article or the owner for the first word, and then find the main noun for the last word. If the main noun is plural, there may not be an article or owner.

Exercise 5-5: Word Order

Rewrite the sentence with all of the blue words in the proper order. Then check the Answer Key.

1. _____ were very expensive.   **Chinese, rugs, his, three**

2. The dogs jumped onto _____.   **couch, my, red, big, leather**

3. He was taking notes in _____ .   **French, a, notebook, tiny**

4. We replaced _____.   **wooden, the, bookshelf, old, brown**

5. She put _____ in the kitchen drawer.   **black, Thai, ten, chopsticks**

Exercise 5-6: Word Order

Rewrite the sentence with all of the blue words in the proper order. For the last two, create your own phrase. Then check the Answer Key.

1. **Japanese saw the students young three I English**

2. **China long only the Italian in on train black We're**

3. **tabletops ten Tunisian tin Todd's tiny are Where**

4. Article Number Color Compound Noun

5. Owner Size Color Material Compound Noun

For the next exercise, think back to Chapter 2, where we studied the five conjunctions: **and**, **but**, **so**, **or**, **because**.

Exercise 5-7: Conjunctions

Listen to the audio and repeat five times.

He was happy _____ he lived in Beijing.

when	**At the time** that he lived in Beijing, he was happy.
whenever	**Every time** that he lived in Beijing, he was happy.
before	**Prior to living** in Beijing, he was happy.
until	**Up to the point** that he lived in Beijing, he was happy, then he wasn't.
because	Living in Beijing made him happy. (cause)
even though	**In spite of living** in Beijing, he was happy (contrary to expectations).
but	Living in Beijing is unusual for happy people.
but then	He used to be happy, but **the change** made him unhappy.
after	Upon moving away from Beijing, he was happy.
while	He was happy **during his stay** in Beijing.
as soon as	**The moment** he moved into his Beijing apartment, he was happy.
unless	Living in Beijing made him unhappy.
so	Happy people move to Beijing.
and	His mood and location were **unrelated events**.

Exercise 5-8: Conjunctions

Select the proper answer. Then check the Answer Key.

They waited	until	the last moment.	☐ by ■ until
1. We won't rest		we find the answer.	☐ although ☐ until
2. They dropped the subject		it was boring.	☐ because ☐ so
3. We planned on going,		we cancelled.	☐ since ☐ but then
4. The old man fainted		he heard the news.	☐ until ☐ as soon as
5. The roof leaked		it rained.	☐ but ☐ whenever
6. I can't help you		you cooperate.	☐ unless ☐ so
7. They kept going		they were exhausted.	☐ as soon as ☐ even though
8. He called me		the earthquake.	☐ right after ☐ until
9. They've been busy		they got here.	☐ ever since ☐ until
10. The dancing started		dark.	☐ after ☐ until

How Many? So Many! Too Many!

In Chapter 4, we worked with **how** in the meaning of *in what way*?

It is good.	He works well.
Is it good?	Does he work well?
How is it?	How does he work?
	How well does he work?

Now, let's look at **to what extent**? We can express this by adding an adjective or an adverb. Let's also review countable and uncountable nouns.

So is an intensifier.	**Too** is excessive.
We had so much fun.	He ate too much.
There were so many people there!	There were too many people there.

Uncountable	**Countable**
So Much / Too Much	**So Many / Too Many**
Did you buy sugar?	Did you buy bananas?
Yes, I bought **so much** sugar!	Yes, I bought **so many** bananas!
I bought **too much** sugar!	I bought **too many** bananas!
How Much	**How Many**
How much sugar did you buy?	**How many** bananas did you buy?
How much did **it** cost?	**How much** did **they** cost?
Single	**Plural**
How often do you buy **it**?	**How often** do you buy **them**?
How long does **it** last?	**How long** do **they** last?

Count Me!

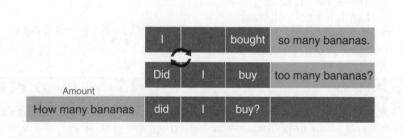

I		bought	so many bananas.
Did	I	buy	too many bananas?

Amount

How many bananas	did	I	buy?

Exercise 5-9: *How + Many* ↻

*Convert each statement to a how question, using either the verb **to be** or a main verb. Then check the Answer Key.*

There are five people in my family.	**How many people are there in your family?**
He has two uncles.	**How many uncles does he have?**

1. There were many cars on the road.
2. We had so many problems.
3. She wanted several alternatives.
4. They made a lot of mistakes.
5. He put two sugars in his coffee.
6. This car has two doors.

7. My aunt has forty pairs of shoes.
8. That boy has six dogs.
9. I only have five minutes to finish this.
10. The student is taking eighteen units.

Don't Count Me!

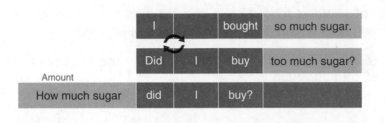

Exercise 5-10: *How + Much* ↻

*Convert each statement to a **how** question, using either the verb **to be** or a main verb. Then check the Answer Key.*

There is not much time.   **How much** time is there?
He does not have much time.   **How much** time does he have?

1. I have too much ink.
2. This ink costs too much.
3. They cost $10 this year.
4. It costs $10 this year.
5. They cost $10 last year.
6. It cost $10 last year.
7. She doesn't have much energy.
8. There wasn't much rice left over.
9. It was a lot of fun.
10. There is a lot smoke in the air.

Exercise 5-11: *How Much / How Many* ↻

*Convert each statement to a **how** question, using either the verb **to be** or a main verb. Then check the Answer Key.*

There's not much water.   **How much** water is there?
There's a drop of water.   **How many** drops of water are there?

1. There's too much noise out here!
2. There are so many singers.
3. There's enough cloth for that dress.
4. You are making three dresses.
5. I don't have enough gas in the car.
6. There are two gas stations there.
7. I don't have much hair.
8. I found several hairs in my sink.
9. You didn't learn much today.
10. You went to four classes today.

How Often?

Let's use the question flip with **how often**.

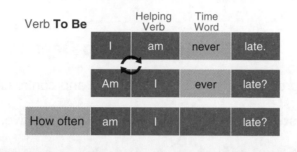

Exercise 5-12: *How + Often — To Be* ↻

*Convert each statement to a **how** question, using the verb **to be**. Pay attention to the verb tenses. You can use either nouns or pronouns in your answers. Check the Answer Key when you're done.*

The grass is watered every day.	**How often is the grass watered?**
The grass is never cut.	**How often is the grass cut?**

1. They are almost always in trouble.
2. The weather is almost always nice.
3. The staff is frequently out of the office.
4. Our dogs are often dirty.
5. His comments were generally ignored.
6. She is usually on the road.
7. Swans are sometimes vicious.
8. History is hardly ever repeated.
9. We are almost never confused.
10. He's never in L.A.

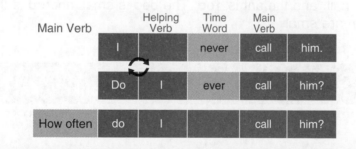

Exercise 5-13: *How + Often — Main Verbs* ↻

*Convert each statement to a **how** question, using main verbs. Then check the Answer Key.*

You frequently go to the gym.	**How often do you go to the gym?**
You go to the gym every day.	**How often do you go to the gym?**

1. We always plan for the future.
2. She almost always had a Plan B.
3. I almost never eat donuts.
4. Ants frequently get into the kitchen.
5. Commuters sometimes take shortcuts.
6. I always do the right thing.

7. She's usually pretty direct.
8. It's often cold in Alaska.
9. This car is generally reliable.
10. He never changes his mind.

Two Bees or Not Two Bees

There are several words and phrases for comparing and contrasting two items.

Both, **each**, **either**, **so**, and **too** are positive. **Neither** is negative.

Either can be used for questions or as a response to a negative statement: **I don't do it. I don't either.**

Exercise 5-14: *Two* Terminology   CD 2 Track 4

Listen to the audio and repeat the phrases relating to the picture.

1. There are **two** bugs.
2. These are **both** insects.
3. They **both** have six legs. **Neither** of them has eight legs like a spider.
4. They **each** have a way of communicating.
5. **One of them** can fly, but **the other** can't.
6. Can **either** of them talk? No, **neither** of them can talk, but **both** of them can sting.
7. One of them **stung** me. It was **either** the ant **or** the bee. **Neither** of them stung you.
8. **The one on the left** is an ant. **The one on the right** is a bee.
9. The bee is small, and the ant is, **too**. The bee is small and **so** is the ant.
10. **Both** of them are small.

Exercise 5-15: *Two* Terminology — Fill in the Blanks

Fill in the blanks, using information about a horse and a zebra. Then check the Answer Key.

1. There are **two** _____.
2. These are **both** _____.
3. They **both** _____. **Neither** of them _____.
4. They **each** _____.
5. **One of them** _____, but **the other** _____.
6. Can **either** of them _____? No, **neither** of them can _____, but **both** of them can _____.
7. **One of them** _____. It is **either** the horse **or** the zebra. **Neither** of them _____.
8. **The one on the left** is a _____. **The one on the right** is a _____.
9. The horse is _____, and the zebra is, **too**. The horse is _____ and **so** is the zebra.
10. The _____ runs fast, and the _____ does, **too**. The _____ runs fast and **so** _____ the zebra.

Exercise 5-16: *Two* Terminology — Make Up Your Own Sentences

Make your own sentences using information about a mobile home and a cabin. Then check the Answer Key.

1. two
2. both
3. both / neither
4. each
5. one of them / the other
6. either / neither / both
7. one of them / either / neither
8. the one on the left / right
9. too / so (is)
10. too / so (main verb)
11. both

Use

Use has several meanings. The most basic is **to utilize** or **to employ**.
Used to is for a repeated past action.
To be used to doing something is to be accustomed to doing something. (habit + verb)
To be used to something. (habit + noun)

Exercise 5-17: *Use*

*Fill in the blank with the proper form of **use**, **to be used**, **to be used to**, or **used to**. Then check the Answer Key.*

1. When I eat, I _____ a fork.   utilize, employ
2. I _____ walking to work.   accustomed to, habit
3. They _____ live in San Francisco.   previously
4. We _____ an oven for baking. (əvən)   utilize, employ
5. An oven _____ for baking.   is utilized, is employed
6. When he eats Chinese food, he _____ chopsticks.   utilize, employ
7. They _____ working hard.   accustomed to
8. She _____ work hard, but she doesn't anymore.   previously
9. Everyone _____ English in class.   utilize, employ
10. English _____ in class.   is utilized, is employed

Exercise 5-18: *Use* — Pronunciation   CD 2 Track 5

Listen to the audio and repeat five times.

1. When I eat, I **yuze** a fork.
2. I'm **usta** walking to work.
3. They **usta** live in San Francisco.
4. We **yuze** an oven for baking. (əvən)
5. An oven **iz yuzd** for baking.
6. When he eats Chinese food, he **yuzez** chopsticks.

7. They're **usta** working hard.
8. She **usta** work hard, but she doesn't anymore.
9. Everyone **yuzez** English in class.
10. English **iz yuzd** in class.

Countable and Uncountable Collections

We have worked with countable and uncountable nouns before. Now, we'll see how individual, countable items (left) form **collections** (right).

Count Items	Don't Count Collections
a painting	art
a statue	
a photograph	
a storm	weather
a sunny day	
a heat wave	
a report	information
a data set	
a phone call	communication
a letter	
a memo	
an e-mail	
a conversation	
a novel	literature
a story	
a poem	

Exercise 5-19: *Much* or *Many* with Countables and Uncountables

*Select **much** or **many**. Then check the Answer Key.*

The dealer bought so _____ painting**s**.

The dealer bought so _____ art.

1. You gave me too _____ information.
2. You gave me too _____ facts.
3. There was not _____ communication.
4. There were not _____ e-mails.
5. She didn't eat _____ dessert.
6. She ate too _____ pies.
7. There's not _____ water in the glass.
8. There're _____ drops of water on the table.
9. How _____ traffic is there?
10. How _____ cars are there?

The dealer bought so **many** paintings.
The dealer bought so **much** art.

Notice the verb change between the singular and the plural.

1. Half **of the lakes** are **frozen**.	Half **of the water** is **frozen**.
2. Both halves **of the book** are **useful**.	The first half **of the book** is **useful**.
3. Some **of the loaves** are **stale**.	Some **of the bread** is **stale**.
4. Not all **of the teas in China** are **green**.	All **of the tea in China** is **excellent**.
5. Half **of the team members** are **late**.	Two-thirds **of the team** is **late**.
6. **Ten percent of the people I know** are **away**.	**Ten percent of the population** is **away**.
7. There are **two** more **hours** to go.	**Two hours** is a long time.
8. There are **$10 bills** in my wallet.	**Ten dollars** is not enough.
9. There are **five** more **miles** until the end.	**Five** miles is too far.
10. There are **two weeks** until graduation.	**Two weeks** isn't enough time.

Exercise 5-20: Half Is . . . Half Are . . .

Select the proper verb. Then check the Answer Key.

> There are ten miles more to go.
> Ten miles is a long way.

1. Half of the oranges _____ packed in boxes.   is / are
2. Most of the orange juice _____ in cartons.   is / are
3. _____ any of the family coming?   is / are
4. _____ any of your brothers or sisters coming?   is / are
5. The first half of the movie _____ fantastic.   was / were
6. Half of the room _____ filled with balloons.   was / were
7. Half of the rooms _____ damaged in the fire.   was / were
8. Both halves of the amulet _____ quite valuable.   was / were
9. We think that 25% _____ a fair commission.   has been / have been
10. We think that 25% of them _____ ready to go.   has been / have been

This next topic is not very common, but it's important for passing tests. Some nouns can be both countable and uncountable, depending how you look at them. For example, the word **experience** can be countable, as there may be **a good experience** or **a bad experience**. In this meaning, it's an **event**.

However, it can also be a collection of events to mean a person's "background." For example, a person's schoolwork and previous jobs form a collection called **experience**. In this way, you can have both **He had many interesting experiences** (countable) and **He didn't have much experience** (uncountable).

An adjective can also make an uncountable noun countable. For example, **life** is uncountable, but you can say **He has a good life**.

Exercise 5-21: *Much* or *Many* with Countables and Uncountables

*Select **much** or **many**. Then check the Answer Key.*

He didn't have _____ experiences.
He didn't have _____ experience.

He didn't have **many** experiences.
He didn't have **much** experience.

1. I need so _____ space for my stuff.
2. I need so _____ spaces for the cars.
3. There were too _____ noises outside.
4. There was too _____ noise outside.
5. There was _____ discussion about it.
6. There were _____ discussions about it.
7. There is too _____ light in here!
8. There are too _____ lights in here!
9. We ate so _____ ice cream. (in a bowl)
10. We ate so _____ ice creams. (on a stick)
11. He didn't have too _____ success there.
12. He didn't have too _____ successes with it.
13. He doesn't have _____ memory left.
14. He doesn't have _____ good memories.

Exercise 5-22: Eureka!

*Fill in the blank with **a**, **an**, **the**, or — (if another word isn't needed). Then check the Answer Key.*

Here is _____ famous **experiment;** _____ **king** buys _____ new **crown** from _____ **crafts**man. _____ **crafts**man says that _____ **crown** is _____ pure **gold,** but _____ **King** thinks that _____ cheaper, lighter metal like _____ **silver** is **in** it, **too**. He **asks** his **friend, Archimedes**, to **find** out if _____ **crafts**man is **telling** _____ **truth**. _____ **silver** is **lighter** than _____ **gold,** so you **need** more than **one** cup of **silver** to **weigh** _____ **same** as **one** cup of **gold**. If he mixes **silver** into _____ **crown,** there will be **more** cups of _____ **metal** in it than in _____ **same** weight of pure **gold. Archimedes** says, "I **have** to figure **out** if there are **more** cups of **metal** in _____ **crown** than in _____ **same** weight of pure **gold**. But, if I **melt** _____ crown to find **out,** it **won't** be _____ **crown** anymore. _____ **king** will be **angry**. How can I find **out** how many **cups** there are without **melting** _____ **crown**?"

     Archimedes decides to **take** _____ **bath**. He **steps** into his **tub** and _____ **over**flowing **water** gives him _____ **idea**. He **fills** _____ **bucket** with **water**. He puts _____ **pound** of **gold** in _____ **bucket**. _____ **cup**ful of **water** spills **out**. **Then** he puts _____ pound of **silver** in _____ bucket. **Two** cupfuls of water **spill** out! **This** is because **silver** weighs **less** than **gold, so** _____ **pound** of it (weight) takes up **more room** (volume) than _____ **pound** of **gold** and **pushes** out **more water**. _____ **King's crown** weighs _____ **pound. Archimedes** puts it into _____ full **bucket**. If **one** cupful of water spills **out,** there is _____ **pound of gold** in _____ **crown**. If **more** than **one** cupful of water spills **out,** it **can't be** pure **gold. This** way, he **doesn't** have to **melt** _____ **crown. All** he has to do is **measure** _____ **water** that spills **out**. It's _____ **great** idea! **Archimedes** gets so **excited** that he **jumps** out of _____ **tub,** and runs **naked down** _____ **street** shouting **"Eureka!"** In **Greek,** this means, "I **found** it!"

     When **Archimedes** does _____ **experiment,** he **finds** that _____ **crown** pushes out **more** water than _____ **equal** weight of **gold** does. **That** means that the **gold** is mixed with **silver**. _____ **crafts**man is **cheating** _____ **King**.

ü	u
put	truth
push	you
pull	two
full	room
cupful	to(w)a

Exercise 5-23: Yer-reekə!

CD 2 Track 6

Listen and repeat.

ACCENT

Hir zə faməs **eksperam'nt; ə king** by zə new **crown** frəmə **crafts**m'n. Thə **crafts**man sez thət thə **crown**iz pyoor **gold**, bət thə king thinks thada cheaper, lyder medəl like silver izinit, **too**. He **asks** his **frend, Arkəmeedeez,** to **fyn** dout if the **crafts**m'n iz **telling** thə **truth. Silver** iz **lyder** thən **gold**, so you **need** more thən **one** cuppa **silver** tə **way** the **same** əz **one** cuppa **gold.** Iffee mixəz **silver** into the **crown,** there'll be **more** cupsa **medəl** init thənin the **same** way dov pyoor **gold. Arkə meedeez** sez, "I **haf**ta figyer **out** if there are **more** cupsa **medəl** in the **crown** thenin the **same** waydov pyoor **gold.** Bədify **melt** the crown tə fyn **dout,** it **won't** be(y)ə **crown** nanymore. The **king**'ll be(y)**angry.** How c'nai **fyn dout** how many **cups** there are without **melting** the **crown?"**

　　Arkəmeedeez d'cidz tə **tay** kə **bath.** He **step** sinto hiz **tub** and thee(y)**over**flowing **wäder** give zima ny deə. He **fill** zə **bucket** with **wäder.** He pütsə **poundə gold** in the **bucket.** A **cup**füllə **wäder** spill **zout. Thene**e pütsə poundə **silver** in the bucket. **Two** cupfulzə wader **spill**out! **This** iz b'cuz **silver** wayz **less** thən **gold,** so(w)ə **poundə**vit take səp **more room** thanə **poundə gold** and **push**əzout more **wäder.** The kingz **crown** wayzə **pound. Arkameedeez** putsidinto(w)ə full **bucket.** If **one** cupfullə wader spill **zout,** therzə **poundə gold**in the **crown.** If **more** thən **one** cupfullə wader spill **zout,** it **cæn't be** pyoor **gold. This** way, he **də**znt haftə **melt** the **crown. Allee** has tə do(w)iz **mezher** the **wäder** that spill **zout.** Itsə **gray** dydeə! **Arkəmeedeez** getsso(w)**excidəd** the dee **jump** soudə the **tub,** and runz **naked down** th' **street** shouding yer-reekə! In **Greek,** this meenz, I **foun** dit!

　　When **Arkəmeedeez** dəz thee(y)**eksperəm'nt,** he **findz** thət the **crown** push zout **more** wäder thanə n**eekwəl** way dəv **gold** dəzz. **That** meenz thət the **gold**iz mixt with **silver.** The **cræfts**man iz **cheading** the **king.**

crown	clown
æ	æo
craftsman	crown
angry	pound
asks	down
bath	shout
have to	found
can't	around

In this section, you will learn both the real and unreal futures, with **will** and **going to**.

	Past	Present	Future
Simple	I did it. ◀	I do it. ●	I will do it. I'm going to do it. ◀
Duo	I had done A before I did B. ◀◀	I have done A before now. ◀●	I will have done A by the time I do B. ▶▶
Unreal Duo	If I had done A, I would have done B. ◀◀	If I did A, I would do B. ●●	If I do A, I will do B. ▶▶

The helping verb **will** is used with both the verb **to be**—**I will be there**—and main verbs—**I will do it**. With **going to**, you will hear native speakers use a very colloquial pronuciation: aimana. This will make **I'm going to try it** sound like: Aimana try it. Trust the phonetics.

Exercise 5-24: Simple Future

Put the sentences in the future. Remember to use the unchanging form of the main verb. Then check the Answer Key.

I speak Italian.
1. The teachers write on the blackboard.
2. Larry rides his bike everywhere.
3. Your cousin flew first class.
4. The managers arrange meetings.
5. I gave many presents.
6. We think about it.
7. They threw it away.
8. Virginia sold her car.
9. The candles burn steadily.
10. Her sister said hello.

I will speak Italian.

The ***simple present*** can be used to indicate the ***near future***.

I have a doctor's appointment at one o'clock tomorrow.
His plane arrives on Sunday night.
There's a party next week.

Exercise 5-25: Negatives

Change the positive to a negative. Then check the Answer Key.

He will make money.
1. The teachers will write on the blackboard.
2. Larry will ride his bike everywhere.
3. Your cousin will fly first class.
4. The managers will arrange meetings.
5. I will give many presents.
6. We will think about it.

He will not make money.

7. They will throw it away.
8. Virginia will sell her car.
9. The candles will burn steadily.
10. Her sister will say hello.

Exercise 5-26: Negative Contractions

Change the positive to a negative contraction. Then check the Answer Key.

He will look at it.
1. The teachers will write on the blackboard.
2. Larry will ride his bike everywhere.
3. Your cousin will fly first class.
4. The managers will arrange meetings.
5. I will give many presents.
6. We will think about it.
7. They will throw it away.
8. Virginia will sell her car.
9. The candles will burn steadily.
10. Her sister will say hello.

He won't look at it.

Exercise 5-27: Negative Contractions

*Change to the other form of the contraction with the negative present of **to be**. Check the Answer Key when you're done.*

He isn't looking at it.
1. They aren't writing on it.
2. He isn't riding it.
3. She isn't flying in one.
4. They aren't arranging them.
5. He isn't giving them.
6. We aren't thinking about it.
7. They aren't throwing it away.
8. Virginia isn't selling it.
9. They aren't burning steadily.
10. She isn't saying hello.

He's not looking at it.

Contrasting *Will Do* and *Going To Do*

Will do and **going to do** are largely interchangeable, but **will** is a bit more formal.

Exercise 5-28: Two Futures

CD 2 Track 7

Listen and repeat.

Will Do	**Going To Do (prior plan)**
I'll call you later.	I'm going to have to call you later. (aimana hafta)
He'll **think** about it.	He's going to **think** about it.

We'll let you know **later**.　　　We're going to let you know **later**.
It'll **happen** before **long**.　　It's going to **happen** before **long**.
You'll have a good time.　　　　You're going to have a good time.

Exercise 5-29: Changing Future Forms

*Change the **will** form to the **going to** form. Use contractions and change nouns to pronouns. Then check the Answer Key.*

He'll go.　　　　　　　　　　　　**He's going to go.**

1. We'll think about it.
2. They'll throw it away.
3. Virginia will sell her car.
4. The candles will burn steadily.
5. Her sister will say hello.

Exercise 5-30: Questions ↻

Change the statements to questions. Then check the Answer Key.

Jane will dance well.　　　　　　**Will Jane dance well?**

1. The teachers will write on the blackboard.
2. Larry will ride his bike everywhere.
3. Your cousin will fly first class.
4. The managers will arrange meetings.
5. I will give many presents.
6. We will think about it.
7. They will throw it away.
8. Virginia will sell her car.
9. The candles will burn steadily.
10. Her sister will say hello.

Exercise 5-31: Questions with Pronouns ↻

Change the statements to questions. Change all nouns to pronouns. (Duzzy, Izzy, Willy?) Check the Answer Key when you're done.

Joe will drink his coffee.　　　　**Will he drink it?**

1. The teachers will write on the blackboard.
2. Larry will ride his bike everywhere.
3. Your cousin will fly in a jet.
4. The managers will arrange meetings.
5. I will give many presents.
6. Bob will think about his classes.
7. Jenny and Norbert will throw it away.
8. Virginia will sell her car.
9. The boys will sit in a row.
10. Her sister will say hello.

"Only One Will"

The *simple future* is used with
until, before, after, when, even if, unless, etc.

I **will call** you when I **get** there.
We **won't rest** until we find out what **is** going on.

Exercise 5-32: Present Tense to Indicate the Future

Rewrite the sentences using the simple present or the continuous form. Then check the Answer Key.

He **will get** a job after he **graduates.**	He's getting a job after he graduates.

1. She **will make** the decision **when** she **is** here.
2. I **won't tell** you **until** she **gets** here.
3. We'll **leave when** it's **over**.
4. He won't get **up until** it's time to **go**.
5. Everyone **will work until** the bell **rings**.
6. They'll **go** home **after** the stores **close**.
7. I'll **take** a walk **even if** it's raining.
8. We'll **go** to bed **when** the sun **sets**.
9. She **was** very rude to me. I **refuse** to speak to her again **until** she **apologizes**.
10. I'll **start after** I **get** organized.
11. We'll do something **soon**, **before** it's too **late**.
12. I won't **call** him **unless** I **need** to.
13. We'll go **shopping even if** it's **snowing**.
14. I will be a **nurse when** I pass the **exam**.
15. I won't **tell** you **until after** we finish **class**.

Exercise 5-33: Present Tense to Indicate the Future CD 2 Track 8

Listen to the motorcycle story again, but this time focus on the use of the present tense to indicate the future. These five instances are indicated in blue.

In eight years, three days **after I win** Mr. Europe, I will be riding a motorcycle on a main street in Milan, Italy. I will be going about 80 miles an hour. All of a sudden, a car will pull in front of me. I'll hit the car and fly about 10 yards. My leg will break in three places. I will be in and out of the hospital for seven months. The doctor will put me in traction for the first month without a cast. **After my leg is a little better**, he will put a cast on. He will give me a lot of antibiotics. Everyone will be very worried about me. The newspapers and TV will report everything that **happens**. It will take me seven months to recover, and it will be a year **before I compete** again. I will still have a scar on my shin, and my right calf won't be as developed as the other one **is**. I'll be lucky to be alive, though.

If . . .

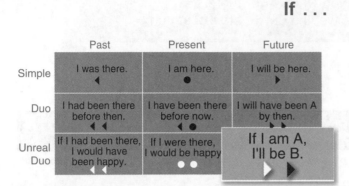

	Past	Present	Future
Simple	I was there. ◀	I am here. ●	I will be here. ▶
Duo	I had been there before then. ◀◀	I have been there before now. ◀●	I will have been A by then. ▶▶
Unreal Duo	If I had been there, I would have been happy. ◁◀	If I were there, I would be happy. ●●	If I am A, I'll be B. ▷▶

The **simple future** can be used with the **simple present** to indicate **an unreal situation**. Notice that both verbs are represented by the symbol for the future, ▶, but now the first triangle is white. This is because it represents something that hasn't happened or won't happen. The **white** symbols are **unreal**. The **black** symbols indicate things that **will happen** if certain conditions are met.

If + To Be

This looks like the present (**If I am A**), but when you ask the question, **Will I be A?**, you can see that it is the future. With the statement **If I am there, I'll be available**, you can ask, **Am I there?** The answer is, "Maybe, maybe not." The same is true with the second half, **Will I be available?** Again, "Maybe, maybe not." We don't know yet, and we won't know until the **if** condition is met.

Exercise 5-34: The Unreal — *To Be*

*Fill in the blank with the proper form of the unreal, using the verb **to be**. Then check the Answer Key.*

Current fact
The store is open. I am inside.

1. The **boxes** are **full**. They are **heavy**.
2. The boxes are **empty**. They are not **heavy**.
3. It's **raining**. You are **cold**.
4. He's **lying**. He is in **trouble**.
5. He is **sorry**. His friends are **understanding**.
6. They are on **time**. They are **satisfied**.
7. The **wheel** is **loose**. The **driver** is **scared**.
8. He is **here**. He is **helpful**.
9. He isn't **here**. He isn't **helpful**.
10. They are **tired**. They stay **home**.

Conjecture about the future
If the store is open, I'll be inside.

Main Verbs

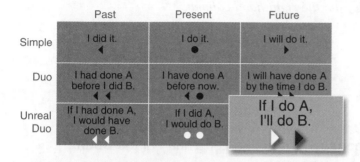

Just as with the verb **to be**, with *main verbs* you will always use the *simple present* form after **if**.

Exercise 5-35: The Unreal — Main Verbs

Fill in the blank with the proper form of the unreal, using main verbs. Use the unchanging form of the main verb for the second half of the sentence. Check the Answer Key when you're done.

Current fact
He goes. He has fun.
1. He has **time**. He goes to the **party**.
2. She runs a red **light**. She gets a **ticket**.
3. She knows all the **answers**. She passes the **test**.
4. He tries **hard**. He **succeeds**.
5. You tell the **truth**. He **appreciates** it.
6. They get to work **late**. They get **fired**.
7. She drives too **fast**. She has an **accident**.
8. He forgets to **pay**. He gets in **trouble**.
9. I lose the ring. He is up**set**.
10. We are **hungry**. We stop for **lunch**.

Conjecture about the future
If he goes, he'll have fun.

Exercise 5-36: Future Tags

All three forms of the future use tags in the same way we have learned. Fill in the correct tag. Then check the Answer Key.

He'll be there,
He's going to do it,
If he is there, he'll help us,
1. She'll think about it,
2. You're going to try,
3. If they like it, they'll get one,
4. Everyone will take the day off,
5. Nobody's going to worry,

won't he?
isn't he?
won't he?

right?

Grammar in a Nutshell

So far, we have studied the simple present, the past, and two forms of the future, as well as the continuous. Let's review all of this in Grammar in a Nutshell.

Exercise 5-37: Grammar in a Nutshell CD 2 Track 9

Listen to the audio and repeat, reading from the right-hand column.

Grammar	Pronunciation
1. **Dogs** eat **bones**.	**däg** zeet **bounz**
2. The **dogs** eat the **bones**.	the **däg** zeet the **bounz**
3. The **dogs** are eating the **bones**.	the **däg** zr reeding the **bounz**
4. The **dogs** ate the **bones**.	the **däg** zate the **bounz**
5. The **dogs**'ll eat the **bones**.	the **däg** zə leet the **bounz**
6. The **dogs** are going to eat the **bones**.	the **däg** zer g'nna eat the **bounz**

Notice how similar the following pairs sound.

Similar sounds: are eating / are reading

Note: Don't ever write *gonna* or *wanna*.

Exercise 5-38: Grammar in a Negative Nutshell CD 2 Track 10

Listen to the audio and repeat, reading from the right-hand column.

Grammar	Pronunciation
1. **Dogs** don't eat **bones**.	**dägz** doe neet **bounz**
2. The **dogs** don't eat the **bones**.	the **dägz** doe neet the **bounz**
3. The **dogs** aren't eating the **bones**.	the **däg** zär needing the **bounz**
4. The **dogs** weren't eating the **bones**.	the **dägz** wrrn deeding the **bounz**
5. The **dogs** won't be eating the **bones**.	the **dägz** wont be$^{(y)}$eeding the **bounz**
6. The **dogs** didn't eat the **bones**.	the **dägz** didn neet the **bounz**
7. The **dogs** won't eat the **bones**.	the **däg** zwoa neet the **bounz**
8. The **dogs** aren't going to eat the **bones**.	the **däg** zärnt g'nna eat the **bounz**

Similar Sounds

The dogs don't eat the bones. The dogs don't need the bones.
The dogs are going to eat the bones. The dogs aren't going to eat the bones.

Exercise 5-39: Grammar in a Nutshell? ↻ CD 2 Track 11

Listen to the audio and repeat, reading from the right-hand column.

Grammar	Pronunciation
1. Do **dogs** eat **bones**?	D' **däg** zeet **bounz**?
2. Do the **dogs** eat the **bones**?	D'the **däg** zeet the **bounz**?
3. Did the dogs eat the bones?	Did the **däg** zeet the **bounz**?
4. Are the **dogs** eating the **bones**?	Är the **däg** zeeding the **bounz**?
5. Were the dogs eating the bones?	Wrr the **däg** zeeding the **bounz**?
6. Will the **dogs** eat the **bones**?	Will the **däg** zeet the **bounz**?

7. Are the **dogs** going to eat the **bones**?	Är thə **dägz** g'nna eat the **bounz**?
8. Were the **dogs** going to eat the **bones**?	Wrr the **dägz** g'nna eat the **bounz**?
9. What eats the **bones**?	W'deets the **bounz**?
10. What ate the **bones**?	W'date the **bounz**?
11. What will eat the **bones**?	Whədə **leet** the **bounz**?
12. What do the **dogs** eat?	W'd' thə **däg** zeet?
13. What did the **dogs** eat?	W'd'd thə **däg** zeet?
14. What will the **dogs** eat?	Wədəll thə **däg** zeet?
15. Where do the **dogs** eat the **bones**?	Where də thə **däg** eat the **bounz**?
16. Where did the **dogs** eat the **bones**?	Where d'd thə **däg** eat the **bounz**?
17. Where will the **dogs** eat the **bones**?	Wherəll thə **däg** zeet the **bounz**?
18. When do the **dogs** eat the **bones**?	When d' th' **däg** zeet the **bounz**?
19. When did the **dogs** eat the **bones**?	When d'd th' **däg** zeet the **bounz**?
20. When will the **dogs** eat the **bones**?	Whenəll the **dag** zeet the **bounz**?
21. Why do the **dogs** eat the **bones**?	Why d' th' **däg** zeet the **bounz**?
22. Why did the **dogs** eat the **bones**?	Why d'd th' **däg** zeet the **bounz**?
23. Why will the **dogs** eat the **bones**?	While the **dag** zeet the **bounz**?
24. How do the **dogs** eat the **bones**?	How d' th' **däg** zeet the **bounz**?
25. How did the **dogs** eat the **bones**?	How d'd th' **däg** zeet the **bounz**?
26. How will the **dogs** eat the **bones**?	Hal thə **däg** zeet the **bounz**?
27. Who gives the **bones** to the **dogs**?	**Who** gives the **bounz** t'th' **dägz**?
28. Who gave the **bones** to the **dogs**?	**Who** gave the **bounz** t'th' **dägz**?
29. Who will give the **bones** to the **dogs**?	**Hool** give the **bounz** t' th' **dägz**?
30. **Who** let the **dogs** out?	**Who** let the **dägz** out?

Exercise 5-40: Grammar in a Nutshell — Pronouns   CD 2 Track 12

Listen to the audio and repeat, reading from the right-hand column.

Grammar	Pronunciation
1. They **eat** them.	they **eed**'m
2. They're **eating** them.	ther **reed**ing'm
3. They were **eating** them.	they wrr **reed**ing'm
4. They'll **eat** them.	thell **leed**em
5. They're going to **eat** them.	ther g'nna **eed**'m

Similar Sounds
They're eating them. / They're reading them.

Exercise 5-41: Grammar in a Negative Nutshell — Pronouns   CD 2 Track 13

Listen to the audio and repeat, reading from the right-hand column.

Grammar	Pronunciation
1. They don't **eat** them.	they doe **need**'m
2. They aren't **eating** them.	they är **need**ing'm
3. They weren't **eating** them.	they wrr **need**ing'm
4. They won't **eat** them.	they woe **need**'em

5. They aren't going to **eat** them.　　they ärn g'nna **eed**'m
6. They weren't going to **eat** them.　　they wrnt g'nna **eed**'m

---

Exercise 5-42: Grammar in a Nutshell? Pronouns ↻　　　CD 2 Track 14

Listen to the audio and repeat, reading from the right-hand column.

Grammar	Pronunciation
1. Do they **eat** them?	d'they **eed**'m?
2. Did they **eat** them?	d'd they **eed**'m?
3. Are they **eating** them?	är they **eed**ing'm?
4. Were they **eating** them?	wrr they **eed**ing'm?
5. Will they **eat** them?	will they **eed**'m?
6. Are they going to **eat** them?	är they g'nna **eed**'m?
7. Were they going to **eat** them?	wrr they g'nna **eed**'m?
8. What **eats** them?	w'**deet** s'm?
9. What **ate** them?	w'**day** d'm?
10. What will **eat** them?	wədə**lee** d'm?
11.What do they **eat**?	whadda they **eat**?
12. What did they **eat**?	whadd'd they **eat**?
13. What will they **eat**?	whaddəll they⁽ʸ⁾**eat**?
14. Where do they **eat** them?	where d'they **eed**'m?
15. Where did they **eat** them?	wherd they **eed**'m?
16. Where will they **eat** them?	wherəll they **eed**'m?
17. When do they **eat** them?	when d'they **eed**'m?
18. When did they **eat** them?	when d'd they **eed**'m?
19. When will they **eat** them?	whenəll they **eed**'m?
20. Why do they **eat** them?	why d'they **eed**'m?
21. Why did they **eat** them?	wide they **eed**'m?
22. Why will they **eat** them?	while they **eed**'m?
23. How do they **eat** them?	how d'they **eed**'m?
24. How did they **eat** them?	howd they **eed**'m?
25. How will they **eat** them?	howəll they **eed**'m?
26. Who **gives** them to them?	who **giv** zem to⁽ʷ⁾'m?
27. Who **gave** them to them?	who **gav**'em to⁽ʷ⁾'m?
28. Who will **give** them to them?	whoəll **giv**'em to⁽ʷ⁾'m?
29. Who let them **out**?	who leddem **out**?

Similar Sounds
Were they going to eat them? / Where are they going to eat them?

Do and Make

These are many useful idiomatic expressions with the verbs **do** and **make**. Just learn them the way they are, as there are no rules for this form.

Do the dishes	**Make** a mistake
Do the laundry	**Make** an appointment
Do the shopping	**Make** a promise

Do homework	**Make** the bed
Do your best	**Make** dinner
Do a favor	**Make** time for
Do a good job	**Make** trouble
Do something over	**Make** a mess
Do the right thing	**Make** a noise
Do something the right way	**Make** money
	Make arrangements

Exercise 5-43: *Do* or *Make*

*Fill in the blank with the proper form of **do** or **make**. Then check the Answer Key.*

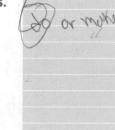

	Do the dishes.	**Make** the bed.
1.	They	the shopping together every week.
2.	They	a lot of mistakes.
3.	He didn't	his homework on time.
4.	She	a huge mess yesterday.
5.	How	you do? It's a pleasure to meet you.
6.	You and I	our best.
7.	He needs to	an appointment.
8.	Why don't you	the right thing?
9.	Why don't you	more money?
10.		the travel arrangements soon!

Stand

Stand is another verb with a wide range of meanings, including **represent**, **defy**, **loiter**, **excel**, **replace**, and **tolerate**.

Einstein was outstanding in his field.
This man is out standing in his field.

stand up (arise)
stand in for someone (take someone's place)
stand pain (tolerate pain)
stand trial (be tried for a crime)
stand guard (protect)
stand on (rest, plant, repose)
stand one's ground (hold a position)
stand on one's own two feet (be independent)
stand by (wait)
stand aside (get out of the way)
stand still (not to move)
be standoffish (be reserved)
stand out (be noticeable)
be outstanding (be exceptional)
stand to reason (be logical)
can't stand someone or something (dislike intensely)
stand a chance (have any opportunity for success)
stand for something (tolerate)

stand for something (represent)
stand up for someone (take someone's side)
stand up to someone (defy someone)
from my standpoint (view or perspective)

Exercise 5-44: *Stand*

*Fill in the blank with the proper form of **stand**. The synonym is on the right. Then check the Answer Key.*

1. The old manager was lenient, but the new one won't stand ____ any infractions of the rules at all.
   tolerate

2. The situation reached a head when one of the clerks stood ____ him and demanded a union meeting to rewrite the regulations.
   defy

3. He realized the depth of feeling in the department when all the employees stood ____ her.
   took her side

4. Without his support, though, the issue didn't stand ____ with management.
   have any hope for success

5. The typist stood her ____ and eventually an amicable solution was worked out.
   held her position

In the calendar, some months have 30 days and some months have 31 days. How many months have 28 days?

Answer: All of them.

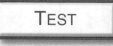

Let's review everything you have learned in Chapter 5. Make sure you get 100% on the test before going on to the next chapter. Check your work using the Answer Key.

Part 1: Underline the word that should be stressed.

1. They took a **long walk.**
2. May I borrow your **laptop?**
3. I ran out of **paper clips.**
4. It was a really **hot day.**
5. They live in a **beautiful house.**
6. Do they have a **fax machine?**
7. Is that a **new shirt?**
8. He has a **broken leg.**
9. What's the **expiration date?**
10. I really like your new **sunglasses!**

Part 2: Fill in the appropriate conjunction.

1. He changed his mind [____] considering the options. ☐ after ☐ because
2. We won't go [____] we have your support. ☐ but ☐ unless
3. He jumped in the pool [____] he got there. ☐ as soon as ☐ while

*Part 3: Fill in the proper article (**a, the, some,** or **none**).*

We were walking down ____ dark street. ____ moon wasn't out, so we couldn't see ____ thing. ____ sidewalk was uneven, and I almost took ____ fall. We were lost, so we figured that ____ best thing would be to go back ____ way we had come. ____ of us knew where we were, so it took quite ____ time to get back home.

*Part 4: Change past or present to future, using **will**.*

1. Charlie went to France.

2. Sam gives a speech.

3. John is reading a book.

4. Marcus did not order shoes from Italy.

5. Did Larry fix my computer?

Part 5: Change the positive statement to a negative contraction.

1. Timmy will answer your questions.

2. Lea will be dancing in Fresno.

3. Jill is going to facilitate the file transfer.

4. The clown will joke with the crowd.

5. Twenty trees will crash to the ground in the storm.

6. The secretary is going to file the forms.

Part 6: *Change the statement to a question.*

1. Shorty will eat his dog food.

2. The cell phone will need to be charged.

3. Nate is going to make a big announcement.

Part 7: *Fill in the blank with* **do** *or* **make**.

1. Could you _____ me a favor, please?
2. Try not to _____ any more mistakes.
3. We need to _____ a final decision.
4. Lucy forgot to _____ her homework.
5. Josie promised to _____ her best.

Part 8: *Fill in the blank with* **up**, **still**, **for**, **out**, *or* **on**.

1. People stand _____ when the President enters the room.
2. What does ASAP stand _____ ?
3. The actors were standing _____ the stage.
4. Stop wiggling! Stand _____ !
5. That red text really stands _____ on the black background.

Using what you have learned, write two paragraphs on the following topics:

1. What is your favorite season, and why?
2. What is your most prized possession?

You can handwrite your paragraphs below or e-mail them to **para@grammar.bz** to be stored. These paragraphs are not graded or reviewed, but simply by writing them, your English will improve.

● ○ ○	Student Paragraph

| Send | Chat | Attach | Address | Fonts | Colors | Save As Draft | Photo Browser | Show Stationery |

To:	para@grammar.bz
Cc:	
Bcc:	
Subject:	Chapter 5

Signature: Corporate ⬍

My name is _____

MIDTERM

Let's review everything you have learned in Chapters 1 through 5. Make sure you get 100% on this test before going on to the next chapter. Check your work using the Answer Key.

Part 1: *Underline the words that should be **stressed**.*

1. The dogs were playing in the yard.
2. The taxi driver put my suitcase in the trunk.
3. There was a big earthquake in San Francisco last week.

Part 2: *Identify the sound in each of the following words.*

1. chance   ☐ æ ☐ ä ☐ ə
2. done   ☐ æ ☐ ä ☐ ə
3. saw   ☐ æ ☐ ä ☐ ə

Part 3: *Fill in the rest of each sentence based on the changing intonation.*

1. **I** didn't hear him say that,
2. I **didn't** hear him say that,
3. I didn't **hear** him say that,
4. I didn't hear **him** say that,
5. I didn't hear him **say** that,
6. I didn't hear him say **that**,

Part 4: *Make a question and change the subject to **who** or **what**.*

1. My family came to visit.
2. The cars were painted again.

Part 5: *Convert each statement to a question.*

1. She was dancing in the park.   Where
2. He graduated in 2009.   When
3. They ordered sushi.   What
4. We cried because it was so sad.   Who

Part 6: *Replace all **nouns** with **pronouns**.*

1. The meetings were cancelled because of the earthquake.

2. My mother is going to visit my brother and me.

Part 7: *Change each sentence to the **plural**.*

1. This building was poorly built.

2. Can the child have some more?

3. That person was not ready.

*Part 8: Fill in the proper **article** (a, an, the).*

1. Do you have ____ moment?
2. That was ____ second time he tried it.
3. It was ____ awkward situation.
4. I know ____ really good Italian restaurant.
5. I know ____ best Italian restaurant.

*Part 9: Fill in the appropriate **conjunction**, using **and**, **so**, **but**, or **or**.*

1. Would you prefer coffee ____ tea?
2. It was late, ____ we went home.
3. We couldn't figure it out, ____ we kept trying in spite of the difficulty.
4. I'd like to travel ____ see the world.

*Part 10: Fill in the appropriate **preposition** of **location** or **direction**.*

1. Please sit next ____ me at the movies tomorrow.
2. He put the pencils ____ the drawer.
3. Leave the report ____ my desk, please.
4. Do you want to come ____ us?
5. I think he wrote his report ____ hand, not ____ the computer.

*Part 11: Fill in the proper **comparison** word.*

1. That's the ____ idea!   **good**
2. The problems were ____ than we thought.   **big**
3. She's much ____ than she used to be.   **happy**
4. I think he earns ____ than we do, but more than he did before.   **little**
5. OMG! He's the ____ dancer! LOL!   **bad**

*Part 12: Fill in the blank with **much** or **many**.*

1. He caused so ____ trouble!
2. He had so ____ problems.
3. How ____ time will it take?
4. How ____ times did you take the test?

*Part 13: Rewrite the sentences, with the **time words** in the proper place.*

1. We used to go to the beach.   (all the time)

2. They talk about it.   (always)

3. Let's do it.   (today)

*Part 14: Change the sentences to the **past**.*

1. I drive fast.
2. She thinks about it every day.

Part 15: Change the sentences to the *continuous*.

1. She laughed.
2. He won't help us this time.
3. She dances and sings well.

Part 16: Change the sentences to the *future*.

1. He works on it all the time.
2. They need more time.

Part 17: Select the *simple present* or *past* tense, or the appropriate *continuous* form.

1. They _____ the new system yesterday.   **start**
2. She _____ lunch at the same restaurant every day.   **eat**
3. They _____ TV when the phone rang.   **watch**
4. He _____ here tomorrow.   **be**

Part 18: Change the *positive* statement to a *negative*.

1. He knows how to do it.
2. She understood.
3. They will try it again.
4. She is ready.

Part 19: Change the statement to a *question*. ↻

1. They were ready.
2. She bought one.

Part 20: Put in the *verb contraction*.

1. She will not tell you.
2. They cannot get here in time.
3. He is not coming.

Part 21: Fill in the proper *tag ending*.

1. You won't tell them,   ?
2. He was late again,   ?
3. She likes it,   ?

Part 22: *Fill in the blank with* **do** *or* **make**.

1. Try not to _____ any mistakes.
2. Nobody wanted to _____ the dishes or _____ their beds.
3. Let's _____ an appointment for next week.

Part 23: *Identify the story order, by putting 1, 2, 3 in the boxes in the proper order.*

☐ He bought a ticket and moved to Marina del Rey.
☐ He will always remember his exciting adventures as a California bodybuilder.
☐ Max wanted to live in America.

Chapter 6: Indirect Speech and the Unreal Duo

In this chapter we will look at intro clauses and indirect speech, **so / such**, and other joiners beyond conjunctions, such as **that**, **when**, and **if**.

For verbs, we will be working with the present unreal duo, opinion words, **do / to do / doing**, the difference between **take / have**, **say / tell**, and **speak / talk,** verbs of probability and obligation, and verbs of perception.

Before we start Chapter 6, let's take a moment to think about applying what you have learned so far. Using the vocabulary, grammar, and pronunciation from Chapters 1 through 5, you can communicate clearly and accurately. Early on, you learned two important patterns in English:

SVO and **modifier + noun**

It is important to force yourself to use these simple patterns. It's very tempting to try to learn the advanced forms, but if you don't have a solid foundation, there is no point in doing that. Students may have several reactions at this point.

"But in my language . . ."
Many people feel that their language is "right," and they are correct. Every language is right. However, people shouldn't try to apply their own rules to English. In some languages, you can change the word order around, you can leave words out or add in different words, you don't conjugate the verb, you always have the verb at the end, and so on. This is fine for your language, but for English, you need to force yourself to use the SVO order. Later, you will gain more flexibility, but you have to have a solid foundation first.

"We don't have that sound/structure/concept in my language."
Well, learn it.

"When I'm talking, I don't have time to think about it."
Yes, you do. Think first, then speak. Instead of just jumping in and saying whatever comes to mind, pause, plan, and then speak. When in doubt, SVO. If you're not sure, SVO. What to do? SVO.

Then, when you are **not** in a conversation with someone, think about the rules and practice applying them. Take your time and think about it. Practice enough that it happens automatically, and you don't have to think about the rules. Repetition, repetition, repetition.

"I think in my language, and then translate to English."
Well, don't. Practice in English. Think in English. Write in English. Count in English. Daydream in English. Repetition, repetition, repetition.

"SVO?"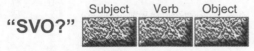

Learn it. Own it. Use it.

From this point on, you will be working at the intermediate level, and you need to have mastered the basics before continuing.

Exercise 6-1: Dictation

Listen to the audio and write the exact transcription in the spaces below. Then check the Answer Key.

DICTATION

1. _____

2. _____

3. _____   *TH = Teeth*

4. _____   *tangle*

5. _____

The Italian Incidents

STORY

One day, I was walking in Marina del **Rey**. I heard some people **talking**. They were **speaking** Italian. They were **talking** about me. They **said** that I was so **big**. They started **saying** some rude **things** about me. They **said**, "**Look** at that guy! He's so **big**! If you stuck a **pin** in him, he would **pop** like a **balloon**!" I **said,** "Hey, I **speak** Italian!" They were really **embarrassed**. They **said** that they were **sorry**. I **told** them that I didn't **care** and I **told** them to go **away**.

Another day, I overheard some **other** people **speaking** Italian. They thought I was **American**, so they started **talking about** me. Before they could **say** anything, I **said**, "Excuse me, but I **speak** Italian." They **said** hello and we **talked about** living in America. They **told** me that they were from Milan. One of them **spoke** English very well. After we **talked** for a while, we **said** goodbye.

Exercise 6-2: "The Italian Incidents" — Pronunciation

Listen to the audio and repeat, focusing on intonation and pronunciation.

One day, I wəz wähking in M'reena Del **Ray**. I hrrrrrd s'm peeple **tähking.** They wrr speekinga **tælian**. They wrrr **täking** əbout me. They sed thə dai wəz so **big**. They starded **saying** s'm rude **thing** zəbout me. They sed, "**Lükət** that guy! Heez so **big**! Ifyu stəckə **pin** innim, heed **päp** lykə **bəlloon**!" I **sed**, "Hey, I **speakə** tælian!" They wrr rilly **emberrast**. They **sed** thət they wrr **särry**. I **told** them thə dai didn't **care** and I **told** 'em tə go⁽ʷ⁾**away**.

Another day, I overhrrd s'mə**ther** peepəl **speaking** ətælian. They thädai wəzza **merək**'n, so they stardəd **talking** əbout me. B'for they cüd **say** anything, I sed, "Eks-kyoozzzz me, bədäi **speekə** tælian." They **sed** hello and we **tähkt** about living in əmerəca. They **told** me thət they were fr'm Milan. wənəvəm spok **Kinglish** very well. æfter we **tähkt** frə while, we sed güd**by**.

NOUNS	This is an important section. You will review how to ask direct questions and learn how to ask questions *indirectly*. You will start by using intro phrases. There will be some word-order

changes that are important to notice and master.

Common and Useful Intro Phrases

You can add a good deal of information with a simple intro phrase before your standard SVO. This can be a one-word adverb, such as **suddenly**, **fortunately**, **actually**, **originally**, **naturally**, **surprisingly**, and so on. See how different the following sentences are:

> **Suddenly,** he stopped the car.
> **Fortunately,** he stopped the car.
> **Actually,** he stopped the car.

The same can be done with *phrases*:

> **As usual,** he stopped the car.
> **As a matter of fact,** he stopped the car.
> **All of a sudden,** he stopped the car.
> **By the way,** he stopped the car.
> **On the other hand,** he stopped the car.
> **Now that you mention it,** he did stop the car.
> **First,** he stopped the car, next he got out.
> **At first,** he stopped the car, but then he kept going.

Joiners

In Chapter 2, we studied the five conjunctions **and**, **but**, **so**, **or**, and **because**. In the broader sense of a conjunction—let's call it a *joiner*—you can link sentences with **that**.

Exercise 6-3: Joining Phrases and Sentences with *That*

*Join the two statements using **that**. Then check the Answer Key.*

It's obvious. He's not ready.	**It's obvious that he's not ready.**

1. They are happy. They won the lottery.

2. You are concerned. They are working too hard.

3. The farmers were happy. It was finally raining.

4. It's not clear. They're telling the truth.

5. We aren't worried. Things aren't going well.

Indirect Speech

With indirect speech, you combine two statements, and they both have the same SVO order. You can replace the **subject** or the **object**:

Subject		
Joe	eats	apples.

I'm not sure	who	eats	apples.

Object		
Joe	eats	apples.

I'm not sure	what	Joe	eats

Exercise 6-4: Indirect Statements ⟳

Change the statement to an indirect statement. The word order is the same; there is no flip. Change the blue text to one of the 5 Ws and how. Check the Answer Key when you're done.

They bought a car.   **I'm not sure what they bought.**

1. They saw **their friends**.

   I'm not sure

2. She did **her homework**.

   They are confused about

3. They went **to the park**.

   It's not clear

4. They did it **on Wednesday**.

   Please confirm

5. They were in trouble **because of all the mistakes**.

   It's clear

6. They got there **by bus**.

   Let us know

7. She didn't ask him **because she didn't want to know the answer**.

   It isn't obvious

8. They thought about **changing the situation**.

   The note didn't indicate

9. Rigel is located **on Orion's belt**.

   In your astronomy class, you learned

10. Jane gave her coat to **her sister**.

    We don't want to know

11. The post office closes **at five**.

    It's not posted

12. I put my keys **on the table**.

    Tell me

13. She moved to France **in** 2007.

    Ask her

14. They bought **some expensive suits**.

    Show me the record of

15. We never watch TV **because we don't have time**.

    you know

Indirect Questions

With indirect questions, the word order for the main sentence doesn't do the question flip. Why? **Because the flip occurs in the introduction.**

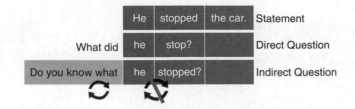

This is true for indirect questions about both the **subject** and the **object**.

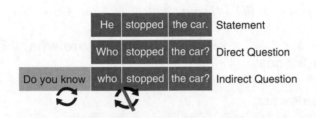

Once again, it's important to remember that with a **who** or **what** question about the **subject**: No flip. You just add the question directly onto the intro phrase without changing the word order.

Right	Wrong, Wrong, Wrong
I don't know why he did it.	I don't know why did he do it?
Can you tell me where she is?	Can you tell me where is she?
Do you know where he went?	Do you know where did he went?
Do you know where he is?	Do you know where is he?

Exercise 6-5: Indirect Yes / No Questions — Subject ↻ ... ↕

*Change the statement to an indirect question by adding either **who** or **what** to the intro phrase provided. Then check the Answer Key.*

The submarine is underwater.   **Do you know what is underwater?**
They told you.   **Does she know who told you?**

1. **He** took the test.
   Do you remember

2. **It** happened.
   Did they find out

3. **Joe** saved him.
   Does he know

4. **The situation** is going on.
   Do they understand

5. **The entire basketball team** was there.
   Did they realize

With *object* questions using the **5 W**s, use the statement word order.

Exercise 6-6: Indirect Yes / No Questions — Object ↻ ... ↻

Change the statement to an indirect question. (There is no question flip in the main sentence.)
*Change the object noun/pronoun to one of the **5 Ws** or **how**. Check the Answer Key when*
you're done.

They bought a car.   **Do you know what they bought?**

1. They saw **their friends**.
   Do you remember

2. She did **her homework**.
   Can you tell me

3. They went **to the park**.
   Do you know

4. They did it **on Wednesday**.
   Does anyone know

5. They were in trouble **because of all the mistakes**.
   Is it clear

6. They got there **by bus**.
   Are we clear on

7. She didn't ask him **because she didn't want to know the answer**.
   Isn't it obvious

8. They thought about **changing the situation**.
   Did the note indicate

9. Rigel is located **on Orion's belt**.
   In your astronomy class, will you learn

10. Jane gave her coat to **her sister**.
    Will you confirm

11. The post office closes **at five**.
    Do you know

12. I put my keys **on the table**.
    Do you know

13. She moved to France **in** 2007.
    Will you be asking her

14. They bought **some expensive suits**.
    Do you have a record of

15. We never watch TV **because we don't have time**.
    Isn't it apparent

16. They lost **their luggage**.
    Will they be able to get back

17. He's **here**.
    Do you know

18. It was **there**.
    Did he explain

19. I got there **by bus**.
    Can you guess

20. You figured it out **with a good deal of hard work**.
    Did you tell them

Exercise 6-7: Subject and Object ↻ ... ↯

Change the statements to indirect questions using the phrase "Do you know ..." (There is no question flip in the main sentence.) Change the subject or object noun/pronoun to one of the 5 Ws or how. Then check the Answer Key.

Jane **saw** Bill.	**Do you know** who **saw Bill?** (subject)
Jane **saw** Bill.	**Do you know** whom* **she saw?** (object)

1. **The car** was in the garage.

2. The car was **in the garage**.

3. **The man** ran quickly to the pool.

4. The man ran **quickly** to the pool.

5. The man ran quickly to **the pool**.

6. **The boys** played baseball.

7. The boys played **baseball**.

8. **The book** cost $10.

9. The book cost **$10**.

*****Whom** replaces **who** when used as an object.

Question Review

As you have seen, there are several types of questions. It's important know if you are asking about the subject or the object.

	Kind	Order	Verb *To Be*	Main Verb
Subject	**Statement**		**He** is there.	**He** likes it.
	Who?	↯	**Who** is there?	**Who** likes it?
	What?	↯	**What** is there?	**What** likes it?
	Yes or no?	↻	**Is he** there?	**Does he** like it?
Object	**Statement**		He is a doctor.	Joe saw **Bill and his dog.**
	Who?	↯	**Who** is a doctor?	**Who** did he see?
	What?	↯	**What** is he?	**What** did he see?
	Where?	↯		**Where** did he see them?
	When?	↯		**When** did he see them?
	Why?	↯		**Why** did he see them?
	How?	↯		**How** did he see them?
	Yes or no?	↻		**Did he** see them?

So and *Such*

So + *adjective*   **Such** + *noun*

There are two similar words that can be used to intensify meaning. You can add **so** to an *adjective* and **such** to a *noun*.

Exercise 6-8: *So* or *Such*?

*Fill in the blank with **so** or **such**. Then check the Answer Key.*

1. That was _Such_ a great movie!
2. She is _So_ worried today.
3. The staff is _So_ busy these days.
4. I don't think it's _Such_ a good idea.
5. He is _Such_ a funny guy!
6. He is _So_ funny!
7. It was _So_ exciting!
8. He was in _Such_ trouble.
9. They are _Such_ liars!
10. They are _So_ dishonest!
11. I am _So_ lucky!
12. I have _Such_ good luck!
13. I am _Such_ a lucky person!
14. That is _Such_ an interesting story!
15. He is _So_ cute!

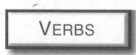

It's Iffy

This section reviews the **present unreal duo**, clarifying the very important distinction between the **future** (what **will** happen), the **present** (what **does** happen), and the **unreal present** (what **would** happen if certain conditions were met). This ties in with **hope** and **wish**.

In Chapter 5, we studied the simple future and the future unreal duo. Now, we are ready to move on to the **present unreal duo**. As usual, let's start with the verb **to be**.

Verb **To Be**	Past	Present	Future
Simple	I was there. ◄	I am here. ●	I will be there. ►
Duo	I had been there before then. ◄◄	I have been there before now.	I will have been A by then. ►►
Unreal Duo	If I had been there, I would have been happy. ◄◄	If I were A, I'd be B. ○ ○	If I am there I will be happy. ►►

Looking at the verb map, you see three things: First, this is the **present** (even though the verb seems to be a past form); second, there are **two events**; third, the events **don't actually happen** (the symbols are white).

The nice thing is that this form doesn't need to be conjugated—it's **were** and **would** for everyone.

Fact	I **am** six feet tall. I **will** try out for the basketball team.
Unreal	If I **were** six feet tall, I **would** try out for the basketball team.

But I'm not.
I am only five feet tall, so I'll stick to baseball.

Fact	He **is** rich. He **lives** in a big mansion in Beverly Hills.
Unreal	If he **were** rich, he **would** live in a big mansion in Beverly Hills.

But he's not.
He lives in a small but charming house in Elkhorn, Nebraska.

You can change either a *present*, *present continuous*, or *future* statement to the present unreal. Notice the relationship between **will** and **would**.

Real	I **will** try it.	I **hope** you **will** try it.
Unreal	I **would** try it if I were you.	I **wish** you **would** try it.

Exercise 6-9: Unreal Duo — Present / *To Be*

*Change the sentences to the present unreal, using **were** and **would**. Then check the Answer Key.*

I am six feet tall. I will try out for the basketball team.
If I were six feet tall, I would try out for the basketball team.

1. It's obvious. I understand it completely.

2. They are in good shape. They will win the competition.

3. We are prepared. She will hire us.

4. I am working on it. I will make the deadline.

5. She is honest. She will not lie.

6. You are not available. You won't offer to help.

7. He is running late. He will call us.

8. It's hot. We're sweating.

9. You are sincere. I trust you completely.

10. I'm sure about it. I recommend it to everyone.

Main Verbs	Past	Present	Future
Simple	I did it. ◄	I do it. ●	I will do it. ►
Duo	I had done A before I did B. ◄◄	I have done A before now.	I will have done A by the time I do B. ►►
Unreal Duo	If I had done A, I would have done B. ◄◄	If I did A, I'd do B. ○ ○	If I do A, I'll do B. ►►

With main verbs, the **present** unreal uses a form that looks like the **past**. The way you can tell it's the present is by asking a question: **If I had time, I would go.**
Do I have time?
You can see that the question identifies the time as the present.

Fact   He weighs 350 pounds. He will become a sumo wrestler in Japan.
Unreal   If he **weighed** 350 pounds, he **would** become a sumo wrestler in Japan.
But he doesn't.
He's quite small, so he just wrestles with his conscience.

Fact   They **know** all the answers. They **teach** the world.
Unreal   If they **knew** all the answers, they **would** teach the world.
But they don't.
So, they just try to do what is right.

Exercise 6-10: Unreal Duo — Present / Main Verbs

Combine the sentences starting with **if**. *Use the present unreal duo. Then check the Answer Key.*

She studies hard. She will succeed.
If she studied hard, she would succeed.

1. You like to ski. You go as often as possible.

2. I will tell you. You won't remember.

3. We practice every day. We will get better.

4. He eats a lot. He is overweight.

5. I study every day. I speak English well.

6. They talk too much. They get in trouble.

7. It works well. We use it everyday.

8. They pay attention. They understand.

9. Everyone knows how to do it. We don't need the instruction manual.

10. It makes us mad. We complain about it.

Intro Phrases with the Unreal Duo

Exercise 6-11: Intro Phrases

*Connect the phrases using **if**. Then check the Answer Key.*

It's not clear. They like it.
It's not clear if they like it.

1. I'm not sure. It works.

2. I'm not sure. It will work.

3. I'm not sure. It worked.

4. He doesn't know. He will be there.

5. I don't know. He was there.

6. I don't know. He is here.

Hope: Real	Wish: Unreal
a possibility in the future	a desire that probably won't happen
hope + will	**wish + would**

Exercise 6-12: *Hope* or *Wish*?

*Fill in the blank with the proper form of **hope** or **wish**. Then check the Answer Key.*

1. I _____ you can help me.
2. I _____ you could help me.
3. They _____ it is true.
4. They _____ it were true.
5. They _____ it was true.
6. They _____ it had been true.
7. You _____ they would take care of it.
8. You _____ they will take care of it.
9. She _____ that he wouldn't argue so much. (but he will)
10. She _____ that he won't argue this time. (maybe he won't)
11. We _____ they stop fighting soon.
12. They _____ they would stop fighting soon.
13. I _____ you're happy.
14. I _____ you were happy.
15. She _____ she will win the lottery.

Opinion Words

	Past	Present	Future
Simple	I had to do it. ◀	I have to do it. ●	I'll have to do it. ▶
Duo	I had done A before I did B. ◀◀	I have done A before now. ◀●	I will have done A by the time I do B. ▶▶
Unreal Duo	If I had done A, I would have done B. ◀◀	If I had to do A, I'd have to do B. ●●	If I have to do A, I'll have to do B. ▶▶

The lighter areas indicate the tenses we've studied up through this chapter, using **have to.**

What Are the Odds?
Action vs. Non-Action

Will	I will do it.	100% probability
Must	I must do it!	strong probability
May	I may do it.	50% possibility
Might	I might do it.	50% possibility
Could	I could do it.	slight possibility
Would . . . if	I would do it if I had time.	unreal
Won't	I won't do it.	0% probability

May and **might** have the same meaning.

Exercise 6-13: Probability

Fill in the blank with the appropriate form of will, must, may, might, could, would, or won't. Then check the Answer Key.

1. I _____ call you **tomorrow**.	100% probability
2. My **boss** says we _____ need to work **over**time.	0% probability
3. I'm not **sure**, but he _____ be **wrong**.	possibility
4. Be **careful**, or you _____ get **hurt**.	slight possibility
5. He _____ be **crazy**; he wants to **swim** across the **lake**!	strong probability
6. She _____ buy a **Mercedes**, if she had more **money**.	unreal
7. It was 20 **degrees** last night; you _____ have been **freezing**!	strong probability
8. If you had **asked** me, I _____ have **told** you.	unreal
9. Don't jump to **conclusions**; he _____ have been at **work**.	slight possibility
10. The **weather** report said that it _____ **rain** this afternoon.	possibility
11. I _____ not give any more **help** even if he **asked** me.	0% probability
12. She _____ wear a **power** suit if she wants to get that **job**!	strong probability
13. My **brother** says he _____ fix my **car**.	slight possibility
14. The **teacher** _____ give us **home**work today — it's **Friday**!	0% probability
15. You _____ **do** it if I **tell** you to.	100% probability

Duty Calls!

have to	I have to do it.	strong obligation
must	I must do it.	strong obligation
had better	I had better do it.	obligation
had better	You had better!	warning
should	I should do it.	obligation
should	I should have done it.	past advice
ought to	I ought to do it.	obligation
may	You may do it.	permission
can	I can do it.	ability
could	Could you do it, please?	polite request

Exercise 6-14: Obligation

*Fill in the blank with the appropriate form of **have to**, **must**, **had better**, **should**, **ought to**, **may**, **can**, or **could**. Then check the Answer Key.*

1. We _____ **think** about it. — strong obligation
2. You _____ get **out** of here, or there'll be **trouble**! — warning
3. You _____ be **care**ful with that **knife**. — warning
4. . . . and the little train said, "I **think** I _____." — ability
5. . . . and the little train said, "I **thought** I _____." — past ability
6. You _____ n't have opened the **gate**; the **dog** got out! — past advice
7. Yes, you _____ **leave** now. — permission
8. I _____ jump **high**. — ability
9. _____ you **help** me with this, please? — polite request
10. You _____ watch **out**! — warning
11. She _____ drink **coffee** in the **morning**. — strong obligation
12. **Americans** have that "_____ do" **spirit**! — ability
13. If you want to earn **money**, you _____ get a **job**. — warning
14. Since you're **tired**, you _____ **rest**. — obligation
15. **One** day, you _____ travel to **Europe**. — possibility

Asking for Advice

Dear Annie, What should I do?

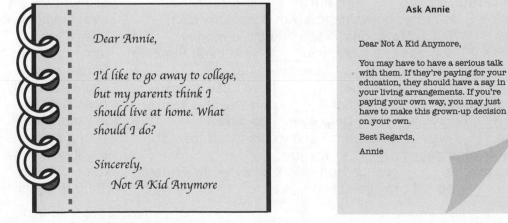

Dear Annie,

I'd like to go away to college, but my parents think I should live at home. What should I do?

Sincerely,

Not A Kid Anymore

Ask Annie

Dear Not A Kid Anymore,

You may have to have a serious talk with them. If they're paying for your education, they should have a say in your living arrangements. If you're paying your own way, you may just have to make this grown-up decision on your own.

Best Regards,

Annie

Exercise 6-15: Three Verb Forms

Fill in the blank with the proper form of the verb, using the simple form, the infinitive, or –ing (**do**, **to do**, **doing**). *Remember that prepositions are followed by –ing. Check the Answer Key when you're done.*

I will _____ that.	**I will do that.**
I want _____ that.	**I want to do that.**
I enjoy _____ that.	**I enjoy doing that.**
1. I want _____ that.	do
2. We plan on _____ that.	do
3. He refused _____ me what he was _____.	tell / do
4. What do you hope _____?	accomplish
5. I appreciate you _____ me with this.	help
6. I anticipate your _____ with this.	help
7. By not _____, you're guaranteeing a poor grade.	study
8. He insisted on _____.	pay
9. You have _____ the report by Friday.	submit
10. The site recommends _____ online.	register
11. We used _____ for long drives in the country.	go
12. I've never heard of _____ it that way.	use
13. He likes _____ fast.	drive
14. My boss won't let me _____ the week off.	take
15. The children promised _____ quietly.	play
16. I don't recall _____ that before.	see
17. Let's have him _____ in early tomorrow.	come
18. I needed _____ him _____ with me.	ask / work
19. We can't put off _____ him any longer!	tell
20. They tried _____ _____ her the bad news.	avoid / tell
21. We'd be interested in _____ your plan.	hear
22. Let's think about _____ it first class.	ship
23. You've got _____ a lot in order to succeed.	practice
24. There's no use _____ about it.	complain
25. There's no point in _____ about it.	worry
26. I prefer _____ it myself.	do
27. I would rather _____ it myself.	do
28. Would you mind _____ me with this?	help
29. Thank you for _____ me with this.	help
30. I _____ him run out of the house yesterday.	see
31. I _____ him to come back in last night.	tell
32. I _____ him go down the stairs at midnight.	hear
33. We hope _____ you again sometime.	see
34. They enjoyed _____ you again.	see
35. We are looking forward to _____ them later on.	meet
36. He asked if I would _____ ready.	be
37. "May I see that?" He asked _____ it.	see
38. "Ed, show me that." He asked Ed _____ it to him.	show
39. They stopped _____. (Their goal was to eat.)	eat
40. They stopped _____. (They were no longer eating.)	eat
41. We can read the reviews online before _____.	decide
42. I was waiting for him _____.	finish
43. We let them _____ outside.	go

44. We allowed them _____ outside.	go
45. We didn't make them _____ outside.	go
46. We had them _____ outside.	go
47. He helped us _____ the project.	do

Say, Tell, Speak, Talk

These verbs are all used to indicate communication. **Say** is the most common. **Tell** is more direction-oriented; you tell someone something. It is similar to **inform**. You also use **tell** with **tell the truth**, **tell a lie**, and **tell a story**. **Speak** is a more formal version of **talk**, and is used with languages, such as **I speak Spanish**. **Talk** is similar to converse. It is also used in phrases such as, **What are you talking about?** or **Who were you talking to?**

Exercise 6-16: *Say, Tell, Speak, Talk*

Fill in the blank with the proper form of ***say***, ***tell***, ***speak***, *or* ***talk***. *Then check the Answer Key.*

What are you _____ about?   What are you talking about?

1. Don't		me that!
2. How do you		*sushi* in English?
3. Let's		this over, OK? Let's discuss this.
4. I'll		you a secret.
5. Don't		French during English class!
6. Don't		the boys about their surprise party.
7. I don't want to		about it anymore.
8. What did you		? Who were you _____ to?
9. Did you		the truth? (Note: **Speak the truth** is not commonly used.)
10. Don't		him what happened.

Exercise 6-17: *Say, Tell, Speak, Talk*   CD 2 Track 17

Now that you are familiar with the four verbs, listen to "The Italian Incidents" again.

One day, I was walking in Marina del Rey. I heard some people **talking.** They were **speaking** Italian. They were **talking** about me. They said that I was so **big**. They started **saying** some rude **things** about me. They said, "**Look** at that guy! He's so **big**! If you stuck a **pin** in him, he'll **pop** like a **balloon**!" I **said,** "Hey, I **speak** Italian!" They were really **embarrassed**. They **said** that they were **sorry**. I **told** them that I didn't **care** and I **told** them to go **away**.

Another day, I overheard some **other** people **speaking** Italian. They thought I was American, so they started **talking about** me. Before they could **say** anything, I said, "Excuse me, but I **speak** Italian." They **said** hello. We **talked about** living in America. They **told** me that they were from Milan. One of them **spoke** English very well. After we **talked** for a while, we **said** goodbye.

Verbs of Perception

Look, **see**, and **watch** are similar in that they are all about visual perception. However, there are two main differences. One is *intentionality*, as you intentionally **look** at something, but you just **see** whatever falls within your field of vision. The other difference is *movement*, as you **look at** something that is stationary, but you **watch** something that is moving.

Exercise 6-18: *Look / See / Watch*

*Fill in the blank with the proper form of **look**, **see**, or **watch**. Then check the Answer Key.*

1. _____ at the sky; it's beautiful!
2. Let's _____ TV for a while.
3. How does this _____?
4. Could you _____ my kids for a minute, please? Keep an eye on them!
5. Cats can _____ in the dark.
6. Could you take a quick _____ at my paper?
7. Do you _____ what I'm saying?
8. We have to _____ our weight. We have to monitor our poundage.
9. Let's wait and _____ how it turns out.
10. We should _____ around for a better job.

Hear and **listen** are also distinguished by intentionality, as you intentionally **listen to** something, but you just **hear** whatever comes in hearing range.

Exercise 6-19: *Hear / Listen*

*Fill in the blank with the proper form of **hear** or **listen**. Then check the Answer Key.*

1. What was that noise? I didn't _____ anything.
2. Would you please _____ when I'm talking to you!
3. Don't _____ to him; he's just talking nonsense.
4. Have you _____ the good news?
5. I'll let you know if I _____ anything about it.
6. _____, we need to re-think this!
7. Can you _____ me now?
8. Stop _____ to the radio and pay attention!
9. _____ carefully, you can _____ the ocean!
10. I've never _____ of such a thing!

Exercise 6-20: Verbs of Perception

Select the proper word. Then check the Answer Key.

1. He _____ like a nice guy.

2. That _____ like a really good plan.

3. How do you _____ about that?

☐ looks
☐ appears
☐ hears
☐ sounds
☐ feel
☐ appear

143

4. With my own eyes, I _____ him take it. ☐ looked
☐ saw

5. With my own ears, I _____ him say it. ☐ listened
☐ heard

6. They _____ to be very responsible. ☐ appear
☐ look

7. It's so cold I can't _____ my fingers. ☐ feel
☐ touch

8. She _____ so young! ☐ looks
☐ appears

9. Don't _____ the stove, it's hot! ☐ feel
☐ touch

10. What are you _____ on your mp3 player? ☐ hearing
☐ listening to

Exercise 6-21: Linking Verbs of Perception

Select the proper verb of perception. Then check the Answer Key.

1. Now that he has gray hair, he _____ much older. ☐ looks
☐ sounds

2. Over the phone, you _____ very young. ☐ sound
☐ look

3. The committee _____ to be reconsidering its position. ☐ appears
☐ feels

4. These are so soft and silky ... they _____ very smooth. ☐ sound
☐ feel

5. You are getting hoarse. You _____ like you're getting sick. ☐ look
☐ sound

Involuntary	Voluntary	Perception or Opinion
He hears a noise.	He listens to the radio.	It sounds good.
We see the colors.	We look at the painting.	They look beautiful.
She felt a shock.	She touched the wire.	She feels sad.
You smelled the coffee.		The coffee smelled good.
You tasted the candy.		The candy tasted good.

Exercise 6-22: Verbs of Perception

Select the proper option. Then check the Answer key.

1. Did you _____ about the accident? ☐ hear
☐ listen
☐ sound

2. Cats can _____ in the dark. ☐ see
☐ look

3. The kids were _____ TV again. ☐ seeing
☐ looking
☐ looking at
☐ watching

4. They weren't ____ to the teacher.

5. He ____ a little tired.

6. Don't ____ the sun during an eclipse.

7. Great speech! That ____ terrific.

8. You____ warm; you might have a fever.

9. Don't____ the wet paint!

10. He's trying to____ his weight.

☐ hearing
☐ listening
☐ sounding
☐ sees
☐ looks
☐ look
☐ look at
☐ heard
☐ sounded
☐ feel
☐ touch
☐ feel
☐ touch
☐ feel
☐ look
☐ look at
☐ watch

Exercise 6-23: *Have* or *Take*?

*Fill in the blank with the proper form of ~~take~~ or **have**. Then check the Answer Key.*

1. What are we ____ for breakfast?
2. I think I'll ____ a nap now.
3. Will they ____ time to finish?
4. Let's ____ a five-minute break.
5. He ____ a shower last night. took
6. We ____ dinner at midnight.
7. Let's ____ a trip to Rio.
8. ____ an aspirin if you ____ a headache.
9. We should ____ turns with this.
10. I think he's ____ piano lessons.

taking

Take

Take is used in its basic meaning of **to lay hold of something, accept,** or **to remove**, but in combination with other words, it has many other meanings. Here are some common combinations.

take after	look like, resemble	take apart	take something to pieces
take aside	get someone alone to talk to him	take away	remove, deduct from
take advantage	benefit by	take advice	receive guidance
take advantage	exploit	take bribes	accept illegal money
take back	make someone nostalgic	take down	make notes or write down in full
take back	retract a statement, admit something was wrong	take down	remove from a high place
take in	absorb information	take it	accept something negative, like criticism

take in	make clothes smaller	take it upon yourself	take responsibility, often without consulting other people
take it out on	abuse someone because you're angry	take notes	write down what was said at a meeting
take off	make great progress	take on	employ
take off	reduce the price of an item	take on	assume responsibility
take off	when a plane departs or leaves the ground	take over	assume control of
take off	remove from an object	take up	fill or occupy time or space
take out	extract, remove, delete	take up	start a new hobby, pastime, etc.
take out	borrow, for instance a library book or a loan	take to	make a habit of something
take place	happen	take out	go out socially with someone, especially on a date
take time	need time	take out	remove from within
take up room	occupy space	take turns	alternate

Exercise 6-24: Take It Easy! Take Five!

*Fill in the blank with the proper form of **take** using the information at the end of the sentence. Then check the Answer Key.*

1. It would be great to have another computer, but unfortunately it would take _____ too much room. **(space)**
2. The prices will never be this low again, so it would be to our benefit to take _____ of them now. **(profit by)**
3. The salesman took _____ the secretary's kind nature to find out the company pricing policy. **(used, exploited)**
4. The dispatcher wasn't sure how much time it would _____ to get through the route so he allowed an extra hour. **(duration)**
5. The typist thought that she should hurry, but the manager told her to take her ___ to avoid making mistakes. **(go at her own pace)**
6. The chairman was sick, so the director took his _____ at the board meeting. **(replace, stand in for)**
7. The committee chairman requested that the secretary take _____ at the meeting. **(write down what was said)**
8. It is illegal not only to offer money for favors, but to take _____. **(accept money)**
9. If they had taken my _____, there wouldn't have been any trouble. **(if they had listened to me)**
10. Neither company could decide who should have responsibility for maintaining the premises, so they settled on taking _____. **(alternating)**

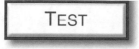

Let's review everything you have learned in Chapter 6. Make sure you get 100% on the test before going on to the next chapter. Check your work using the Answer Key.

Part 1: Fill in the blank to complete each response.

1. Did he do it?   Yes,
2. Did he do it?   No,
3. Will they call you?   No,
4. Can they try it?   Yes,
5. Would she like that?   No,

Part 2: Rewrite the sentences, replacing **Who** with **He** or **She**.

1. Who did it?

2. Who should do it?

Part 3: Start each sentence with **I don't know who**.

1. He did it.

2. They like them.

Part 4: Answer the question using **We can't figure out**.

1. Do you know who did it?

2. Do you know who makes them?

Part 5: Convert from a statement to a **What** question.

1. He did it.

2. They will buy them.

Part 6: Convert from a statement to a **Where** question.

1. He did it there.

2. They will go to the park.

Part 7: Convert from a statement to a **When** question.

1. He did it then.

2. We dance on Wednesdays.

Part 8: *Convert from a statement to a **How** question.*

1. He did it quickly.

How did he do it so quickly

2. She paints beautifully.

How does she paint so beautifully

Part 9: *Respond using **I'm not sure if.***

1. Did he do it?

2. Do we need one?

3. Will he do it?

Part 10: *Answer the question using **Because** and your own words.*

1. Why do people drive so fast?

2. Why is the sky blue?

Part 11: *Fill in the blank with the proper form of **say**, **tell**, **speak**, or **talk**.*

1. What did you _____?
2. Could you _____ me who was there?
3. What are you _____ about?
4. Sam always _____ the truth.
5. Do you _____ any other languages?

Part 12: *Select the proper verb of **obligation** or **probability**.*

1. It's very late. You _____ tired!

☐ will be
☐ must be

2. He's making a lot of mistakes. He _____ a beginner.

☐ will be
☐ may be

3. There's a slight possibility that he _____ on time today.

☐ will be
☐ could be

4. I need to do this now. It _____ completed immediately.

☐ will be
☐ has to be

5. _____ I help you?

☐ may
☐ will

6. He is very smart. He _____ answer your questions.

☐ can
☐ may

7. I have a deadline. I _____ work faster.

☐ should
☐ will be

Using what you have learned, write two paragraphs on the following:

1. If you could travel to any country, where would you go and what would you do?
2. If you could have one super power, what would it be?

You can handwrite your paragraphs below or e-mail them to **para@grammar.bz** to be stored. These paragraphs are not graded or reviewed, but simply by writing them, your English will improve.

```
○ ● ○                          Student Paragraph

Send  Chat  Attach  Address  Fonts  Colors  Save As Draft        Photo Browser   Show Stationery

     To:  para@grammar.bz
     Cc:
     Bcc:
 Subject:  Chapter 6
                                                    Signature: Corporate

My name is _____
```

Chapter 7: Reverse Modifiers and Opinion Words

This chapter covers a different form of *adjective*, a phrase that comes after the noun. Additionally, we will work with **something / nothing**, **else**, and **time words**. We will contrast **how**: **quality** vs. **degree**, as well as do a thorough review of **how + 5 W**s.

DICTATION

For verbs, we'll learn the *present real duo*, review all verbs we've studied to date using **there**, along with the phrasal verb **turn**, and go over the differences between **there is**, **it is**, and **it has**.

Exercise 7-1: Dictation
CD 2 Track 18

Listen to the audio and write the exact transcription in the spaces below. Then check the Answer Key.

1. _____

2. _____

3. _____

4. _____

5. _____

STORY

The Boy Who Cried Wolf

The **strangest** thing is happening. There's a **flight** attendant **who** keeps **calling** me and leaving **messages** on my **machine**. Six **months** ago, I flew from **Italy** to LA**X** on TW**A**. The attendant **knew** who I **was** and we **chatted** a little. After I had **been** here for a while, I started getting **phone** messages from her. I never called her **back**, but she started calling more and **more**. She would **say** things like she wanted to go **out** with me, and that she **loved** me! My **girl**friend is **furious**. I **told** her that I hadn't **given** this woman my **phone** number. I **suppose** that she got it from the **computer** at the **air**line. My **girl**friend doesn't **trust** me, however. Because of my little **joke** with the **flowers** (I'll tell you about this soon!), she thinks that I want to chase other **women**. I **guess** it's just like the little **boy who** cried **wolf**. When he was **kidding**, everyone **believed** him, but he did it **once** too **often**, and then when the wolf really **came**, no one **believed** him. I **swear**, I don't know **who** this woman is or **why** she is calling me!

Exercise 7-2: "The Boy Who Cried Wolf" — Pronunciation
CD 2 Track 19

Listen to the audio and repeat, focusing on intonation and pronunciation.

Thə **strangest** thingiz hæppəning. Therzə **fly**də tendənt who keeps **cälling** me and leaving **mess'j'z** än my **m'sheen**. Six **mənts**a go, I flew fr'm **Idə**ly to LA**X** än TW**A**. The[(y)]ettendənt **knew** who I **wəz** and we **chædd'd** a liddle. æfter I had **bin** hir frə while, I starded gedding **phone** mess'j'z fr'mmer. I never call der **bæck**, but she starded **cälling** more and **more**. Sheed **say** things like she wännəd to go **out** with me, and that she **ləvd** me! My **girl**frend iz **furiəs**. I **told**er that I hadn't **given** this wüm'n my **phone** number. I **s'poz** that she gäddit from the **c'mpuder** at the **air**line. My **girl**friend dəzznt **trəst** me, however. B'cuz of my liddle **joke** with the **flowers** (all tell you[(w)]about this soon), she thinks thə dai wänt to chase əther **wimmen**. I **guess** it's just like the liddle **boy** who cried **wüf**. Whenee wəz **kidding**, everyone **believe** dim, bəddee did it **once** too[(w)]**offen**, and then when the wüf rilly **came**, no one **believe** dim. I **swear**, I don't know **who** this wüm'n iz or **why** sheez **cälling** me.

Exercise 7-3: *What, But, That*   CD 2 Track 20

Listen to the audio and repeat, focusing on intonation and pronunciation.

	What	But	That
a	wədə	bədə	thədə
I	wədäi	bədäi	thədäi
I'm	wədäim	bədäim	thədäim
I've	wədäiv	bədäiv	thədäiv
if	wədif	bədif	thədif
it	wədit	bədit	thədit
it's	wədits	bədits	thədits
is	wədiz	bədiz	thədiz
isn't	wədizn^t	bədizn^t	thədizn^t
are	wədr	bədr	thədr
aren't	wədärn^t	bədärn^t	thədärn^t
he	wədee	bədee	thədee
he's	wədeez	bədeez	thədeez
her	wədr	bədr	thədr
you	wəchew	bəchew	thəchew
you'll	wəchül	bəchül	thəchül
you've	wəchoov	bəchoov	thəchoov
you're	wəchr	bəchr	thəchr

Exercise 7-4: *What, But, That* in Context   CD 2 Track 21

Listen to the audio and repeat, focusing on intonation and pronunciation.

1. I don't know what it **means.**
    I don$^{(t)}$know wədit **meenz**
2. But it **look**s like what I **need.**
    bədi$^{(t)}$**lük** sly kwədäi **need**
3. But you **said** that you **wouldn't.**
    bəchew **sed** thəchew **wüdnt**
4. I **know** what you **think.**
    I **know** wəchew **think**
5. But I don't **think** that he **will.**
    bədäi don$^{(t)}$**think** thədee **will**
6. He said that if we can **do** it, he'll **help.**
    he sed the diff we k'n **do**$^{(w)}$it, hill **help**
7. But isn't it **easier** this **way?**
    bədizni **dee**zier thi sway?
8. We **want** something that isn't **here.**
    we **wänt** something thədizn^t **here**
9. You'll **like** it, but you'll **regret** it **later.**
    yül **lye** kit, bəchül r'**gre** dit **laydr**
10. But he's not **right** for what I **want.**
    bədeez nät **right** fr wədäi **wänt**
11. It's **amazing** what you've **accomplished.**
    its amazing wəchoovəc**cäm**plisht
12. What if he **forgets?**
    wədifee fr**gets**
13. **OK**, but aren't you **missing** something?
    OK, bədärn^t chew **miss**ing səmthing
14. I think that he's **OK** now.
    I think thədeez **OK** næo
15. She **wanted** to, but her **car** broke down.
    She **wän**əd to, bədr **cär** broke dæon
16. We **think** that you're taking a **chance.**
    We think thəchr taking a **chænce**
17. They don't know what it's **about.**
    They don't know wədit sə**bæot**

| NOUNS | This noun section covers *reverse modifiers*, **how** with *quality* and *degree*, a review of the *question* forms, **something**, **something else**, and *time words*. |

Reverse Modifiers: *That* or *Who*

As you know, adjectives come *before* the noun.

Nice people go far in life.
The **helpful** assistant is not here today.
I met a **really nice** girl.

Now, you can also put a modifier *after* the noun by using **who**.

People **who are nice** go far in life.
The assistant **who helped us** is not here today.
I met a girl who was **really nice**.

This also works with –**ing** or –**ed** modifiers.

The **dancing** man is over there.
The man **who is dancing** is over there.

The **embarrassed** children hid their faces.
The children **who were embarrassed** hid their faces.
The children **who hid their faces** were embarrassed.

Exercise 7-5: Regular Adjective to Reverse Adjective

*Flip the adjective in each of the following sentences. If the subject is a person, use **who**. If the subject is not a person, use **that**. Check the Answer Key when you're done.*

Evil people get their just rewards.
People who are evil get their just rewards.
1. The **loudly ticking** bomb is about to go off.

2. The **well-known** facts are not in dispute.

3. The **recently admitted** audience clapped loudly.

4. A **two-year-old** child can't read.

5. The **downsized salesmen** protested loudly.

Exercise 7-6: Reverse Adjective to Regular Adjective

Flip the adjective in each of the following sentences. Then check the Answer Key.

A situation that is familiar is often more comfortable.
A familiar situation is often more comfortable.

1. A person **who is illiterate** can't work for the government.

2. An object **that was unidentified** flew over the city.

3. The car **that was recently purchased** runs really well.

4. The players **who were eliminated** cheered for the remaining contestants.

5. The detective **who retired** has written a book about his experiences.

You may be wondering why there are two similar but different ways to modify a noun (**nice people** and **people who are nice**). They are similar in that they both give information about the noun. They are different in several significant ways, however.

Reverse modifiers are used for *emphasis* or *clarification*. However, there are many instances where you can't use a simple adjective because there is too much information in the reverse modifier, such as *The guy **who runs the donut shop** speaks Thai* or *The certificate **that I requested** hasn't arrived yet*. You can't say, *The donut shop running guy speaks Thai*. You can say, *The requested certificate hasn't arrived yet*, but then it's not clear who requested it.

When we talk, we can throw in as many words as we like in order to get our point across. In writing, however, being concise is better. In editing, you will often find yourself going back and forth between the two forms, in order to find the best way to present the information. Let's look at the various possibilities.

When the speaker is immediately familiar with the topic or it's an obvious characteristic, the adjective comes before the noun.

> It's a **green** car.
> He's a **good** teacher.
> It's a **good** idea.

The emphasis is on the noun.

The **reverse** adjective lets you start with the noun and then develop the description. You can use more complex phrases and more detailed verb tenses.

> It's a car **that runs on water**.
> He's a teacher **who thrives on challenges**.
> It's an idea **whose time has come**.

The rhythm also lets you stress both the noun and the main word of the modifier.

As you get into the higher levels of speaking, reading, and writing, you'll notice that these two forms are used together.

Constantly barking **dogs that have been left home alone** are often bored.
Densely populated **areas that suffer from a lack of medical facilities** are a breeding ground for disease.

Compacting Sentences: *That* or *Who*

Now that we've discussed reverse modifiers, let's look at another approach to the same thing. You can join two sentences by changing the subject of the second sentence into **that** or **who**. We'll call this *compacting*. **That** is for *things*, and **who** is for *people*. However, you will hear Americans using **that** for people, as well.

> **The man** is nice. **He** is over there.
> The man **who is nice** is over there.
> The man **who is over there** is nice.

> **A book** is well written. **It** may be out of print.
> A book **that is well written** may be out of print.
> A book **that is out of print** may be well written.

You'll notice that the meaning of the sentence changes with the position of the **blue clause**. In the first example, the focus is on the man's location, and the fact that he is nice is secondary (The man **who is nice** is over there). In the second example, his personality is primary and his location is secondary (The man **who is over there** is nice).

Exercise 7-7: Compacting Subjects

*Combine the two sentences, using **that** or **who** to replace the **subject** of the second sentence. Then check the Answer Key.*

My brother lives in California. He likes to surf.
My brother **who lives in California** likes to surf.
My brother, **who likes to surf,** lives in California.

1. **The kids** are playing on the swings. **They** are having a great time.

2. **The house** was painted blue. **It** is next door to us.

3. **My sister** is married. **She** is very happy.

4. **The teacher** gave us a test today. **She** will grade it later.

5. **The dress** doesn't fit anymore. **It** would be better off given to someone else.

Note the punctuation difference between *My brother who lives in California likes to surf* and *My brother, who lives in California, likes to surf*. In the first sentence, I have more than one brother and the sentence distinguishes that brother from the one who lives somewhere else. In the second sentence, I only have one brother and I'm giving more information about him. **That** changes to **which** when you add commas: *The pen **that** I have in my pocket is blue* and *The pen, **which** I have in my pocket, is blue*. (Traditionally, these are called restrictive and non-restrictive clauses.)

Now, we will compact **object**-**subject**. All you have to do is replace the second subject with **who** or **that**.

	Object	**Subject**	
That	I need a **car**.	**It**	should run really well.
	I need a **car**	**that**	runs really well.
Who	I see a **girl**.	**She**	is wearing a red dress.
	I see a **girl**	**who**	is wearing a red dress.

Exercise 7-8: Compacting Objects

*Combine the two sentences, using **that** or **who** to replace the **object** of the second sentence. Then check the Answer Key.*

She met a guy. He didn't know much.   **She met a guy who didn't know much.**
We saw a movie. It was hilarious.   **We saw a movie that was hilarious.**
1. I met **a man**. **He** had nine kids.

2. We heard a **rumor**. **It** wasn't true at all.

3. I like **people**. **They** are nice.

4. There was a **mistake** in his report. **It** caused a lot of problems.

5. They will organize a **protest**. **It** will change everything.

In the following exercise, use **where** for *location*, **when** for *time*, and **whose** for *possession*.

Exercise 7-9: It's All Relative

*Fill in the blanks with **who**, **whose**, **where**, **when**, or **that**. Then check the Answer Key.*

I'd like to **welcome** you to our **company**, **introduce** you to the people _____ **work** here, and tell you about the **job** _____ you'll be **doing**. Mr. **Edwards** is the man _____ **started** this company. **This** room is _____ we hold our weekly **meetings** at 8:00 am (ay day **yem**), although **morning** is usually _____ we make most of our **calls**. This is Mr. **Roberts**, _____ you'll be working with. **Finally**, here's the room _____ **you** will be working and the **ID** card _____ you'll need to carry at all times. This is the **best** company _____ I've ever **worked** for.

How Does It Work?

How tells the *manner* of something. It answers the question, "In what way?" We will use:

1. Adverbs: **easily**, **quickly**, **fast**, **roughly** (words ending in –**ly** are adverbs)
2. Phrases: **in a hurry**, **by himself**, **all alone**
3. Supporting words: **by**, **with**, **like**, **as**, **the way**

The supporting words have rules:

	Example	Structure
1.	He does it **like** a pro.	like + noun
2.	He does it **by** work**ing** hard.	by + ing
3.	He broke it **with** a hammer.	with + noun
4.	He does it **the way** he learned.	the way + phrase
5.	He does it **as** he was taught.	as + phrase

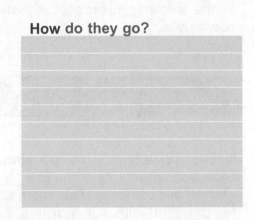

Does	it	go	fast?
How	does	it	go?

Exercise 7-10: How Questions of Manner ↻

*Convert each statement to a **how** question. Change any nouns to pronouns. Remember to use the unchanging form of the main verb. **How** replaces the **adverb**. Check the Answer Key when you're done.*

The cars go fast.   **How do they go?**
1. It works **well**.
2. She got rich **by working hard**.
3. He drives **like a maniac**.
4. We opened it **with a letter opener**.
5. They found it **by searching online**.
6. He did it **like I showed him**.
7. He did it **the way he was taught**.
8. He did it **as he was taught**.
9. We traveled **by plane**.
10. He made friends **by being friendly**.

How also tells the *extent* of something. It answers the question, "How much?" or "To what extent?"

Exercise 7-11: *How* Questions of Extent ↻

*Convert each statement to a **how** question. Change the nouns to pronouns. Remember to use the unchanging form of the main verb. **How** replaces the **modifying adverb**. Check the Answer Key when you're done.*

The cars go really fast.

How fast do they go?

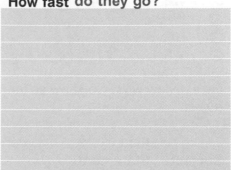

1. It works **extremely well**.
2. She got **really rich**.
3. He drives **too fast**.
4. We opened it **very slowly**.
5. They found it **surprisingly late**.
6. He was **SO dumb**!
7. It was **mind-bogglingly ridiculous**.
8. They were **blazingly furious**.
9. Her house was **outlandishly modern**.
10. His hands were **bizarrely small**.

Exercise 7-12: 5 W Review ↻

*Convert each statement to a **how** question. Change the nouns to pronouns. Then check the Answer Key.*

The Pilgrims celebrated Thanksgiving in Massachusetts over 300 years ago by having a feast with the Indians because they were happy to be alive.

↻ **Who** celebrated it?
↻ **What** did they celebrate?
↻ **Where** did they celebrate it?
↻ **When** did they celebrate it?
↻ **Why** did they celebrate it?
↻ **How** did they celebrate it?
↻ **Did** they celebrate it? (Yes/No)

1. In 1969, with great courage and technical expertise, Neil Armstrong landed Apollo 11 on the moon in order to win the space race.

↻ Who
↻ What
↻ Where
↻ When
↻ Why
↻ How
↻ Y/N:

2. Over 500 years ago, Christopher Columbus sailed a ship across the Pacific, from Spain to America, with the goal of establishing a new trade route.

↻ Who
↻ What
↻ Where
↻ When
↻ Why
↻ How
↻ Y/N:

3. In 1863, Friedrich Miescher, a Swiss physician, first isolated DNA after discovering a microscopic substance on discarded surgical bandages as he was trying to isolate nuclein.

↻ Who
↻ What
↻ Where

↻ When
↻ Why
↻ How
↻ Y/N:

Let's review what we know so far about statements and questions about the *subject* and *object*.

	Kind	Order	Verb *To Be*	Main Verb
Subject	**Statement**		**He** is there.	**He** likes it.
	Who?	↻	**Who** is there?	**Who** likes it?
	What?	↻	**What** is there?	**What** likes it?
	Yes or No?	↻	**Is he** there?	**Does he** like it?
Object*	**Statement**		He is a doctor.	He saw them with her.
	Who?	↻	**Who** is he?	**Who** did he see?
	What?	↻	**What** is he?	**What** did he see?
	Where?	↻	**Where** is he?	**Where** did he see it?
	When?	↻	**When** is lunch?	**When** did he see it?
	Why?	↻	**Why** is he there?	**Why** did he see them?
	How?	↻	**How** is he?	**How** did he see them?
				Who did he see with her?**
	Yes or No?	↻	**Is** he a doctor?	**Did** he see them?

*The term **object** is used here, but with the verb **to be**, it's technically a *complement*.
Whom is the grammatically correct term, but it's not often heard in conversation.
With whom did he see her? would sound awkward and stilted in everyday speech.

Some or *Any*

Some is used in a positive sentence, and **any** is used with negatives, questions, or in a very broad sense.

Thing	Place	Person	
anything	anywhere	anyone	
something	somewhere	someone	**+ else**
nothing	nowhere	no one	
everything	everywhere	everyone	
What else?	**Where else?**	**Who else?**	
Time	Way	Reason	
When else?	**How else?**	**Why else?**	

Something else = another thing
Somewhere else = another place
Someone else = another person

Exercise 7-13: Something Else

*Change the **bold words** to an **else** phrase. Then check the Answer Key.*

1. I saw **another person**.

2. There was **no other thing** there.

3. **At what other time** could we do it? (wennelse kwee du^(w)it?)

4. **What other person** will be there?

5. We need **all the other things**.

6. Let's go **to another place**.

7. **For what other reason** would he do it?

8. They can't go **to any other place**.

9. Do you know **all the other people**?

10. **In what other way** can we do it?

11. **Every other place** is full.

12. Give it to **another person**.

13. Will there be **any more things** needed?

14. I can't find it **in any other place**.

15. **Another person** must have taken it.

Time Words

	Before **Ago**	Now **For**	Later **In**
Hour	an **hour** ago	for an **hour**	in an **hour**
Day	yesterday	today	tomorrow
Week	last **week**	this **week**	next **week**
Month	last **month**	this **month**	next **month**
Year	last **year**	this **year**	next **year**
Time	**last** time	**this** time	**next** time

Exercise 7-14: *Ago / For / In*

*Fill in the blank with **ago**, **for**, or **in**. Then check the Answer Key.*

It's six o'clock now. I'll eat dinner _____ an hour, at seven o'clock. I was supposed to meet Tom an hour _____ at five o'clock, but he wasn't there. I waited _____ fifteen minutes, (from 5:00 to 5:15) and then I had to leave without him. He'll probably call me _____ a couple of minutes, at 6:15.

During or *While*

During + Noun
We talked **during** lunch.
He thought of it **during** the meeting.

While + Phrase (-ing)
He talked **while** eating.
He talked **while** they were eating lunch.

Exercise 7-15: *During* or *While*

*Fill in the blank with **during** or **while**. Then check the Answer Key.*

1. The **phone** rang _____ I was in the **shower**.
2. We never **see** each other _____ the **week**, only on **week**ends.
3. _____ the **war**, there wasn't enough **food**.
4. I broke my **racket** _____ I was teaching my **friend** how to **serve**.
5. My **boss** got sick _____ **lunch** and had to go **home**.
6. It's not polite to **interrupt** _____ someone is **talking**.
7. What kind of places did you **visit** _____ you were in **Mexico**?
8. _____ the **discussion**, I realized that I didn't under**stand** him at **all**.
9. What do you **do** _____ the **day**?
10. It is easy to make **mistakes** _____ learning something **new**.
11. _____ you're at the **store**, could you get some bread and **milk**, please?
12. Most of the **damage** happened _____ the **storm**.
13. _____ my **first** year of **high** school, I read over forty **books**.
14. It was **good** _____ it **lasted**.
15. The **quarter**back was **tackled** _____ he was **running** for a **touch**down.
16. I can't **believe** you left _____ he was still **talking**!
17. Don't talk _____ the **micr**ophone is on — the audience can **hear** you.
18. It started **raining** _____ I was walking **home** yesterday.
19. The **baby** never cries _____ the **night**.
20. You can't **talk** _____ a **test**.

Deadlines and Boundaries

I will work **until** 8:00 and then stop. (up to, but no later than)
I will be back **by** 6:00. (before, a time window)
I will be back **at** 6:00. (right at 6:00)

Exercise 7-16: *By / Until*

*Fill in the blank with **by** or **until**. Then check the Answer Key.*

1. I **waited** for him at the station _____ five **o'clock**.
2. I finished **reading** the re**port** _____ two **thirty**.
3. We **talked** _____ midnight.
4. The **work** was so **tiring** that we were **exhausted** _____ **noon**.
5. The job was **tiring**, but we kept **working** _____ **five**.
6. Will you be done_____ the time I get back?
7. The **teacher** kept **explaining** _____ everyone **understood**.
8. _____ the **time** we got to the **meeting**, everyone **else** was **gone**.

9. We kept looking _____ we found it.
10. _____ **Christmas**, I'll have saved **five** hundred **dollars**.
11. The **chairman** of the **meeting** spoke _____ he was **hoarse**.
12. You can **think** about it, but I need to **know** _____ **Monday**, and no **later**.
13. We can **study** _____ **ten**, but **then** we have to go to **bed**.
14. We have to start **studying** _____ **six**.
15. She **waited** _____ she was the **last** person **there**, and then **she** went home, **too**.

For	**Since**
Time span, duration.	**A date, a time in the past.**
for 10 minutes, for a year,	since 1965, since last year,
for the rest of my life	since I came to America

Exercise 7-17: *For or Since*

Fill in the blank with for or since. Then check the Answer Key.

1. I've been **waiting** _____ half an **hour**, but no one has **helped** me.
2. **America** has been a **nation** _____ 1776.
3. **America** has been a **nation** _____ more than **200 years**.
4. He is a different **man** _____ he got **married**.
5. My **friend** has been on a **diet** _____ six **months**.
6. We've **known** each other _____ two **years**.
7. He's been in France _____10 **years** now.
8. He's **been** there _____ 1999.
9. I've wanted to **travel** _____ a long **time**.
10. My **boss** has been **happy** ever _____ his **promotion**.

Ago / Before	**In / After / Later**
Ago	**In**
a time + **ago**	**In** + a time in the future
a week **ago**, a minute **ago**	**In** a week, **in** a minute
Before	**After**
Before + time	After + time
Before 1972	After a week, after that
Before + -ing	
Before working	**Later (relative time)**
	Time + later
Before + noun	A week later
Before work	

Exercise 7-18: *Ago / Before / In / After / Later*

Fill in the blank with ago, before, in, after, or later. Then check the Answer Key.

1. The **project** will be **completed** _____ a **month**.
2. It was first **proposed** over a **year** _____.
3. The **staff analyzed** the **cost** _____ **starting**. (They analyzed and then they started.)

4. _____ a **week**, they **realized** that it would be really **expensive**.
5. She graduated in **May**, and a month _____, in **June**, she got **married**.
6. The **day** _____ **Wednesday** is **Thursday**.
7. The **day** _____ **Tuesday** is **Monday**.
8. _____ accepting his **invitation**, she **asked** to meet his **family**.
9. _____ being **promoted**, he worked **harder** than **ever**.
10. Personal **computers** were **introduced** several **years** _____.

Notice the **position** of the words in the chart below. Each one has either a positive or negative meaning.

Yet Up to now, so far	**Yet** is used in negative statements and questions: **He is not here yet.** **Is he here yet?**
Already Previous	**Already** is used in *positive* statements and questions: **He is already here.** **Is he already here?**
Still Continuing	**Still** is used in both positive and negative statements, and questions: **He is still here.** **He still isn't here.** **Is he still here?**
Anymore Discontinued	**Anymore** is used in negative statements: **He isn't here anymore.** **Anymore** is a single word in this case, but it can also be a two-word phrase: **I don't buy books anymore because I don't need any more books.**
No longer Discontinued	**No longer** is used in negative statements. **He is no longer here.** It usually comes in the *middle* of a sentence. **No longer** has the same meaning as **not anymore,** but it's more formal.

Exercise 7-19: *Yet / Already / Still / Anymore*

Fill in the blank with **yet,** **already,** **still,** *or* **anymore.** *Then check the Answer Key.*

1. It isn't time to **go** _____.
2. Have you **finished** _____?
3. We've _____ **seen** that movie.
4. I can't **talk** about it _____.
5. It hasn't stopped **raining** _____, has it? No, it's _____ **raining**.
6. We have _____ finished the **test**.
7. **Polio** used to be **incurable**, but it **isn't** _____.
8. He's **only** had this **umbrella** for a **week**, and it's _____ **broken**.
9. I've studied **French** for ten **years**, but I _____ don't **speak** it well.
10. The **doctor** had **explained** about **lung** problems, but the **patient** _____ **smoked**.

Exercise 7-20: *Yet / Already / Still / Anymore*

*Fill in the blank with **yet**, **already**, **still**, or **anymore**. Then check the Answer Key.*

The **Cubans** and the **Americans** haven't settled their **differences** ____. They are ____ arguing about **communism** and **capitalism**. They've ____ **discussed** it many **times**. **Most people** don't hope for a speedy **resolution** ____ because it has gone **on** for so **long**.

The *present real duo* is used when something from the past connects with the present. This is either through a repeated action, or a continuation of a past action into the present. You can't use words like **later** or **yesterday** with this tense. Words like **ago** and **never** are frequently used, however.

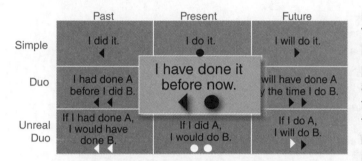

In English, time is important. Verbs tell us when something happened. Verb tenses are like a puzzle. It's important to see how all the pieces fit together, what their relationships are, and how they can change. With the present real duo—a combination of the past and the present—it's like you are pulling the past up into the present.

If you say, **I did A. I also did B**, you should use the *simple past*. However, if you want to relate the past action of A to the present, as in, **I have done A many times before now**, you should use the *present real duo*.

Simple Past	Present Real Duo
Indicates that something is over.	Indicates that the situation is ongoing or there is still some relationship to the past.
You **lived** in L.A. for two years.	You **have lived** in L.A. for two years.
◄	◄●
You don't live in L.A. anymore.	You still live in L.A.

Today is February 28

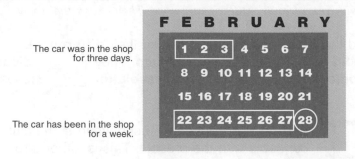

The car was in the shop for three days.

The car has been in the shop for a week.

The car was in the shop for three days, three weeks **ago**. (2/1 to 2/3)
The car has been in the shop **for** a week now. (2/22 until now)

50 Irregular Verbs

be	was / were	**been**	to know	knew	**known**
become	became	**become**	to leave	left	**left**
begin	began	**begun**	to lose	lost	**lost**
break	broke	**broken**	to make	made	**made**
bring	brought	**brought**	to mean	meant	**meant**
catch	caught	**caught**	to meet	met	**met**
choose	chose	**chosen**	to put	put	**put**
come	came	**come**	to read	read	**read**
do	did	**done**	to ride	rode	**ridden**
drink	drank	**drunk**	to run	ran	**run**
drive	drove	**driven**	to say	said	**said**
eat	ate	**eaten**	to see	saw	**seen**
fall	fell	**fallen**	to sell	sold	**sold**
feel	felt	**felt**	to send	sent	**sent**
fight	fought	**fought**	to sit	sat	**sat**
find	found	**found**	to speak	spoke	**spoken**
fly	flew	**flown**	to stand	stood	**stood**
forget	forgot	**forgotten**	to take	took	**taken**
give	gave	**given**	to teach	taught	**taught**
get	got	**gotten**	to tell	told	**told**
go	went	**gone**	to think	thought	**thought**
grow	grew	**grown**	to throw	threw	**thrown**
have	had	**had**	to understand	understood	**understood**
hear	heard	**heard**	to win	won	**won**
hold	held	**held**	to write	wrote	**written**

Exercise 7-21: "Have You Ever Been to Mexico?"

Fill in the blanks with the present duo. Then check the Answer Key.

I _____ (go) to **Mexico** three **times** this year. My **brother** _____ never _____ (be) there. We _____ (talk) about it several **times**, but he _____n't ever _____ (find) the **time** to go. He _____ (be waiting) for a long **time**! We _____ (make) **plans** to go **later** this **year**, but he _____n't _____ (decide) **when**. When we **do** go, it'll be **great**.

Exercise 7-22: "A Has-Been or a Wannabe?"

Fill in the blanks with the present duo. Then check the Answer Key.

America is a good country, but it ____ **(be)** slowly crumbling ever since the Vietnam War. ____ we ____ **(learn)** the lessons of the past? Can we say that we ____ **(provide)** all of our children with a good education? We ____ **(devote)** far, far too much time, energy and money on the military. This country ____ **(arrive)** at a crossroads, and we can either survive and become stronger, or fall by the wayside in global significance.

Earlier in this chapter, you learned several *time words* that can be used with the present duo and the simple past. These key words—**since**, **yet**, **already**—will tell you which tense to use.

Exercise 7-23: Present Duo vs. Simple Past

Fill in the blanks with either the present duo or the simple past. Then check the Answer Key.

1. I ____ here since 1965.	live
2. I ____ here in 1965.	move
3. He ____ to get a better job.	never try
4. When he was 18, he ____ from L.A. to New York.	drive
5. Hey, someone ____ my spot!	take
6. It ____ three times today!	happen
7. They ____ working on your project, but they ____ yet.	start / not finish
8. When they ____, they went home.	finish
9. When they ____, they'll let you know.	finish
10. He ____ hard last week.	work
11. He ____ hard lately.	be working
12. It ____ yesterday.	rain
13. It ____ for a week.	be raining
14. ____ this movie yet?	(you) see
15. You ____ in that chair for three hours!	sit
16. You ____ down with a thud!	sit
17. You ____ that car for 10 years.	drive
18. You ____ like a maniac yesterday.	drive
19. You ____ so much in life in such a short time.	see
20. I ____ you take it.	see

Exercise 7-24: Present Duo vs. Simple Present

Fill in the blanks with either the present duo or the simple present. Then check the Answer Key.

1. You ____ that theater for years.	like
2. I ____ that movie.	like
3. When they ____, they'll let you know.	finish
4. They ____ on time because they are efficient.	finish
5. That lady ____ tomatoes.	grow
6. They ____ in her backyard for 60 years.	grow
7. You ____ this office well for a long time now.	manage

8. I _____ to cope with life.   **manage**
9. You _____ into such a lovely young lady.   **grow**
10. She _____ flowers.   **grow**

The V Sound

People have trouble with the V sound. They either make it sound like a W or a B. The easiest way to get a good V is to start with F. Say **fffffffffffffffffff**. Now, leave everything in exactly the same position—your upper teeth should be almost touching your lower lip—and put your finger on your throat. Make your throat vibrate and say **vvvvvvvvvvvvvvvv**.

Exercise 7-25: *V as in Victory*   CD 2 Track 22

Listen to the audio and repeat five times.

	P	B	F	V	W
1.	Perry	berry	fairy	very	wary
2.	pat	bat	fat	vat	wax
3.	Paul	ball	fall	vault	wall
4.	pig	big	fig	vim	wig
5.	purr	burr	fur	verb	were

There Is or *It Has*

You have learned how to use **have** as well as **there is / there are**. We will now contrast the two forms. With **have**, we need an identified subject, such as **We have**, **They had**, or **I will have**. Frequently, though, the speaker just wants to point out the existence of something by indicating a subject. In this case, use **there + be**. Both forms are correct, but **there is** is more common and colloquial.

There	**Have**
There is a car in the garage.	We have a car in the garage.
There are five people in my family.	I have five people in my family.
There isn't much time left.	We don't have much time left.
There aren't a lot of options for us this time.	We don't have a lot of options this time.
There was a war in 1812.	They had a war in 1812.
There was a big celebration last night.	Someone had a big celebration.
There wasn't enough food for everyone.	People didn't have enough food.
There weren't many people in the store.	The store didn't have many people in it.
There's going to be a party at my house.	We're going to have a party.
There won't be another opportunity.	We won't have another opportunity.
There can't be any noise during the play.	We can't have any noise during the play.

Exercise 7-26: *There or Have*

*Change each **have** sentence to a **there** sentence. Then check the Answer Key.*

I have a lot of books in my room.　　**There are** a lot of books in my room.

1. We don't have enough **time.**

2. We had a lot of exciting **stuff** to **do.**

3. You have no **need** to buy new **clothes. (kloz)**

4. They had no **reason** to arrange the **meeting.**

5. They had many **reasons** to arrange the **meeting.**

6. **Every**one had a lot of **trouble** with the **fax** machine. **(fakss m'sheen)**

7. We had many **hard**working **people** in the **office.**

8. You don't have to go to **work** today.

9. They had a lot of **seals** on the beach.

10. We will have **peace** someday.

11. We didn't have a **class** on **Friday**.

12. That **town** has a lot of **butter**flies.

13. They had a **shirt** on the floor.

14. We had no **need** to **do** that.

15. The **room** had a lot of **balloons.**

There Is or It Is

There + be is used to point out the existence or location of something. **It** is a pronoun, so it replaces a noun. With **it**, you always have to introduce the noun first. If you start out with, **It** was a _____. People will say or think, "**What** was a _____?" **It** is used with weather, time, color, and adjectives.

Weather

It's sunny.	**It's** sprinkling.	**It's** drizzling.	**It's** raining.	**It's** pouring.
It's hot.	**It's** snowing.	**It's** cold.	**It's** stormy.	**It's** humid.
It's clear.	**It's** overcast.	**It's** windy.	**It's** cloudy.	**It's** muggy.
It's icy.	**It's** freezing.	**It's** beautiful.	**It's** foggy.	**It's** smoggy.

Time

It's noon.	**It's** midnight.	**It's** five o'clock.	**It's** early.	**It's** late.
It's Wednesday.	**It's** January.	**It's** winter.	**It's** 2009.	**It's** time to go.

Just because the topic is weather, however, you still need to follow the rules:

There was a storm. It was stormy.

Exercise 7-27: *There* or *It*

*Fill in the blanks with either **there** + **be** or **it** + **be**. Then check the Answer Key.*

1. _____ a small **house** near us. _____ three **trees** in front.
2. _____ a **car**wash near here? Yes, _____ one on **Front** Street.
3. We **wanted** to go to the **beach**, but _____ not enough **time**.
4. _____ time to **go**? No, _____ still **early**.
5. _____ an **ocean** between the U.**S.** and **Europe**.
6. A few **days** ago, _____ a **storm**. _____ terrible. _____ a lot of **damage**. There _____ a lot of **injuries**.
7. _____ **eight** colors in the **rain**bow.
   (Roy G. Biv is a mnemonic device for the colors: red, orange, yellow, green, blue, indigo, violet.)
8. Last **winter**, _____ very **cold**. _____ a lot of **snow**. _____ **snowy**.
9. After the **lecture** tomorrow, _____ an **opportunity** to ask **questions**.
10. _____ **no** need to get dressed **up**. We're **just** going to the **donut** shop.
11. They live on a busy **street**. _____ a lot of **noise** from the **traffic**.
12. _____ three **4**s in **twelve**.
13. _____ an **accident** in **Venice** yesterday, but _____n't **serious** and _____n't any **injuries**.
14. Where is the **car**? She said that _____ over **there**.
15. _____ many **people** there tomorrow.
16. We're **bored**. _____ nothing to **do** in this place. _____ **boring**.
17. I **hope** that _____ someone to meet me at the airport tomorrow.
18. I was **hoping** that _____ someone to meet me at the **air**port, but _____n't anyone **there**.
19. _____ too much **pressure** on us last year.
20. He doesn't **like** where he **lives** because _____ **better** to be **closer** to **work**.
21. _____ my **birth**day yesterday.
22. _____ a **museum** there, but it burned **down**. (**myoozím**)
23. I **wish** _____ n't **raining**. I **wish** _____ n't so much **rain** here. I **wish** _____ n't so **rainy** here in Seattle.
24. Do you think _____ a better **way** to **do** this?
25. Do you think _____ a long **way** from **Rome** to **Madrid**?
26. How far _____ from **Rome** to **Madrid**?
27. _____ **nice** to live in a **cabin** in the **mountains**.
28. _____ used to be a **theater** on **First** Street, but it closed a few **months** ago. (munts)
29. That **building** is now a **super**market. _____ used to be a **theater**.
   (It's the same building, converted to a supermarket.)
30. That **building** is a **super**market. _____ used to be a **theater** there.
   (It's a different building in the same location.)
31. I wanted to visit the **museum**, but _____ n't enough **time**.
32. _____ time to **leave**?
33. _____ anything on **TV** early in the **morning**.
34. _____ **trouble** at the **game** last night. They had to **cancel** it **because** of that.
35. The **room** was completely **empty**. _____ n't anything **there**.
36. Look in the desk **drawer**, _____ some **paper** clips there.

Verb Review

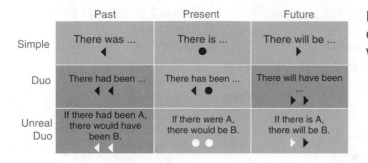

	Past	Present	Future
Simple	There was ... ◀	There is ... ●	There will be ... ▶
Duo	There had been ... ◀ ◀	There has been ... ◀ ●	There will have been ... ▶ ▶
Unreal Duo	If there had been A, there would have been B. ◀ ◀	If there were A, there would be B. ● ●	If there is A, there will be B. ▶ ▶

Here is a comprehensive review of various verb tenses, opinion words, and tag endings.

Facts

	There is / are	Present fact
100%	There was / were	Past fact
	There will be	Future fact
	There has / have been	Present fact
	There had been	Past fact
	There will have been	Future fact

Opinions and Obligations

	There had better be	Obligation or warning
90%	There must be, has to be	Strong probability, strong obligation
	There must have been	Strong probability
	There had to be	Strong probability
	There should be	Present probability, obligation, opinion, advice, suggestion
75%	There should have been	Past probability, obligation, opinion, advice, suggestion
50%	There may / might be	Present possibility
	There might have been	Past possibility
25%	There could be	Present slight possibility
	There could have been	Past slight possibility
	If there were, there would be . . .	Present unreal
0%	If there had been, There would have been . . .	Past unreal
	If there is, there will be . . .	Future unreal

Exercise 7-28: Verb Review

*Using the previous page as a guide, select the proper verb. Be mindful of the difference between **strong** and **weak possibilities** and **probabilities**. Fill in the blank with **is, was, were, will be, has been, have been, had been, may be, might be, should be, could be, must be, would be, will have been, may have been, must have been, should have been, would have been**, or **could have been**. Then check the Answer Key.*

1. There _____ a good **chance** that it will **rain** tomorrow. Present fact
2. There _____ an **earth**quake in **Tokyo** yesterday. Past fact
3. There _____ a lot of **problems** with the **fax** lately. Present duo fact
4. The **news**paper says that there _____ a **storm** next week. Future fact
5. They're not **sure**, but there _____ a **tornado**, too. Present or future possibility

6. My **brother** thinks that there _____ a **soda** machine in every **class**room.   Opinion

7. **Otherwise**, there _____ some thirsty **people**.   Present or future slight possibility

8. There _____ a better **way** to lose **weight**!   Present strong opinion
9. There _____ more **time** if everyone **got** here **earlier**.   Present unreal
10. By **this** time next **year**, there _____ 25 **births**.   Future duo fact
11. The re**port** wasn't clear, but there _____ a **problem** with the **phone**.   Past possibility

12. Before we had **cars**, there _____ a lot of **horses**.   Past strong probability
13. My **parents** think that there _____ more **home**work last year.   Past opinion

14. If **Bob** hadn't forgotten the **map**, there wouldn't _____ any **problems**.   Past unreal

15. It was **dangerous** to **drive** so fast; there _____ an **accident**.   Past slight possibility

16. **Joe** didn't know that there _____ an **earth**quake.   Past duo
17. Sam's **letter** said that if there _____ any **trouble**, he'd come right **back**.   Reported speech

18. The **guests** _____ **chatting** prior to the **interruption**.   Past duo
19. The **president** _____ **persuasive**, since **everyone** agreed to **try** it.   Past strong probability

20. If **I** _____ you, there _____ an **investigation**.   Present unreal

---

Exercise 7-29: Change to the Past

Rewrite each sentence, changing the verb to the past tense. Then check the Answer Key.

I should ask him about his plans. **I should have asked** him about his plans.

1. He must be able to think quickly. (probability)

2. He must be able to think quickly. (obligation)

3. It might be better to wait for them.

4. He says that they shouldn't go. (change both verbs)

5. If they take my car, they won't have to wait for the bus.

6. If they took my car, they wouldn't have to wait for the bus.

7. You can go home at five today. (ability)

8. He isn't supposed to take Jim's car without asking.

9. They say that they will be here until next week.

10. Al may use your car for the rest of the week. (possibility)

11.Al may use your car for the rest of the week. (permission)

12. I wish I knew what he wanted.

13. He knows what he's doing.

14. I forget why we did it.

Exercise 7-30: Tag Endings

Fill in the blank with the proper tag ending. Then check Answer Key.

1. The new clerk is very slow, ?
2. But he can improve, ?
3. She doesn't type very well, ?
4. They lost their way, ?
5. You don't think so, ?
6. I don't think it's easy, ?
7. I'm your friend, ?
8. You won't be coming, ?
9. He keeps the books, ?
10. You couldn't tell, ?
11. We have to close the office, ?
12. We have closed the office, ?
13. We had to close the office, ?
14. We had the office closed, ?
15. We had already closed the office, ?
16. We'd better close the office, ?
17. The office has closed, ?
18. The office is closed, ?
19. The office will be closed, ?
20. The office has been closed, ?
21. You'll be working late tonight, ?
22. We've done our best, ?
23. He should have been here by now, ?
24. He should be promoted, ?
25. I didn't send the fax, ?
26. I won't get a raise this year, ?
27. You use the computer, ?
28. You're used to the computer, ?
29. You used to use the computer, ?
30. I can use the phone, ?
31. We don't have to fill in all these forms, ?
32. They have all kinds of trouble with their computer, ?
33. He'd rather work overtime, ?
34. You never used to work Saturdays, ?
35. That wouldn't be possible, ?
36. The police have never done that, ?

37. I'd better get going,   ?
38. That's better,   ?
39. They didn't have to buy them all,   ?
40. They would reschedule,   ?

Remember: **Am I not** is not standard.

Turn

Turn usually indicates some kind of change.

Verb	Meaning	Verb	Meaning
turn into something	change or become	turn up	increase the volume
turn out well	succeed	turn up	appear
turn out badly	fail	turn down	decrease the volume
turn out to be	be other than supposed	turn down	refuse or reject
turn over / turnover	flip / employee hiring cycle	turn up	find or discover
turn 25	become that age	a turning point	a directional change
		turn around	change directions 180°

<hr/>

Exercise 7-31: *Turn*

Fill in the blank with the appropriate preposition. Then check the Answer Key.

1. When the project was first introduced, no one had any idea that it would turn _____ so well. **(succeed)**

2. Although he wanted the promotion, he turned it _____ because it would have meant moving again. **(refused or rejected)**

3. During the hectic reorganization of the office, many files were mislaid and who knows when or where they'll turn _____ again. **(appear)**

4. At the time, everyone involved thought it would be a good idea, but it turned _____ to be a disaster. **(other than supposed)**

5. At first, the tracking system was more of a nuisance, but over the years, it turned _____ one of the wisest investments the company ever made. **(change or become)**

6. I love that song! Turn it _____! **(increase the volume)**

7. We all thought he was lazy but he turned _____ to be the hardest worker of us all. **(be other than supposed)**

8. I can't believe that my brother has turned _____. **(become the age of 30)**

9. It's a sign of bad management to have such high _____. **(employee hiring cycle)**

10. When you're finished with the test, turn your papers _____. **(flip)**

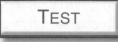

TEST Let's review everything you have learned in Chapter 7. Check your work using the Answer Key. Make sure you get 100% on the test before going on to the next chapter.

Part 1: Select the proper form.

1. He's the person _____ created the infrastructure. who/whose/that/what
2. That's the idea _____ changed everyone's way of thinking. who/whose/that/what
3. I'm not sure _____ idea that was. who/whose/that/what
4. This is not _____ I wanted! who/whose/that/what
5. I hope it _____ work out. will/is/was/were
6. I wish it _____ possible. will/is/was/were
7. If there _____ time right now, we would take care of it. is/were/had been
8. If there _____ time tomorrow, we will take care of it. is/were/had been
9. If there _____ time yesterday, we would have taken care of it. is/were/had been
10. You _____ there yesterday. should be/should have been
11. When I was young, I _____ well. could dance/could have danced
12. I'm sorry you had to walk. You _____ me. could call/could have called

Part 2: Fill in the proper tag ending.

1. We have to finish quickly, ?
2. They had to redo it, ?
3. She has been there before, ?
4. They had never acted like that before, ?
5. The school will be closed Thursday, ?
6. She has good grades, ?
7. He had better think about it, ?
8. They'd rather play, ?

Part 3: Select the proper form.

1. He enlisted in the army two years _____. for/ago/in
2. He's been in the army _____ two years now. for/ago/in
3. He'll be getting out _____ a couple of days. for/ago/in
4. They thought it over _____ the meeting. during/while
5. We chatted amiably _____ the intermission. during/while
6. _____ you're up, could you get me a glass of water? during/while
7. What do you do _____ the day? during/while
8. It's not safe to talk on the phone _____ driving. during/while
9. We plan on working _____ 10:00. by/until
10. We need to start _____ 7:00. by/until
11. They have been here _____ ten years. for/since
12. They have been here _____ 2001. for/since
13. Let me call you back _____ a couple of minutes, OK? in/after
14. He had to take another call, but he called me back _____ a few minutes. in/after
15. Have you finished _____? yet/already/still/anymore

16. They have _____ finished.   yet/already/still/anymore
17. The others are _____ working on it. (continuing)   yet/already/still/anymore
18. We don't want to do this _____.   yet/already/still/anymore

Part 4: *Change from the simple present to the present duo.*

1. I watch TV.

2. They do the dishes.

3. People make mistakes.

4. Things fall in an earthquake.

5. The situation gets better.

6. The shredder tears the paper.

7. The children are well behaved.

8. The competitors bring their own gear.

9. The cats drink the milk.

10. Dennis broke his leg.

Part 5: *Change from the simple past to the present duo.*

1. Everyone saw that movie.

2. Joe stole the books.

3. Louise took the test.

4. The teacher chose the participants.

5. The idea became more popular.

6. The students learned the lessons.

7. His parents were informed of the decision.

8. The CEO was thinking about it.

9. Many people forgot to answer.

10. The horses ate the hay.

Part 6: *Choose either the simple past or the present real duo.*

1. He _____ about it many times before today.
   ☐ thought
   ☐ has thought

2. Jennie _____ it two years ago.
   ☐ bought
   ☐ has bought

3. We _____ to the mall this morning.
   ☐ drove
   ☐ have driven

4. I _____ such a thing in my life.
   ☐ never saw
   ☐ have never seen

5. Our friends _____ about it again last night.
   ☐ talked
   ☐ have talked

6. Until now, _____ a good deal of discretion.
   ☐ they always used
   ☐ they've always used

7. Do you think he _____ his homework yet?
   ☐ did
   ☐ has done

8. The dogs _____ all day yesterday.
   ☐ barked
   ☐ have barked

9. Have you ever _____ to the races before?
   ☐ went
   ☐ gone

10. I think he _____ home.
    ☐ already went
    ☐ has already gone

11. He _____ about it all of the time.
    ☐ thinks
    ☐ has thought

12. He _____ about it for years.
    ☐ thinks
    ☐ has thought

13. We _____ to start studying now.
    ☐ need
    ☐ have needed

14. We _____ to start studying for quite some time now.
    ☐ need
    ☐ have needed

15. Jennie _____ there in 1968.
    ☐ lived
    ☐ has lived

16. Jennie _____ there since 1968.
    ☐ lived
    ☐ has lived

17. The janitor _____ in Fresno until December.
    ☐ worked
    ☐ has worked

18. The janitor _____ here for the past three months.
    ☐ worked
    ☐ has worked

 Using what you have learned, write two paragraphs on the following topics:

1. What one indulgence would you enjoy if there were no consequences?
2. If you could change one law, what would that be?

You can handwrite your paragraphs below or e-mail them to **para@grammar.bz** to be stored. These paragraphs are not graded or reviewed, but simply by writing them, your English will improve.

Student Paragraph									
Send	Chat	Attach	Address	Fonts	Colors	Save As Draft		Photo Browser	Show Stationery

To: para@grammar.bz

Cc:

Bcc:

Subject: Chapter 7

Signature: Corporate

My name is _____

Chapter 8: Complex Intonation, the Past Unreal Duo, and the Causative

In this chapter we'll review common courtesy, as well as direct and indirect questions. We have worked with **how** (in terms of how many times), and now we will look at it from the perspective of *extent* and *dimensions*. We have also worked with prepositions of location and direction, as well as with phrasal verbs. Here, we'll examine a variety of verbs with **to**, **for**, **of**, **about**, **on**, **with**, and **from**.

> DICTATION

For verbs, we will learn the *past unreal duo* and the *causative* (**let, have, get, make, force, allow, permit, persuade, convince**).

Exercise 8-1: Dictation   CD 2 Track 23

Listen to the audio and write the exact transcription in the spaces below. Then check the Answer Key.

1. _____

2. _____

3. _____

4. _____

5. _____

The Flower Incident

> STORY

My **girl**friend, **Eve**, sometimes gets **jealous**. I **tell** her that I'm too **busy** and too **tired** to be looking at other **women**, but she doesn't **trust** me. **One** time, as a **joke** to teach her a **lesson**, I ordered a **big** bouquet of **flowers** and **had** a girl **sign** them, "Love, **Sabrina**." I **had** them delivered to my house. When Eve came **home**, she **saw** them and **asked** me who had given me **flowers**. I just **shrugged**, so she looked at the **card**. When she saw "**Sabrina**," she was really **mad**. I **laughed** a lot, but she **made** me apologize and **had** me give the flowers **away**. She didn't **let** me **near** her for the rest of the **day**. Bit by **bit**, she's gently **forcing** me to be a better **person** by not **allowing** that kind of **behavior**. She's been trying to **get** me to **change** for a long **time**.

Exercise 8-2: "The Flower Incident" — Pronunciation   CD 2 Track 24

Listen to the audio and repeat, focusing on intonation and pronunciation.

My **girl**friend, **Eve**, səmtymz gets **jellǝs**. I **tell**er the dime too **bizzy** and too **tired** t' be looking at other **wimmen**, bǝt she doesn't **trǝst** me. **One** time, ezza **joke** t' teacher ǝ **lessǝn**, I order dǝ **big** bokay ǝv **flowerz** and hadǝ girl **syn**em, "Luv, **S'breena**." I had them d'liverd to my house. Wheneev came **home**, she **säh** em and **askt** me who h'd given me **flowerz**. I jǝst **shrugd**, so she lükt at the **cärd**. When she säh "**S'breena**," she wǝz rilly **mäd**. I **læfft** ǝ lät, but she made me ǝpälǝgize and had me give the flowers **away**. She didn't let me **near** her fr the restǝv the **day**. Bit by **bit**, she's gently forcing me to be a better **person** by not allowing that kind of behavior. She's been trying to get me to **change** for a long **time**.

| NOUNS |

This is an important section because you will learn how to show appreciation, ask for a favor, apologize, and ask for an apology, as well as review how to ask questions, both *directly* and *indirectly*.

Common Courtesy

The social graces are largely the same in every culture, but the terminology is quite specific to each language.

Appreciation

There are several ways to show appreciation, such as a direct **Thank you!** or **Thank you very much. Thanks!** is more casual, as is **Thanks a lot!** To be more specific, you can add **for –ing**, such as **Thank you for helping me with this**. You can add expressions such as **That was really nice of you**, **I really appreciate it**, **You've been very helpful**, **I appreciate your consideration / kindness / support / help / cooperation**. You can also use a short phrase such as **Thanks for the ride!** Sometimes people will show general appreciation with **Thank goodness!**

Acknowledging Appreciation

The most common acknowledgement is **You're welcome**. You'll also hear **Sure!**, **No problem**, **No prob**, **My pleasure**, **I was glad to help**, **That's OK**, or **Any time!** You can also say, **Thank *you*!** with the emphasis on **you**.

Giving Praise

When you want to let someone know that you are pleased with the effort, you can say **Excellent work!** or **Good job!** or **Nice report!**

Invitations

Would you like to get together for coffee?
Would you like to get together some time?
Would you like to come visit?
If you're ever in the neighborhood, feel free to drop by.
We're having a party on Saturday; would you like to come?
Would you like to be part of our study group?
Would you like to join us for lunch some time?

Phone Terminology

If someone has mis-dialed, you say **I think you have the wrong number**. If you can't hear a person due to phone static, say **You're breaking up. Could you say that again?** Or, **Pardon me, I can't hear you.** If you hear another phone ring on their end, you can say, **Do you need to get that?**

Asking a Favor

Could you do me a favor?
Would you please open the window?
Would you mind opening the window?
Would you mind if I opened the window?
May I open the window?
Could you help me with this, please?
It would mean so much to me if you could _____.
Could you give me a ride to _____?
Excuse me, can I get by?
Would it be possible to _____?
Excuse me, where's the restroom?
Could you lend me _____?
Could I borrow _____?
Could you help me out with _____?
Could you explain _____?
Could you let me know when _____?

Apologizing

Sad to say, the time comes when we all need to apologize. As soon as you realize that you have hurt someone's feelings, insulted someone, forgotten to do something, broken something, or committed some other social error, the best apology is direct and heartfelt. **I'd like to apologize for what happened the other day. I'm sorry I was so rude / so late. I shouldn't have done that / been late. There is no excuse for it and it won't happen again.** One thing you want to avoid is saying, **Sorry, but . . .** , which is not a real apology.

There are lighter ways to express regret or to acknowledge a mistake, such as **Sorry I'm late!** or **Excuse me for stepping on your foot. Pardon me** is a bit more formal than **Excuse me** and is sometimes used ironically or sarcastically. It's also used to have someone repeat something. Of course, as we all know, the real apology is not doing it again.

Not Accepting an Apology

There are times when the offender's behavior is so egregious or so often repeated that it is simply not in your best interest to accept the apology, no matter how it is offered. At this point, you can say **I'm sorry, but I simply can't forgive you for what you have done**, or **I'm sorry, I can't excuse this behavior yet again.** Or **I can't accept your apology. What you did was wrong and you should have known better.**

You can give yourself a little breathing room by saying something along the lines of **I have given this a great deal of thought, and discussed it with others. What you did was hurtful and I need to take some time to get some perspective on this.**

Requesting an Apology

Ideally, we all learn manners by the age of six or seven, but there are times when someone has offended or insulted you, lied, cheated, stood you up, or broken something, and you need to let him or her know how you feel. You can say **I am upset that you said that. I'd like an apology.** Or **That was uncalled for. I think you should apologize**, or **I think you owe me an apology.**

Accepting an Apology

Even if the apology is hollow or poorly delivered, you can graciously accept by saying, **Thank you, I appreciate your apology.** If the person seems sincerely contrite, you can say **Thank you, I accept your apology and we can put this behind us.**

Intonation and Attitude

There are certain sounds in any language that are considered nonsense syllables yet impart a large amount of information to the informed listener. Each language has a different set of these sounds, such as **eto ne** in Japanese, **em** in Spanish, **eu** in French, and **um** in English. These are the sounds that a native speaker makes when he is thinking out loud—holding the floor, but not yet committing to actually speaking.

Exercise 8-3: Intonation of Empathy — CD 2 Track 25

These are very common sounds. They can be nasalized or not, and said with the mouth open or closed. Intonation is the most important point. Listen and repeat.

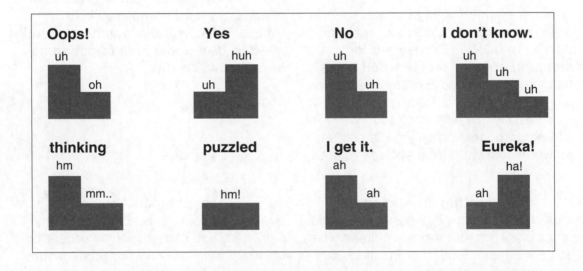

Oops! uh / oh

Yes huh / uh

No uh / uh

I don't know. uh / uh / uh

thinking hm / mm..

puzzled hm!

I get it. ah / ah

Eureka! ha! / ah

L and R

Let's start with L because it's easy, especially at the beginning of a word. Say **la-la-la**. Feel the tip of your tongue on the bumps behind your top teeth. The secret to the L is that you must always touch your tongue to these bumps. Where people run into trouble is at the end of a word, like **call** or **well**. They end up sounding like **caw** or **weo**. There are a couple of ways to deal with this. First, you can use word connections. For example, if you put a word starting with a vowel right after the final L, you can then make the L into the beginning letter of the second word. **Call Ann** becomes **cäh länn**, instead of **caw ænn**.

The second trick is to add a little schwa just before and after the L. Putting all of those words on a staircase will show just how many extra sounds you have to put in to make it "sound right." For example, if you were to pronounce **fail** as [fal], the sound is too abbreviated for the American ear—we need to hear the full [fayələ].

Exercise 8-4: Final L with Schwas   CD 2 Track 26

Listen and repeat. Do not round your lips for a final L.

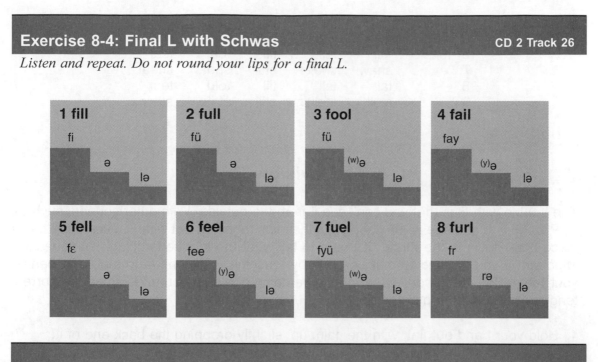

Exercise 8-5: Comparing L with T, D, and N Sounds

For this exercise, concentrate on the different ways in which the air comes out of the mouth when producing L, T, D, and N sounds. Look at the drawings to see the correct position of the tongue.

T/D **Plosive** A puff of air comes out over the tip of the tongue. The tongue is somewhat tense.	
	N **Nasal** Air comes out through the nose. The tongue is completely relaxed.
L **Lateral** Air flows around the sides of the tongue. The tongue is very tense. The lips are *not* rounded!	

Exercise 8-6: L Combos   CD 2 Track 27

Don't think about spelling. Listen and repeat.

	ərəl	äl	ɛl	il	ol	eel
1.	Earl	all	ell	ill	old	eel
2.	curl	call	kell	kill	cold	keel
3.	hurl	hall	hell	hill	hole	heel

181

4. pearl	Paul	pell	pill	pole	peel
5. world	wall	well	will		we're
6. furl	fall	fell	fill	foal	fear
7.	shawl	shell	shill	shoal	shear
8.	tall	tell	till	told	tear
9.	stall	stellar	still	stole	steer

The Invisible R

The trouble with R is that you can't see it from the outside. With other sounds, such as B, P, or M, you can see when people put their lips together, but with R, everything takes place back down in the throat. It's hard to tell what the tongue is doing. It's especially important if you're used to making an R by touching your tongue to the ridge behind your teeth. So, what *should* your tongue be doing? To help you understand the correct tongue movements in pronouncing the R, use your hand.

1. Hold your hand out flat, with the palm up, slightly dropping the back end of it. That's basically the position your tongue is in when you say **ah** [ä], so your flat hand will represent this sound.

2. Now, to go from **ah** to **er**, take your fingers and curl them up slightly. Again, your tongue should follow that action. The sides of your tongue should come up a bit, too. When the air passes over that hollow in the middle of your tongue (look at the palm of your hand), that's what creates the **er** sound.

Try it using both your hand and tongue simultaneously. Say **ah**, with your throat open (and your hand flat), then curl your tongue up (and your fingers) and say **errr**. The tip of the tongue should be aimed at a middle position in the mouth, but never touching, and your throat should relax and expand. R, like L, has a slight schwa in it. This is what pulls the **er** down so far back in your throat.

Exercise 8-7: R Combos CD 2 Track 28

Don't think about spelling. Listen and repeat.

	ər	är	ɛr	or	eer	æwr
1.	earn	art	air	or	ear	hour
2.	heard	hard	hair	horse	here	how're
3.	pert	part	pair	pour	peer	power
4.	word		where	war	we're	
5.	first	far	fair	four	fear	flower
6.	rather	cathartic	there	Thor	theory	11th hour
7.	sure	sharp	share	shore	shear	shower
8.	churn	char	chair	chore	cheer	chowder
9.	turn	tar	tear	tore	tear	tower
10.	stir	star	stair	store	steer	

Complex Intonation

Exercise 8-8: Descriptions and Compound Nouns — CD 2 Track 29

To review, an adjective and noun make a description, and the second word is stressed. Two nouns make a compound noun, and the first word is stressed. Listen and repeat.

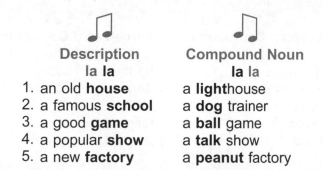

Description	Compound Noun
la **la**	**la** la
1. an old **house**	a **light**house
2. a famous **school**	a **dog** trainer
3. a good **game**	a **ball** game
4. a popular **show**	a **talk** show
5. a new **factory**	a **peanut** factory

Three-Word Phrases

Exercise 8-9: Modifying Descriptions — CD 2 Track 30

*When you modify a **descriptive phrase** by adding an adjective or adverb, keep the original intonation pattern and add another stress point. Listen and repeat.*

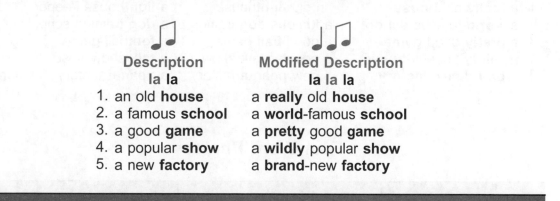

Description	Modified Description
la **la**	la la **la**
1. an old **house**	a **really** old **house**
2. a famous **school**	a **world**-famous **school**
3. a good **game**	a **pretty** good **game**
4. a popular **show**	a **wildly** popular **show**
5. a new **factory**	a **brand**-new **factory**

Exercise 8-10: Modifying Compounds — CD 2 Track 31

*When you modify a **compound noun,** keep the same pattern, leaving the new adjective unstressed. Listen and repeat.*

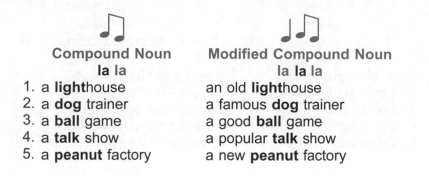

Compound Noun	Modified Compound Noun
la la	la **la** la
1. a **light**house	an old **light**house
2. a **dog** trainer	a famous **dog** trainer
3. a **ball** game	a good **ball** game
4. a **talk** show	a popular **talk** show
5. a **peanut** factory	a new **peanut** factory

183

Exercise 8-11: Three-Word Compound Nouns   CD 2 Track 32

*The next step is to combine **three things:** Light + house + keeper. Leave the stress on the first word:* **ligh**thouse keeper. *Although you are now using three words, they still mean **one new thing**. Listen and repeat.*

Two-Word Compound **la la**	Three-Word Compound **la la la**
1. a **ligh**thouse	a **ligh**thouse keeper
2. a **dog** trainer	a **dog** training school
3. a **ball** game	a **foot**ball game
4. a **talk** show	a **talk** show host
5. a **peanut** factory	a **peanut** factory violation

Exercise 8-12: Three-Word Phrase Summary   CD 2 Track 33

Listen and repeat.

Modified Description **la la la**	Modified Compound **la la la**	Three-Word Compound **la la la**
1. a **really** old **house**	an old **ligh**thouse	a **ligh**thouse keeper
2. a **world**-famous **school**	a famous **dog** trainer	a **dog** training school
3. a **pretty** good **game**	a good **ball** game	a **foot**ball game
4. a **wildly** popular **show**	a popular **talk** show	a **talk** show host
5. a **brand**-new **factory**	a new **peanut** factory	a **peanut** factory violation

Four-Word Phrases

Exercise 8-13: Multiple Modifiers with Compound Nouns   CD 2 Track 34

When you continue to modify a compound noun, keep the original intonation pattern and add another stress point. Listen and repeat.

Modified Compound **la la la**	Double Modified Compound **la la la la**
1. an old **ligh**thouse	a **really** old **ligh**thouse
2. a famous **dog** trainer	a **world**-famous **dog** trainer
3. a good **ball** game	a **pretty** good **ball** game
4. a popular **talk** show	a **wildly** popular **talk** show
5. a new **peanut** factory	a **brand**-new **peanut** factory

Exercise 8-14: Modifying Three-Word Compound Nouns   CD 2 Track 35

When you continue to modify a set phrase, you maintain the original intonation pattern and simply add an unstressed modifier.

Three-Word Compound la la la	Modified Three-Word Compound la la la la
1. a **light**house keeper	an old **light**house keeper
2. a **dog**-training school	a famous **dog**-training school
3. a **foot**ball game	a good **foot**ball game
4. a **talk** show host	a famous **talk** show host
5. a **peanut** factory violation	a new **peanut** factory violation

Exercise 8-15: Building Up to Five-Word Phrases   CD 2 Track 36

Listen and repeat.

1. It's a **pot**.	*noun*
2. It's **new**.	*adjective*
3. It's a new **pot**.	*description (noun)*
4. It's brand **new**.	*description (adjective)*
5. It's a **brand**-new **pot**.	*modified description*
6. It's a **tea**pot.	*two-word compound*
7. It's a new **tea**pot.	*modified compound*
8. It's a **brand**-new **tea**pot.	*modified compound*
9. It's a **tea**pot lid.	*three-word compound*
10. It's a new **tea**pot lid.	*modified three-word compound*
11. It's a **brand**-new **tea**pot lid.	*modified three-word compound*

1. It's a **house**.	It's a **school**.
2. It's **old**.	It's **famous**.
3. It's an old **house**.	It's a famous **school**.
4. It's really **old**.	It's world-**famous**.
5. It's a **really** old **house**.	It's a **world**-famous **school**.
6. It's a **light**house.	He's a **dog** trainer.
7. It's an old **light**house.	He's a famous **dog** trainer.
8. It's a **really** old **light**house.	He's a **world**-famous **dog** trainer.
9. He's a **light**house keeper.	It's a **dog**-training school.
10. He's an old **light**house keeper.	It's a famous **dog**-training school.
11. He's a **really** old **light**house keeper.	It's a **world**-famous **dog**-training school.

1. It's a **game**.	It's a **show**.
2. It's **good**.	It's **popular**.
3. It's a good **game**.	It's a popular **show**.
4. It's really **good**.	It's really **popular**.
5. It's a **really** good **game**.	It's a **wildly** popular **show**.
6. It's a **ball** game.	It's a **talk** show.

7. It's a good **ball** game.
8. It's a **pretty** good **ball** game.
9. It's a **foot**ball game.
10. It's a good **foot**ball game.
11. It's a **pretty** good **foot**ball game.

It's a popular **talk** show.
It's a **wildly** popular **talk** show.
She's a **talk** show host.
She's a popular **talk** show host.
She's a **wildly** popular **talk** show host.

Exercise 8-16: Intonation of Numbers   CD 2 Track 37

*In short phrases (such as #1 and #2 below), **-teen** can be thought of as a separate word in terms of intonation. In longer phrases, the number + **-teen** becomes one word. Listen and repeat.*

1. How **old** is he?
    He's four**teen**. [for**téen**]
    He's **for**ty. [**fór**dy]

2. How long has it **been**?
    Fourteen **years**.
    Forty **years**.

3. How **old** is he?
    He's **four**teen years **old**.
    He's **for**ty years **old**.

How Long, How Well, How Far, How Big

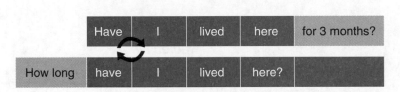

Let's use several **how** questions. They explain *extent*, *duration*, and *dimension*. Between **what** and **how** questions, there are some word-order changes that are important to notice and master.

What is the **distance**?	How **far** is it?
What is the **age**?	How **old** is it?
What is the **price**?	How **much** is it? How much does it cost?
What is the **frequency**?	How **often**? How frequently?
What is the **quantity**? (uncountable)	How **much**?
What is the **quantity**? (countable)	How **many**?
What is the **duration**?	How **long** is it? How long does it last?
What is the **length**?	How **long** is it?
What is the **width**?	How **wide** is it?
What is the **height**?	How **tall** is it?
What is the **thickness**?	How **thick** is it?

How? When? Where? How Often? How Much?

How do I do it?	**When do I do it?**	**How often do I do it?**
I do it **quickly**.	I do it **every day**.	I **always** do it.
I do it **rudely**.	I do it **all of the time**.	I **almost always** do it.
I do it **easily**.	I've **already** done it.	I **usually** do it.
I do it **suddenly**.	I'm doing it **right now**.	I **frequently** do it.
I do it **early**.	I'm doing it **at this time**.	I **generally** do it.
I do it **well**.	I'll do it **later**.	I **often** do it.
I do it **quite well**.	I'll do it **later today**.	I **don't often** do it.
I do it **extremely well**.	I'll do it **then**.	I **hardly ever** do it.
I do it **so well**.	I'll do it **right then**.	I **rarely** do it.
I do it **too well**.	I'll do it **again**.	I **never** do it.
I do it **well enough**.	I'll do it **first**.	I **haven't ever** done it.
I do **such** a good job.	I did it **last**.	I'm **not** doing it.
I do it **much better**.	I'll do it **next**.	I **don't** do it.
I do it **too much**.	I'm only doing it **once**.	
I do it **too many times**.	I **haven't** done it **lately**.	**How much do I do it?**
		(degree)
I do it **often**.	I've done it **recently**.	I **definitely** do it.
I do it **too often**.	I'll do it **when I can**.	I **obviously** do it.
I don't do it **often enough**.	I do it **every so often**.	I **absolutely** insist on doing it.
I do it **right**.	I do it **every once in a while**.	I **totally** forgot to do it.
I do it **just right**.	**Where do I do it?**	I **completely** understand how to do it.
I do it **perfectly**.	I do it **here**.	I don't **exactly** know how to do it.
I do it **alone**.	I do it **there**.	I'll **probably** do it.
I **just** do it.	I do it **everywhere**.	I **barely** do it.

Exercise 8-17: *How* + Adjective

*Convert each statement to a **how** question. Then check the Answer Key.*

The book is 300 pages long.	**How long is it?**

1. That tree is as wide as a building.
2. The car weighs two tons.
3. The notebook has 10 pages.
4. This chair is fairly old.
5. That painting is a million dollars.
6. I brush my hair every morning.
7. She ate three ice cream sandwiches.
8. She ate so much ice cream!
9. This building is 10 stories tall.
10. That meeting was four hours long.

As you've seen, there is a relationship between certain adjectives and the noun form (How **long** is it? What is the **length**?). The next step is to include the verb form. You can do this by adding **–en** to the noun **(lengthen)**.

Exercise 8-18: Nouns to Verbs

Convert each statement from the –en verb to **make** *and an* **adjective**. *Then check the Answer Key.*

We need to shorten this report.

1. Lengthen this dress.
2. It weakened the system.
3. We need to strengthen our industries.
4. Could you tighten this knot?
5. I need to loosen my tie.
6. It only deepened my love for them.
7. It will heighten the suspense.
8. We hope it will lessen the damage.
9. Let's try to broaden its appeal.
10. Try to widen the gap between them.
11. You should thicken the sauce a little.
12. This lamp will brighten the room.
13. Use this to whiten your teeth.
14. Could you darken the room, please?
15. The farmer fattened the turkey.

We need to make this report shorter.

Let's review the relationships between nouns, verbs, and adjectives. As you know, a noun is a person, place, thing, or idea. Verbs are action words. Adjectives modify nouns. The adjective endings are –y, –ed, –able, –ible, –al, –ful, –ic, –ive, –less, –ous, –ent, –ant, etc.

Noun	Adjective	Verb
1. It's a **cloud**.	It's **cloud**y.	It clouded our **judg**ment.
2. It's an a**chiev**ement.	It's a**chiev**able.	We a**chie**ved it.
3. It gave us a big **scare**.	It's **scar**y.	It **scared** us.
4. It has great **beauty**.	It's **beau**tiful.	She beautified the **garden**.
5. It's an at**trac**tion.	It's at**trac**tive.	Honey at**tracts** flies.
6. We took **care**.	He's **care**ful / **care**less.	We **cared** for them.
7. He has a **book**.	He's **book**ish.	He **booked** a flight.
8. We had no **int**erest in it.	It was **int**eresting.	The book **int**erested us.
9. She has **con**fidence.	She is **con**fident.	She con**fid**ed in us.
10. We have **power**.	We are **power**ful.	The sun **powers** our lights.
11. There was con**fus**ion.	I'm con**fus**ed.	It con**fus**ed us.
12. It's an an**im**ation.	It was **an**imated.	Let's **an**imate this a little.
13. We were in **awe**.	It was **awe**some / **aw**ful!	I was awed by the **sight**.
14. It's absolute per**fec**tion.	It was **per**fect.	We want to per**fect** this.
15. It's an a**na**lysis.	He is ana**ly**tic.	Let's **ana**lyze this.
16. What's the **diff**erence?	How is it **diff**erent?	It **diff**ers from the others.
17. Do you have any ad**vice**?	It was ad**vis**ory.	We ad**vise** you not to do it.
18. He has no worries.	He was not worried.	It didn't worry him.
19. We did it with great **ease**.	It was **eas**y.	He **eased** into it.
20 It's a bi**o**graphy.	It's bio**graph**ical.	I wrote a bi**o**graphy.
21. It was an an**noy**ance.	It was an**noy**ing. He was an**noy**ed.	He an**noy**ed us. It an**noy**ed him.
22. It's an image / imagery. He has no imagi**na**tion.	It's **ima**ginary. He's **ima**ginative.	I can't **ima**gine such a thing.

Prepositions

To is the most commonly used preposition. It's usually pronounced **tə** or **də**.

We first saw prepositions of *location* in Chapter 2, prepositions of *direction* in Chapter 3, and prepositions of *manner* and *time* in Chapter 4. We have seen phrasal verbs in every chapter, including **get**, **take**, **put**, **stand**, **give**, and **turn**. We have worked with the infinitive in the high-frequency phrases **want to do**, **like to do**, **have to do**, **need to do**, **try to do**, **hope to do**, and **plan to do**.

add to	Just **add** water **to** this mix!
adjust to	We can't **adjust to** daylight savings time.
agree to	They **agreed to** work on it a little more.
apologize to	Everyone **apologized to** the mayor.
be up to	I don't think he's **up to** the job!
belong to	Does this glove **belong to** you?
get around to	I hope to **get around to** it before long.
get back to	It's time to **get back to** work.
get through to	We couldn't get **through to** him on his cell phone.
get used to	It was hard to **get used to** the cold weather.
happen to	Do you know what **happened to** the car?
introduce to	I'd like to **introduce** you **to** my cousin.
invite someone to	Let's **invite** Susie **to** the party.
lead to	I'm afraid that it will **lead to** more trouble.
listen to	I try not to **listen to** talk radio in the car.
look forward to	We **look forward to** hearing back from you.
object to	I think he **objected to** the general idea, not the specifics.
occur to	It didn't **occur to** him that the others would mind.
prefer A to B	Children generally **prefer** candy **to** vegetables.
refer to	What do you think he was **referring to**?
relate to	It's hard to **relate to** people who are so completely different.
stick to	He's trying to **stick to** his diet.
talk to	Who were you **talking to**?

Note: I **prefer** A to B is the same as I **like** A **better than** B, but it's a bit more formal.

Exercise 8-19: *To*

Fill in the blanks with the words listed below. Then check the Answer Key.

I'd like to _introduce_ you to my cousin, and _invite_ you to our company party. If you _agree_ to do this, you'll be able to _talk_ to a lot of fun people. If you _happen_ to be busy that day, let me know. I'm having trouble _getting used_ to your new schedule! Anyway, I ____ to seeing you there!

love
Susie

happen	**invite**	**agree**	**talk**
getting used	**introduce**	**look forward**	

For

For is also very commonly used in verb + preposition phrases. It's pronounced **fer**.

apologize for	I'd like to **apologize for** my outburst.
apply for	He's **applying for** a new job today.
ask for	What did you **ask for**?
blame someone for	Why did they **blame** him **for** their mistake?
forgive someone for	We need to **forgive** him **for** being so rude.
have a reason for	Do you **have a good reason for** doing that?
keep for	Let's **keep** this **for** later.
listen for	I think they're **listening for** their cue.
look for	What are you **looking for**?
pay for	We have to **pay for** the new supplies one way or another.
prepare for	Nobody was **prepared for** the attack.
provide for	The contract **provides for** all services.
search for	They **searched for** hours, but couldn't find it.
send for	The president **sent for** the ambassador.
substitute for	Margarine is a good **substitute for** butter.
thank someone for	I'd like to **thank** you **for** your support.
vote for	Who did you **vote for**?
wait for	What are you **waiting for**?
wish for	Don't **wish for** the impossible.
work for	They **worked for** that company for 30 years.

Exercise 8-20: *For*

Fill in the blanks with the words listed below. Then check the Answer Key.

Could I _____ you for a favor? I _____ for the inconvenience, but I have a good _____ for asking. I'm _____ for a new apartment and I can't _____ for the real estate agent. I _____ for three apartments, but I wasn't able to get any of them. I wasn't _____ for this, and I'm starting a new job on Monday, so I really hope this _____ for me!

ask	**looking**	**wait**	**applied**
reason	**works out**	**apologize**	**prepared**

Of + About

accuse someone of	Are you **accusing** him **of** lying?
become of	Whatever **became of** Joe Smith?
consist of	The training **consists of** two main parts.
dream of	I **dream of** joining the Peace Corps.
get rid of	Let's **get rid of** these old magazines.
hear of	I've never **heard of** such a thing!
remind someone of	You really **remind** me **of** my sister.
suspect someone of	I **suspect** him **of** taking my notebook.
take advantage of	The bank took **advantage of** the farmer.
take care of	We **took care of** our mother for years.
think of	I can't **think of** anything else. Can you?
argue about	What are they **arguing about** this time?

complain about	Stop **complaining about** everything!
dream about	I **dream about** living in France.
forget about	Don't **forget about** the report that's due.
hear about	Have you **heard about** Bob's new job?
learn about	When did you **learn about** it?
see about	Well, let's **see about** that!
think about	I **think about** it all of the time.
wonder about	We **wonder about** his competence.
worry about	Actually, we **worry about** it a lot.

Of and **about** can be similar.
Remind someone **of** / remind someone **about**
Dream **of** / dream **about**
Hear **of** / hear **about**
Think **of** / think **about**
Learn **of** / learn **about**

Exercise 8-21: *Of* and *About*

Fill in the blanks with the words listed below. Then check the Answer Key.

1. Did you _____ about what happened last week?
2. They _____ your brother of taking someone's wallet!
3. They said he _____ of it, but kept the money. What was he _____ of?
4. It's all we can _____ about! I wonder what will _____ of him.

hear	talk	got rid
thinking	accused	become

On

agree on	Let's **agree on** one thing, OK?
blame something on	Don't try to **blame** that **on** me!
comment on	No one **commented on** the lack of documentation.
compliment someone on	He **complimented** her **on** her excellent work.
congratulate someone on	She **congratulated** him **on** his promotion.
concentrate on	It's hard to **concentrate on** this when it's so noisy.
decide on	We couldn't **decide on** the best way to do it.
depend on	I really **depend on** my support staff.
insist on	He **insisted on** doing it his way.
keep on	Let's **keep** the pressure **on** the competition.
rely on / depend on	Don't **rely on** / **depend on** him. He'll always let you down.
spend money on	Don't **spend** money **on** useless junk.
spend time on	You have **spent** a lot of time **on** that project.
waste money on	We **wasted** a lot of **money on** technical issues.
waste time on	It's a shame to **waste time on** meaningless things.

Exercise 8-22: *On*

Fill in the blanks with the words listed below. Then check the Answer Key.

I'd like to _____ you on your recent promotion. I hear that the bosses _____ on you for the position at the last meeting. As a matter of fact, the CEO _____ on your being selected, and said that future contracts depended on your continued involvement, and that you need to _____ on the big projects. They really _____ on you!

insisted   congratulate   decided   concentrate   rely

With

agree with someone	I couldn't **agree with** you more! I **agree with** you 100%.
argue with someone	Never **argue with** a crazy person.
catch up with	Try to **catch up with** the rest of the group, OK?
communicate with	I've tried, but I just can't **communicate with** him.
compare with	It's a great deal if you **compare** it **with** the others.
deal with	You'll just have to **deal with** it on your own.
get along with	He's very hard to **get along with**.
have patience with	Try to have **patience with** him.

Exercise 8-23: *With*

*Fill in the blanks with **communicating**, **get along**, **agree**, **patience**, **argue**, or **deal**. Then check the Answer Key.*

Have you noticed that the new chef doesn't _____ with the rest of the staff? I think he has a problem _____ with others. Whether you _____ with a person or not, you don't have to _____ with them. He needs to have more _____ with everyone and _____ with them as individuals.

From

borrow from	Could I **borrow** a dollar **from** you? Could you lend me a dollar?
come from	So, where do you **come from**, originally?
get back from	When did you **get back from** Scotland?
keep something from	We can't **keep** this **from** management any longer.
prevent from	You have to **prevent** him **from** making more mistakes.
protect from	You have to **protect** the lawn **from** the freezing weather.
recover from	It's hard to **recover from** such a disaster.
separate from	Let's consider this **separate from** the other issues.
stop from	**Stop** him **from** doing that again!
subtract from	**Subtract** that **from** the total, and add it to the balance.

Exercise 8-24: *From*

*Fill in the blanks with **get back**, **prevent**, **stop**, **recovered**, or **keeping**. Then check the Answer Key.*

So, when did you _____ from your vacation? I hear you had a pretty bad cold at the beginning. Have you _____ from it? It's hard to _____ yourself from getting sick, but it helps to wash your hands a lot. With children, you need to _____ them from touching their faces. Hey, are you still under the weather? Are you _____ something from me?

Exercise 8-25: Preposition Review

*Fill in the blank with **to, for, of, on, with, about, out, at, in, out, than, up,** or **from**. Then check the Answer Key.*

1. Let's agree   disagree.
2. You get what you pay   .
3. We just have to deal   this and move on.
4. He really needs to work   his presentation skills.
5. What are you talking   ?
6. Where did that come   ?
7. We should take care   that problem quickly.
8. It took a while to get used   his style.
9. Let's take advantage   the situation right away.
10. Could you ask the manager   a recommendation?
11. This saddle used to belong   Roy Rogers.
12. We've got to prepare   all possibilities.
13. We've got to get ready   the party.
14. We're looking forward   seeing how well he does.
15. Try comparing these results   the monthly ones.
16. What are you so worried   ?
17. In order to recover   the shock, she had to take a long walk.
18. It's not realistic to object   starting this project.
19. It's important to get along   one's colleagues and co-workers.
20. I happen   think that it wasn't an accident.

21. Don't try		prevent them from trying new things.
22. Let's think		it before making a decision.
23. They prefer actions		meetings.
24. I've been searching		this file for three days now.
25. You need to talk		your friends before making a decision.
26. Not many people agree		the last administration.
27. I think we should apply		a government grant.
28. It could happen		anyone!
29. Let's take care		this, once and for all.
30. It's natural to worry		the future.
31. I'm sorry to have been late		responding.
32. We can't rely		him any more.
33. We have to depend		them for information.
34. They had to start over due		his interference.
35. According		the news, the house burned to the ground.
36. Don't leave		the most important information!
37. I prefer		do it this way.
38. It's hard to deal		his mood swings.
39. What do you think		this?
40. Based		our calculations, we need to order more.
41. She simply didn't agree		his conclusions.
42. We hope to agree		the terms of the contract later this week.
43. He agreed		work harder.
44. Thank you so much		helping us with this.
45. Please take care		this immediately.
46. She forgot		lock the door again.
47. Do you believe		ghosts?
48. We have to get rid		all the old furniture.
49. They have been very kind		me.
50. I'm not good		fixing things.
51. Sugar is not good		you.
52. Look		the picture.
53. Look		the mirror.
54. We are very proud		how well you have done.
55. Are you scared		the dark?
56. A friend of mine called		invite me to the party.
57. I would like		invite you to my house for dinner.
58. The new one is different		the old one.
59. This one is better		the other one.
60. It is similar		the original version.
61. We have to fill		a lot of forms to see a doctor.
62. Please fill		this section of the form.
63. The room filled		quickly.
64. Have you ever heard		Michelangelo?
65. Have you heard		the accident?
66. I was		to leave.
67. We saw our friends		the concert.
68. They were		the front row.
69. We hope to see you		Saturday.
70. We hope to see you		5:00.
71. We hope to see you		the summer.

72. We hope to see you _____ June.
73. We hope to see you _____ Saturday afternoon.
74. We hope to see you _____ the afternoon.
75. We hope to see you _____ your birthday.
76. We hope to see you _____ your birthday party.
77. We hope to see you _____ the weekend.
78. We hope to see you _____ Los Angeles.
79. We met him _____ the way to the store.
80. We hope he doesn't get _____ the way this time.
81. _____ the way, they already know.
82. We wanted to go, but _____ the end, we decided to stay home.
83. The movie was good, but _____ the end, the dog died, so we were sad.
84. We decided _____ see it later.
85. We decided _____ the red one.
86. If you're upset, do something _____ it.
87. Come _____ lunch with us.
88. We just came _____ lunch.
89. I'm _____ my lunch break.
90. What are you having _____ lunch?
91. Come _____ us to lunch.
92. He pointed _____ each of the differences.
93. He pointed _____ the exit.
94. Give it _____ me!
95. We weren't sure he'd show _____ .
96. They were making fun _____ us.
97. If you don't know, look it _____ .
98. It's close _____ being done.
99. Make _____ your mind!
100. Could you drop me off _____ the corner?

VERBS

Here, we will learn the *past unreal duo* and the *causative* (**let**, **have**, **get**, **make**, **force**, **allow**, **permit**, **persuade**, **convince**).

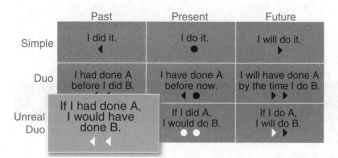

	Past	Present	Future
Simple	I did it. ◀	I do it. ●	I will do it. ▶
Duo	I had done A before I did B.	I have done A before now. ◀●	I will have done A by the time I do B. ▶▶
Unreal Duo	If I had done A, I would have done B. ◀◀	If I did A, I would do B. ●●	If I do A, I will do B. ▶▶

Past Unreal Duo

Looking at the verb map, you see three things: First, this is the *past*; second, there are *two events*; third, the events *didn't actually happen* (the symbols are white).

Fact	He weighed 350 pounds. He became a sumo wrestler in Japan.
Unreal	If he **had weighed** 350 pounds, he **would have** become a sumo wrestler.

But he didn't.
He was quite small, so he just wrestled with his conscience.

Fact	They **knew** all the answers. They **taught** the world.
Unreal	If they **had known** all the answers, they **would have** taught the world.

But they didn't.
So, they just tried to do what was right.

Exercise 8-26: Past Unreal Duo — Main Verbs

Rewrite the sentences, changing from the real past to the past unreal duo. Then check the Answer Key.

She **studied** hard. She **succeeded**.
~~If~~ she **had studied** hard, she **would have** succeeded.

1. You liked to ski. You went as often as possible.

2. I told you. You didn't remember.

3. We practiced every day. We got better.

4. He ate too much. He was overweight.

5. I studied every day. I spoke English well.

6. They talked too much. They got in trouble.

7. It worked well. We used it every day.

8. They paid attention. They understood.

9. Everyone knew how to do it. We did not need the instruction manual.

10. It made us mad. We complained about it.

Exercise 8-27: Past Unreal Duo — Pronunciation

CD 2 Track 38

Listen to the following and repeat five times.

1. If yood lykt to ski, youdə gänə zäffə nəz pässəbəl.
2. Ifyd tol joo, you wüdn nə r'membrd.
3. If weed præctist evry day, weedə gättn bedder.
4. Ifee deetn too much, heedə bin overweight.
5. Ifyd stədied evry day, I wüdə spokən English well.
6. If theyd talkt too much, they wüdə gättn in trouble.
7. Ifid wrrkt well, weedə yooz dit every day.

8. If theyd pay dəttention, they wüdə vənderstood.
9. Ifevry one had known howdə do it, we wüdn needəd the instruction manual.
10. Ifid made us mad, we wüdəv complain da boudit.

Exercise 8-28: That's a Big If!

Select the proper form of the unreal duo — past, present, or future. Then check the Answer Key.

1. If he had had a bike, he _____ it.
   Did he have a bike? No.
   - ☐ will ride
   - ☐ would ride
   - ☐ would have ridden

2. If he has a bike, he _____ it.
   Will he have a bike? Maybe, maybe not.
   - ☐ will ride
   - ☐ would ride
   - ☐ would have ridden

3. If he had a bike, he _____ it.
   Does he have a bike? No.
   - ☐ will ride
   - ☐ would ride
   - ☐ would have ridden

4. If you _____ on time, we won't be late.
   - ☑ are ready
   - ☐ were ready
   - ☐ had been ready

5. If you _____ on time, we wouldn't be late.
   - ☐ are ready
   - ☑ were ready
   - ☐ had been ready

6. If you _____ on time, we wouldn't have been late.
   - ☐ are ready
   - ☐ were ready
   - ☑ had been ready

7. _____ if they got what they wanted.
   - ☐ They'll be happy
   - ☑ They'd be happy
   - ☐ They'd have been happy

8. _____ if they'd gotten what they wanted.
   - ☐ They'll be happy
   - ☐ They'd be happy
   - ☑ They'd have been happy

9. _____ if they get what they want.
   - ☑ They'll be happy
   - ☐ They'd be happy
   - ☐ They'd have been happy

10. If I _____ you, I'd think it over.
   - ☐ am
   - ☐ are
   - ☑ were
   - ☐ would be

Causative Verb Map

	Past	Present	Future
Simple	I had him do it. ◄	I have him do it. ●	I will have him do it. ►
Duo	I'd had him do A before he did B. ◄ ◄	I've had him do it. ◄ ●	I'll've had him do A before he does B. ► ►
Unreal Duo	If I'd had him do A, I'd've had him do B. ◄ ◄	If I had him do A, I'd have him do B. ○ ○	If I have him do A, I'll have him do B. ► ►

A caused B to happen: A wants it to happen, but B doesn't necessarily want to do it.

The teacher **had** the students study.

The teacher **made** the students study.

The teacher **got** the students **to** study by promising them good grades.

The teacher **forced** the students **to** study.

The teacher **caused** the students **to** study.

A allowed B to happen: B wants to do it and A gives permission.

The teacher **let** the students take a break.

The teacher **allowed** the students **to** take a break.

The teacher **permitted** the students **to** take a break.

Exercise 8-29: Giving Permission

*Change to **let**, **allow**, and **permit**. Then check the Answer Key.*

He wants to go to the beach. She says OK.

She lets
She allows
She permits

> him go to the beach.

I would like to think about it. He says OK.

He lets
He allows
He permits

We need to try again. They said OK.

They let
They allow
They permit

Exercise 8-30: Causing an Action

*Change to **have**, **make**, and **get**. Then check the Answer Key.*

We want them to come back later.

We have
We make
We get

> them come back later.

They wanted him to change the settings.
They had
They made
They got

She needed us to work on it.
She had
She made
She got

Causative: Something Causes Something

It has to do with:
1) Who **wants** something
2) Who is **in charge**

The causative is the intersection of power and desire.

POWER DESIRE

Giving Permission
let
permit _____ to do (formal)
allow _____ to do (formal)
give someone permission to do something

Causing an Action
have (routine situation)
get _____ to do (persuasion)
talk someone into doing
persuade someone to do
convince someone to do
compel someone to
make (a little force)
force _____ to do (strong)

Let

Let's start with **let**. In this case, the boss is in charge and Ben wants to do something. Ben says to his boss, "Joe, can I leave early today?" The boss says, "Yes."

> The boss **gives** Ben **permission to** leave early.
> The boss **lets** Ben leave early.
> The boss **allows** Ben **to** leave early.
> The boss **permits** Ben **to** leave early.

Have

Ben's hair is too long and his car is dirty. He goes to the salon and says, "Pierre, please cut my hair." It is Pierre's job to cut people's hair. Pierre cuts Ben's hair. **Have** indicates a normal situation.

> Ben **had** him cut his hair.
> Ben took his car to the carwash to **have** them wash it.

Get

The next month, Ben went to the salon and Pierre was very, very busy. He said, "Sorry, Ben. There's no time for me to cut your hair today." Ben says, "I will give you an extra $10."

> Ben **gets** Pierre **to** cut his hair.
> Ben **talks** Pierre **into** cutting his hair.

Ben **persuades** Pierre **to** cut his hair.
Ben **convinces** Pierre **to** cut his hair.

Make

Ben's house was very dirty. His housekeeper was very lazy. Ben said, "Sam, clean the house now!" Sam said, "I'm tired. I don't want to clean the house." Ben said, "If you don't clean the house, you're fired."

Ben **made** Sam clean the house.

Make does not always indicate coercion. It can be used to intensify an action.

The student **shortened** the report. The student **made** the report shorter.
The gardener **beautified** the garden. The gardener **made** the garden beautiful.

Force

The prisoner didn't want to go back into his cell. The guards pushed him in.

The guards **forced** the prisoner **to** go back into the cell.

Exercise 8-31: Causing an Action

*Change to the correct form of **let**, **have**, **make**, or **get**. Then check the Answer Key.*

Sam said to the teacher, "May I borrow this book?"
The teacher **let** Sam borrow the book.
Ed said to the barber, "Take a little off the sides, please."
Ed **had** the barber take a little off the sides.
The boss said, "Clean up this mess!"
The boss **made** us clean up the mess.
Betty said, "Bob, could you please help me with this? That would be great!"
Betty **got** Bob **to** help her.

1. Please meet us in Sacramento.
   We are _____ them meet us in Sacramento.
2. Take out the trash!
   I _____ him take out the trash.
3. I'd really appreciate it if you would take out the trash. I'll help you with your project!
   I _____ him to take out the trash.
4. Take out the trash, please.
   I _____ him take out the trash.
5. Please, please, please ask questions.
   I can't _____ you to ask questions.
6. Come in to work and I'll give you overtime pay.
   The boss tried to _____ the worker to come in to work.
7. Come in at 9:00.
   The boss _____ the worker come in at 9:00.

8. Come in at 9:00 or you're fired!
   The boss _____ the worker come in at 9:00.

9. Can I borrow this? Sure!
   My friend _____ me borrow it.

10. Go borrow some money from your parents, please.
    My friend _____ me borrow some money from my parents.

11. I'd really like it if you would make some delicious Thai curry.
    He _____ me to make Thai curry even though I was really busy.

12. Can we study on our own? No, you may not.
    The teacher didn't _____ us study on our own.

13. Empty your pockets!
    The police _____ us empty our pockets.

14. Do the dishes, please.
    My mom _____ me do the dishes.

15. I'd like everyone to sit down.
    Can I _____ everyone to sit down, please?

Let's review everything you have learned in Chapter 8. Make sure you get 100% on the test before going on to the next chapter. Check your work using the Answer Key.

Part 1: *Fill in the appropriate preposition.*

1. We just can't get used _____ the time change this year.
2. Did they have a good reason _____ their actions?
3. What ever became _____ that box of old papers?
4. What on earth are they arguing _____?
5. Have you decided _____ a strategy?
6. Compared _____ the previous year, we are doing very well.
7. Where did this report come _____?
8. I hope you don't object _____ this schedule change.
9. We were simply not prepared _____ the demands of the job.
10. I'm not sure what you're referring _____.
11. I don't recall agreeing _____ those terms!
12. There is no substitute _____ good quality.
13. The new employee really reminds me _____ my cousin.
14. Well, we'll just have to see _____ that!
15. They insisted _____ doing it a particular way.
16. We just don't have time to deal _____ this right now!
17. I don't know if we'll ever recover _____ the shock.
18. Did you happen _____ find out who will be there?
19. We didn't think there was anything to apologize _____.
20. Many people prefer _____ skip breakfast.

Part 2: *Change each question to the standard **how** question.*

1. What is the **distance**?
2. What is the **age**?
3. What is the **price**?
4. What is the **frequency**?
5. What is the **quantity**? (uncountable)
6. What is the **quantity**? (countable)

7. What is the **duration**?
8. What is the **length**?
9. What is the **width**?
10. What is the **height**?
11. What is the **thickness**?

Part 3: *Fill in the proper form of the past, present, or future unreal duo.*

1. If he had thought of it, he _____ the e-mail.	**send**
2. If he thinks of it, he _____ the e-mail.	**send**
3. If he thought of it, he _____ the e-mail.	**send**
4. We would go to the beach if the weather _____ better.	**be**
5. We would have gone to the beach if the weather _____ better.	**be**
6. We will go to the beach if the weather _____ good.	**be**

Part 4: *Indicate if the following sentences are correct or not.*

1. This sentence is correct: **He has always permitted them to go.** ☐ True ☐ False
2. This sentence is correct: **He has usually let them to go.** ☐ True ☐ False
3. This sentence is correct: **He didn't want to make them to go.** ☐ True ☐ False
4. This sentence is correct: **He has never allowed them to go.** ☐ True ☐ False
5. This sentence is correct: **He can't force them to go.** ☐ True ☐ False

Part 5: *Fill in the blank with the past real duo.*

1. He _____n't _____ the test before the bell rang.	**finish**
2. We _____n't _____ it was serious until the test results came back.	**think**
3. They _____ always _____ that cheaper was better.	**think**
4. She _____ always clearly _____ what the problem was.	**understand**
5. I _____n't _____ how much it meant to them.	**realize**

Part 6: *Rewrite the sentences, changing from the real past to the past unreal duo.*

1. You studied. You learned.

2. It was impossible. You stopped trying.

3. They showed me how to do it. It wasn't scary anymore.

Part 7: *Choose the proper verb form.*

1. Edward _____ to the bank yesterday.	**go**
2. Joe _____ English for three years now.	**speak**
3. The girls _____ English long before they came to the States.	**speak**
4. She _____ that she would support them in every way.	**always say**
5. We _____ about the problem for a month before it was officially reported.	**know**
6. They _____ really hard last year.	**study**

Part 8: *Convert each statement from the –en verb to **make** an **adjective**.*

1. Could you shorten this essay?
2. Let's straighten this row.
3. She tried to loosen the knot.

Using what you have learned, write two paragraphs on the following topics:

1. If you had to write a book, what would the subject be?
2. Tell your favorite joke.

You can handwrite your paragraphs below or e-mail them to **para@grammar.bz** to be stored. These paragraphs are not graded or reviewed, but simply by writing them, your English will improve.

Student Paragraph

Send   Chat   Attach   Address   Fonts   Colors   Save As Draft   Photo Browser   Show Stationery

To: para@grammar.bz

Cc:

Bcc:

Subject: Chapter 8

Signature: Corporate ⬍

My name is _____

Chapter 9: Comprehension and Reported Speech

DICTATION

In earlier chapters, we learned the various ways to use and modify nouns. This chapter presents a series of comprehension exercises, so you can make sure you understand rapid, natural speech. For verbs, we will be working with reported speech, the past unreal duo, and the phrasal verb **give**.

Exercise 9-1: Dictation   CD 2 Track 39

Listen to the audio and write the exact transcription in the spaces below. Then check the Answer Key.

1. _____

2. _____

3. _____

4. _____

5. _____

The Bodyguard Incident

STORY

In **Italy**, in addition to being a **professional bodybuilder**, I'm also a **bodyguard**. I protect the president of a **famous car company** and an **international tennis star**, among others. One day, I was working in a **club** when a **fight** broke out on the floor. There were four or five guys involved, but **one** in particular was **very aggressive**. I think he was **high** on **coke**. He came into the office where I was and started **shouting** at me. He broke a **bottle** and **attacked** me; he **tried** to slash my **throat** with it. I wasn't about to **hit** him — he was **crazy** and he was holding **broken glass** — so I pulled out a **gun** and **shot** him. I'm a **good shot** because I was in the **Italian army** for two **years**. I shot him in the **leg**, not in the **body**, which would have **killed** him. That would have been a **big problem**. As it **was**, we had to go to **court**, which was a **big headache**.

Exercise 9-2: "The Bodyguard Incident" — Pronunciation   CD 2 Track 40

Listen to the audio and repeat, focusing on intonation and pronunciation.

In **Idəly**, in əddition tə being ə **pr'fessional bädy**builder, I mälso ə **bädy**gärd. I pr'tect the prezədent əvə **faym's cär cəmpəny** and an **innernæshənəl tennis star**, əməng əthrrz. One day, I wəz working innə **cləb** whenə **fight** broke out än the **floor**. There were four or five **guyz** invälvd, bət **one** in p'ticulər wəz **very aggressive**. I thinkee wəz **hi**⁽ʸ⁾än **coke**. He came into thee⁽ʸ⁾äffiss where I wəz and stärdəd **shæuding** at me. He broke **bäddle** and əttækt me; he **tried** tə slæsh my **throat** with it. I wəznt əbout tə **hidd**im — he wəz **crazy** and he wəz holding **brokən glæss** — so⁽ʷ⁾I püll doudə **gən** and **shädd**im. Im ə **güd shät** b'cuz I wəzzin thee⁽ʸ⁾**ətælyən**

204

ärmy fər two **yirz**. I shäddim in the **leg**, nät in the **bädy**, which wüdəv **kill** dim. Thæt wüda binna **big präbləm**. Az it **wəz**, we had tə godə **court**, which wəzzə **big hedake**.

NOUNS

This section includes a general comprehension lesson, both with listening and reading. You will identify specific information, determine the gist, and draw conclusions.

Listening Comprehension

Exercise 9-3: The Story of Human Language
CD 2 Track 41

Listen to the audio and fill in the blanks. Then check the Answer Key.

"I _____ who is not interested in language," wrote the bestselling author and psychologist Steven Pinker. _____ that language fascinates us so. It not _____, placing us head and _____ the most proficient animal communicators, but it also beguiles us with its endless mysteries.

For example, _____?
Why isn't there just one language? _____ change, _____, is that change _____ growth? _____ extinct? Consider how a single tongue spoken 150,000 years ago has evolved into the estimated 6,000 languages _____.

Exercise 9-4: Polar Bears and Global Warming
CD 2 Track 42

Select the appropriate response based on the audio. Then check the Answer Key.

1. Polar bears have been listed as an _____.	☐ dangerous species ■ endangered species
2. This will reduce the risk that they_____.	☐ become extinct ☐ become a stink
3. They will have new _____ under the Endangered Species Act.	☐ protections ☐ detections
4. The U.S. government cannot _____ the bears' existence.	☐ check the eyes ☐ jeopardize
5. The government could consider tougher _____ to clean up the air.	☐ majors ☐ measures
6. Scientists believe carbon _____ emissions cause global warming.	☐ dioxide ☐ the oxide
7. Unless global warming is _____, the bears will be extinct by 2100.	☐ tamed ☐ stemmed
8. There are about _____ polar bears worldwide.	☐ 25,000 ☐ 2,500

9. There are about _____ polar bears in Alaska.   ☐ 4,700
                                                        ☐ 470
10. Polar bears tend to be _____ to blend in with the   ☐ black
    snow.   ☐ white

Exercise 9-5: Physics   CD 2 Track 43

Listen to the audio and fill in the blanks. Then check the Answer Key.

"It doesn't ____ to understand modern physics," says Professor Richard Wolfson. ____ touch the very basis of physical reality, altering our commonsense notions of ____. Both have reputations for being bewilderingly complex. But the basic ideas behind relativity and quantum physics are, in fact, simple ____. The essence of relativity is summed up in a single, concise sentence: ____ uniform motion.

Exercise 9-6: The History of the English Language   CD 2 Track 44

*Listen to the audio and select **True** or **False**. Then check the Answer Key.*

1. The origins of English are Germanic.   ☐ True ☐ False
2. It has a 2,500-year history.   ☐ True ☐ False
3. English is only spoken in America.   ☐ True ☐ False
4. English is the international language of business and trade. ☐ True ☐ False
5. There are many literary and cultural achievements in English. ☐ True ☐ False

---

Exercise 9-7: Economics   CD 2 Track 45

*Listen to the audio and check the box that best reflects the **gist** of the text. Then check the Answer Key.*

☐ Everyone is trained to be an economist, and we all save money based on our sophisticated understanding of the fundamentals of economics.

☐ Economic issues play a large part in our everyday lives, and it's important to have a deeper understanding of the fundamentals.

☐ It doesn't pay to be a good economist in working, buying, saving, investing, paying taxes, and voting.

Exercise 9-8: The Joy of Science

CD 2 Track 46

*Listen to the audio and identify **specific facts**. Then check the Answer Key.*

People should be acquainted with the second ____ of thermodynamics. This law deals with the diffusion of ____ and has many ____ consequences. Also important are Newton's laws, the periodic table of elements, the double-helix ____ DNA, and scores of other masterpieces of ____.

Exercise 9-9: Drawing a Conclusion

CD 2 Track 47

Read the text and listen to the audio. Then select the most logical conclusion. Check the Answer Key when you're done.

Question of Value

Our lives are filled with everyday questions of fact and finance. Which investment brings the highest return? What school district is the house in? What will this candidate actually do if elected? But the really fundamental questions of our lives are questions of neither fact nor finance. The really fundamental questions are questions of value. These are the deep questions that apply to every aspect of our lives. What is it that gives something genuine value? What things are really worth striving for? What is it that makes life worth living? Are there values that transcend cultural differences? Is all value subjective?

☐ Finances are the most fundamental question in our lives.
☐ The fundamental questions in our lives pertain to value.
☐ Values transcend all cultural differences.

Exercise 9-10: Listening for Specific Facts

CD 2 Track 48

Listen to the audio and determine if each item is true or false. Then check the Answer Key.

1. Africa is the world's second-largest continent. ☐ True ☐ False
2. It covers 16 percent of the Earth's total surface area. ☐ True ☐ False
3. There are 406 countries in Africa, not including the island groups. ☐ True ☐ False
4. The earliest hominids were discovered in Africa. ☐ True ☐ False
5. There are no glaciers in Africa. ☐ True ☐ False

Reading Comprehension

Exercise 9-11: John F. Kennedy

Read the selection and answer the questions. Then check the Answer Key.

John Fitzgerald Kennedy, who was often referred to by his initials, JFK, was the 35th president of the United States, serving from 1961 until his assassination in 1963. Kennedy was born in Massachusetts on May 29, 1917.

In the 1960 U.S. presidential election, Kennedy defeated Richard Nixon, in one of the closest races in American history. To date, he is the only practicing Roman Catholic to have been President. He was also the youngest man elected to the office, at the age of 43. JFK is the only president to have won a Pulitzer **Prize**. During his administration, events included the Bay of **Pigs** invasion, the Cuban **missile** crisis, the building of the Berlin **Wall**, the **space** race, the civil **rights** movement, and the early part of the Vietnam **War**.

Kennedy was assassinated on November 22, 1963, in Dallas, Texas. **Lee** Harvey **Oswald** was charged with the crime but was murdered **two** days **later** by Jack **Ruby**, before he could be put on trial. The **Warren** Commission concluded that Oswald was the assassin, but allowed for the probability of conspiracy. The event turned out to be an important moment in U.S. history because of how it profoundly affected the nation. Today, Kennedy continues to rank highly in public opinion ratings of former U.S. presidents.

1. What does JFK stand for?
2. Who were the two candidates in the 1960 election?
3. How old was Kennedy when he was elected?
4. What's another word for **murdered**?
5. Who killed JFK?
6. Was Lee Harvey Oswald the only gunman?
7. What happened to Oswald?
8. What's another word for **profoundly**?
9. How do people feel about Kennedy now?

Exercise 9-12: Rice

Read the selection and answer the questions. Then check the Answer Key.

Rice is a staple food for a large part of the world's population, providing more than one fifth of the calories consumed worldwide, making it the second-most-consumed cereal grain. The rice plant grows about 2 to 5 feet high and is a flowering plant.

Rice is composed of the grain and the husk. The grain is mainly used as food, but the vitamins, including B-complex, are found in the husk. Most people prefer to eat polished rice without the husk, but this can create a vitamin deficiency because polished rice doesn't have many vitamins.

Much of the rice that we eat comes from southeastern Asia and grows in all countries that have a warm and moist climate, including India, China, and Japan. The traditional method for cultivating rice is to flood the fields after planting the seedlings. This simple method requires planning and maintenance of the water supply, but reduces the growth of weeds and deters vermin. Flooding is not mandatory, but all other methods of irrigation require more effort in weed and pest control and different methods of fertilization.

What are the two edible parts of rice? _____

Rice grows in all the countries with climates that are:
A. ☐ cool and moist   C. ☐ warm and moist
B. ☐ warm and dry   D. ☐ cool and dry

What is another word for **consumed** in the first sentence? _____

Why is rice husk important?
A. ☐ because it tastes good   B. ☐ because it has many vitamins

Why do people who don't eat rice husk suffer from various deficiencies? Explain in one sentence. _____

The following story has been in circulation on the Internet and the radio for the past 25 years. It's generally attributed to a church newsletter in Ohio, but this can't be verified. Take this with a grain of salt!

Exercise 9-13: Gin-Soaked Raisins

Read the following passage and answer the questions. The prepositions have been highlighted. Check the Answer Key when you're done.

Gin-Soaked Raisins Bring Relief to Arthritic Patient

When we heard this, we felt obligated **to** share it. It must be noted, however, that the claim is unsubstantiated, and is offered **to** you exactly as it is. Here is an unusual recipe **for** arthritic relief:

Empty one box **of** golden raisins **into** a large, shallow container. Pour **in** enough gin (the cheapest you can buy) **to** completely cover the raisins. Let it stand uncovered **until** all the liquid disappears (about seven days). Stirring occasionally helps the evaporation process. Then, put the raisins **in** a covered container and eat just nine raisins a day. If you don't like raisins, put them **on** your cereal or **in** a salad.

I began eating nine raisins a day **on** October 10. **By** November 10, my knees, which had sounded **like** castanets whenever I bent **over**, no longer clicked so loudly, and I was able **to** walk **up** and **down** those small steps **from** the sidewalk **to** the street **outside** our building **without** turning sideways **to** go one step **at** a time or hang **on to** a parked car. I could bend my head back to look **at** the stars **without** leaning **against** a tree or fence or holding the back of my neck **for** support. A couple weeks later, the swelling and pain were gone **from** my arthritic toes. By December, I could close my fingers **into** fists. **Before** October 10, a knife would slide **through** either hand. My whole body feels more limber; I can do exercises, including hugging my knees **to** my chest and rocking back and forth, **without** back pain. I can handle needles and pins **with** greater ease.

A friend **in** Massachusetts gave me this recipe last September. She had learned **about** it this past summer **from** her podiatrist, who had noticed her difficulty **in** getting **up to** leave his office. He learned **of** it **from** one **of** his patients, whose toes and knees were no longer swollen and who could stretch her hands flat **on** the table — all after just two months **of** eating nine raisins a day. **Before** her retirement, she was the assistant dean **of** a medical school. **On** a return trip **to** visit former colleagues, a friend told her that the school's specialist in rheumatology was prescribing this recipe

to all his patients! (The podiatrist and his friends have been eating these raisins and have been playing their best golf **in** more than 30 years; they are **in** their 70's.)

Why does this recipe bring such fantastic results? As far back as early Biblical times, the people **of** India and Egypt discovered the healing properties **of** juniper berries. Gin is made **from** natural grains and juniper berries. Even if you are **on** medication that advises **against** alcohol, you can eat nine raisins a day. Most of the alcohol has evaporated and the small amount would be insignificant. That comes **from** my own physician.

In your own words, what is the main idea of the article?

_____

_____

What ingredient in gin helps healing and reduces swelling?

_____

_____

Exercise 9-14: Gin-Soaked Raisins — Pronunciation   CD 2 Track 49

Listen and repeat.

ACCENT

Jin-Soakt Rayzinz Bring R'leef to Arthridic Paysh'nt
When we hrrd this, we felt äbləgadəd to share it. It məst be nodəd, however, thət thə claim iz ənsəbstænshee⁽ʸ⁾adəd, and iz äfferd to you eggzækly əzidiz. Hirzən unuzhu⁽ʷ⁾al rəsəpee for ärthridic r'lief:

Empty one bäx of golden ray-zinz into a large shællow c'ntainer. Pour in ənəf jin (the cheapest you c'n buy) to c'mpleetly cəver the ray-zinz. Ledit stænd əncəverd until äll the likwid disəppirz (about 7 dayz). Stirring əccazhənəlly helps thee⁽ʸ⁾əvæporashən präcess. Then, püt the ray-zinz in a cəverd cəntainer and eat jəst nine ray-zinz ə day. If you don't like ray-zinz, put them än your cire⁽ʸ⁾əl or innə sæləd.

I b'gæn eeding 9 ray-zinz a day än äctober 10. By November 10, my kneez, which had soundəd like cæstənets whenever I bent over, no länger clickt so loudly and I wəz abəl to wälk up and down thoz smällə steps from the sidewalk to the street outside är bilding without turning sidewayz to go one stepədə time or hæng on to a pärkt cär. I cüd bend my head bæck to lük at the stärz without leaning agenst a tree or fence or holding the bæck of my neck for s'pport. A cəpəl of weeks lader, the swelling and pain wr gän from my ärthridic toz. By D'cember, I cüd cloz my fingrz into fists. B'fore äctober 10, a nyf wüd slyd thru either hænd. My whole bädy feelz more limber; I c'n do exercizəz, including həgging my kneez to my chest and räcking bæckən forth, without bæck pain. I c'n hændle needəlz and pinz with greader eez.

A friend in Mæssə chussetts gave me this rəsəpee læst September. She had lrnd aboudit this pæst summer frommer p'dy⁽ʸ⁾ətrist, who had nodist her diffəcəlty in gedding əp to leeviz äffice. He lrrrndəvit frəm wənəviz patients, whooz toz and kneez were no länger swollen and who cüd stretch her hænds flædän the table — ällæf ter just 2 mənts əveeding 9 raisinz a day. B'fore her r'tirement, she wəz thee⁽ʸ⁾əssistant dean əvə medəcal school. ännə r'turn trip to vizit former cälleegz, a friend told her that the schoolz speshəlist in roomətälⱥgy wəz pr'scribing this resəpee to all his patients! (The p'dy⁽ʸ⁾ətrist and his frenz have been eeding theez ray-zinz and have been playing their best gälf in more th'n thirdee yirz — they are in their sevendeez.)

Why dəz this resəpee bring səch fæntæstic r'zəlts? Az fär bæck az erly biblⱥcəl timz, the people of India and Egypt d'scəverd the healing präperdeez ov junəper berreez. Jin is made from næchrəl grainz and junəper berreez. Even if you are än medⱥcation thət ədvizəz əgenst ælkəhäl, you c'n eat 9 ray-zinz a day. Most ov the ælkəhäl haz əvæporadəd and the small amount wüd be insig nifⱥcənt. That cəmz frəm my own fⱥzishən.

Exercise 9-15: Review

Identify the appropriate word. Then check the Answer Key.

1. I can't get _____ how well he's dealing with this! ☐ up ☐ over
2. Don't put it _____ any longer. ☐ up ☐ off
3. Nobody can stand _____ his dictatorial ways. ☐ — ☐ up
4. That plane will take _____ at 9:15 a.m. ☐ up ☐ off
5. A tadpole turns _____ a frog. ☐ up to ☐ into
6. It's hard to get _____ jury duty. ☐ out of ☐ at
7. Keep trying! Don't give _____! ☐ up ☐ out
8. It certainly didn't turn _____ the way we expected! ☐ out ☐ up
9. Please put your coat _____ when you get home. ☐ off ☐ away
10. Could you turn _____ the radio, it's too loud. ☐ down ☐ away
11. What's his point? I'm not sure what he's getting _____. ☐ from ☐ at
12. That basketball player really stands _____ in a crowd. ☐ up ☐ out
13. It's time to _____ your homework. ☐ do ☐ make
14. Do it now! There's no point in putting it _____. ☐ away ☐ off
15. I'm sorry, we don't give _____ personal information. ☐ out ☐ up
16. What time do you get _____ work? ☐ off ☐ out
17. Because I was moving, I gave _____ all of my old CDs. ☐ away ☐ off
18. Don't worry, it'll turn _____ sooner or later. ☐ away ☐ up
19. It's important to stand _____ what you believe in. ☐ up to ☐ up for
20. I can't believe he turned _____ that job offer! ☐ down ☐ away
21. What time would you like to _____ lunch? ☐ take ☐ have
22. The children need to _____ a nap. ☐ have ☐ take
23. I hope they didn't _____ a mistake. ☐ make ☐ do
24. You need to _____ a shower after working out. ☐ have ☐ take
25. Did you _____ an appointment? ☐ make ☐ take
26. Did he _____ a promise? ☐ make ☐ do
27. Do you _____ good notes in class? ☐ take ☐ make
28. Their teacher didn't _____ them talk in class. ☐ let ☐ allow
29. They _____ us repaint the whole house. ☐ got ☐ had
30. We _____ him to change his mind. ☐ had ☐ got

VERBS

In this section, we'll learn about reported speech, the past real duo, and the phrasal verb **give**. This section also includes synopses of **would**, **had**, **be**, **to**, and **there**, as well as a comprehensive version of "Grammar in a Nutshell."

He Said, She Said

The verb changes when speech is reported.

Direct Speech	Reported Speech
"I **do** it."	I said that I **did** it.
"I **did** it."	I said that I **had done** it.
"I **will do** it."	I said that I **would do** it.

When you say something directly, you need to use quotation marks.

"I need to go," he said.

When you use reported speech, two things happen. The quotation marks disappear, and you push the verb tense back in order to match when the report is.

He said that he needed to go.

Exercise 9-16: Reported or Indirect Speech

Change the direct statement to a reported statement using the provided phrase. Then check the Answer Key.

He doesn't like it.   **He said that he didn't like it.**

1. She does that everyday.
   I thought that
2. He will do it later.
   He said that
3. They left early.
   She believed that
4. Your friends left.
   I thought that
5. He'll call you when he has time. (Hint: Both verbs change.)
   He said that
6. You need to take a bath.
   She believed that
7. She wants him to do his homework.
   I thought that
8. These shoes are too small.
   He said that
9. She looks great in that dress.
   She believed that
10. The computer crashed.
    I thought that

Past Unreal Duo

	Past	Present	Future
Simple	I did it. ◀	I do it. ●	I'll do it. ▶
Real Duo	I'd done A before I did B.	I've done it. ◀ ●	I'll've done A before I do B. ▶ ▶
Unreal Duo	If I had done A, I would've done B. ◀ ◀	If I did A, I'd do B. ◀ ●	If I do A, I'll do B. ▶ ▶

As you learned with the present unreal duo, you can link two events in time that are contrary to fact.

The **past unreal duo** clarifies the distinction between what actually took place and what hypothetically could have taken place.

(Traditionally, this is known as the past subjunctive conditional.)

Exercise 9-17: Past Unreal Duo

Change from the past to the past unreal duo. Then check the Answer Key.

He studied hard. He did well.
If he had studied hard, he would have done well.
If he had studied hard, he could have done well.

1. She saved her money. She lived comfortably.

2. They considered all of the options. They were prepared.

3. We planted a garden. We have a lot of vegetables.

4. I didn't watch the road. I got in an accident.

5. We didn't do the laundry. We didn't have anything to wear.

Let's do a review of the verbs we've studied so far.

Exercise 9-18: Verb Tense Understanding

Fill in the blank with the proper verb form. Then check the Answer Key.

1. The accident _____ yesterday.
   - ☐ happens
   - ■ happened

2. Nobody _____ what will happen tomorrow.
   - ☐ knows
   - ☐ will know

3. I _____ you in the morning.
   - ☐ call
   - ☐ will call

4. They _____ it many times over the years, but never succeeded.
   - ☐ try
   - ☐ have tried

5. There _____ a possibility for it later.
   - ☐ may be
   - ☐ has been

6. He _____ to England.
   - ☐ has never gone
   - ☐ has never went

7. You ____ that yesterday, right?
- [ ] did
- [ ] have done
- [ ] had done

8. You ____ that before, right?
- [ ] did
- [ ] have done
- [ ] had done

9. You ____ that before I met you, right?
- [ ] did
- [ ] have done
- [ ] had done

10. He will ____ the water.
- [ ] drink
- [ ] drinks

11. I ____ going to the store yesterday.
- [ ] was
- [ ] will be

12. He ____ travel by train, but now he prefers his car.
- [ ] used to
- [ ] is used to

13. He ____ driving on the right side of the road.
- [ ] used to
- [ ] is used to

14. She ____ working really hard right now.
- [ ] was
- [ ] is

15. I ____ not born yesterday.
- [ ] was
- [ ] am

16. Do you think they ____ figure it out?
- [ ] will be able to
- [ ] are

17. She ____ survive the storm.
- [ ] didn't
- [ ] don't

18. He ____ off the roof this morning.
- [ ] fell
- [ ] falls

19. Don't ____ over spilled milk.
- [ ] cried
- [ ] cry

20. He ____ the house last year.
- [ ] paints
- [ ] painted

Three *Theres*

There	They're	Their
There was a fire.	**They're** at the party.	It's **their** turn.

Exercise 9-19: Three *Theres*

Select the proper form. Then check the Answer Key.

1. ____ will be an earthquake within the next 50 years.
- [ ] There
- [ ] They're
- [ ] Their

2. That's not ____ first time to work on this.
- [ ] there
- [ ] they're
- [ ] their

3. I think ____ not coming back.
- [ ] there
- [ ] they're
- [ ] their

Four *2s*

1 Preposition	3 Number
We went **to** the party.	I bought **two** hats.
2 Also	4 Excess
I have one, **too**.	There were **too** many people there.

Exercise 9-20: Four *2s*

Identify the proper form. Then check the Answer Key.

1. Don't eat _____ much!   ☐ 1 ☐ 3 ☐ 2 ☐ 4

2. We like it, _____.   ☐ 1 ☐ 3 ☐ 2 ☐ 4

3. They bought _____ of them.   ☐ 1 ☐ 3 ☐ 2 ☐ 4

4. Let's go _____ the beach!   ☐ 1 ☐ 3 ☐ 2 ☐ 4

Four *Hads*

1 Possession	3 Obligation
I **had** a bicycle.	I **had** to do it. I **had** better do it now.
2 Causative	4 Past Real Duo
I **had** him do it.	I **had** never done that before.

Exercise 9-21: Four *Hads*

*Identify which form of **had** is being used. Then check the Answer Key.*

1. I **had** to finish my homework before going out.   ☐ 1 ☐ 3 ☐ 2 ☐ 4

2. They **had** us wait at the office while they investigated the situation.   ☐ 1 ☐ 3 ☐ 2 ☐ 4

3. He **had** a ticket.   ☐ 1 ☐ 3 ☐ 2 ☐ 4

4. They **had** never had a pineapple before they went to Hawaii.   ☐ 1 ☐ 3 ☐ 2 ☐ 4

Four *Woulds*

1 Unreal Duo	3 Repeated Past
If I were you, I **would**n't do that.	When I was little, I **would** always play in the yard.
If I had been there, I **would** have done it.	
I wish he **would** do it.	
I **would** rather do it later.	

2 Polite	4 Reported Speech
Would you please help me with this?	"I will do it."
I **would** like a glass of water.	He said that he **would** do it.

Exercise 9-22: Four *Woulds*

*Identify which form of **would** is being used. (Remember: **Would** is always followed by the simple form of the main verb.) Check the Answer Key when you're done.*

1. I **would** like to try it again, please.   ☐ 1   ☐ 3   ☐ 2   ☐ 4

2. He told me that he **would** do it later.   ☐ 1   ☐ 3   ☐ 2   ☐ 4

3. When I lived in France, I **would** always speak French.   ☐ 1   ☐ 3   ☐ 2   ☐ 4

4. If you were sure, you **would**n't be nervous about it.   ☐ 1   ☐ 3   ☐ 2   ☐ 4

Seven Forms with *To Be*

1 –ing
He is runn**ing**.
It is excit**ing** (to me).
It is rain**ing**.
It's go**ing** to rain.

2 Adjective (quality, nationality, color, time, etc.)
He is **nice / happy / hungry / funny**.
He is **gone / back / available / ready**.
It is **wrong / right / stressful**.
He is **Italian**.
It is **blue**.
It is **Tuesday**.
It's **9:00**.
It's **January**.

3 –ed
It is clos**ed**.
He is excit**ed** (by it).
He is interest**ed** / confus**ed** / worri**ed**.
He is surpris**ed** / annoy**ed** / irritat**ed**.

4 Noun / Pronoun (person, place, thing, idea)
He is **a doctor**.
It's **mine**.

5 Preposition
He is **at** the park.
He is **like** the other people.

6 Passive
It was **written** by Shakespeare.
It **got** stolen.

7 Conjunction
It was **because** we wanted it that way.
It's **when** he quit that we started worrying.

Exercise 9-23: Seven *Bes*

*Identify the correct use of **be**. Look for the key word or form in the chart above. Hints for the first seven are in bold. Check the Answer Key when you're done.*

1. He wasn't surpris**ed** by their offer.

☐ 1 ☐ 3 ☐ 5
☐ 2 ☐ 4 ☐ 6
☐ 7

2. It isn't **available** right now.

☐ 1 ☐ 3 ☐ 5
☐ 2 ☐ 4 ☐ 6
☐ 7

3. This is so exci**ting**!

☐ 1 ☐ 3 ☐ 5
☐ 2 ☐ 4 ☐ 6
☐ 7

4. I think it's an automatic **response**. (noun)

☐ 1 ☐ 3 ☐ 5
☐ 2 ☐ 4 ☐ 6
☐ 7

5. It was heard **by** over a million people. (A million people heard it.)

☐ 1 ☐ 3 ☐ 5
☐ 2 ☐ 4 ☐ 6
☐ 7

6. I will be **in** L.A. for six weeks. (preposition)

☐ 1 ☐ 3 ☐ 5
☐ 2 ☐ 4 ☐ 6
☐ 7

7. It's **why** we had to tell you.

☐ 1 ☐ 3 ☐ 5
☐ 2 ☐ 4 ☐ 6
☐ 7

8. It's not like everything else.

☐ 1 ☐ 3 ☐ 5
☐ 2 ☐ 4 ☐ 6
☐ 7

9. It's wrong.

☐ 1 ☐ 3 ☐ 5
☐ 2 ☐ 4 ☐ 6
☐ 7

10. They are Indonesian.

☐ 1 ☐ 3 ☐ 5
☐ 2 ☐ 4 ☐ 6
☐ 7

11. That wasn't Wednesday; it was Tuesday.

☐ 1 ☐ 3 ☐ 5
☐ 2 ☐ 4 ☐ 6
☐ 7

12. It was a mistake.

☐ 1 ☐ 3 ☐ 5
☐ 2 ☐ 4 ☐ 6
☐ 7

13. We have been in the back office for three hours.

☐ 1 ☐ 3 ☐ 5
☐ 2 ☐ 4 ☐ 6
☐ 7

14. It's going to be awful.

☐ 1 ☐ 3 ☐ 5
☐ 2 ☐ 4 ☐ 6
☐ 7

15. It's a little stressful.

☐ 1 ☐ 3 ☐ 5
☐ 2 ☐ 4 ☐ 6
☐ 7

16. It's not done yet.

☐ 1 ☐ 3 ☐ 5
☐ 2 ☐ 4 ☐ 6
☐ 7

17. They weren't very excited about it.

☐ 1 ☐ 3 ☐ 5
☐ 2 ☐ 4 ☐ 6
☐ 7

18. The kids got really sunburned at the beach.

☐ 1 ☐ 3 ☐ 5
☐ 2 ☐ 4 ☐ 6
☐ 7

19. Oh, no! It's gone.

☐ 1 ☐ 3 ☐ 5
☐ 2 ☐ 4 ☐ 6
☐ 7

20. The website has been seen by millions.

☐ 1 ☐ 3 ☐ 5
☐ 2 ☐ 4 ☐ 6
☐ 7

Grammar in a Bigger Nutshell

All through this book, we have studied intonation. Here we will look at it in a single sentence with the various verb tenses.

Subject		Object
The **show**		a **house**
The **talk** show		a **light**house
The **talk** show host		a **light**house keeper
The popular **talk** show host		an old **light**house keeper
The **wildly** popular **talk** show host	interviewed	a **really** old **light**house keeper

The **wildly** popular **talk** show host interviewed a **really** old **light**house keeper.
Thə **wildly** päpyəlrr **täk** show host dinnerview də **rilly** old **lyt** hæous keeper.

Exercise 9-24: Verb Tense Understanding   CD 2 Track 50

*Listen to the audio and repeat. No matter how complex the verb gets, remember to follow the basic **Dogs** eat **bones** intonation, where you stress the nouns. We will build up one complex noun for the subject, and another one for the object.*

dinner viewz
1. The **wildly** popular **talk** show host interviews **really** old **light**house keepers all the time.

dizinner viewing
2. The **wildly** popular **talk** show host is interviewing a **really** old **light**house keeper right now.

dinner viewdə
3. The **wildly** popular **talk** show host interviewed a **really** old **light**house keeper last week.

də linner viewə
4. The **wildly** popular **talk** show host will interview a **really** old **light**house keeper next week.

də dinner viewə
5. The **wildly** popular **talk** show host would interview a **really** old **light**house keeper if she could **find** one.

dədə vinner viewdə

6. The **wildly** popular **talk** show host would have interviewed a **really** old **light**house keeper if she'd been able to **find** one.

thədə zinner viewdə

7. The **wildly** popular **talk** show host that has interviewed a **really** old **light**house keeper is living in France now.

də zinner viewdə

8. The **wildly** popular **talk** show host has interviewed a lot of **really** old **light**house keepers over the years.

də dinner viewdə

9. The **wildly** popular **talk** show host had interviewed a **really** old **light**house keeper before the huge storm in the Atlantic knocked over his lighthouse.

dələ vinner viewdə

10. The **wildly** popular **talk** show host will have interviewed a lot of **really** old **light**house keepers by the end of the season.

dädə inner viewə

11. The **wildly** popular **talk** show host ought to interview a **really** old **light**house keeper.

shü dinner viewə

12. The **wildly** popular **talk** show host should interview a **really** old **light**house keeper.

shüd•n ninner view

13. The **wildly** popular **talk** show host shouldn't interview **really** old **light**house keepers because it confuses the audience.

shüdə vinner viewdə

14. The **wildly** popular **talk** show host should've interviewed a **really** old **light**house keeper so an expert could have been heard.

shüd•nə vinner viewdə

15. The **wildly** popular **talk** show host shouldn't have interviewed a **really** old **light**house keeper because the audience was completely confused.

cü dinner viewə

16. The **wildly** popular **talk** show host could interview a **really** old **light**house keeper.

cüd•n ninner viewenny

17. The **wildly** popular **talk** show host couldn't interview any **really** old **light**house keepers because they were all on strike that month.

cüdə vinner viewdə

18. The **wildly** popular **talk** show host could've interviewed a **really** old **light**house keeper, but instead she went with a **very** attractive **lion** tamer.

cüd•nə vinner viewdə

19. The **wildly** popular **talk** show host couldn't have interviewed a **really** old **light**house keeper because none of them were in town last month.

my dinner viewə

20. The **wildly** popular **talk** show host might interview a **really** old **light**house keeper.

mydə vinner viewdə
21. The **wildly** popular **talk** show host might've interviewed a **really** old **light**house keeper, but we're not sure because the schedule was shredded earlier today.

məss dinner viewə
22. The **wildly** popular **talk** show host must interview a lot of **really** old **light**house keepers because she completely understands the issues. (probably)

məss də vinner viewdə
23. The **wildly** popular **talk** show host must've interviewed a lot of **really** old **light**house keepers because she completely understood the issues. (probably)

cə ninner viewə
24. The **wildly** popular **talk** show host can interview a **really** old **light**house keeper if she has time at the end of the show.

cæn dinner view
25. The **wildly** popular **talk** show host can't interview any **really** old **light**house keepers due to the union rules about discussing maritime issues with civilians.

Give

To give one's opinion	I'd like to give my opinion on that.
It is given that ...	It's given that the process needs to change.
To give up	They won't ever give up!
To give someone the benefit of the doubt	Let's give him the benefit of the doubt.
To give in	He held out for a while, but then gave in.
To give away	She gave away all of her worldly goods.
To give away	He gave away the end of the movie.
To give back	Let's hope they give us the money back.
To give off	The heater is giving off a strange odor.
To give out	Our old car finally gave out.

Exercise 9-25: *Give*

Select the proper option. Then check the Answer Key.

1. The boss insisted on paying, so we finally gave _____. ☐ in ☐ away
2. The director knew he was right, so he refused to give _____. ☐ up ☐ away
3. The junior execs were reluctant to give their _____. ☐ opinion ☐ benefit of the doubt
4. In government, _____ massive debt is a fact of life. ☑ it's given that ☐ it's given away

5. He protested so well that they gave him the ____.   ☐ opinion   ☑ benefit of the doubt
6. Don't give ____ the ending of the story!   ☐ back   ☑ away
7. Let's give ____ these old clothes and toys.   ☑ back   ☑ away
8. I'm sorry, we don't give ____ personal information.   ☑ out   ☐ off
9. We think you should give it ____ to him.   ☑ back   ☑ away
10. The fire is giving ____ a lot of smoke!   ☐ out   ☑ off

TEST Let's review everything you have learned in Chapter 9. Make sure you get 100% on the test before going on to the next chapter. Check your work using the Answer Key.

Part 1: Fill in the proper word. Don't forget to capitalize the first letter.

1. _____ he do it yesterday?
2. _____ he do it tomorrow?
3. _____ he doing it right now?
4. _____ he ever done it before?
5. _____ he do it if he had time?

Part 2: Select the proper verb form.

1. _____ you like it?   ☐ Do   ☐ Does
2. The director _____ the staff later.   ☐ inform   ☐ will inform
3. He _____ never figured it out.   ☐ has   ☐ hasn't
4. She _____ figured it out, if she had thought about it.   ☐ will   ☐ would   ☐ would've
5. She _____ figure it out, if she thought about it.   ☐ will   ☐ would   ☐ would've
6. She _____ figure it out when she thinks about it.   ☐ will   ☐ would   ☐ would've

*Part 3: Convert to a reported statement using **I said that** or **I thought that**.*

1. He does it.

2. She will buy one.

3. They have opened a new branch.

4. They designed a wonderful plaza.

5. We are trying our hardest.

Part 4: *Fill in the blank with the appropriate **give** phrase.*

1. I'm sorry, we can't give _____ that information.
2. Keep trying! Don't give _____!

Part 5: *Fill in the blank with the appropriate **preposition**.*

1. That plane will take _____ at 9:15 a.m.
2. It certainly didn't turn _____ the way we expected!

Part 6: *Change from the past to the past unreal duo.*

1. He thought about it. He reconsidered.

2. They brought their laptops. They got a little work done.

Part 7: *Fill in the blank with **their / they're / there**.*

1. _____ is a spot on my tie.
2. I tried to borrow _____ car.
3. She thinks _____ not really trying.

Part 8: *Fill in the blank with **to / too / two**.*

1. I have _____ go now.
2. I have _____ hours to finish.
3. I have _____ much to do.

Using what you have learned, write two essays on the following:

1. How many scars do you have and how did you get them?
2. Explain an aspect of American culture or habits that you find strange or confusing.

You can handwrite your paragraphs below or e-mail them to **para@grammar.bz** to be stored. These paragraphs are not graded or reviewed, but simply by writing them, your English will improve.

	Student Paragraph	
Send Chat Attach Address Fonts Colors Save As Draft		Photo Browser Show Stationery

To: para@grammar.bz

Cc:

Bcc:

Subject: Chapter 9

Signature: Corporate

My name is _____

Chapter 10: Comprehension and the Passive Voice

Here, we pull together all of the elements you have studied in comprehension exercises, along with word order, prefixes, synonyms, *doubt* vs. *question*, and **only**. For verbs, you will learn the passive voice, and the past and future real duo.

Exercise 10-1: Dictation	CD 2 Track 51

Listen to the audio and write the exact transcription in the spaces below. Then check the Answer Key.

1. _____
   _____

2. _____
   _____

3. _____
   _____

4. _____
   _____

5. _____
   _____

6. _____
   _____

7. _____
   _____

8. _____
   _____

9. _____
   _____

10. _____
    _____

The Army Incident

STORY	What a Surprise . . . Max Doesn't Think It Through

When I was **younger**, I was really **crazy**. I didn't **think** things **through** — I would just do **whatever** I **felt** like, no matter **what** the **consequences** would be. I felt **sorry** for whoever got in my **way**, because, **basically**, I just ran **over** them. When I was in the **army**, I wanted to go work **out** in the **gym**, but my commanding **officer** wanted me to do some **work**. I really needed to work **out** because I was getting **ready** for a **competition**, but the **officer** just wouldn't **listen** to me. He kept **yelling** at me to get **working**, so I grabbed a **machine** gun and started **firing**. The guy ran so **fast** and **jumped** behind a **wall**. If he hadn't been so **quick**, I'm sure I would have **shot** him. I **really** wasn't **thinking**. Of **course**, I got in **all** kinds of **trouble**. They put me in the **brig** for a couple of **days** and they wanted to **court** martial me. **Fortunately**, my **father**, who is a **doctor** and famous **bicyclist**, was able to get me **out** and to get the **charges** dropped. He was **so mad** at me that he didn't **speak** to me for a **year**. I **really** didn't think that one **through**.

Exercise 10-2: "The Army Incident" — Pronunciation	CD 2 Track 52

Listen to the audio and repeat, focusing on intonation and pronunciation.

ACCENT	When I wuz **younger**, I wuz rilly **crazy**. I didn't **think** thingz **thru** — I wüd just do **whadever** I **felt** like, no mædder **what** the **cänsequences** wüd be. I felt **särry** for whoever gät in my **way**,

b'cuz, **basaklee**, I just ran **over** them. When I was in the **army**, I wänted to go work **out** in the **gym**, but my commanding **äfficer** wänted me t' do some **work**. I rilly needed to work **out** because I was gedding **reddy** for a **cämpetition**, but the **äfficer** just wüdn **lissen** to me. He kept **yelling** at me t' get **working**, so I græbbed a **m'cheen** gun and stärded **firing**. The guy ræn so **fast** and **jumpt** b'hind a **wall**. If he hædn't been so **quick**, I'm sure I wüda **shät** him. I **rilly** wuzn't **thinking**. Of **corss**, I gät in **äll** kindza **trubble**. They püt me in the **brig** for a coupla **dayz** and they wänted t' **court** märtial me. **Forchunately**, my **fäther**, who izza **däctor** and famous **bicyclist**, wuzable to get me **out** and t' get the **chärges** dräpt. He wuz **so mad** at me that he didn't **speak** t' me fora **yir**. I **rilly** didn't think that one **thru**.

M, N, Ng

Let's work on the three nasal consonants—M, N, and the NG combination. These sounds come out through the nose. For each one, the air is blocked in the mouth in one of three locations.

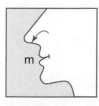 **M** is the easiest and most obvious. Like **B**, the lips come together, and the air can't get out, so it has to come out through the nose.

 **N** is similar to **T**, but it is more relaxed. It fills the mouth, touching the insides of all the teeth, leaving no room for the air to escape, except through the nose.

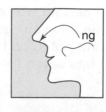 **NG** is back in the throat with [g]. The back of the tongue presses back, and again, the air comes out through the nose.

Exercise 10-3: Nasal Consonants — CD 2 Track 53

Let's contrast nasal and non-nasal consonants. Listen and repeat.

	Initial		Middle		Final	
m/b	my	by	grammer	grabber	rim	rib
n/d	no	dough	bunny	buddy	Ben	bed
ng/g	wrong answer	green	finger	digger	wrong	log

Exercise 10-4: Ending Nasal Consonants — CD 2 Track 54

Here we'll focus on the final sounds. Listen and repeat.

M	N	ND	NG
rum^ə	run^ə	round	rung^ə
some	son	sound	sung
dumb	torn	found	tongue
palm	pond	pound	song

The Held T

When you have an **N** immediately after a **T**, don't pop the **T**. Leave the tongue in the **T** position and hum. (There is no T and no ə.) Another point to remember is that you need a sharp upward sliding intonation up to the "held T," then a quick drop for the N.

T

nnnnn

written	sentence
gotten	certain
forgotten	mountain
important	button
eaten	rotten

Exercise 10-5: "Held T" Before N — CD 2 Track 55

Read the following sentences out loud. Remember, there is no "uh" sound before the N.

1. He'd **forgotten** the **rotten written sentence.**
2. She wasn't **certain** who had **written** it.
3. They **certainly** haven't **gotten** a new **mountain** bike.
4. It's **important** not to be **frightened**.
5. The **kitten** has **eaten** the **button**.

NOUNS

In this section, we focus on word order, prefixes, synonyms, colloquial expressions such as **doubt** vs. **question**, and the position of **only** in a sentence.

Word Order

One of the most important elements in both written and spoken English is proper word order. The main form that you use is SVO, but here is a synopsis of the three most common instances where the word order changes.

The Question Flip ↻

When you change from a sentence to a question, the word order reverses.

He is here.
Is he here?

This also shows up with tag endings.

He is here.
He is here, isn't he?

Reverse Modifiers

With noun descriptions, you can either use a standard adjective before the noun or a clause after it.

nice people
people who are nice

Active and Passive

When you change from the active voice to the passive, you reverse the position of the subject and the object.

Dogs eat bones.
Bones are eaten by dogs.

Only

The word **only** has several meanings, including **just**, **one**, **simply**, **merely**, and **but**, and this is determined by the word order. It tends to modify the word that is right next to it.

Exercise 10-6: *Only*   CD 2 Track 56

Listen to the audio and repeat, focusing on intonation and meaning.

Only my brother told the truth (No one else did).
My **only** brother told the truth. (I only have one brother.)
My brother **only** told the truth. (He didn't say anything else.)
My brother told **only** the truth. (He never lied.)
My brother told the **only** truth. (There is only one truth.)
My brother told the truth **only** if people wanted to hear it. (In the case that)
My brother told the truth, **only** to find that no one wanted to hear it. (negative result)
My brother told the truth, **only** this time, everyone was glad to hear it. (But this time)

Exercise 10-7: *Only*

Check the box with the appropriate response. Then check the Answer Key.

1. This information is for your eyes only.
   - ☐ It's for your viewing.
   - ☐ It's not for your ears.

2. He's an only child.
   - ☐ He doesn't have any siblings.
   - ☐ He is very young.

3. He's only a child.
   - ☐ He doesn't have any siblings.
   - ☐ He is very young.

4. Only we call on Wednesdays.
   - ☐ No one else calls.
   - ☐ That's the only day we call.

5. We only call on Wednesdays.
   - ☐ No one else calls.
   - ☐ That's the only day we call.

Doubt and *Question*

Both **doubt** and **question** indicate a lack. **Doubt** is a feeling of uncertainty or a lack of conviction, whereas a **question** is used to gain information.

Exercise 10-8: *Doubt / Question*

Select the appropriate response. Then check the Answer Key.

1. I have to say that I _____ that he'll be there.
   - ☐ doubt
   - ☐ question

2. He had a _____ about the lesson.
   - ☐ doubt
   - ☐ question

3. It was simply a _____ of time. (not if, but when)
   - ☐ doubt
   - ☐ question

4. Without a _____, he'll arrange it.
   - ☐ doubt
   - ☐ question

5. I don't _____ it for a moment.
   - ☐ doubt
   - ☐ question

6. The widow _____ the banker's rosy promises.
   - ☐ doubted
   - ☐ questioned

7. The detective _____ the suspect about where he had been.
   - ☐ doubted
   - ☐ questioned

8. We have our _____ about him.
   - ☐ doubts
   - ☐ questions

9. The students had a lot of _____ for the teacher about the test.
   - ☐ doubts
   - ☐ questions

10. I'd like to ask a _____.
    - ☐ doubt
    - ☐ question

Prefixes

It's useful to know the basic prefixes, as you can then guess the meaning of a word that you aren't familiar with. There are common changes, such as –**pel** to –**ulsion** (propel / propulsion); –**vert** to –**version** (convert / conversion); –**tend** to –**tention** (attend / attention). The unstressed syllable is neutral (con**vert** / cən**vert**, re**duce** / rə**duce**). There is an intonation change between the noun (**pro**duce) and the verb (pro**duce**).

Listen and repeat. The intonation is marked for you.

	-vert	-tend	-pel	-tract	-port	-duce/duct
a-	a**vert**	at**tend**	ap**pel**late	at**tract**	ap**por**tion	ad**duce**
con/com-	con**vert**	con**tend**	com**pel**	con**tract**	com**port**	con**duct**
di/dis/de-	di**vert**	dis**tend**	dis**pel**	dis**tract**	de**port**	de**duct**/de**duce**
e/ex-	e**vert**	ex**tend**	ex**pel**	ex**tract**	ex**port**	**ed**ucate
in/im-	in**vert**	in**tend**	im**pel**	in**tract**able	im**port**	in**duce**
pro/pre/per	per**vert**	pre**tend**	pro**pel**	pro**tract**	pro**por**tion	pro**duce**
re-	re**vert**	re**tain**	re**pel**	re**tract**	re**port**	re**duce**

The following is a portion of President Barack Obama's inaugural speech, given on January 21, 2009. The first section is the standard text, with the intonation marked for you. The second section is the phonetic transcription. The third section is a simplified version of the speech.

Listen and repeat.

My fellow citizens, I **stand** here **today humbled** by the task **before** us, **grateful** for the **trust** you have **bestowed**, **mindful** of the **sacrifices borne** by our **ancestors**. I thank President **Bush** for his **service** to our **nation**, as well as the **generosity** and **cooperation** he has shown through**out** this **transition**.

My fellow cidəzənz, I stænd hir təday həmbəld by the tæsk bəforəs, gratfəl fr thə trəst yoov bəstowd, mindfəl əv thə sæcrəfysəz born by är æncestrrz. I thænk Prezədent Büsh for hiz srrvəs to(w)är nation, az welləz thə genərasədy and co(w)äperation he yəz shown thru(w)out this trænzition.

Americans, I am here today with great respect for the job ahead of us. I thank you for the trust you have given to me. I know how much the previous generations have given up and done without. I thank President Bush for his hard work for our country, and for the help he has given me during the transition.

Forty-four **Americans** have now **taken** the presidential **oath**. The **words** have been **spoken** during **rising** tides of **prosperity** and the **still** waters of **peace**. **Yet**, **every** so **often** the **oath** is **taken** amidst gathering **clouds** and raging **storms**. At these **moments**, **America** has carried on **not simply** because of the **skill** or **vision** of **those** in high **office**, but because **We** the **People** have remained **faithful** to the

ideals of our **forebearers**, and **true** to our founding **documents**. So it has **been**. So it must **be** with **this** generation of **Americans**.

Fordy-for əmerəcənz həv now takən the prezədenshəloath. Thə wrrdzəv bin spokən dyuring rizing tyd zəv präsperədy and thə still wäder zəv pees. Yet, evry so^(w)äffen thee^(y)oathiz takən əmidst gæthering clæodz and raging stormz. ət theez moments, əmerəcə həz kerry dän nät simply bəcəzəv thə skill or vizhən əv thozin high^(y)äffəs, bət bəcəz We thə Peepəl həv rəmaind faithfəl tə thee^(y)idee^(y)əlz əv our forbearerz, and tru to^(w)är founding däcyəmənts. So^(w)it haz bin. So^(w)it must be with this genaration'v əmerəcənz.

Up to now, forty-four Americans have made this statement to be president. They have said these words while our country was rich and peaceful. But, sometimes, they said them while we were poor or at <u>war</u>. At these times, America has continued, not only because of elected people who work hard or understand what needs to be done, but because Americans have stayed with the best ideas of the previous generations and have followed the Constitution. This is how it has been. This is how it has to be with us.

That we are in the **midst** of **crisis** is now well under**stood**. Our **nation** is at **war**, against a **far**-reaching **net**work of **violence** and **hatred**. Our **economy** is badly **weakened**, a **consequence** of **greed** and **irresponsibility** on the part of **some**, but **also** our collective **failure** to make hard **choices** and **prepare** the **nation** for a new **age**. **Homes** have been **lost**; **jobs shed**; **businesses shuttered**. Our **health** care is too **costly**; our **schools** fail too **many**; and **each** day brings further **evidence** that the ways we use **energy strengthen** our **adversaries** and **threaten** our **planet**.

That we are in the midst of crisis is now well understüd. Är nashən izzət war, əgenst ə **fär**-reaching **net**wrrk əv **violence** and **hatred**. Är **ecänomy** iz bædly **week**ənd, ə **cäns**əquents əv **greed** and **irrespänsibility** än thə pärdəv **səm**, bəd**älso** är cəllectəv fay-yəlyer tə make härd choisəz and prəpar thə nation frə new age. Homzəv bin läst; jäbs shed; biznessəz shədderd. Är helth care iz too cästly; är schoolz fail too many; and **each** day bringz further **evədents** thət thə wayz we yuz energy strengthən är ædversereez and threat'n är plænət.

People now understand that we are in the middle of a huge problem. Our country is at war against a wide system of fighting and hate. Our economy is weak. This is a result of some greedy, irresponsible people. It is also the result of our group failure to make hard choices and prepare the country for a new time. People have lost their homes and their jobs, and businesses have closed. Our hospitals are too expensive. Our schools don't teach children well enough. And every day shows us that our energy use makes our enemies stronger and is bad for the earth.

These are the **indicators** of **crisis**, subject to **data** and **statistics**. Less **measurable** but no less **profound** is a **sapping** of **confidence** across our **land** — a nagging **fear** that America's **decline** is **inevitable**, that the next **generation** must **lower** its **sights**.

Theez är thee^(y)indəcaderz əv crysəs, səbject tə dadə and stətistəcs. Less mezhrəbəl bət no less prəfound izə sæpping əv cänfədənts əcräss är lænd — ə nægging fear thəd əmerəcəz decline izinevətəbəl, thət thə next genəration məst lower its sights.

These are the signs of big problems. You can see this in the numbers in the reports. It is not as easy to measure the decrease in confidence in America, but it is equally important. There is a continuing fear that America will fail and the next generation will have to accept less in life.

Today I say to **you** that the **challenges** we face are **real**. They are **serious** and they are **many**. They will not be met **easily** or in a **short** span of **time**. But **know this**, **America** — they **will** be **met**. On **this** day, we **gather** because we have chosen **hope** over **fear**, **unity** of **purpose** over **conflict** and **discord**. On this **day**, we come to **proclaim** an **end** to the petty **grievances** and false **promises**, the **recriminations** and worn-out **dogmas**, that for far too **long** have **strangled** our **politics**.

Təday I say də **you** thət thə **chælləngəz** we face är **real**. They är **siree**[(y)]**us** and they är **many**. They will nät be met **eezəly** or innə **short** span əv **time**. But know **this**, əmerəcə — they **will** be **met**. Än this day, we **gæ**ther bəcəz we həv chozən ho po ver fir, yunədy əv prpəs over **cæn**flict and discord. Än this day, we cəm tə **prəclaim** ənend tə thə peddy greevəncəz and false **präm**əsəz, thə rəcrimənashənz and wor nout **dägmə**z, thət fr fär too läng həv **stræn**gəld är **päl**ətics.

I am telling you today that we are facing real challenges. They are serious and there are a lot of them. It will not be easy to fix these problems and it will take a long time. But we will fix them. We are here together today because we think hope is better than fear. We think that we should all work together instead of fighting and arguing. We are here to say that this is the end of small complaints and false promises. We have to stop blaming each other and using old ideas. This has held our politics back.

We remain a young **nation**, but in the words of **Scripture**, the **time** has **come** to set **aside** childish **things**. The **time** has **come** to **reaffirm** our enduring **spirit**; to **choose** our better **history**; to carry **forward** that precious **gift**, that noble **idea**, **passed** on from generation to **generation**: the **God**-given **promise** that **all** are **equal**, **all** are **free**, and **all** deserve a chance to **pursue** their **full** measure of **happiness**.

We rəmainə yəng **nation**, bəddin thə wrrdz əv **Scripchər**, thə **time** həz **cəm** tə sedə **side** childish **thingz**. Thə **time** həz **cəme** tə ree[(y)]**əffirm** är endyuring **spirət**; tə **chooz**ar bedder **histry**; tə carry **forwrrd** thæt preshəs **gift**, thæt nobəl **ideə**, **pæst** än frəm generation tə **genəration**: thə **Gäd**-givən **präməs** thə**däller** eekəl, **äller free**, and **äll** dəzervə chænts tə **prrsue** their **füll** mezher əv **hæpp**inəss.

We are still a young country. As it says in the Bible, it is time to stop acting like children. It is time to talk about our lasting spirit. It is time to choose a better path for our history. It is time to carry forward that valuable gift, that noble idea, that has been passed on from generation to generation. It is a promise from God that all people are equal, everyone is free, and we all should have the chance of as much happiness as possible.

Synonyms

A synonym is a word with a meaning that is similar to another word. For example, synonyms for *sarcastic* are *ironic, sardonic, mocking*, and *satirical*. These are all words indicating mockery, but there are important nuances.

One of the first things a child learns in elementary school is to use synonyms in order to avoid repeating the same word over and over again. The following is a student writing sample. You'll notice that the word **cook** is used in various forms 13 times. In the rewrite, the word has been replaced all but three times.

Repetitive Wording

Have I ever told you how lucky I am? Yesterday my husband **cooked** a cake! It was the most delicious cake I had ever eaten in my life. You may know that I'm not good at **cooking**. If I had had to **cook**, I would have **cooked** instant noodles. When I was in Thailand, my dad and my two sisters did all the **cooking**. If I had wanted to eat something and I didn't know how to **cook** it, I just told them what it looked like, and they would **cook** it and it always turned out very delicious. When I decided to get married, everyone got worried. That was because I knew nothing about **cooking**. First I told my husband-to-be that I didn't know how to **cook**, but he said that was OK, he would teach me. Do you know what Thai potato curry looks like? Steve **cooked** it for me. It was so good and I liked it. He taught me how to **cook**. Today I can **cook** almost everything he likes and also some Thai foods. I hope I will be a perfect **cook** soon. When I visit my family in Thailand, I will show them how good I am.

With Synonyms

Have I ever told you how lucky I am? Yesterday my husband **made** a cake! It was the most delicious cake I had ever eaten in my life. You may know that I'm not a good **cook**. If I had had to **make dinner**, I would have **heated up** instant noodles. When I was in Thailand, my dad and my two sisters **made** all the meals. If I wanted to eat something and I didn't know how to **prepare** it, I just told them what it looked like, and they would **take care of** it and it always turned out very delicious. When I decided to get married, everyone got worried. That was because I knew nothing about **the kitchen**. I told my husband-to-be that, but he said that was OK, he would teach me. Do you know what Thai potato curry looks like? He **fixed** it for me once. It was so good and I liked it. He taught me how to **cook**. Today I can **make** almost everything he likes and also some Thai foods. When I visit my family in Thailand, I will show them how good I am.

VERBS

In this section, you will learn the true passive and the various imitation passives, as well as six useful verbs, and the past and future real duo.

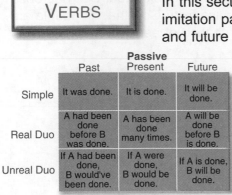

	Past	**Passive** Present	Future
Simple	It was done.	It is done.	It will be done.
Real Duo	A had been done before B was done.	A has been done many times.	A will be done before B is done.
Unreal Duo	If A had been done, B would've been done.	If A were done, B would be done.	If A is done, B will be done.

The Passive

There are two ways of giving information. The most direct is called the **active voice** (SVO), as in **The dogs ate the bones**. With the active voice, the subject (the dogs) does something to the object (the bones). You can flip this order so the subject receives the action (**The bones were eaten by the dogs**).

The passive voice always includes a form of *be*, such as *am, is, was, were, are,* or *been*. Another way to recognize it is that it may include "by," such as *It was developed by a team of engineers*.

The active voice is more common and is generally preferred as it makes your communications stronger and more dynamic. Overuse of the passive voice will make you sound flat and uninteresting. There are instances where the passive voice should be used, however, such as in scientific writing, where it gives the appearance of objectivity.

1 Let's start with the active voice. You did something and you admit it. I **broke** the cup.	**3** One step further away, it turns into a description, and doesn't involve you at all. The cup **is broken**.
2 Next, you remove yourself a bit. This is the true passive voice. The cup **was broken** (by me). The cup **got broken** (by me).	**4** Finally, you blame the cup. The cup **broke**.

With these particular verbs, it's common to put the focus on the **action**, rather than on the **cause**.	It broke. It bent. It creased. It crinkled. It crumpled. It folded. It rumpled. It wrinkled. It chipped. It cracked. It crumbled.	It crashed. It crushed. It fractured. It ripped. It shattered. It smashed. It snapped. It splintered. It split. It tore. It healed.

Exercise 10-11: Switching Between Active and Passive

Change to the opposite form. Then check the Answer Key.

A watched B.
A was folded by **B.**

B was watched by A.
B folded A.

1. The boys washed the cars.

2. The papers were handed out by the teacher.

3. The dentist cleaned her teeth.

4. Everyone was upset by his remarks.

5. Gold was discovered by the miners.

6. Snow covered the fields.

7. The plan will be revised by the committee.

8. Our intelligence has been insulted by the media.

9. The patient should have been informed by the doctor.

10. The mailman will have delivered the package by 5:00 p.m.

Exercise 10-12: Active to No-Blame Passive

*Change to **no-blame**. Then check the Answer Key.*

They opened it.   **It opened.**
1. Joe tore the paper.

2. Sammy rocked the boat.

3. Edna crashed the car.

4. Gloria fractured her leg.

5. The suspect burned the evidence.

6. Angela overflowed the tub.

7. Ben tipped over the vase.

8. The drycleaner wrinkled his shirt.

9. Edgar chipped his tooth.

10. The wind snapped the branch.

Exercise 10-13: Passive Voice

Fill in the blanks using the appropriate words from the following list. Then check the Answer Key.

Soybeans _____ in Asia more than 3,000 years ago. A mural shows tofu and soy milk _____ in northern China. The earliest written reference to soy milk didn't occur for another 1,200 years, when soy milk _____ in a Chinese poem, "Ode to Tofu."

Travelers from Europe _____ with soybeans and the foods _____ them — especially miso, soy sauce, and tofu. Soybeans arrived in the United States in the 1700s, _____ Europe by several people including Benjamin Franklin.

Soy-based infant formulas _____ in the United States in 1909, and in 1910 the world's first soy dairy _____ by a Chinese biologist. By the end of the first World War, soy milk _____ commercially in New York. Within 15 years, manufacturers _____ with added nutrients such as calcium.

became acquainted	was started	brought from	made from
was mentioned	being made	were first cultivated	
were introduced	were experimenting	was being produced	

Six Useful Verbs

MANAGE	TURN OUT
He **managed** to pay his bills, even though he didn't earn very much.	He thought he had no cash, but it **turned out** that he had $5 in his back pocket.
HAPPEN TO	**USED TO**
By chance, he **happened to** forget his wallet that day.	This kind of thing **used to** happen to him all the time.
END UP	**WOUND UP**
He thought he would have to write a check, but he **ended up** doing dishes to pay his bill.	He started out in the kitchen, but somehow **wound up** in the back office working on the company taxes.

Exercise 10-14: 6 Useful Verbs

Select the most appropriate of the six verbs. Then check the Answer Key.

1. It was hard, but we _____ to find a spot.
2. Did anyone _____ pick up the dry-cleaning?
3. When she was young, she _____ hike a lot.
4. He seemed honest, but he _____ not to be.
5. They started out in L.A., but _____ in New York.
6. It didn't _____ the way we expected.
7. If you _____ see him, say hello for me.
8. Didn't you _____ live in L.A.?
9. He wanted to be a doctor, but _____ working as an auto mechanic.
10. They _____ to scrape together the basic costs.

Past Duo

	Past	Present	Future
Simple	I did it. ◄	I do it. ●	I'll do it. ►
Real Duo	I'd done A before I did B. ◄◄	...ve done it. ◄●	I'll've done A before I do B. ►►
Unreal Duo	done A, I would've done B. ◄◄	If I did A, I'd do B. ◄●	If I do A, I'll do B. ►►

As you learned with the present duo, you can link two events in time.

The **past duo** expresses the idea that something happened before another action in the past. It can also show that something happened before a specific time in the past.

This is traditionally called the past perfect.

Exercise 10-15: Past Duo

Using the provided phrase, change the past or present to the past duo. Then check the Answer Key.

1. He has never been to Los Angeles.

   Until he was invited by the university last year,

2. He lost his wallet.

   He didn't have any money because

3. He frequently traveled there.

   Ron was very familiar with Paris as

4. We didn't make a reservation.

   We couldn't get a hotel room since

5. Fred was in college for ten years.

   By the time he graduated,

6. They owned their house for 20 years.

   They felt bad about moving because

Present and Past Duo Review

Exercise 10-16: Past Duo and Present Duo

Fill in the blanks with the most appropriate verb form, including the simple past and the present and past duo. Then check the Answer Key.

1. You may _____ (hear) of Ernest Hemingway. He _____ (be) an American novelist who _____ (die) in 1961. Prior to his death, he _____ (write) over a dozen novels.
2. Every year, Joyce and Blake _____ (spend) a few days at a hotel in Fiji. They _____ (go) there for years.
3. Sam _____ (go) for a bike ride after school yesterday. He _____ (want) some exercise because he _____ (sit) in a stuffy classroom all day.
4. It _____ (be) six months since I've seen my cousins.
5. Lee was driving over to pick up his wife. Outside her office, he met a couple of people he knew. They wanted to go out for coffee, but he _____ (arrange) to meet his wife for dinner and didn't have time.

Exercise 10-17: When Did Those Two Things Happen?

Select the correct answer. Then check the Answer Key.

1. We _____ to Paris.

   ☐ have never been
   ☐ had never been

2. We _____ to Paris **before** the Olympics.

   ☐ have never been
   ☐ had never been

3. Oh, dear! The sink _____!

   ☐ has overflowed
   ☐ had overflowed

4. The house_____ **by the time** the plumber arrived.
  - ☐ has flooded
  - ☐ had flooded

5. We _____ time to clean it up **yet**.
  - ☐ haven't had
  - ☐ hadn't had

6. We_____ such a mess **before** that event.
  - ☐ haven't ever seen
  - ☐ hadn't ever seen

7. _____ thinking about moving out.
  - ☐ We've already started
  - ☐ We'd already started

8. _____ of moving **until** that happened.
  - ☐ We've never thought
  - ☐ We'd never thought

9. _____ in 20 years.
  - ☐ We haven't moved
  - ☐ We hadn't moved

10. At the beginning of the year, we _____ this possibility!
  - ☐ haven't foreseen
  - ☐ hadn't foreseen

Future Real Duo

So far, you have learned the **present** duo (I have never done that before.) and the **past** duo (I had never done that before last year).

Now, we are going to add the **future** duo, which is two completed actions in the future. Key words are *by*, *by the time*, and *before*.

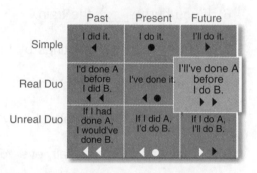

Exercise 10-18: Future Real Duo

Using the provided phrase, change the future or present duo to the future duo. Use the supporting words where provided. Check the Answer Key when you're done.

He **has saved** enough to buy a car.
By next year, he **will have saved** enough to buy a car.

1. Will she learn French before she goes to Paris?

2. I have figured out when I'll graduate.
   By Christmas,

3. He'll finish it.
   by midnight.

4. They'll turn it in.
   before the deadline.

5. She's running out of options.
   before she hears back about the decision.

Future Review

Exercise 10-19: Three Futures

Select the correct tense. Then check the Answer Key.

1. We _____ tomorrow.
   - ☐ will finish
   - ☐ will have finished

2. Do you think you _____ over it by then?
   - ☐ will get
   - ☐ will have gotten

3. If you tell me when, _____ sure to be there.
   - ☐ I'll be
   - ☐ I'll have been

4. _____ you at 8:00 sharp.
   - ☐ I'll call
   - ☐ I will've called

5. Hurry, or they _____ all the food by the time we get there!
   - ☐ will eat
   - ☐ will have eaten

6. If you hurry, _____ the train.
   - ☐ you'll catch
   - ☐ you'll have caught

7. _____ through six meetings by the time you get here.
   - ☐ We'll sit
   - ☐ We'll have sat

8. Do you think _____ this time?
   - ☐ they'll help
   - ☐ they'll have helped

9. Don't worry, _____ all about it by tomorrow.
   - ☐ he'll forget
   - ☐ he'll have forgotten

10. He thinks that if he's fair, everyone _____ him.
    - ☐ will like
    - ☐ will have liked

Exercise 10-20: Verb Review

Select the correct answer. Then check the Answer Key.

1. Joseph _____ groceries last week.
   - ☐ buys
   - ☐ bought

2. I think he _____ it tomorrow.
   - ☐ do
   - ☐ will do

3. Let's _____ him on Friday.
   - ☐ call
   - ☐ to call
   - ☐ calling

4. He _____ out the warehouse right now.
   - ☐ vacuums
   - ☐ is vacuuming

5. Shirley _____ supplies once a month.
   - ☐ orders
   - ☐ is ordering

6. The rec center _____ since 1998.
   - ☐ is open
   - ☐ has been open

7. The hard drive _____.
   - ☐ is corrupt
   - ☐ has corrupted

8. My car _____ many times since May.
   - ☐ stalls
   - ☐ has stalled

9. Ted and Marge _____ away ten years ago.
   - ☐ moved
   - ☐ have moved

10. Joanie _____ on the rowing team since Tuesday.
- ☐ was
- ☐ has been

11. I hope _____ this by Wednesday.
- ☐ finish
- ☐ to finish
- ☐ finishing

12. We wish he _____ be more open about it.
- ☐ will
- ☐ would

13. Everyone hopes they _____ succeed.
- ☐ will
- ☐ would

14. The insurance company _____ by the new agent.
- ☐ is called
- ☐ was called

15. We will _____ by his assistant no later than 5:00.
- ☐ be informed
- ☐ have been informed

16. "I will go," said Tom. He said that he _____.
- ☐ will go
- ☐ would go

17. She _____ here for two years next month.
- ☐ will be
- ☐ will have been

18. If he had taken an aspirin, he _____ have a headache.
- ☐ won't
- ☐ wouldn't

19. If the report _____ clear, we could act on it.
- ☐ was
- ☐ were

20. I'm not sure if I _____ help you.
- ☐ can
- ☐ could

21. He is very motivated, _____ he?
- ☐ isn't
- ☐ doesn't

22. Stewart arranges things very well, _____ he?
- ☐ isn't
- ☐ doesn't

23. The weather has been great, _____ it?
- ☐ isn't
- ☐ hasn't

24. George broke his promise, _____ he?
- ☐ wasn't
- ☐ didn't

25. Candy won't be there, _____ she?
- ☐ will
- ☐ won't

26. That would be nice, _____ it?
- ☐ won't
- ☐ wouldn't

27. Maurice had never been there, _____ he?
- ☐ has
- ☐ had
- ☐ hasn't
- ☐ hadn't

28. Benny wanted to play. The coach _____ play.
- ☐ let him
- ☐ let him to

29. They intended _____ the board soon.
- ☐ notify
- ☐ to notify
- ☐ notifying

30. Someone suggested _____ the subway.
- ☐ take
- ☐ to take
- ☐ taking

TEST	Let's review everything you have learned in Chapter 10. Check your work using the Answer Key.

Part 1: *Select the proper form.*

1. By summer, he _____ in Somalia for a decade.
   - ☐ will be
   - ☐ will have been

2. Next time, they _____ before they come over.
   - ☐ call
   - ☐ will call

3. She isn't sure if she _____ help us.
   - ☐ can
   - ☐ could

4. They have several _____. Would you mind if they asked them?
   - ☐ doubts
   - ☐ questions

5. The commissioner had grave _____ about the testing process.
   - ☐ doubts
   - ☐ questions

6. When I was 16, I _____ in swim meets.
   - ☐ participated
   - ☐ was participated

7. I was _____ English by a college professor.
   - ☐ learned
   - ☐ taught

8. When I was in college, I _____ my husband.
   - ☐ met
   - ☐ was met

9. When I got off the train, I _____ by my sister.
   - ☐ met
   - ☐ was met

10. The product _____ the rigorous standards.
    - ☐ didn't meet
    - ☐ wasn't met

Part 2: *Select the proper form.*

1. I hope you _____ it.
   - ☐ like
   - ☐ would like

2. I hope he _____ find it.
   - ☐ will
   - ☐ would

3. I hoped he _____ take it, but he didn't.
   - ☐ will
   - ☐ would

4. I wish he _____ go.
   - ☐ can
   - ☐ could

5. I wished he _____, but he didn't.
   - ☐ went
   - ☐ had gone

6. I hope he _____ interested.
   - ☐ is
   - ☐ were

7. I wish he _____ interested, but he's not.
   - ☐ is
   - ☐ were

8. I hoped he _____ interested.
   - ☐ was
   - ☐ were

9. I wished he _____ interested.
   - ☐ has been
   - ☐ had been

10. I had hoped that he _____ interested, but he wasn't.
    - ☐ will be
    - ☐ would be

Part 3: *Fill in the proper tag ending.*

1. They have to change the rules, _____ ?
2. They have changed the rules, _____ ?
3. They had to change the rules, _____ ?
4. They had the rules changed, _____ ?
5. They had already changed the rules, _____ ?
6. They'd better change the rules, _____ ?
7. They'd rather change the rules, _____ ?
8. The rules have changed, _____ ?
9. The rules will be changed, _____ ?
10. The rules have been changed, _____ ?

Part 4: *Select the proper form.*

1. "I will do it." I said that I _____ it.
   - ☐ will do
   - ☐ would do

2. They found it. They thought they _____ it.
   - ☐ found
   - ☐ had found

3. She isn't ready. She told us that she _____ ready.
   - ☐ isn't
   - ☐ wasn't

4. If you have time, we _____ to the park.
   - ☐ will go
   - ☐ would go
   - ☐ would've gone

5. If you had time, we _____ to the park.
   - ☐ will go
   - ☐ would go
   - ☐ would've gone

6. If you'd had time, we _____ to the park.
   - ☐ will go
   - ☐ would go
   - ☐ would've gone

7. If they _____ interested, they would join.
   - ☐ are
   - ☐ were
   - ☐ had been

8. If they _____ interested, they would've joined.
   - ☐ are
   - ☐ were
   - ☐ had been

9. If they _____ interested, they will join.
   - ☐ are
   - ☐ were
   - ☐ had been

10. People will be happy if that _____ true.
    - ☐ is
    - ☐ was
    - ☐ were

Using what you have learned, write an essay using the following topics:

1. What childhood friends would you like to reconnect with?
2. If you had to move, what would you miss most about your home?

You can handwrite your essay below or e-mail it to **para@grammar.bz** to be stored. These paragraphs are not graded or reviewed, but simply by writing them, your English will improve. For this final essay, review the outline format, the writing structure checklist, and the technical editing checklist.

Student Paragraph
Send Chat Attach Address Fonts Colors Save As Draft Photo Browser Show Stationery

To: para@grammar.bz

Cc:

Bcc:

Subject: Chapter 10

Signature: Corporate

My name is _____

Outline Format

You'll notice that this is the same format you first learned in Chapter 1: Introduction, Body, and Conclusion. The number of main points, subpoints, and sub-subpoints will change depending on how much information you have and how much detail and supporting material you need to use. Don't use more than five main points in your essay.

Introduction

I. Attention-getting statement — Get the reader's attention by telling a short or humorous story, asking a question, using a quotation, etc.
II. Thesis statement — State the specific purpose of your essay.
III. Preview statement — Give an overview of all of your main points.

Body

I. First main point
    A. Subpoint
        1. Sub-subpoint
        2. Sub-subpoint
    B. Subpoint
        1. Sub-subpoint
        2. Sub-subpoint
        3. Sub-subpoint

II. Second main point
    A. Subpoint
        1. Sub-subpoint
        2. Sub-subpoint
    B. Subpoint
        1. Sub-subpoint
        2. Sub-subpoint
        3. Sub-subpoint
    C. Subpoint

Conclusion

I. Summary statement — Review all of your main points.
II. Concluding statement — Prepare a closing statement that ends your presentation smoothly.

Writing Structure Checklist

1. ☐ There are at least 200 words.
2. ☐ There are at least 15 periods (i.e., 15 complete sentences).
3. ☐ The introduction has 2–3 sentences, the main paragraph 10–11, and the conclusion 2–3.
4. ☐ The introduction captures the reader's interest.
5. ☐ There is a clear topic sentence in the first paragraph. This is an opinion that needs support and is not just a simple fact.
6. ☐ The introduction does not use the words **I agree**, **I disagree**, **I think, in my opinion**, etc.
7. ☐ The main body paragraph gives 2–3 different reasons or a combination of reasons and examples that support the topic sentence in the introduction.
8. ☐ There is a single voice, with no shifting between I / you / we / they.
9. ☐ Vocabulary, idioms, prepositions, and word order sound natural.
10. ☐ Every sentence connects to the sentence before and after it in some way; synonym, antonym, repeated word, word form, etc.
11. ☐ There are at least four different sentence types.

Technical Editing Checklist

1. ☐ The mechanical aspects of punctuation, spelling, capitalization, and indenting are correct.
2. ☐ There are no sentence fragments. Every sentence can be turned into a yes/no question.
   Complete: I was tired. (Was I tired?)
   Fragment: Because I was tired. (You can't ask, I was tired because?)
3. ☐ Every two-part sentence has a joiner (for, and, but, or, yet, so).
4. ☐ All future time clauses use the simple present tense.
   Correct: When I go...
   Incorrect: When I will go...
5. ☐ There is an **article** (a, an, the) or other **modifier** (my, one, that, etc.) before every **single** countable noun.
6. ☐ There are proper plural noun modifiers such as **these** and **those**.
7. ☐ There is an **–S ending** on every plural noun, with the few exceptions of **men**, **women**, **people**, **children**, etc.
8. ☐ **The** is only used to mean something specific. It is not used with general things, such as **life**, **nature**, **kindness**.
9. ☐ Each **he** / **she** / **it** / **they** refers back to a specific noun that it matches (i.e., singular / singular & plural / plural).
10. ☐ The simple form is used after these helping verbs: can / could / will / would / may / might / must / shall / should (e.g., I can **go**).
11. ☐ The simple form is used after **do**, **does**, or **did** (Did he **go**?, not Did he **went**?).
12. ☐ A comma is used with **which**, but not with **that**.

Let's review everything you've learned in Chapters 6 through 10. Check your work using the Answer Key.

*Part 1: Join the two statements using **that**.*

1. We are sad. We lost the game.

2. He is happy. His friends arrived safely.

Part 2: Rewrite each sentence starting with the indicated phrase.

1. They finished it.
   It's not clear who

2. It's wonderful.
   She said that

3. They can't swim.
   I thought that

Part 3: Change the statement to an indirect question by adding the statement to the intro phrase.

1. She bought groceries.
   Do you remember that

2. They got married.
   Did you know that

3. The new store opened.
   Did you hear that

Part 4: Change the statement to an indirect question, using your own intro phrase.

1. They went **there**.

2. **That girl** won an award.

3. He drove to California **on Wednesday**.

*Part 5: Fill in the blank with **so** or **such**.*

1. He was _____ worried about his lost dog.
2. We are _____ good friends.
3. Her teacher is _____ prepared to teach class every day.
4. I had _____ an amazing time at the concert!

Part 6: *Fill in the blank with the proper form of* **hope** *or* **wish**.

1. She   she had a million dollars.
2. She   you will give her a million dollars.
3. We   you have a nice day.
4. We   it were a nice day.

Part 7: *Complete the sentence with the appropriate probability verb.*

1. I _____ be able to go with you.   0% probability
2. You _____ finish your homework before you go out   strong probability
   tonight.
3. She _____ help you.   slight possibility
4. We _____ complete the sale tomorrow.   100% probability
5. He _____ know the answer; let's ask him.   50% possibility

Part 8: *Complete the sentence with the appropriate verb of obligation.*

1. We _____ followed directions.   past advice
2. She _____ catch up, or she'll be left behind!   obligation
3. You _____ be four feet tall to go on this ride.   strong obligation
4. I _____ only bench-press fifty pounds.   ability
5. You _____ eat dessert after you finish your meal.   permission

Part 9: *Fill in the blank with the proper form of* **say, tell, speak,** *or* **talk**.

1. Please   your sister that I called.
2. Don't   that! It's not true!
3. You should   with the sales associate if you have a question.
4. We were   loudly in the library.

Part 10: *Select the proper word.*

1. Did you _____ that noise? It surprised me!   ☐ listen to
        ☐ hear
2. We should _____ his advice; he knows what he's talking   ☐ listen to
   about.   ☐ hear
3. It _____ like a UFO! I'm serious!   ☐ appeared
        ☐ looked
4. We _____ everywhere but couldn't find it.   ☐ looked
        ☐ saw
5. The babysitter _____ the children while their parents were   ☐ looked at
   out.   ☐ watched
6. Your singing _____ very professional.   ☐ looks
        ☐ sounds

Part 11: Flip the adjective in each of the following sentences.

1. The **very hungry** caterpillar wouldn't stop eating.

2. The **bright red** car was the fastest at the race.

3. A person **who is funny** can make other people laugh.

4. Water **that has frozen** is called ice.

Part 12: Compact the sentences.

1. **The flowers** are blooming. **They** grow in the garden.

1. I know **a girl**. **She** can speak three languages.

*Part 13: Convert the following statement to **Who**, **What**, **Where**, **When**, **Why**, and **How** questions.*
My grandmother eagerly takes the bus to the market every day to sell scarves that she has knitted.

1. Who
2. What
3. Where
4. When
5. Why
6. How

*Part 14: Change the **bold words** to an **else** phrase.*

1. We went to **the other store** to find milk.

2. He talked to **the other salesperson**.

Part 15: Select the proper form.

1. He hasn't worked there _____ three years. ☐ for ☐ ago ☐ in
2. We moved into this house two weeks _____. ☐ for ☐ ago ☐ in
3. She listens to music _____ she rides the bus. ☐ during ☐ while
4. You weren't paying attention _____ the meeting. ☐ during ☐ while
5. You have to turn in your paper _____ Friday. ☐ by ☐ until
6. She won't give up _____ they find her purse. ☐ by ☐ until
7. I've known about that _____ yesterday. ☐ for ☐ since
8. We'll call you _____ lunch. ☐ in ☐ after
9. The judge has not _____ heard all of the arguments. ☐ yet ☐ already ☐ still
10. Have you _____ finished eating? ☐ yet ☐ already ☐ still

Part 16: *Fill in the proper* **tag ending**.

1. They have to listen to you, _____ ?
2. They haven't changed, _____ ?
3. They had already done it, _____ ?
4. She will have finished it by then, _____ ?
5. We've been good, _____ ?

Part 17: *Convert each statement to a* **how question**.

1. That ride was so scary!
2. We bought 60 pounds of potatoes.
3. There are 60 minutes in an hour.

Part 18: *Convert each statement from the —en verb to* **make** *and an* **adjective**.

1. He lifts weights to strengthen his body.
2. This lamp lightens the room.
3. This polish hardens the surface.

Part 19: *Fill in the blank with* **to, for, of, on, with, about, out, at, in, out, than, up,** *or* **from**.

1. I like to think _____ all the good times with my friends.
2. We need to get _____ the store before it closes.
3. We want to take advantage _____ the sale before it ends.
4. Who does this purse belong _____ ?
5. He is preparing _____ his trip to Hawaii.
6. She is getting ready _____ the dance tonight.
7. Who is taking care _____ the children after school?
8. He refuses to ask _____ help.
9. I am looking forward _____ my upcoming vacation.
10. They work _____ at the gym three days a week.

Part 20: *Indicate if each sentence is grammatically correct.*

1. We made them to stand up. ☐ Yes ☐ No
2. We allow them to stand up. ☐ Yes ☐ No
3. We force them to stand up. ☐ Yes ☐ No
4. We permit them to stand up. ☐ Yes ☐ No
5. We let them to stand up. ☐ Yes ☐ No

Part 21: *Change the direct statement to a reported statement.*

1. She calls her sister every day.
   I thought that

2. They will talk to him tomorrow.
   We believed that

3. He'll wake up early when he has to work.
   He said that

Part 22: *Fill in the blank with **their / they're / there**.*

1. Have you seen _____ house? It's gorgeous.
2. _____ not coming back until Saturday.
3. _____ is something wrong with that picture.

Part 23: *Fill in the blank with **to / too / two**.*

1. I ate _____ much last night!
2. I ate _____ pieces of pie.
3. I didn't mean _____ eat so much, but I couldn't help myself!

Part 24: *Check the box with the appropriate meaning of the sentence.*

1. We were the only ones at the party.
   - ☐ Nobody else was having a party.
   - ☐ Nobody else was at the party.
2. He is only hosting the party in town.
   - ☐ He is not doing anything but hosting.
   - ☐ Nobody else is hosting the party.

Part 25: *Select the appropriate response.*

1. If I _____ his judgment, he will become defensive.
   - ☐ doubt
   - ☐ question
2. If you have any _____, I will answer them.
   - ☐ doubts
   - ☐ questions
3. I _____ that she would arrive on time.
   - ☐ doubted
   - ☐ questioned

Part 26: *Change to the opposite form (passive or active).*

1. The stylist cut the girl's hair.

2. The newspapers were distributed by the paperboy.

3. We vacuumed all of the carpets.

Part 27: *Change to no-blame.*

1. Leslie broke the plate.

2. We burned the wood.

3. Joe rolled the tire down the street.

Part 28: *Fill in the blank with the proper form of* **take** *or* **have**.

1. The baby _____ three naps a day.
2. We're _____ company at four.
3. They _____ a short coffee break at ten.
4. Everyone _____ a good time at the party.
5. We're _____ a trip next month.

Part 29: *Fill in the blank with the appropriate preposition.*

1. We got lost and wound _____ 30 miles from our destination.
2. People who succeed don't give _____ easily.
3. I have faith that my lost watch will turn _____ sooner or later.
4. The cake didn't turn _____ the way I had hoped. Oops!
5. If you happen _____ be in the area, stop by and see us.
6. They turned _____ our offer to buy their house.
7. Everyone booed when he gave _____ the ending of the story.
8. She used _____ go there all the time.
9. After the fight, he ended _____ with a black eye.
10. The athlete's knee finally gave _____ after sustaining multiple injuries.

Answer Key

Dictation Placement Test (100 words)

Soccer, a team sport played between two teams of eleven players, is considered to be the most popular sport in the world. It is played on a rectangular grass or artificial turf field, with a goal at each end. The object of the game is to score by maneuvering the ball into the opposing goal. In general play, the goalkeepers are the only players allowed to use their hands or arms to touch the ball. The rest of the team use their feet, head or body. The team that scores the most goals by the end of the match wins.

Grammar Placement Test – Basic

1. a. am b. are c. is
2. a. These tests are easy. b. The trees are tall.
3. Shelly is not in Europe.
4. Is your brother in college?
5. a. I am always late. b. I am late every day.
6. a. feeds b. tell
7. a. He reads one. b. They fly it. c. She plans them.
8. a. on b. on c. in d. under
9. a. and b. but c. so
10. a. Lou does not know Ed. Lou doesn't know Ed. b. The cars do not go fast. The cars don't go fast.
11. a. Does it rain every day? b. Do you like it?
12. the worst
13. a. into b. away
14. a. thought b. saw c. had
15. Morgan did not hear a noise. Morgan didn't hear a noise.
16. a. Did James drive to New York? b. Did Andrea and Sarah walk to work?
17. James frequently drove to New York.
18. a. wasn't he? b. aren't I?
19. a. didn't they? b. did she?
20. a. some b. a
21. a. a b. the
22. a. — b. a
23. a. much b. many
24. a. is sleeping b. work
25. Is the store being remodeled?
26. a. up b. off
27. a. Charlie will go to France. b. Marcus won't order shoes from Italy. Marcus will not order shoes from Italy. c. Will Larry fix my computer?
28. Timmy will not answer your questions. Timmy won't answer your questions.
29. Will the cell phone need to be charged?
30. a. do b. make c. make
31. a. talking b. told
32. a. for b. with

Grammar Placement Test – Advanced

1. a. We don't know who did it. b. We don't know who makes them. c. We don't know who will take care of it.

2. a. What did he do? b. What will they buy? c. Where did he do it? d. When did he do it? e. How did he do it? f. How does she paint?
3. a. I'm not sure if he did it. b. I'm not sure if we need one.
4. a. I thought that he did it. b. I thought that she would buy one. c. I thought that we were trying our hardest.
5. a. must be b. may be c. could be d. has to e. may f. can g. should h. to see i. going j. manage k. to give l. to keep m. going n. to tell o. leaving p. take q. try r. see s. look t. hear u. listen v. who w. that x. whose y. what z. will aa. were bb. were cc. is dd. Had been ee. should have been ff. could dance gg. could have called
6. a. don't we b. didn't they c. hasn't she d. had they e. won't it f. doesn't she g. hadn't he / shouldn't he h. wouldn't they
7. a. ago b. for c. in d. during e. during f. While g. during h. while i. until j. by k. for l. since m. in n. after o. yet p. already q. still r. any more
8. a. for b. on c. to d. of e. on f. with g. to h. to
9. a. They have done the dishes. They've done the dishes. b. Things have fallen in earthquakes. c. The situation has gotten better. d. The competitors have brought their own gear. e. Everyone has seen that movie. f. The students have learned the lessons. g. The CEO has been thinking about it. h. Many people have forgotten the answer.
10. a. has thought b. bought c. have never seen d. has done e. has already gone f. has thought g. have needed h. lived i. has lived
11. a. They do it perfectly. b. They usually do it. c. They do it here. d. They do it at night. e. They definitely do it.
12. a. let b. allow c. permit d. had e. make f. get g. looks h. sounds i. feels
13. a. The ancient Egyptians built the pyramids. b. The accusation stunned our friends. c. The design committee selected the colors. d. A professional speaker will present your ideas.
14. a. have always been b. had reported c. will have really thought this through d. wouldn't have missed e. will all be promoted f. would have g. will definitely take h. let i. we'd walk j. we would've walked

Exercise 1-1: Dictation

1. She is very nice.
2. This is an apple.
3. You and I are in this together.
4. He's in the other room.
5. They're not available for comment right now.

Exercise 1-20: A or An

1. a
2. an
3. A, an
4. an
5. a

Answer Key

Exercise 1-24: A or The

1.	The	6.	The/A
2.	a	7.	the/a
3.	the	8.	a
4.	a	9.	the
5.	a	10.	a

Exercise 1-27: Here or There

1. This
2. That
3. These
4. Those
5. These
6. These
7. Those
8. These
9. Those
10. That

Exercise 1-29: Asking Questions

1. That is Ed.
2. This is a garden.
3. Those are paper clips.
4. Those people are men.
5. That is a donut.
6. These are coffee cups.
7. This is my friend.
8. This is a teapot.
9. These are cowboys.
10. Those are teachers.

Exercise 1-31: Replacing Subject Nouns with Pronouns

1.	They	6.	They
2.	She	7.	You
3.	They	8.	It
4.	They	9.	It
5.	We	10.	She

Exercise 1-34: Replacing Nouns with Pronouns

1.	it	6.	us
2.	them	7.	you
3.	him	8.	us
4.	her	9.	it
5.	them	10.	it

Exercise 1-36: Replacing Nouns with Pronouns — It or One

1.	it	6.	it
2.	one	7.	it
3.	it	8.	it
4.	one	9.	one
5.	one	10.	one

Exercise 1-38: Replacing the Nouns

1. They are in it.
2. He is watching it.
3. She is near it.
4. They are on it.
5. He is holding one.
6. He is in a good one.
7. They are in it.
8. We/They are in it.
9. We are good ones.
10. You are on one.
11. It is in his back one.
12. They are in it.
13. It is on it.
14. They are in a different one.
15. They are in it.

Exercise 1-40: Possessive Modifiers

1.	their	6.	his	11.	his
2.	his	7.	his	12.	my
3.	her	8.	our	13.	Her
4.	Her	9.	our	14.	its
5.	his	10.	your	15.	their

Exercise 1-41: Possessive Pronouns

1.	theirs	6.	his	11.	his
2.	his	7.	his	12.	mine
3.	hers	8.	ours	13.	hers
4.	hers	9.	ours	14.	its
5.	his	10.	theirs	15.	ours

Exercise 1-43: The Verb To Be — Is or Are

1.	is	6.	is	11.	are
2.	is	7.	are	12.	are
3.	are	8.	are	13.	are
4.	is	9.	are	14.	is
5.	are	10.	is	15.	are

Exercise 1-44: The Verb To Be — Am, Is, Are

1.	is	6.	am
2.	are	7.	is
3.	are	8.	are
4.	is	9.	are
5.	is	10.	is

Exercise 1-46: Contractions

1. They're happy.
2. It's here.
3. They're dirty.
4. It's wet.
5. They're late.
6. It's fast.
7. He's French.
8. They're easy.
9. She's your friend.
10. It's fun.

Exercise 1-48: Negatives

1. The teachers are not happy.
2. My bus is not here.
3. The dogs are not dirty.
4. My hair is not wet.
5. You are not silly.
6. The clock is not fast.
7. Tom is not French.
8. These reports are not easy.
9. I am not your friend.
10. This is not fun.

Exercise 1-49: Negative Contractions

1. They are not happy. They aren't happy.
2. It is not here. It isn't here.
3. They are not dirty. They aren't dirty.
4. It is not wet. It isn't wet.
5. You are not silly. You aren't silly.
6. It is not fast. It isn't fast.
7. He is not French. He isn't French.
8. They are not easy. They aren't easy.
9. I am not your friend. (*This verb form does not have a contraction.*)
10. This is not fun. This isn't fun.

Exercise 1-50: Questions

1. Are the teachers happy?
2. Is my bus here?
3. Are the dogs dirty?
4. Is my hair wet?
5. Are you silly?
6. Is the clock fast?
7. Is Tom French?
8. Are these reports easy?
9. Am I your friend?
10. Is this fun?

Exercise 1-51: Questions with Pronouns

1. Are they happy?
2. Is it here?
3. Are they dirty?
4. Is it wet?
5. Are you silly?
6. Is it fast?
7. Is he French?
8. Are they easy?
9. Am I one?
10. Is this fun?

Exercise 1-52: Making a Tag Question

1. aren't they?
2. is it?
3. aren't they?
4. isn't it?
5. aren't you?
6. isn't it?
7. isn't he?
8. are they?
9. aren't I?
10. isn't it?

Exercise 1-53: Contractions, Negatives, and Questions

	Statement	Negative	Question
I	I am here.	I am not here.	Am I here?
You	You are here.	You aren't here.	Are you here?
He	He is here.	He isn't here.	Is he here?
She	She is here.	She isn't here.	Is she here?
It	It is here.	It isn't here.	Is it here?
We	We are here.	We aren't here.	Are we here?
They	They are here.	They aren't here.	Are they here?

Chapter 1 Test

Part 1:
1. He
2. She
3. They

Part 2:
1. They are in it.
2. They are in it.

Part 3:
1. am
2. are
3. are
4. are
5. is
6. is
7. is
8. am
9. is
10. are

Part 4:
1. These tests are easy.
2. There are books.
3. Those men are hungry.
4. The trees are tall.
5. My sisters are nurses.

Part 5:
1. It's a good idea.
2. That's old.
3. We're here.
4. You're there.
5. I'm in class.
6. She's late.
7. He's funny.

Part 6:
1. Shelly is not in Europe.
2. Paul and Larry are not here.
3. The girls are not tired.

Part 7:
1. The boys aren't outside.
2. Charlie isn't happy.
3. My eyes aren't closed.

Part 8:
1. Is your brother in college?
2. Is his bike in the shop?
3. Is my watch fast?

Part 9:
1. Is it in it (there)?
2. Is he in it (there)?
3. Is it in it (there)?

Part 10:
1. He is <u>never</u> rude.
2. I am late <u>every day</u>.
3. We are <u>often</u> confused.
4. She is sleepy <u>in the morning</u>.
5. You are <u>usually</u> right.

Part 11:
1. Bob, friend
2. boys, car
3. teacher, room
4. students, happy
5. dogs, yard

Part 12:
1. æ
2. ə
3. ä

Exercise 2-1: Dictation

1. They don't even want to think about it.
2. We can't afford to make any more mistakes.
3. They don't know about the plan to start over again.
4. Does he know how to set the access code for the front door?
5. Do you know how to work the new coffee machine?

Answer Key

Exercise 2-11: Noun and Pronoun Review

1. She studies it.
2. They need long ones.
3. They ask hard ones.
4. He breaks it.
5. They make it.
6. He forgets it.
7. They take it.
8. She wants one.
9. She likes to cook them.
10. They need warm ones.

Exercise 2-13: Replacing Nouns

1. They saw it.
2. She plays it.
3. We took one.
4. He married her.
5. They gave it to us.

Exercise 2-14: Prepositions of Location

1. under
2. over
3. through
4. beside
5. behind
6. behind
7. next to
8. under
9. on
10. from
11. in
12. in front of
13. on
14. in
15. under
16. for
17. in
18. at
19. on
20. in

Exercise 2-16: Conjunctions — *And, But, So, Or, Because*

1. so
2. and
3. so
4. because
5. so
6. but
7. and
8. but
9. so
10. and

Exercise 2-17: Changing Main Verbs (Regular)

1. speaks
2. lives in
3. need
4. seems
5. give
6. wants
7. make
8. sends
9. gets
10. takes

Exercise 2-18: Changing Main Verbs (Adding –es)

1. goes
2. does
3. boxes
4. buzzes
5. kisses
6. catches
7. pushes

Exercise 2-19: Changing Main Verbs (Adding –ies)

1. studies
2. cries
3. tries
4. flies
5. fries
6. denies

Exercise 2-20: Changing Main Verbs (*Go*)

1. goes
2. go
3. go
4. goes
5. go

Exercise 2-21: Changing Main Verbs (*Do*)

1. do
2. do
3. does
4. does
5. do

Exercise 2-22: Changing Main Verbs (*Have)*

1. has
2. have
3. have
4. have
5. has

Exercise 2-23: Adding *Do* for Emphasis (I, You, We, They)

1. The kids do play at the park.
2. The dogs do get dirty.
3. You do forget many things.
4. These reports do need work.
5. I do work too hard.

Exercise 2-24: Adding *Does* for Emphasis (He, She, It)

1. My bus does come late.
2. My boss does need this done.
3. The clock does cost a lot.
4. Tom does make mistakes.
5. The car does run well.

Exercise 2-25: Adding *Do* or *Does* for Emphasis

1. The kids do play at the park.
2. My bus does come late.
3. The dogs do get dirty.
4. My boss does need this done.
5. You do forget many things.
6. The clock does cost a lot.
7. Tom does make mistakes.
8. These reports do need work.
9. I do work too hard.
10. The car does run well.

Exercise 2-26: Adding *Can*

1. The kids can play at the park.
2. My bus can come late.
3. The dogs can get dirty.
4. My boss can get things done.
5. You can forget many things.
6. The clock can cost a lot.
7. Tom can make mistakes.
8. These reports can change every day.
9. I can work too hard.
10. The car can run well.

Exercise 2-27: Adding a Verb + *To*

1. like to, hope to, want to
2. needs to, has to, tries to, wants to
3. want to, like to
4. wants to, has to, needs to, tries to, likes to
5. try to, have to, need to, like to
6. wants to, likes to, tries to, hopes to
7. wants to, likes to, hopes to, tries to
8. hope to, try to, need to, like to
9. try to, have to, need to, want to
10. tries to, likes to

Exercise 2-28: Adding *Not*

1. The kids do not play at the park.
2. My bus does not come late.
3. The dogs cannot get dirty.
4. My boss does not need this done.
5. You do not forget many things.
6. The clock does not cost a lot.
7. Tom cannot make mistakes.
8. These reports do not need work.
9. I do not work too hard.
10. The car cannot run well.
11. My sister does not want to help him.
12. I do not have to study.
13. We do not need to practice.
14. They do not like to dance together.
15. He does not want to take the test.

Exercise 2-29: Changing to a Contraction

1. The kinds don't play at the park.
2. My bus doesn't come late.
3. The dogs don't get dirty.
4. My boss doesn't need this done.
5. You don't forget many things.
6. The clock doesn't cost a lot.
7. Tom doesn't make mistakes.
8. These reports don't need work.
9. I don't work too hard.
10. The car doesn't run well.
11. My sister doesn't want to help him.
12. I don't have to study.
13. We don't need to practice.
14. They don't like to dance together.
15. He doesn't want to take the test.

Exercise 2-30: Making a Question from an Emphatic Statement

1. Do the kids play at the park?
2. Does my bus come late?
3. Can the dogs get dirty?
4. Does my boss need this done?
5. Do you forget many things?
6. Does the clock cost a lot?
7. Can Tom make mistakes?
8. Do these reports need work?
9. Do I work too hard?
10. Does the car run well?
11. Can my sister help him?
12. Do I have to study?
13. Do we need to practice?
14. Do they like to dance together?
15. Does he hope to pass the test?

Exercise 2-31: Making a Question from a Regular Statement

1. Can the kids play at the park?
2. Does my bus come late?
3. Can the dogs get dirty?
4. Does my boss need this done?
5. Do you forget many things?
6. Does the clock cost a lot?
7. Can Tom make mistakes?
8. Do these reports need work?
9. Do I work too hard?
10. Does the car run well?
11. Can my sister help him?
12. Do I have to study?
13. Do we need to practice?
14. Do they like to dance together?
15. Does he hope to pass the test?

Exercise 2-32: Making a Question with Pronouns

1. Do they play there?
2. Does it come late?
3. Can they get dirty?
4. Does he/she need this done?
5. Do you forget them?
6. Does it cost a lot?
7. Can he make them?
8. Do they need work?
9. Does Bob work too hard?
10. Does it run well?
11. Does she want to help him/her?
12. Do I have to study it?
13. Do we need to practice it?
14. Do they like to dance together?
15. Does he hope to pass it?

Exercise 2-34: Making a Tag Question

1.	do they	8.	don't they?
2.	doesn't it?	9.	don't I?
3.	can't they?	10.	does it?
4.	doesn't he/she?	11.	isn't he?
5.	don't you?	12.	is she?
6.	doesn't it?	13.	aren't they?
7.	can't he?	14.	aren't I?
		15.	am I?

Exercise 2-35: Making a Tag Assertion

1.	do they!	8.	don't they!
2.	doesn't it!	9.	don't I!
3.	can't they!	10.	does it!
4.	doesn't he/she!	11.	isn't he!
5.	don't you!	12.	is she!
6.	doesn't it!	13.	aren't they!
7.	can't he!	14.	aren't I!
		15.	am I!

Exercise 2-36: Identifying Intent

1.	?	6.	!
2.	!	7.	?
3.	!	8.	?
4.	?	9.	!
5.	?	10.	!

Exercise 2-37: Contractions, Negatives, and Questions

	Statement	Negative	Question
I	I do it.	I don't do it.	Do I do it?
You	You do it.	You don't do it.	Do you do it?
He	He does it.	He doesn't do it.	Does he do it?
She	She does it.	She doesn't do it.	Does she do it?
It	It does it.	It doesn't do it.	Does it do it?
We	We do it.	We don't do it.	Do we do it?
They	They do it.	They don't do it.	Do they do it?

Answer Key

Exercise 2-38: Commands
1. Don't give up!
2. They aren't to be informed!
3. Don't try again!
4. Let's not think about it!
5. Don't bring it back!

Chapter 2 Test

Part 1:
1. He buys a new one.
2. They fly it.
3. She plans them.
4. It tells a good one.
5. They bark at him.

Part 2:
1. on
2. under
3. in
4. besides, next to, near
5. under

Part 3:
1. and
2. but
3. so
4. or
5. because

Part 4:
1. speaks
2. eat
3. goes to
4. likes
5. bark at
6. feeds
7. has
8. tell
9. doesn't speak
10. is

Part 5:
1. They do see him every day.
2. He does tell the truth.
3. We do have fun.

Part 6:
1. The boy can see the toys.
2. The girl can speak well.
3. This book can be helpful.

Part 7:
1. Lou does not know Ed.
2. It does not work well.
3. The cars do not go fast.
4. The well is not dry.
5. The boys are not in the house.

Part 8:
1. George doesn't work in Las Vegas.
2. Sandy doesn't sell seashells.
3. The team members don't play every day.
4. Big cities aren't often crowded.
5. It isn't really hot today.

Part 9:
1. Does it rain every day?
2. Does he call us all of the time?
3. Do you like it?
4. Are they very kind?
5. Is he in trouble?

Part 10:
1. doesn't he
2. isn't she
3. don't they
4. aren't they

Part 11:
3, 2, 1

Exercise 3-1: Dictation
1. His latest plan was even more dangerous than any of the ones in the past.
2. The kids learned the hard way that there was an easier solution.
3. She didn't understand the instructions on the package.
4. They didn't even try to clarify the situation.
5. I pretended that everything was OK.

Exercise 3-4: *A* or *Some*
1. some
2. some
3. a
4. a
5. a
6. some
7. a
8. some
9. some
10. a

Exercise 3-5: *A* or *The*
1. the
2. a
3. a
4. the, the
5. the
6. a
7. a
8. the
9. the
10. a
11. the
12. the
13. an, a, a, the, a
14. the
15. a
16. the
17. the
18. the
19. a, the
20. The, a
21. the, the
22. the, the
23. the
24. a
25. the
26. the
27. a
28. the
29. the
30. the, a
31. a, the
32. the
33. a
34. An, a, the
35. a, the

Exercise 3-6: Short Comparison Words
1. the best
2. cheaper
3. the worst
4. hot
5. smarter
6. the tallest
7. warm
8. colder
9. better
10. easier
11. the oldest
12. happy
13. harder
14. nice
15. big
16. faster
17. the best
18. more
19. richer
20. farther

Exercise 3-7: Long Comparison Words
1. the most interesting
2. a delicious
3. more obedient
4. difficult
5. more expensive
6. wonderful
7. the most unusual
8. more complicated
9. the most important
10. a wonderful

Exercise 3-8: Long and Short Comparison Words
1. more effective
2. cheaper
3. more dangerous
4. the most important
5. richer
6. better
7. scarier
8. the longest

9. earlier
10. the closest

Exercise 3-12: Change to the Past

1. The teachers wrote on the blackboard.
2. Larry rode his bike everywhere.
3. Your cousin flew first class.
4. The managers arranged meetings.
5. I gave many presents.
6. We thought about it all the time.
7. They threw it away every day.
8. Virginia had long hair.
9. Happy people had good luck.
10. Her sister said hello.
11. The kids wanted to ride their bikes.
12. Students tried to pass tests.
13. Ed liked to go to the gym.
14. The class hoped to have a party.
15. Everyone needed to have more fun.

Exercise 3-13: Change to the Emphatic

1. The teachers did write on the blackboard!
2. Larry did ride his bike everywhere!
3. Your cousin did fly first class!
4. The managers did arrange meetings!
5. I did give many presents!
6. We did think about it all of the time!
7. They did throw it away every day!
8. Virginia did have long hair!
9. Happy people did have good luck!
10. Her sister did say hello!
11. The kids did want to ride their bikes!
12. The students did try to pass the tests!
13. Ed did like to go to the gym!
14. The class did hope to have a party!
15. Everyone did need to have more fun!

Exercise 3-14: Change to the Negative

1. The teachers did not write on the blackboard.
2. Larry did not ride his bike everywhere.
3. Your cousin did not fly first class.
4. The managers did not arrange meetings.
5. I did not give many presents.
6. We did not think about it all of the time.
7. They did not throw it away every day.
8. Virginia did not have long hair.
9. Happy people did not have good luck.
10. Her sister did not say hello.
11. The kids did not want to ride their bikes.
12. The students did not try to pass the tests.
13. Ed did not like to go to the gym.
14. The class did not hope to have a party.
15. Everyone did not need to have more fun.

Exercise 3-15: Change to Negative Contractions

1. The teachers didn't write on the blackboard.
2. Larry didn't ride his bike everywhere.
3. Your cousin didn't fly first class.
4. The managers didn't arrange meetings.
5. I didn't give many presents.
6. We didn't think about it all of the time.
7. They didn't throw it away every day.
8. Virginia didn't have long hair.
9. Happy people didn't have good luck.
10. Her sister didn't say hello.

11. The kids didn't want to ride their bikes.
12. Students didn't try to pass tests.
13. Ed didn't like to go to the gym.
14. The class didn't hope to have a party.
15. Everyone didn't need to have more fun.

Exercise 3-16: Change the Positive to Negative Contractions

1. They didn't write on it.
2. He didn't ride it everywhere.
3. He/She didn't fly first class.
4. They didn't arrange them.
5. I didn't give them.
6. We didn't think about it all of the time.
7. They didn't throw it away every day.
8. She didn't have it.
9. They didn't have it.
10. She didn't say hello.
11. They didn't want to ride them.
12. They didn't try to pass them.
13. He didn't like to go to it.
14. They didn't need to have one.
15. Everyone didn't need to have it.

Exercise 3-17: Change the Emphatic to a Question

1. Did the teachers write on the blackboard?
2. Did Larry ride his bike everywhere?
3. Can your cousin fly first class?
4. Did the managers arrange meetings?
5. Can I give many presents?
6. Did we think about it all of the time?
7. Did they throw it away every day?
8. Did Virginia have long hair?
9. Can happy people have good luck?
10. Did her sister say hello?
11. Did the kids want to ride their bikes?
12. Did students try to pass tests?
13. Did Ed like to go to the gym?
14. Did the class hope to have a party?
15. Did everyone need to have more fun?

Exercise 3-18: Change a Regular Statement to a Question

1. (Did/Didn't/Could/Couldn't) the teachers write on the blackboard?
2. (Did/Didn't/Could/Couldn't) Larry ride his bike everywhere?
3. (Did/Didn't/Could/Couldn't) your cousin fly first class?
4. (Did/Didn't/Could/Couldn't) the managers arrange meetings?
5. (Did/Didn't/Could/Couldn't) I give many presents?
6. (Did/Didn't/Could/Couldn't) we think about it all of the time?
7. (Did/Didn't/Could/Couldn't) they throw it away every day?
8. (Did/Didn't/Could/Couldn't) Virginia have long hair?
9. (Did/Didn't/Could/Couldn't) happy people have good luck?
10. (Did/Didn't/Could/Couldn't) her sister say hello?

11. (Did/Didn't) the kids want to ride their bikes?
12. (Did/Didn't/Could/Couldn't) the students try to pass the tests?
13. (Did/Didn't) Ed like to go to the gym?
14. (Did/Didn't) the class hope to have a party?
15. (Did/Didn't) everyone need to have more fun?

Exercise 3-19: Change to Pronouns

1. Did they write on it?
2. Did he ride it everywhere?
3. Did he/she fly first class?
4. Can they arrange them?
5. Did I give them?
6. Did he think about her all of the time?
7. Can he throw it away every day?
8. Did she have it?
9. Did they have it?
10. Can she say it?
11. Did they want to ride them?
12. Can they try to pass them?
13. Did he like to go to it?
14. Did they hope to have one?
15. Did everyone need to do them?

Exercise 3-20: Change a Regular Statement to a Question

1. (Do/Don't/Could/Couldn't) they write on it?
2. (Did/Didn't/Could/Couldn't) he ride it everywhere?
3. (Does/Doesn't/Can/Can't) he/she fly first class?
4. (Did/Didn't/Could/Couldn't) they arrange them?
5. (Did/Didn't/Could/Couldn't) I give them?
6. (Do/Don't/Can/Can't) we think about it all of the time?
7. (Did/Didn't/Could/Couldn't) they throw it away every day?
8. (Does/Doesn't/Can/Can't) she have it?
9. (Did/Didn't/Could/Couldn't) they have it?
10. (Does/Doesn't/Can/Can't) she say hello?
11. (Did/Didn't) they want to ride them?
12. (Do/Don't/Can/Can't) they try to pass them?
13. (Did/Didn't) he like to go to it?
14. (Do/Don't) they hope to have it?
15. (Did/Didn't) everyone need to do them?
16. (Did/Didn't/Could/Couldn't) they jump over it?
17. (Does/Doesn't) she like it?
18. (Does/Doesn't) he want it?
19. (Does/Doesn't) he always lose it with him?
20. (Did/Didn't/Could/Couldn't) they get in trouble again?
21. (Did/Didn't/Could/Couldn't) he burn it?
22. (Does/Doesn't/Can/Can't) it get it?
23. (Did/Didn't/Could/Couldn't) he/she drop out of it?
24. (Did/Didn't/Could/Couldn't) they fall in it?
25. (Do/Don't/Can/Can't) they give them?
26. (Did/Didn't/Could/Couldn't) they find them?
27. (Did/Didn't/Could/Couldn't) it burn it?
28. (Did/Didn't/Could/Couldn't) they lose it?
29. (Did/Didn't/Could/Couldn't) he/she forget to get it?
30. (Did/Didn't/Could/Couldn't) she change it?

Exercise 3-21: Change to a Tag Question

1. didn't they?
2. didn't he?
3. didn't he/she?
4. didn't they?
5. didn't I?
6. didn't we?
7. didn't they?
8. didn't she?
9. didn't they?
10. didn't she?
11. didn't they?
12. didn't they?
13. didn't he?
14. didn't it?/didn't they?
15. didn't they?

Exercise 3-22: Change to a Tag Question — All Verbs

1. don't I?
2. don't you?
3. didn't you?
4. do you?
5. did you?
6. didn't we?
7. can't they?
8. isn't she?
9. aren't I?
10. didn't she?
11. are they?
12. am I?
13. weren't there?
14. wasn't there?
15. was there?

Exercise 3-23: Past Tense Review

thought, was, was, wanted, tried, worked, invented, was, handled, replied, were, taught

Exercise 3-26: *Get*

1. along
2. back
3. fired
4. used
5. sick
6. down
7. together
8. even
9. upset
10. ahead
11. excited
12. bored
13. off
14. away
15. divorced
16. tired
17. together
18. impatient
19. lost
20. dressed
21. ahead
22. worried
23. back
24. into
25. tired of
26. in an accident
27. undressed
28. rid of
29. in trouble
30. better
31. there
32. up
33. bored
34. down
35. in an argument
36. along
37. worse
38. started
39. rid of
40. back
41. drunk
42. hired
43. hungry

Chapter 3 Test

Part 1:
1. the best
2. bigger
3. nice
4. the warmest
5. more interesting

Part 2:
1. over / above / on top of
2. through / into / by / inside of

Part 3:
1. Sam lived in Chicago.
2. We thought about it.
3. We saw him at the gym.
4. You found many good opportunities.
5. I knew the answer.
6. She said anything!
7. Charlie did not make mistakes.
8. Did Laura get in trouble?
9. We had enough time.
10. It took too long!

11. I was hungry.
12. You were right.
13. He was over there.
14. We were not on the committee.
15. She was going to the party.

Part 4:
1. Morgan did not hear the news.
2. Gordon did not follow the rules.
3. The girl was not confused.
4. The boys were not late again.

Part 5:
1. He didn't buy it.
2. She didn't go with him.
3. She wasn't on it.
4. They weren't in it.

Part 6:
1. Did James drive to New York?
2. Is Susie in back?
3. Did Andrea say hello?
4. Were Fred and Jim outside?
5. Do I like pie?

Part 7:
1. Edgar buys groceries all the time.
2. Sam and Charlie never fly the kite.
3. Moira organized her schedule every once in a while.
4. The book often tells a good story.
5. The dogs barked at passers-by all day.

Part 8:
1. wasn't he?
2. aren't you?
3. weren't they?
4. aren't I?
5. isn't it?
6. didn't they?
7. don't you?
8. didn't they?
9. don't I?
10. did she?

Part 9:
1. a
2. a
3. the
4. a, some

Part 10:
1. tired
2. used to
3. done
4. together
5. lost

Exercise 4-1: Dictation

1. They're thinking about having a meeting and making a final decision.
2. Sam thinks that Ed won't know what to say about the latest business development.
3. He was talking to his boss about the increase in sales for the month of May.
4. I needed to buy some fruit and other groceries for the meeting.
5. We are thinking about trying the new plan.

Exercise 4-5: Countable and Uncountable Nouns (*A / —*)

1. —, (All)
2. —, (Some)
3. —, (All)
4. —, (Some)
5. a
6. —, (Some)
7. a
8. —, (Some)
9. —
10. a

Exercise 4-6: Countable and Uncountable Nouns (*A / An Some / —*)

1. a
2. some
3. —
4. some
5. a
6. an
7. —, —
8. a
9. A, —
10. a, —

Exercise 4-7: *Much* or *Many*

1. many
2. much
3. much
4. many
5. many
6. much
7. much
8. many
9. many
10. much

Exercise 4-9: Prepositions of Time

1. in
2. on
3. on
4. in
5. on
6. in
7. at
8. in
9. at
10. in

Exercise 4-10: Prepositions of Manner

1. in
2. by
3. in
4. in
5. in
6. by
7. by
8. on
9. for
10. to
11. of

Exercise 4-11: Jack and the Beanstalk

Once upon **a** time, there was **a** poor widow and her son Jack. One day, **the** widow said, "Jack, we don't have **any** food. Take **the** cow to **—** town and sell her so that we can have **some** money for **—**food." Jack said OK and went to **—** town, leading **the** cow behind him. Very soon, he came back alone. "See what I got for our cow, Mother," he said happily. "I sold her to **a** man for **—** three magic beans." When Jack's mother heard that he traded **the** cow for three beans, she was very angry. "Jack!" she yelled. "Three beans can't keep us from starving!" She threw **the** beans out of **the** window. Jack went to **—** bed.

The next morning, they saw **a** huge vine. **The** vine rose above **the** house and disappeared into **the** clouds. Jack climbed up **the** vine and soon disappeared into **the** clouds, too. At **the** top of **the** vine, Jack saw **a** huge castle. **The** door was ten times his size. He called out, "Excuse me, do you have **any** food for **a** hungry boy?" **The** door opened, and Jack saw **a** woman who was as tall as **a** tree. She picked him up by his shirt and put him on **the** table. "So, you're hungry? Well, I'll give you **a** bite to eat. But watch out for my husband!" She handed Jack **a** slice of bread as big as **a** mattress, and **a** piece of **—** cheese high enough to sit on. But before Jack could eat, he heard **—** giant-sized footsteps and **a** voice said, "Wife, where's my dinner?" Jack hid out of sight in **the** shadows. Then he heard **the** giant say, "Fee, fie, fo, fum, I smell the blood of an Englishman!" **The** giant didn't want Jack to take **the** goose that laid golden eggs. One thing led to another, and there was **a** huge fight between Jack and **the** giant. Jack grabbed the goose and ran. **The** giant ended up chasing Jack down **the** beanstalk. Fortunately, Jack got to **the** bottom first, grabbed **an**, ax, and chopped it down. **The** giant fell to his death and Jack and his mother lived happily ever after with the goose.

Exercise 4-14: Reading Comprehension

Synonyms:
1. hearing-impaired
2. hard of hearing

True or False:

1.	False	4.	False
2.	True	5.	False
3.	False	6.	False

How do most languages convey information: Spoken word

What does sign language use: Visual signals

List three reasons why people who can hear might also need to learn sign language:
1. Scuba divers for use underwater
2. Firefighters and policemen to communicate silently
3. Dog-trainers to train dogs

Exercise 4-18: Present Continuous

1. I'm having lunch right now.
2. Bob's sick right now.
3. It's raining in California today.
4. It's not/It isn't raining in California right now.
5. He's working hard for a change.
6. She's dancing well this week.
7. He's thinking about it at the moment.
8. He's not/He isn't thinking about it for the moment.
9. She's making cookies tonight.
10. They're not/They aren't drinking coffee these days.

Exercise 4-19: Past Continuous

1. The teachers were writing on the blackboard when the bell rang.
2. Larry was riding his bike when it started raining.
3. Your cousin was flying first class until he ran out of money.
4. The managers were still arranging the meetings before the conference.
5. I was not working hard last year, but I am now.
6. We were thinking about it before the situation changed.
7. They were throwing it away until they realized its value.
8. Virginia was not selling her car until she won the lottery.
9. The candles were burning steadily even though it was windy.
10. Her sister was saying hello when he rudely interrupted.

Exercise 4-20: Continuous Negative Contractions

1. They aren't writing on it. They're not writing on it.
2. He isn't riding it. He's not riding it.
3. He/She isn't flying first class. He's/She's not flying first class.
4. They aren't arranging them. They're not arranging them.
5. I'm not giving them.
6. We aren't thinking about it. We're not thinking about it.
7. They aren't throwing it away. They're not throwing it away.
8. She isn't selling it. She's not selling it.
9. They aren't burning steadily. They're not burning steadily.
10. She wasn't saying hello.

Exercise 4-21: Continuous Questions

1. Are they writing on it?
2. Are they riding them?
3. Is he/she flying first class?
4. Are they arranging them?
5. Am I giving them?
6. Were we thinking about it?
7. Were they throwing it away?
8. Was she selling it?
9. Are they burning steadily?
10. Was she saying hello?

Exercise 4-23: Simple Present vs. Continuous Present

1.	go	26.	is having
2.	are going	27.	are having
3.	has	28.	have
4.	is wearing	29.	gets
5.	is having	30.	take
6.	has	31.	am taking
7.	likes	32.	buys
8.	wants	33.	is buying
9.	think	34.	is selling
10.	is thinking	35.	sells
11.	am	36.	is walking
12.	is	37.	walks
13.	is being	38.	dances
14.	is being	39.	is dancing
15.	is making	40.	works
16.	do you make	41.	is working
17.	are you making	42.	are eating
18.	Are you waiting	43.	eat
19.	Will you wait	44.	plays
20.	is having	45.	is playing
21.	has	46.	is writing
22.	are having	47.	writes
23.	had/were having	48.	does
24.	is having	49.	is doing
25.	had	50.	doesn't

Exercise 4-24: Getting It Right

1.	along, divorced	6.	excited	11.	confused
2.	up	7.	better	12.	behind
3.	on	8.	rid of	13.	dressed
4.	away	9.	back	14.	even
5.	used	10.	annoyed	15.	together

Exercise 4-26: *Who* and *What* — *To Be*

1. Who is worried?
2. What was expensive?
3. What were filled in?
4. Who was on duty?
5. What is playing?

Exercise 4-27: *Who* and *What* — Main Verbs

1. Who told Lou/him?
2. What closed early?
3. Who left early?
4. What left the station/it?
5. What rang loudly?

Exercise 4-28: Yes / No Question Review — *To Be*

1. Is she excited about the party?
2. Is the party very exciting?
3. Weren't we invited?
4. Isn't he ready yet?
5. Is Bob sick?

Exercise 4-29: Yes / No Question Review – Main Verbs

1. Do they like to swim?
2. Can he tell you the answer?
3. Didn't you eat breakfast?
4. Does Bob have a headache?
5. Doesn't Ella want one?

Exercise 4-30: *Five W* Questions — *To Be*

1. What is he jumping on?
2. Where is the book?
3. When was he here?
4. What time was he here?
5. Why isn't he tired?

Exercise 4-31: *Five W* Questions — Main Verbs

1. Where does she shop?
2. Who did Janice tell?
3. When did he start work?
4. Why did he stop?
5. Where does he want to move?

Exercise 4-32: *How* Questions — *To Be*

1. How were they?
2. How is she?
3. How were they?
4. How is it?
5. How will it be?

Exercise 4-33: *How* Questions — *To Be*

1. How excited were they?
2. How happy is she?
3. How bad were they?
4. How burned is it?
5. How old is it?

Chapter 4 Test

Part 1:
1. an
2. a
3. an
4. an
5. a

Part 2:
1. some
2. a
3. some
4. a
5. some

Part 3:
1. a
2. the
3. the
4. a
5. the

Part 4:
1. —
2. a
3. —
4. —
5. —

Part 5:
1. on, at
2. to

Part 6:
1. much
2. many
3. many
4. much
5. many

Part 7:
1. He is being silly.
2. They are working hard.
3. You were choosing one.
4. He was losing the race.
5. I was writing to him.

Part 8:
1. is sleeping
2. works
3. was thinking
4. is / was
5. is being

Part 9:
1. Lou does not know Ed.
2. The cars do not go fast.

Part 10:
1. Does it rain every day?
2. Is it raining?
3. Do you like it?
4. Are you in charge?

Part 11:
1. but your brother may.
2. but my sister may.
3. he really, really doesn't like dogs.
4. but he tolerates them.
5. but he does like cats.

Part 12:
1. Who is starting the game now?
2. What fell off the shelf?

Part 13:
1. Where are they sitting?
2. When did we leave?
3. What did she look at?
4. Why did he laugh?

Exercise 5-1: Dictation

1. I'm going to have to think about it a little bit more.
2. We'll wait around for them to make the delivery.
3. We're going to Hawaii for the first time next week.

4. They'll let you know your schedule in the morning.
5. If it weren't so difficult we'd do it ourselves.

Exercise 5-3: Noun Intonation

1.	time	11.	truck	21.	egg
2.	time	12.	truck	22.	egg
3.	hair	13.	hot	23.	butter
4.	hair	14.	coffee	24.	knife
5.	hot	15.	wedding	25.	towels
6.	deal	16.	cake	26.	towels
7.	cell	17.	house	27.	house
8.	plan	18.	key	28.	house
9.	note	19.	hair	29.	base
10.	walk	20.	brush	30.	ball

Exercise 5-4: Noun Intonation

1. short, alley, super
2. air, Angeles
3. school, amusement, hours, sun
4. President, White, C.
5. math, book, text
6. swim, day, summer
7. recipes, junk
8. boy, ring, birth
9. dog, look, porch, day
10. break, down

Exercise 5-5: Word Order

1. His three Chinese rugs
2. my big red leather couch
3. a tiny French notebook
4. the old, brown wooden bookshelf
5. ten black Thai chopsticks

Exercise 5-6: Word Order

1. I saw the three young Japanese English students.
2. We're on the only long, black Italian train in China.
3. Where are Todd's ten tiny Tunisian tin tabletops?
4. *Answers will vary.*
5. *Answers will vary.*

Exercise 5-8: Conjunctions

1. until
2. because
3. but then
4. as soon as
5. whenever
6. unless
7. even though
8. right after
9. ever since
10. after

Exercise 5-9: *How + Many*

1. How many cars were on the road?
2. How many problems did we have?
3. How many alternatives did she want?
4. How many mistakes did they make?
5. How many sugars did he put in his coffee?
6. How many doors does this car have?
7. How many pairs of shoes does my aunt have?
8. How many dogs does that boy have?
9. How many minutes do I have to finish this?
10. How many units is the student taking?

Exercise 5-10: *How + Much*

1. How much ink do I have?
2. How much does this ink cost?
3. How much do they cost this year?
4. How much does it cost this year?
5. How much did they cost last year?
6. How much did it cost last year?
7. How much energy does she have?
8. How much rice was left over?
9. How much fun was it?
10. How much smoke is in the air?

Exercise 5-11: *How Much / How Many*

1. How much noise is out here?
2. How many singers are there?
3. How much cloth is there for that dress?
4. How many dresses are you making?
5. How much gas do I have in the car?
6. How many gas stations are there?
7. How much hair do I have?
8. How many hairs were in my sink?
9. How much did you learn today?
10. How many classes did you go to today?

Exercise 5-12: *How + Often — To Be*

1. How often are they in trouble?
2. How often is the weather nice?
3. How often is the staff out of the office?
4. How often are our dogs dirty?
5. How often were his comments ignored?
6. How often is she on the road?
7. How often are swans vicious?
8. How often is history repeated?
9. How often are we confused?
10. How often is he in L.A.?

Exercise 5-13: *How + Often — Main Verbs*

1. How often do we plan for the future?
2. How often did she have a Plan B?
3. How often do I eat donuts?
4. How often do ants get into the kitchen?
5. How often do commuters take shortcuts?
6. How often do I do the right thing?
7. How often is she direct?
8. How often is it cold in Alaska?
9. How often is the car reliable?
10. How often does he change his mind?

Exercise 5-15: *Two Terminology — Fill in the Blanks*

The following are sample answers. Your answers will differ.

1. There are two animals.
2. These are both quadrupeds.
3. They both have four legs. Neither of them can fly.

4. They each have a specific type of coloring.
5. One of them is striped, but the other isn't.
6. Can either of them fly? No, neither of them can fly, but both of them can run fast.
7. One of them is wild. It is either the horse or the zebra. Neither of them is native to Alaska.
8. The one on the left is a horse. The one on the right is a zebra.
9. The horse is a quadruped, and the zebra is, too. The horse is a quadruped and so is the zebra.
10. The horse runs fast, and the zebra does, too. The horse runs fast and so does the zebra.

Exercise 5-16: *Two* Terminology — Make Up Your Own Sentences

The following are sample answers. Your answers will differ.

1. These are two places to live.
2. Both usually have four walls and a roof.
3. Both are common in the United States, but neither is considered to be a luxury home.
4. Each has its own different attraction for people.
5. One of them has wheels. The other doesn't.
6. Either can be found anywhere in the United States. Neither is typically used for schools. Both of them are legal residences.
7. One of them is made of metal. Either can be used as a permanent home. Neither of them is usually more than one story tall.
8. The one on the left is a mobile home. The one on the right is a cabin.
9. A mobile home is a house, and a cabin is, too. A mobile home is a house, and so is a cabin.
10. A cabin has a front door, and a mobile home does, too. A cabin has a front door, and so does a mobile home.
11. Both of them are usually fairly small.

Exercise 5-17: *Use*

1. use
2. am used to
3. used to
4. use
5. is used
6. uses
7. are used to
8. used to
9. uses
10. is used

Exercise 5-19: *Much* or *Many* with Countables and Uncountables

1.	much	6.	many
2.	many	7.	much
3.	much	8.	many
4.	many	9.	much
5.	much	10.	many

Exercise 5-20: Half Is ... Half Are ...

1.	are	6.	was
2.	is	7.	were
3.	Is	8.	were
4.	Are	9.	has been
5.	was	10.	have been

Exercise 5-21: *Much* or *Many* with Countables and Uncountables

1.	much	8.	many
2.	many	9.	much
3.	many	10.	many
4.	much	11.	much
5.	much	12.	many
6.	many	13.	much
7.	much	14.	many

Exercise 5-22: Eureka!

Here is **a** famous experiment; **a** king buys **a** new crown from **a** craftsman. **The** craftsman says that **the** crown is = pure gold, but **the** king thinks that **a** cheaper, lighter metal like = silver is in it, too. He asks his friend, Archimedes, to find out if **the** craftsman is telling **the** truth. = silver is lighter than = gold, so you need more than one cup of silver to weigh **the** same as one cup of gold. If he mixes silver into **the** crown, there will be more cups of = metal in it than in **the** same weight of pure gold. Archimedes says, "I have to figure out if there are more cups of metal in **the** crown than in **the** same weight of pure gold. But, if I melt **the** crown to find out, it won't be **a** crown anymore. **The** king will be angry. How can I find out how many cups there are without melting **the** crown?"

Archimedes decides to take **a** bath. He steps into his tub and **the** overflowing water gives him **an** idea. He fills **a** bucket with water. He puts **a** pound of gold in **the** bucket. **A** cupful of water spills out. Then he puts **a** pound of silver in **the** bucket. Two cupfuls of water spill out! This is because silver weighs less than gold, so **a** pound of it (weight) takes up more room (volume) than **a** pound of gold and pushes out more water. **The** king's crown weighs **a** pound. Archimedes puts it into **a** full bucket. If one cupful of water spills out, there is **a** pound of gold in **the** crown. If more than one cupful of water spills out, it can't be pure gold. This way, he doesn't have to melt **the** crown. All he has to do is measure **the** water that spills out. It's **a** great idea! Archimedes gets so excited that he jumps out of **the** tub and runs naked down **the** street shouting "Eureka!" In Greek, this means, "I found it!"

When Archimedes does **the** experiment, he finds that **the** crown pushes out more water than **an** equal weight of gold does. That means that the gold is mixed with silver. **The** craftsman is cheating **the** king.

Exercise 5-24: Simple Future

1. The teachers will write on the blackboard.
2. Larry will ride his bike everywhere.
3. Your cousin will fly first class.
4. The managers will arrange meetings.

5. I will give many presents.
6. We will think about it.
7. They will throw it away.
8. Virginia will sell her car.
9. The candles will burn steadily.
10. Her sister will say hello.

Exercise 5-25: Negatives

1. The teachers will not write on the blackboard.
2. Larry will not ride his bike everywhere.
3. Your cousin will not fly first class.
4. The managers will not arrange meetings.
5. I will not give many presents.
6. We will not think about it.
7. They will not throw it away.
8. Virginia will not sell her car.
9. The candles will not burn steadily.
10. Her sister will not say hello.

Exercise 5-26: Negative Contractions

1. The teachers won't write on the blackboard.
2. Larry won't ride his bike everywhere.
3. Your cousin won't fly first class.
4. The managers won't arrange meetings.
5. I won't give many presents.
6. We won't think about it.
7. They won't throw it away.
8. Virginia won't sell her car.
9. The candles won't burn steadily.
10. Her sister won't say hello.

Exercise 5-27: Negative Contractions

1. They're not writing on it.
2. He's not riding it.
3. She's not flying in one.
4. They're not arranging them.
5. He's not giving them.
6. We're not thinking about it.
7. They're not throwing it away.
8. Virginia's not selling it.
9. They're not burning steadily.
10. She's not saying hello.

Exercise 5-29: Changing Future Forms

1. We're going to think about it.
2. They're going to throw it away.
3. She's going to sell it.
4. They're going to burn steadily.
5. She's going to say hello.

Exercise 5-30: Questions

1. Will the teachers write on the blackboard?
2. Will Larry ride his bike everywhere?
3. Will your cousin fly first class?
4. Will the managers arrange meetings?
5. Will I give many presents?
6. Will we think about it?
7. Will they throw it away?
8. Will Virginia sell her car?
9. Will the candles burn steadily?
10. Will her sister say hello?

Exercise 5-31: Questions with Pronouns

1. Will they write on it?
2. Will he ride it everywhere?
3. Will he/she fly in it?
4. Will they arrange them?
5. Will I give them?
6. Will he think about them?
7. Will they throw it away?
8. Will she sell it?
9. Will they sit in one?
10. Will she say hello?

Exercise 5-32: Present Tense to Indicate the Future

1. She's making the decision when she is here.
2. I'm not telling you until she gets here.
3. We're leaving when it's over.
4. He's not getting up until it's time to go.
5. Everyone's working until the bell rings.
6. They're going home after the stores close.
7. I'm taking a walk even if it's raining.
8. We're going to bed when the sun sets.
9. She was very rude to me. I'm refusing to speak to her again until she apologizes.
10. I'm starting after I get organized.
11. We're doing something soon, before it's too late.
12. I'm not calling him unless I need to.
13. We're going shopping even if it's snowing.
14. I'm going to be a nurse when I pass the exam.
15. I'm not telling you until after we finish class.

Exercise 5-34: The Unreal — *To Be*

1. If the boxes are full, they'll be heavy.
2. If the boxes are empty, they won't be heavy.
3. If it's raining, you'll be cold.
4. If he's lying, he'll be in trouble.
5. If he is sorry, his friends will be understanding.
6. If they are on time, they'll be satisfied.
7. If the wheel is loose, the driver will be scared.
8. If he is here, he'll be helpful.
9. If he isn't here, he won't be helpful.
10. If they are tired, they'll stay home.

Exercise 5-35: The Unreal — Main Verbs

1. If he has time, he'll go to the party.
2. If she runs a red light, she'll get a ticket.
3. If she knows all the answers, she'll pass the test.
4. If he tries hard, he'll succeed.
5. If you tell the truth, he'll appreciate it.
6. If they get to work late, they'll get fired.
7. If she drives too fast, she'll have an accident.
8. If he forgets to pay, he'll get in trouble.
9. If I lose the ring, he'll be upset.
10. If we are hungry, we'll stop for lunch.

Exercise 5-36: Future Tags

1. won't she?
2. aren't you?
3. won't they?
4. won't they?
5. are they?

Exercise 5-43: *Do* or *Make*

1.	do	6.	do
2.	make	7.	make
3.	do	8.	do
4.	made	9.	make
5.	do	10.	Make

Exercise 5-44: *Stand*

1. for
2. up to
3. up for
4. a chance
5. ground

Chapter 5 Test

Part 1:

1.	walk	6.	fax
2.	lap	7.	shirt
3.	paper	8.	leg
4.	day	9.	expiration
5.	house	10.	sun

Part 2:

1. after
2. unless
3. as soon as

Part 3:

We were walking down **a** dark street. **The** moon wasn't out, so we couldn't see **a** thing. **The** sidewalk was uneven, and I almost took **a** fall. We were lost, so we figured that **the** best thing would be to go back **the** way we had come. **None** of us knew where we were, so it took quite **some** time to get back home.

Part 4:

1. Charlie will go to France.
2. Sam will give a speech.
3. John will read a book.
4. Marcus will not order shoes from Italy.
5. Will Larry fix my computer?

Part 5:

1. Timmy won't answer your questions.
2. Lea won't be dancing in Fresno.
3. Jill isn't going to facilitate the file transfer. / Jill's not going to facilitate the file transfer.
4. The clown won't joke with the crowd.
5. Twenty trees won't crash to the ground in the storm.
6. The secretary isn't going to file the forms. / The secretary's not going to file the forms.

Part 6:

1. Will Shorty eat his dog food?
2. Will the cell phone need to be charged?
3. Is Nate going to make a big announcement?

Part 7: *Part 8:*

1.	do	1.	up
2.	make	2.	for
3.	make	3.	on
4.	do	4.	still
5.	do	5.	out

Chapters 1–5 Midterm

Part 1:

1. dogs, yard
2. taxi, suit, trunk
3. earth, Francisco, week

Part 2:

1. æ
2. ə
3. ä

Part 3:

1. but you might have.
2. but that's not true at all.
3. but he put it in an e-mail to me.
4. but I did hear someone else say it.
5. but I know that's what he thinks.
6. but I heard him say something else.

Part 4:

1. Who came to visit?
2. What were painted again?

Part 5:

1. Where was she dancing?
2. When did he graduate?
3. What did they order?
4. Who cried because it was so sad?

Part 6:

1. They were cancelled because of it.
2. She is going to visit us.

Part 7:

1. These buildings were poorly built.
2. Can the children have some more?
3. Those people were not ready.

Part 8: *Part 9:*

1.	a	1.	or
2.	the	2.	so
3.	an	3.	but
4.	a	4.	and
5.	the		

Part 10: *Part 11:*

1.	to	1.	best
2.	in	2.	bigger
3.	on	3.	happier
4.	with	4.	less
5.	by, on	5.	worst

Part 12:

1. much
2. many
3. much
4. many

Part 13:

1. We used to go to the beach all the time.
2. They always talk about it.
3. Let's do it today.

Part 14:

1. I drove fast.
2. She thought about it every day.

Part 15:

1. She was laughing.
2. He won't be helping us this time.
3. She was dancing and singing well.

Part 16:

1. He will work on it all the time.
2. They will need more time.

Answer Key

Part 17:

1. They started the new system yesterday.
2. She eats lunch at the same restaurant every day.
3. They were watching TV when the phone rang.
4. He will be here tomorrow.

Part 18:

1. He doesn't know how to do it.
2. She didn't understand.
3. They won't try it again.
4. She's not ready. / She isn't ready.

Part 19:

1. Were they ready?
2. Did she buy one?

Part 20:

1. She won't tell you.
2. They can't get here in time.
3. He's not coming. / He isn't coming.

Part 21:	*Part 22:*	*Part 23:*
1. will you?	1. make	2, 3, 1
2. wasn't he?	2. do, make	
3. doesn't she?	3. make	

Exercise 6-1: Dictation

1. Who even knows if they should've used 93658321 as the registration number?
2. None of the e-mails got answered, so the account was closed by the bank.
3. You've got to want to talk about the process and how to fix it.
4. I really hope you know what you're doing.
5. I wish it were possible, but it's not.

Exercise 6-3: Joining Phrases and Sentences with *That*

1. They are happy that they won the lottery.
2. You are concerned that they are working too hard.
3. The farmers were happy that it was finally raining.
4. It's not clear that they're telling the truth.
5. We aren't worried that things aren't going well.

Exercise 6-4: Indirect Statement

1. I'm not sure who they saw.
2. They are confused about what she did.
3. It's not clear where they went.
4. Please confirm when they did it.
5. It's clear why they were in trouble.
6. Let us know how they got there.
7. It isn't obvious why she didn't ask him.
8. The note didn't indicate what they thought about.
9. In your astronomy class, you learned where Rigel is located.
10. We don't want to know who Jane gave her coat to.
11. It's not posted when the post office closes.
12. Tell me where I put my keys.
13. Ask her when she moved to France.
14. Show me the record of what they bought.
15. You know why we never watch TV.

Exercise 6-5: Indirect Yes / No Questions

1. Do you remember who took the test?
2. Did they find out what happened?
3. Does he know who saved him?
4. Do they understand what is going on?
5. Did they realize who was there?

Exercise 6-6: Indirect Yes / No Questions

1. Do you remember who they saw?
2. Can you tell me what she did?
3. Do you know where they went?
4. Does anyone know when they did it?
5. Is it clear why they were in trouble?
6. Are we clear on how they got there?
7. Isn't it obvious why she didn't ask him?
8. Did the note indicate what they thought about?
9. In your astronomy class, will you learn where Rigel is located?
10. Will you confirm who Jane gave her coat to?
11. Do you know when the post office closes?
12. Do you know where I put my keys?
13. Will you be asking her when she moved to France?
14. Do you have a record of what they bought?
15. Isn't it apparent why we never watch TV?
16. Will they be able to get back what they lost?
17. Do you know where he is?
18. Did he explain where it was?
19. Can you guess how I got there?
20. Did you tell them how you figured it out?

Exercise 6-7: Subject and Object

1. Do you know what was in the garage?
2. Do you know where the car was?
3. Do you know who ran quickly to the pool?
4. Do you know how the man ran to the pool?
5. Do you know where the man ran quickly?
6. Do you know who played baseball?
7. Do you know what the boys played?
8. Do you know what cost $10?
9. Do you know what the book cost?

Exercise 6-8: *So or Such*?

1. such	6. so	11. so
2. so	7. so	12. such
3. so	8. such	13. such
4. such	9. such	14. such
5. such	10. so	15. so

Exercise 6-9: Unreal Duo — Present / *To Be*

1. If it were obvious, I would understand it completely.
2. If they were in good shape, they would win the competition.
3. If we were prepared, she would hire us.
4. If I were working on it, I would make the deadline.
5. If she were honest, she would not lie.
6. If you were not available, you wouldn't offer to help.
7. If he were running late, he would call us.

8. If it were hot, we would be sweating.
9. If you were sincere, I would trust you completely.
10. If I were I sure about it, I would recommend it to everyone.

Exercise 6-10: Unreal Duo — Present / Main Verbs

1. If you liked to ski, you would go as often as possible.
2. If I told you, you wouldn't remember.
3. If we practiced every day, we would get better.
4. If he ate a lot, he would be overweight.
5. If I studied every day, I would speak English well.
6. If they talked too much, they would get in trouble.
7. If it worked well, we would use it everyday.
8. If they paid attention, they would understand.
9. If everyone knew how to do it, we wouldn't need the instruction manual.
10. If it made us mad, we would complain about it.

Exercise 6-11: Intro Phrases

1. I'm not sure if it works.
2. I'm not sure if it will work.
3. I'm not sure if it worked.
4. He doesn't know if he'll be there.
5. I don't know if he was there.
6. I don't know if he is here.

Exercise 6-12: *Hope* or *Wish*?

1. hope
2. wish
3. hope
4. wish
5. hoped
6. wished
7. hoped/wish(ed)
8. hope
9. wishes
10. hopes
11. hope
12. wish
13. hope
14. wish
15. hopes

Exercise 6-13: Probability

1. will
2. won't
3. may/might
4. could
5. must
6. would
7. must
8. would
9. could
10. might/may
11. would
12. must
13. could
14. won't
15. will

Exercise 6-14: Obligation

1. have to / must
2. had better
3. had better
4. can
5. could
6. should
7. may
8. can
9. Could
10. had better
11. has to
12. can
13. had better
14. should / had better
15. may

Exercise 6-15: Three Verb Forms

1. to do
2. doing
3. to tell, doing
4. to accomplish
5. helping
6. help
7. studying
8. paying
9. to submit
10. registering
11. to go
12. using
13. to drive
14. take
15. to play
16. seeing
17. come
18. to ask, to work
19. telling
20. to avoid, telling
21. hearing
22. shipping
23. to practice
24. complaining
25. worrying
26. to do
27. do
28. helping
29. helping
30. saw
31. told
32. heard
33. to see
34. seeing
35. meeting
36. be
37. to see
38. to show
39. to eat
40. eating
41. deciding
42. to finish
43. go
44. to go
45. go
46. go
47. do

Exercise 6-16: *Say, Tell, Speak, Talk*

1. tell
2. say
3. talk
4. tell
5. speak
6. tell
7. talk
8. say, talking
9. tell
10. tell

Exercise 6-18: *Look / See / Watch*

1. Look
2. watch
3. look
4. watch
5. see
6. look
7. see
8. watch
9. see
10. look

Exercise 6-19: *Hear / Listen*

1. hear
2. listen
3. listen
4. heard
5. hear
6. Listen
7. hear
8. listening
9. Listen, hear
10. heard

Exercise 6-20: Verbs of Perception

1. looks
2. sounds
3. feel
4. saw
5. heard
6. appear
7. feel
8. looks
9. touch
10. listening to

Exercise 6-21: Linking Verbs of Perception

1. looks
2. sound
3. appears
4. feel
5. sound

Answer Key

Exercise 6-22: Verbs of Perception

1. hear
2. see
3. watching
4. listening
5. looks
6. look at
7. sounded
8. feel
9. touch
10. watch

Exercise 6-23: *Have* or *Take*

1. having
2. take
3. have
4. take
5. took
6. had
7. take
8. Take, have
9. take
10. taking

Exercise 6-24: Take It Easy! Take Five!

1. up
2. advantage
3. advantage of
4. take
5. time
6. place
7. notes
8. bribes
9. advice
10. turns

Chapter 6 Test

Part 1:
1. he did.
2. he didn't.
3. they won't.
4. they can.
5. she wouldn't.

Part 2:
1. He/She did it.
2. He/She should do it.

Part 3:
1. I don't know who did it.
2. I don't know who likes them. / I don't know who they like.

Part 4:
1. We can't figure out who did it.
2. We can't figure out who makes them.

Part 5:
1. What did he do?
2. What will they buy?

Part 6:
1. Where did he do it?
2. Where will they go?

Part 7:
1. When did he do it?
2. When do we dance?

Part 8:
1. How did he do it?
2. How does she paint?

Part 9:
1. I'm not sure if he did it.
2. I'm not sure if we need one.
3. I'm not sure if he'll do it.

Part 10:
Answers may vary.

Part 11:
1. say
2. tell
3. talking
4. tells / told
5. speak

Part 12:
1. must be
2. may be
3. could be
4. has to be
5. May
6. can
7. should

Exercise 7-1: Dictation

1. There should have been some kind of explanation during the meeting while everyone was together.
2. They must have forgotten to lock the storage door when they left.
3. We shouldn't have listened in on their conversation while they were discussing private matters.
4. You didn't really think they were going to let you get away with it, did you?
5. He hopes he can deal with it on his own, doesn't he?

Exercise 7-5: Regular Adjective to Reverse Adjective

1. The bomb that is ticking loudly is about to go off.
2. The facts that are well known are not in dispute. / The facts that are known well are not in dispute.
3. The audience that was recently admitted clapped loudly.
4. A child who is two years old can't read.
5. The salesmen who were downsized protested loudly. / The salesmen who had been downsized protested loudly.

Exercise 7-6: Reverse Adjective to Regular Adjective

1. An illiterate person can't work for the government.
2. An unidentified object flew over the city.
3. The recently purchased car runs really well.
4. The eliminated players cheered for the remaining contestants.
5. The retired detective has written a book about his experiences.

Exercise 7-7: Compacting Subjects

1. The kids who are playing on the swings are having a great time. / The kids, who are having a great time, are playing on the swings.
2. The house that was painted blue is next door to us. / The house that is next door to us was painted blue.
3. My sister who is married is very happy. / My sister, who is married, is very happy. / My sister who is very happy is married. / My sister, who is very happy, is married.
4. The teacher who gave us a test today will grade it later. / The teacher, who gave us a test today, will grade it later.
5. The dress that doesn't fit anymore would be better off given to someone else. / The dress that would be better off given to someone else doesn't fit anymore.

Exercise 7-8: Compacting Objects

1. I met a man who had nine kids.
2. We heard a rumor that wasn't true at all.
3. I like people who are nice.
4. There was a mistake in his report that caused a lot of problems.
5. They'll organize a protest that will change everything.

Exercise 7-9: It's All Relative

I'd like to welcome you to our company, introduce you to the people **who** work here, and tell you about the job **that** you'll be doing. Mr. Edwards is the man **who** started this company. This room is **where** we hold our weekly meetings at 8:00 am, although morning is usually **when** we make most of our calls. This is Mr. Roberts, **who(m)** you'll be working with. Finally, here's the room **where** you will be working and the ID card **that** you'll need to carry at all times. This is the best company **that** I've ever worked for.

Exercise 7-10: *How* Questions of Manner

1. How does it work?
2. How did she get rich?
3. How does he drive?
4. How did we open it?
5. How did they find it?
6. How did he do it?
7. How did he do it?
8. How did he do it?
9. How did we travel?
10. How did he make friends?

Exercise 7-11: *How* Questions of Extent

1. How well does it work?
2. How rich did she get?
3. How fast does he drive?
4. How slowly did we open it?
5. How late did they find it?
6. How dumb was he?
7. How ridiculous was it?
8. How furious were they?
9. How modern was her house?
10. How small were his hands?

Exercise 7-12: 5 W Review

1. Who landed on it? What did he land on? Where did he land? When did he land on it? Why did he land on it? How did he land on it? Did he land on it?
2. Who sailed across it? What did he sail across? Where did he sail? When did he sail? Why did he sail? How did he sail? Did he sail (across it)?
3. Who discovered it? What did he discover? Where did he discover it? When did he discover it? Why did he discover it? How did he discover it? Did he discover it?

Exercise 7-13: Something Else

1. someone else
2. nothing else
3. When else
4. Who else
5. everything else
6. somewhere else
7. Why else
8. anywhere else
9. everyone else
10. How else
11. Everywhere else
12. someone else
13. anything else
14. anywhere else
15. Someone else

Exercise 7-14: *Ago / For / In*

It's six o'clock now. I'll eat dinner **in** an hour, at seven o'clock. I was supposed to meet Tom an hour **ago** at five o'clock, but he wasn't there. I waited **for** fifteen minutes, (from 5:00 to 5:15) and then I had to leave without him. He'll probably call me **in** a couple of minutes, at 6:15.

Exercise 7-15: *During* or *While*

1.	while	11.	While
2.	during	12.	during
3.	During	13.	During
4.	while	14.	while
5.	during	15.	while
6.	while	16.	while
7.	while	17.	while
8.	During	18.	while
9.	during	19.	during
10.	while	20.	during

Exercise 7-16: *By / Until*

1.	until	8.	By
2.	by	9.	until
3.	until	10.	By
4.	by	11.	until
5.	until	12.	by
6.	by	13.	until
7.	until	14.	by
		15.	until

Exercise 7-17: *For* or *Since*

1.	for	6.	for
2.	since	7.	for
3.	for	8.	since
4.	since	9.	for
5.	for	10.	since

Exercise 7-18: *Ago / Before / In / After / Later*

1.	in	6.	after
2.	ago	7.	before
3.	before	8.	Before / After
4.	After	9.	After
5.	later	10.	ago

Exercise 7-19: *Yet / Already / Still / Anymore*

1.	yet	6.	already
2.	yet	7.	anymore
3.	already	8.	already
4.	anymore / yet	9.	still
5.	yet, still	10.	still

Exercise 7-20: *Yet / Already / Still / Anymore*

The Cubans and the Americans haven't settled their differences **yet**. They are **still** arguing about communism and capitalism. They've **already** discussed it many times.

Most people don't hope for a speedy resolution **anymore** because it has gone on for so long.

Exercise 7-21: "Have You Ever Been to Mexico?"

I **have gone** to Mexico three times this year. My brother **has** never **been** there. We **have talked** about it several times, but he **has**n't ever **found** the time to go. He **has been waiting** for a long time! We **have made** plans to go later this year, but he **has**n't **decided** when. When we do go, it'll be great.

Exercise 7-22: "A Has-Been or a Wannabe?"

America is a good country, but it **has been** slowly crumbling ever since the Vietnam War. **Have** we **learned** the lessons of the past? Can we say that we **have provided** all of our children with a good education? We **have devoted** far, far too much time, energy and money on the military. This country **has arrived** at a crossroads, and we can either survive and become stronger, or fall by the wayside in global significance.

Exercise 7-23: Present Duo vs. Simple Past

1. have lived
2. moved
3. has never tried
4. drove
5. took
6. has happened
7. started / haven't finished
8. finished
9. have finished
10. worked
11. has been working
12. rained
13. has been raining
14. Have you seen
15. have been sitting
16. sat
17. drove / have driven / have been driving
18. drove
19. have seen
20. saw

Exercise 7-24: Present Duo vs. Simple Present

1. have liked
2. like
3. finish / have finished
4. finish
5. grows
6. have grown
7. have managed
8. manage / have managed
9. have grown
10. grows

Exercise 7-26: *There* or *Have*

1. There is not enough time.
2. There was a lot of exciting stuff to do.
3. There is no need to buy new clothes.
4. There was no reason to arrange the meeting.

5. There were many reasons to arrange the meeting.
6. There was a lot of trouble with the fax machine.
7. There were many hardworking people in the office.
8. There is no need to go to work today.
9. There were a lot of seals on the beach.
10. There will be peace someday.
11. There was no class on Friday.
12. There are a lot of butterflies in that town.
13. There was a shirt on the floor.
14. There was no need to do that.
15. There were a lot of balloons in the room.

Exercise 7-27: *There* or *It*

1. There is, There are
2. Is there, there is
3. there was
4. Is it, it's
5. There's
6. there was, It was, There was, There were
7. There are
8. it was, There was, It was
9. there will be
10. There's
11. There is / There must be
12. There are
13. There was, it was, there were
14. it was
15. There will be
16. There's, It's
17. there will be
18. there would be, there was
19. There was
20. it is/ it would be
21. It was
22. There was
23. it were, there were, it were
24. there is
25. it is
26. is it
27. It is / It would be
28. There
29. It
30. There
31. there was
32. Is it
33. There isn't
34. There was
35. There was
36. there are / there might be

Exercise 7-28: Verb Review

1. is
2. was
3. have been
4. will be
5. may be / might be
6. should be
7. could be
8. must be
9. would be
10. will have been
11. might have been
12. must have been
13. should have been
14. have been
15. could have been
16. had been
17. were
18. had been
19. must have been
20. were, would be

Exercise 7-29: Change to the Past

1. He must have been able to think quickly.
2. He had to be able to think quickly.
3. It might have been better to wait for them.
4. He said that they shouldn't have gone.
5. If they took my car, they wouldn't have to wait for the bus.
6. If they had taken my car, they wouldn't have had to wait for the bus.
7. You were able to go home at five today.
8. He wasn't supposed to take Jim's car without asking.
9. They said that they would be here until next week.
10. Al may have used your car for the rest of the week.
11. Al was allowed to use your car for the rest of the week.
12. I wish I had known what he wanted.
13. He knew what he was doing.
14. I forgot why we had done it.

Exercise 7-30: Tag Endings

1.	isn't he/she	21.	won't you
2.	can't he	22.	haven't we
3.	does she	23.	shouldn't he
4.	didn't they	24.	shouldn't he
5.	do you	25.	did I
6.	do I	26.	will I
7.	aren't I	27.	don't you
8.	will you	28.	aren't you
9.	doesn't he	29.	didn't you
10.	could you	30.	can't I
11.	don't we	31.	do we
12.	haven't we	32.	don't they
13.	didn't we	33.	wouldn't he
14.	didn't we	34.	did you
15.	hadn't we	35.	would it
16.	hadn't we / shouldn't we	36.	have they
17.	hasn't it	37.	hadn't I / shouldn't I
18.	isn't it	38.	isn't it
19.	won't it	39.	did they
20.	hasn't it	40.	wouldn't they

Exercise 7-31: *Turn*

1.	out	6.	up
2.	down	7.	out
3.	up	8.	thirty
4.	out	9.	turnover
5.	into	10.	over

Chapter 7 Test

Part 1:

1.	who	7.	were
2.	that	8.	is
3.	whose	9.	had been
4.	what	10.	should have been
5.	will	11.	could dance
6.	were	12.	could have called

Part 2:

1.	don't we	5.	won't it
2.	didn't they	6.	doesn't she
3.	hasn't she	7.	hadn't he
4.	had they	8.	wouldn't they

Part 3:

1.	ago	10.	by
2.	for	11.	for
3.	in	12.	since
4.	during	13.	in
5.	during	14.	after
6.	While	15.	yet
7.	during	16.	already
8.	while	17.	still
9.	until	18.	anymore

Part 4:

1. I have watched TV.
2. They have done the dishes.
3. People have made mistakes.
4. Things have fallen in an earthquake.
5. The situation has gotten better.
6. The shredder has torn the paper.
7. The children have been well behaved.
8. The competitors have brought their own gear.
9. The cats have drunk the milk.
10. Dennis has broken his leg.

Part 5:

1. Everyone has seen that movie.
2. Joe has stolen the books.
3. Louise has taken the test.
4. The teacher has chosen the participants.
5. The idea has become more popular.
6. The students have learned the lessons.
7. His parents have been informed of the decision.
8. The CEO has been thinking about it.
9. Many people have forgotten to answer.
10. The horses have eaten the hay.

Part 6:

1.	has thought	10.	has already gone
2.	bought	11.	thinks
3.	drove	12.	has thought
4.	have never seen	13.	need
5.	talked	14.	have needed
6.	they've always used	15.	lived
7.	has done	16.	has lived
8.	barked	17.	worked
9.	gone	18.	has worked

Exercise 8-1: Dictation

1. Let's have him get a haircut and then make him make an appointment for a job interview.
2. We can't let her see what the house looks like or she'll get really mad.
3. If he'd been paying attention, this never would have happened.
4. They would never have acted like that if you hadn't been so demanding.
5. If you'd thought about it, you would have come to a different conclusion.

Exercise 8-17: *How* + Adjective

1. How wide is it?
2. How much does it weigh?
3. How many pages does it have?
4. How old is it?
5. How much is it?
6. How often do you brush it?
7. How many did she eat?

8. How much did she eat?
9. How tall is it?
10. How long was it?

Exercise 8-18: Nouns to Verbs

1. Make this dress longer.
2. It made our system weaker.
3. We need to make our industries stronger.
4. Could you make this knot tighter?
5. I need to make my tie looser.
6. It only made my love for them deeper.
7. It will make the suspense higher.
8. We hope it will make the damage less.
9. Let's try to make its appeal broader.
10. Try to make the gap between them wider.
11. You should make the sauce a little thicker.
12. This lamp will make the room brighter.
13. Use this to make your teeth whiter.
14. Could you make the room darker, please?
15. The farmer made the turkey fatter.

Exercise 8-19: *To*

I'd like to **introduce** you to my cousin, and **invite** you to our company party. If you **agree** to do this, you'll be able to **talk** to a lot of fun people. If you **happen** to be busy that day, let me know. I'm having trouble **getting used** to your new schedule! Anyway, I **look forward** to seeing you there!

Exercise 8-20: *For*

Could I **ask** you for a favor? I **apologize** for the inconvenience, but I have a good **reason** for asking. I'm **looking** for a new apartment and I can't **wait** for the real estate agent. I **applied** for three apartments, but I wasn't able to get any of them. I wasn't **prepared** for this, and I'm starting a new job on Monday, so I really hope this **works out** for me!

Exercise 8-21: *Of* and *About*

1. hear
2. accused
3. got rid / thinking
4. talk / become

Exercise 8-22: *On*

I'd like to **congratulate** you on your recent promotion. I hear that the bosses **decided** on you for the position at the last meeting. As a matter of fact, the CEO **insisted** on your being selected, and said that future contracts depended on your continued involvement, and that you need to **concentrate** on the big projects. They really **rely** on you!

Exercise 8-23: *With*

Have you noticed that the new chef doesn't **get along** with the rest of the staff? I think he has a problem **communicating** with others. Whether you **agree** with a

person or not, you don't have to **argue** with them. He needs to have more **patience** with everyone and **deal** with them as individuals.

Exercise 8-24: *From*

So, when did you **get back** from your vacation? I hear you had a pretty bad cold at the beginning. Have you **recovered** from it? It's hard to **prevent** yourself from getting sick, but it helps to wash your hands a lot. With children, you need to **stop** them from touching their faces. Hey, are you still under the weather? Are you **keeping** something from me?

Exercise 8-25: Preposition Review

1.	to	51.	for
2.	for	52.	at
3.	with	53.	in
4.	on	54.	of
5.	about	55.	of
6.	from	56.	to
7.	of	57.	to
8.	to	58.	from
9.	of	59.	than
10.	for	60.	to
11.	to	61.	out
12.	for	62.	in
13.	for	63.	up
14.	to	64.	of
15.	to	65.	about
16.	about	66.	about
17.	from	67.	at
18.	to	68.	in
19.	with	69.	on
20.	to	70.	at
21.	to	71.	in
22.	about	72.	in
23.	to	73.	on
24.	for	74.	in
25.	to	75.	on
26.	with	76.	at
27.	for	77.	on
28.	to	78.	in
29.	of	79.	on
30.	about	80.	in
31.	in	81.	By
32.	on	82.	in
33.	on	83.	at
34.	to	84.	to
35.	to	85.	on
36.	out	86.	about
37.	to	87.	to
38.	with	88.	from
39.	of	89.	on
40.	on	90.	for
41.	with	91.	with
42.	on	92.	to
43.	to	93.	at
44.	for	94.	to
45.	of	95.	up
46.	to	96.	of
47.	in	97.	up
48.	of	98.	to
49.	to	99.	up
50.	at	100.	at

Exercise 8-26: Past Unreal Duo — Main Verbs

1. If you had liked to ski, you would have gone as often as possible.
2. If I had told you, you wouldn't have remembered.
3. If we had practiced every day, we would have gotten better.
4. If he had eaten too much, he would have been overweight.
5. If I had studied every day, I would have spoken English well.
6. If they had talked too much, they would have gotten in trouble.
7. If it had worked well, we would have used it every day.
8. If they had paid attention, they would have understood.
9. If everyone had known how to do it, we would not have needed the instruction manual.
10. If it had made us mad, we would have complained about it.

Exercise 8-28: That's a Big If!

1. would have ridden
2. will ride
3. would ride
4. are ready
5. were ready
6. had been ready
7. They'd be happy
8. They'd have been happy
9. They'll be happy
10. were

Exercise 8-29: Giving Permission

He wants to go to the beach. She says OK.
She lets him go to the beach.
She allows him to go to the beach.
She permits him to go to the beach.

I would like to think about it. He says OK.
He lets me think about it.
He allows me to think about it.
He permits me to think about it.

We need to try again. They said OK.
They let us try again.
They allow us to try again.
They permit us to try again.

Exercise 8-30: Causing an Action

We want them to come back later.
We have them come back later.
We make them come back later.
We get them to come back later.

They wanted him to change the settings.
They had him change the settings.
They made him change the settings.
They got him to change the settings.

She needed us to work on it.
She had us work on it.
She made us work on it.
She got us to work on it.

Exercise 8-31: Causing an Action

1. having	6. get	11. got
2. made	7. had	12. let
3. got	8. made	13. made
4. had	9. let	14. had
5. get	10. had	15. get

Chapter 8 Test

Part 1:

1. to	11. to	
2. for	12. for	
3. of	13. of	
4. about	14. about	
5. on	15. on	
6. to	16. with	
7. from	17. from	
8. to	18. to	
9. for	19. for	
10. to	20. to	

Part 2:

1. How far is it?	7. How long is it?
2. How old is it?	8. How long is it?
3. How much is it?	9. How wide is it?
4. How often is it?	10. How tall is it?/
5. How much is it?	How high is it?
6. How many are there?	11. How thick is it?

Part 3:

1. would have sent
2. will send
3. would send
4. were
5. had been
6. is

Part 4:

1. True
2. False
3. False
4. True
5. True

Part 5:

1. had, finished
2. had, thought
3. had, thought
4. had, understood
5. had, realized

Part 6:

1. If you had studied, you would have learned.
2. If it had been impossible, you would have stopped trying.
3. If they had shown me how to do it, it wouldn't have been scary anymore.

Part 7:

1. went
2. has spoken
3. had spoken
4. always said / had always said
5. had known
6. studied

Answer Key

Part 8:
1. Could you make this essay shorter?
2. Let's make this row straighter.
3. She tried to make the knot looser.

Exercise 9-1: Dictation

1. Bob said he didn't understand how to operate the fax machine.
2. Bill indicated that he wasn't interested in upgrading to a better system.
3. Do you think they knew who the developer of the process was?
4. Nobody can figure out who took the access code to the private elevator.
5. The notes indicated that more resources would have been helpful.

Exercise 9-3: The Story of Human Language

"I **never met a person** who is not interested in language," wrote the bestselling author and psychologist Steven Pinker. **There are good reasons** that language fascinates us so. It not **only defines humans as a species**, placing us head and **shoulders above even** the most proficient animal communicators, but it also beguiles us with its endless mysteries.

For example, **how did different languages come to be?** Why isn't there just one language? **How does a language** change, **and when it does**, is that change **indicative of decay or** growth? **How does a language become** extinct? Consider how a single tongue spoken 150,000 years ago has evolved into the estimated 6,000 languages **used around the world today.**

Exercise 9-4: Polar Bears and Global Warming

1. endangered species
2. become extinct
3. protections
4. jeopardize
5. measures
6. dioxide
7. stemmed
8. 25,000
9. 4,700
10. white

Exercise 9-5: Physics

"It doesn't **take an Einstein** to understand modern physics," says Professor Richard Wolfson. **Relativity and quantum physics** touch the very basis of physical reality, altering our commonsense notions of **space and time, cause and effect**. Both have reputations for being bewilderingly complex. But the basic ideas behind relativity and quantum physics are, in fact, simple **and comprehensible by anyone.** The essence of relativity is summed up in a single, concise sentence: **The laws of physics are the same for all observers in** uniform motion.

Exercise 9-6: The History of the English Language

1. True
2. False
3. False
4. True
5. True

Exercise 9-7: Economics

✓ Economic issues play a large part in our everyday lives, and it's important to have a deeper understanding of the fundamentals.

Exercise 9-8: The Joy of Science

People should be acquainted with the second **law** of thermodynamics. This law deals with the diffusion of **heat** and has many **profound** consequences. Also important are Newton's laws, the periodic table of elements, the double-helix **structure of** DNA, and scores of other masterpieces of **scientific discovery**.

Exercise 9-9: Drawing a Conclusion

✓ The fundamental questions in our lives pertain to value.

Exercise 9-10: Listening for Specific Facts

1. True
2. False
3. False
4. True
5. True

Exercise 9-11: John F. Kennedy

1. John Fitzgerald Kennedy
2. JFK and Richard Nixon
3. 43
4. assassinated
5. Lee Harvey Oswald
6. He may have been, but there is a probability of a conspiracy.
7. He was murdered two days later by Jack Ruby.
8. deeply
9. He continues to rank highly in public opinion ratings of former U.S. presidents.

Exercise 9-12: Rice

What are the two edible parts of rice? **The grain and the husk.**
Rice grows in all the countries with climates that are: **C. warm and moist**
What is another word for **consumed** *in the first sentence?* **eaten**
Why is rice husk important? **B. because it has many vitamins**
Why do people who don't eat rice husk suffer from various deficiencies? **(Answers may vary.)**

Exercise 9-13: Gin-Soaked Raisins

In your own words, what is the main idea of the article? **Eating raisins soaked in gin is a remedy for arthritic pain.**
What ingredient in gin helps healing and reduces swelling? **Juniper berries**

Exercise 9-15: Preposition Review

1.	Over	16.	off
2.	off	17.	away
3.	—	18.	up
4.	off	19.	up for
5.	into	20.	down
6.	out of	21.	have
7.	up	22.	take
8.	out	23.	make
9.	away	24.	take
10.	down	25.	make
11.	at	26.	make
12.	out	27.	take
13.	do	28.	let
14.	off	29.	had
15.	out	30.	got

Exercise 9-16: Reported or Indirect Speech

1. I thought that she did that every day.
2. He said that he would do it later.
3. She believed that they had left early.
4. I thought that your friends left.
5. He said that he would call you when he had time.
6. She believed that you needed to take a bath.
7. I thought that she wanted him to do his homework.
8. He said that these shoes were too small.
9. She believed that she looked great in that dress.
10. I thought that the computer had crashed.

Exercise 9-17: Past Unreal Duo

1. If she had saved her money, she would / could have lived comfortably.
2. If they had considered all of the options, they would / could have been prepared.
3. If we had planted a garden, we would / could have had a lot of vegetables.
4. If I hadn't watched the road, I would / could have gotten in an accident.
5. If we hadn't done the laundry, we wouldn't have had anything to wear.

Exercise 9-18: Verb Tense Understanding

1.	happened	11.	was
2.	knows	12.	used to
3.	will call	13.	is used to
4.	have tried	14.	is
5.	may be	15.	was
6.	has never gone	16.	will be able to
7.	did	17.	didn't
8.	have done	18.	fell
9.	did/had done	19.	cry
10.	drink	20.	painted

Exercise 9-19: Three *Theres*

1. There
2. their
3. they're

Exercise 9-20: Four *2s*

1.	4 (too)	3.	3 (two)
2.	2 (too)	4.	1 (to)

Exercise 9-21: Four *Hads*

1.	3 (obligation)	3.	1 (possession)
2.	2 (causative)	4.	4 (past real duo)

Exercise 9-22: Four *Woulds*

1. 2 (polite)
2. 4 (reported speech)
3. 3 (repeated past)
4. 1 (unreal duo)

Exercise 9-23: Seven *Bes*

1.	3 (−ed)	11.	4 (noun/pronoun)
2.	2 (adjective)	12.	4 (noun/pronoun)
3.	1 (−ing)	13.	5 (preposition)
4.	4 (noun/pronoun)	14.	1 (−ing)
5.	6 (passive)	15.	2 (adjective)
6.	5 (preposition)	16.	2 (adjective)
7.	7 (conjunction)	17.	3 (−ed)
8.	5 (preposition)	18.	6 (passive)
9.	2 (adjective)/	19.	2 (adjective)
	3 (passive)	20.	6 (passive)
10.	2 (adjective)		

Exercise 9-25: *Give*

1.	in	6.	away
2.	up	7.	away
3.	opinion	8.	out
4.	it's given that	9.	back
5.	benefit of the doubt	10.	off

Chapter 9 Test

Part 1:

1. Did
2. Will
3. Is
4. Has
5. Would

Part 2:

1. Do
2. will inform
3. has
4. would've
5. would
6. will

Part 3:

1. I said that he did it. / I thought that he did it.
2. I said that she would buy one. / I thought that she would buy one.
3. I said that they had opened a new branch. / I thought that they had opened a new branch.
4. I said that they had designed a wonderful plaza. / I thought that they had designed a wonderful plaza.
5. I said that we were trying our hardest. / I thought that we were trying our hardest.

Part 4:

1. out
2. up

Part 5:

1. off
2. out

Part 6:

1. If he had thought about it, he would/could have reconsidered.

2. If they had brought their laptops, they would/could have gotten a little work done.

Part 7:
1. There
2. their
3. they're

Part 8:
1. to
2. two
3. too

Exercise 10-1: Dictation

1. Sam couldn't explain why he had done it, could he?
2. The alarm had been turned off by the time the police arrived.
3. All but one of the teams will have been eliminated by the end of the tournament.
4. I hope you'll have learned your lesson by then.
5. She'll have mastered the intermediate level by August of next year.
6. It was reported in the news last Friday that many of the schools that had been built in the 1950s were being closed due to problems with the structure and condition of the classrooms.
7. Nobody was more surprised than the chairman about the sudden and rapid drop in the value of the stocks of the printing company.
8. Long before it was popular, there were many people who took advantage of trading goods and property among themselves instead of buying things new at the various stores in the neighborhood.
9. It seems unbelievable now, but people really used to believe that the earth was flat and that you would fall off if you sailed out past the horizon.
10. They say that travel is broadening, but there are people who have never been anywhere except between the covers of a book and they can be considered as informed and as experienced as anyone who has traveled around the world.

Exercise 10-7: *Only*

1. It's for your viewing.
2. He doesn't have any siblings.
3. He is very young.
4. No one else calls.
5. That's the only day we call.

Exercise 10-8: *Doubt / Question*

1. doubt
2. question
3. question
4. doubt
5. doubt
6. questioned
7. questioned
8. doubts
9. questions
10. question

Exercise 10-11: Switching Between Active and Passive

1. The cars were washed by the boys.
2. The teacher handed out the papers.
3. Her teeth were cleaned by the dentist.
4. His remarks upset everyone.
5. The miners discovered gold.
6. The fields were covered with/by snow.
7. The committee will revise the plan.
8. The media has insulted our intelligence.
9. The doctor should have informed the patient.
10. The package will have been delivered by the mailman by 5:00 p.m.

Exercise 10-12: Active to No-Blame Passive

1. The paper tore.
2. The boat rocked.
3. The car crashed.
4. Her leg fractured.
5. The evidence burned.
6. The tub overflowed.
7. The vase tipped over.
8. His shirt wrinkled.
9. His tooth chipped.
10. The branch snapped.

Exercise 10-13: Passive Voice

Soybeans **were first cultivated** in Asia more than 3,000 years ago. A mural shows tofu and soy milk **being made** in northern China. The earliest written reference to soy milk didn't occur for another 1,200 years, when soy milk **was mentioned** in a Chinese poem, "Ode to Tofu."

Travelers from Europe **became acquainted** with soybeans and the foods **made from** them — especially miso, soy sauce, and tofu. Soybeans arrived in the United States in the 1700s, **brought from** Europe by several people including Benjamin Franklin.

Soy-based infant formulas **were introduced** in the United States in 1909, and in 1910 the world's first soy dairy **was started** by a Chinese biologist. By the end of the first World War, soy milk **was being produced** commercially in New York. Within 15 years, manufacturers **were experimenting** with added nutrients such as calcium.

Exercise 10-14: Six Useful Verbs

1. managed
2. happen to
3. used to
4. turned out
5. ended up / wound up
6. turn out
7. happen to
8. used to
9. wound up / ended up
10. managed

Exercise 10-15: Past Duo

1. Until he was invited by the university last year, he had never been to Los Angeles.
2. He didn't have any money because he had lost his wallet.
3. Ron was very familiar with Paris as he had frequently traveled there.
4. We couldn't get a hotel room since we hadn't made a reservation.
5. By the time he graduated, Fred had been in college for ten years.
6. They felt bad about moving because they had owned their house for 20 years.

Exercise 10-16: Past Duo and Present Duo

1. have heard, was, died, had written
2. spend, have gone
3. went, wanted, had sat
4. has been
5. had arranged

Exercise 10-17: When Did Those Two Things Happen?

1. have never been
2. had never been
3. has overflowed
4. had flooded
5. haven't had
6. hadn't ever seen
7. We've already started
8. We'd never thought
9. We haven't moved
10. hadn't foreseen

Exercise 10-18: Future Real Duo

1. Will she have learned French before she goes to Paris?
2. By Christmas, I'll have figured out when I'll graduate.
3. He'll have finished it by midnight.
4. They'll have turned it in before the deadline.
5. She'll have run out of options before she hears back about the decision.

Exercise 10-19: 3 Futures

1. will finish
2. will have gotten
3. I'll be
4. I'll call
5. will have eaten
6. you'll catch
7. We'll have sat
8. they'll help
9. he'll have forgotten
10. will like

Exercise 10-20: Verb Review

1. bought
2. will do
3. call
4. is vacuuming
5. orders
6. has been open
7. is corrupt
8. has stalled
9. moved
10. has been
11. to finish
12. would
13. will
14. was called
15. have been informed
16. would go
17. will have been
18. wouldn't
19. were
20. can
21. isn't
22. doesn't
23. hasn't
24. didn't
25. will
26. wouldn't
27. had
28. let him
29. to notify
30. taking

Chapter 10 Test

Part 1:

1. will have been
2. will call
3. can
4. questions
5. doubts
6. participated
7. taught
8. met
9. was met
10. didn't meet

Part 2:

1. like
2. will
3. would
4. could
5. had gone
6. is
7. were
8. was
9. had been
10. would be

Part 3:

1. don't they
2. haven't they
3. didn't they
4. didn't they
5. hadn't they
6. hadn't they
7. wouldn't they
8. haven't they
9. won't they
10. haven't they

Part 4:

1. would do
2. had found
3. wasn't
4. will go
5. would go
6. would've gone
7. were
8. had been
9. are
10. is

Chapters 6-10 Review Test

Part 1:

1. We are sad that we lost the game.
2. He is happy that his friends arrived safely.

Part 2:

1. It's not clear who finished it.
2. She said that it was wonderful.
3. I thought that they couldn't swim.

Part 3:

1. Do you remember that she bought groceries?
2. Did you know that they got married?
3. Did you hear that the new store opened?

Part 4:

Intro phrases will vary. Your answer will differ.

1. Do you know where they went?
2. Do you know who won an award?
3. Do you remember when he drove to California?

Part 5:

1. so
2. such
3. so
4. such

Part 6:

1. wishes
2. hopes
3. hope
4. wish

Part 7:

1. won't
2. must
3. could
4. will
5. may / might

Part 8:

1. should have
2. had better / should
3. must
4. can
5. may

Part 9:

1. tell
2. say
3. speak
4. talking

Part 10:

1. hear
2. listen to
3. looked
4. looked
5. watched
6. sounds

Answer Key

Part 11:
1. The caterpillar that was very hungry wouldn't stop eating.
2. The car that was bright red was the fastest at the race.
3. A funny person can make other people laugh.
4. Frozen water is called ice.

Part 12:
1. The flowers that grow in the garden are blooming. / The flowers that are blooming grow in the garden.
2. I know a girl who can speak three languages.

Part 13:
1. Who takes the bus?
2. What does she take? / What does she sell?
3. Where does she take it? / Where does she go?
4. When does she take it? / When does she go to the market?
5. Why does she take it?
6. How does she take it?

Part 14:
1. We went somewhere else to find milk.
2. He talked to someone else.

Part 15:
1. in
2. ago
3. while
4. during
5. by
6. until
7. since
8. after
9. yet
10. already

Part 16:
1. don't they
2. have they
3. hadn't they
4. won't she
5. haven't we

Part 17:
1. How scary was it?
2. How much did you buy? / How many pounds did you buy?
3. How many are there?

Part 18:
1. He lifts weights to make his body stronger.
2. This lamp makes the room lighter.
3. This polish makes the surface harder.

Part 19:
1. about
2. to
3. of
4. to
5. for
6. for
7. of
8. for
9. to
10. out

Part 20:
1. No
2. Yes
3. Yes
4. Yes
5. No

Part 21:
1. I thought that she called her sister every day.
2. We believed that they would talk to him tomorrow.
3. He said that he would wake up early when he had to work.

Part 22:
1. their
2. They're
3. There

Part 23:
1. too
2. two
3. to

Part 24:
1. Nobody else was at the party.
2. He is not doing anything but hosting.

Part 25:
1. question
2. questions
3. doubted

Part 26:
1. The girl's hair was cut by the stylist.
2. The paperboy distributed the newspapers.
3. All of the carpets were vacuumed by us.

Part 27:
1. The plate broke.
2. The wood burned.
3. The tire rolled down the street.

Part 28:
1. takes
2. having
3. took
4. had
5. taking

Part 29:
1. up
2. up
3. up
4. out
5. to
6. down
7. away
8. to
9. up
10. out

Grammar Glossary

5 Ws – *Who, what, where, when, why*. This general category of question words also includes *how*.

ability – The capacity to do something, which is important in the selection of the helping verb, such as *can* or *could*. See *helping verb*.

absolute – An adjective used when not comparing, such as *good*. See *comparative* and *superlative*.

acronym – Initial letters representing an entire phrase, such as *ASAP* for *as soon as possible*.

active voice – Where the subject does something to the object, such as *The rain damaged the crops*. This is considered to be more powerful and straightforward than the passive voice. It also uses fewer words, which is generally good. See *passive voice*.

adjective – A type of modifier, specifically for nouns (*a nice day*). Possessive adjectives indicate ownership, such as **his** book or **her** plan.

adverb – A type of modifier, specifically for verbs (*He ran fast*) or adjectives (*They are very upset*). There are five types of adverbs (manner, time, frequency, extent, degree). See *5 Ws*.

alveolar ridge – The bumpy ridge just behind the top teeth, where *T, D, N, L, S, Z, Sh, Zh, J, Ch* are formed.

antonym – A word opposite in meaning from another, such as *good* and *bad*. See *synonym*.

aptitude – See *test*.

article – A specific type of noun modifier that lets you know if the thing is *singular* (a book, an apple, the car) or *plural* (the cars); or *new information* (a book, an apple) or *known information* (the books, the apples). See *modifier*.

auxiliary verb – See *helping verb*, *verb*, and *modal*.

base form – Another name for the *plain form*. See *verb*.

brackets – A way to set off information [ ], similar to parentheses ( ).

cadence – Rhythm of a spoken sentence, the use of pitch changes to create a noticeable and informative pattern of information. See *intonation*.

capitalize – To use a capital for the first letter of a personal or place name, such as *Bob* or *New York*.

causative – Verbs that produce an effect or cause someone or something to do something, such as *let, permit, allow, make, have, get*. The causative involves a combination of *desire* and *power*. *Let* indicates that the *doer* has the desire to do something and the *permitter* has the power to grant permission. *Force* indicates that the doer

doesn't want to participate, but doesn't have the power to resist.

clause – A group of words containing a subject and a verb. Some clauses are *independent*, which means they express a complete thought (*I laughed* or *Sam walked into the room*). Some clauses are *dependent*, which means they cannot stand alone without an independent clause (***Although I laughed**, I was crying on the inside* or *Sam walked into the room, **unaware that he had forgotten to button his shirt***). See *sentence*.

colloquial – Familiar way of speaking, not formal or literary.

colon – A punctuation mark (:) that separates lists or clauses. Also used in time (10:00) and ratios (10:1).

comma – A punctuation mark (,) indicating a pause between parts of a sentence. Also used with large numbers, such as 1,000.

command – To give an order, such as *Help!, Stop!,* or *Come here!*

comparative – An adjective used when comparing two things, such as *A is **better** than B*. See *absolute* and *superlative*.

complement – Similar to the *object* of a sentence, but it comes after the verb **to be**, not a main verb. With a main verb, you have the SVO pattern, but with the verb **to be**, it's SVC, because objects are always nouns (*Bob sees **Betty***) and the complement after the verb **to be** can be a noun (*I am a **teacher***), an adjective (*I am **happy***), or an adverb (*I am **here***). In this book, complements are treated as objects.

complex intonation – Going beyond the basic SVO pattern, where the subject and the object are stressed for new information, complex intonation can stress a single noun up through a five-word pattern such as **bright** red **fire** truck paint.

compound noun – Two nouns that form a new word such as *talk show*. The stress always goes on the first word, **talk** show. The first word can also be a gerund, **swimming** pool, or an adjective, **hot** dog.

conditional – See *duo*.

conjugate – To change verb tenses (*he is, they are; he was, they were*) based on time and person. This includes past, present, future, simple, and duo forms, real and unreal.

conjunction – A word such as *and, but, if,* or *or*, used to connect nouns, verbs, clauses, or sentences.

consonant – A speech sound where the air flow is blocked at some point, as opposed to a vowel, where the air flows freely. This is why *Y* and *W* are sometimes considered vowels. The American *R* acts like a vowel, whereas the British *R* does not. There are two types of consonant, *voiced* and *unvoiced*. When the vocal cords vibrate, the consonant is spoken or voiced. When they don't, it is whispered or unvoiced. See *vowel*.

continuous – A verb form that indicates an ongoing action or something that is happening right now, such as *He is reading a book*. Also known as *progressive*. See *-ing*.

contraction – A shortened form of a verb plus another word, generally a noun or a pronoun. Examples are *I'm, he's, you've, can't, isn't*.

countable noun – A noun that can have a number attached, such as *one chair* or *ten minutes*. See *uncountable noun*.

dangling participle – A present participle is a verb ending in *-ing*. It is called *dangling* when the subject of the *-ing* verb and the subject of the sentence do not agree, such as *Hurrying to get to work, Bob's car broke down*. The subject is *Bob's car*, but the car isn't doing the *hurrying*. It would be better to say, *While Bob was hurrying to work, his car broke down*. This term is often used humorously. See *participle* and *verb*.

dash – A punctuation mark (—), slightly longer than a hyphen, used to indicate a pause.

definite article – *The* is called *definite* because it refers to something specific, known, or previously mentioned, as opposed to *a* or *an*. See *article* and *modifier*.

demonstrative – One of four noun modifiers that indicate proximity and number (how far and how many): *this, that, these, those*. See *modifier*.

descriptive – A style of instruction that focuses on how things actually *are*, rather than how they *should be*, or how traditional rules would dictate. The program in this book is descriptive. See *prescriptive*. Also a noun modified with an adjective, as opposed to a *compound noun*.

determiner – See *modifier*.

diagnostic – See *test*.

direct speech – Uses quotation marks and a person's exact words, such as *Tom said, "I have to go."* See *indirect speech*.

directional preposition – See *preposition*.

duo – Any of the six forms that require two separate events or states, such as the future real duo (*He will have finished[1] by the time you are ready to go[2].*) or the past unreal duo (*He would have gone[1] if he had been ready[2].*) The second event or state is often unmentioned in the present

real duo (*I've never been there before.*). The three real duo forms are also known as the *present*, *past*, and *future perfect*.

emphatic form – An intense way to present information. With the verb *to be*, the verb is stressed but not changed (*She is happy!*). With main verbs, the verb *to do* is added and stressed (*She does like it!*).

exclamation – A short remark indicating surprise, joy, anger, excitement, pain, or a command, such as *Hey!, Wow!, Ouch!, Oh, no!*, or *Stop!*

exclamation mark – A punctuation mark (!) used to indicate urgency, such as *Hey!* or *Stop!*

figurative – Departing from the literal, actual meaning of a word to a metaphorical meaning, such as *His heart turned to stone*. See *literal*.

future tense – A time frame that has not yet happened and can use *will* (*I will call you tomorrow*), *going to* (*He's going to try again*), or even the *simple present* (*I have a doctor's appointment next week*).

gerund – An *-ing* form, where the verb works like a noun, such as ***Swimming** is fun* (subject), *I like **swimming*** (object), *She is afraid of **swimming*** (object of the preposition), *a **swimming** pool* (compound noun). See *-ing*.

grammar – The whole structure and system of a language, including syntax, morphology, phonology, and semantics. In plain English, it is the rules of a language.

helping verb – Any of the 23 verbs that go along with the main verb: *may, might, must, be, being, been, am, are, is, was, were, do, does, did, should, could, would, have, had, has, will, can, shall*. Also called *auxiliary verbs*.

hyphen – A punctuation mark (-), used to join words, such as *third-grader*.

if clause – The conditional half of the unreal duo, such as ***If I were you**, I wouldn't do that*.

-ing – There are three *-ing* forms. 1) The **continuous**, where the verb acts like a **verb** (*He is swimming.*) 2) A **participle**, where the verb acts like an **adjective** (*a **speeding** car* or ***hoping** to go*). 3) A **gerund**, where the verb works like a **noun** (***Swimming** is fun* or *a **swimming** pool*).

indefinite article – *A* and *an* are called indefinite because they refer to any member of a group, as opposed to *the*. See *article* and *modifier*.

indirect speech – Does not use quotation marks and adjusts the words a person used, such as *Tom* *said that he had to go* or *I'm not sure if he is still here*. See *direct speech*.

infinitive – *To* + the basic form of a verb, such as *to go*.

inflection – In speech, inflection is the modulation of intonation or pitch when speaking. For verbs, it is the changing of the base form to indicate time, person, or number. For speech, see *intonation*. For verbs, see *conjugate*.

interjection – See *exclamation*.

intonation – This is a broad category that encompasses speech, music, pitch change, word and syllable stress, cadence, rhythm, phrasing, inflection, and the staircase. Intonation is initially used to introduce new information via the nouns, or to indicate if a noun is compound or not. It is used secondarily to indicate contrast or opinion.

intransitive verb – A verb that cannot have an object, such as *I laughed*. See *verb*.

lax vowel – One of the vowels produced with relaxed muscles, such as *ih, eh, uh*. See *vowel*.

liaison – A word connection, such as *Gotcha* for *Got you*.

literal – The use of words in their actual meaning. See *figurative*.

locational preposition – See *preposition*.

main verb – A verb that expresses action, such as *go* or *have*, as contrasted with the verb *to be* or a *helping verb*. Every sentence needs a main verb. See *verb*.

manner – The way something is done or how it happens. See *adverb*.

manner adverb – See *adverb*.

mnemonic device – A memory aid used to remember difficult material, such as *Roy G. Biv* for the colors of the rainbow or *bones, stones, tones*, and *thrones* for the four divisions of anthropology (physical anthro, archeology, linguistics, and cultural anthro).

modal – Traditionally, this is not actually a *tense*, but rather a *mood*. Modals are a type of helping verb. They indicate probability, potential, ability, duty, obligation: *can, could, have to, have got to, had better, may, might, must, ought to, shall, should, will, would*. *Would* is used with the present and past unreal duo.

modifier – A broad term that includes articles, adjectives, adverbs, and demonstratives. Also called a *determiner*. See *reverse modifier*.

morpheme – The smallest possible sound unit with meaning, such as *break*. In plain English, it is a word, a prefix, or a suffix. For instance, *unbreakable* is made up of three morphemes –*un, break, able*. See *phoneme*.

negative – Expressing negation through denial, refusal, or refutation, using words such as *no, not, never, nor, neither, none*. See *positive*.

non-standard – Any formulation of speech that is not commonly heard; generally considered to be unacceptable. See *standard*.

noun – A person, place, thing, or idea.

   noun, singular – One thing, such as *a chair*. See *noun, plural*.

   noun, plural – When there is more than one thing, it's most common to add an S, such as *book / books*. Irregular plural nouns include *children, mice, men*, and *feet*. Plurals include *these* and *those*. See *modifier*.

   noun, countable – See *countable noun*.

   noun, uncountable – See *uncountable noun*.

   noun, common – A general item, such as *country* or *woman*. Common nouns are not capitalized.

   noun, proper – The name of a specific person, place, or thing such as *United States* or *Mary*. Proper nouns are capitalized.

object – In plain English, it's the back end of the SVO sentence, such as *Bob sees **Betty***. The object is always a noun. See *subject*.

object pronoun – See *pronoun*.

obligation – Duty, which is important in the selection of the helping verb, such as *have to, should*, or *must*. See *helping verb*.

paragraph – A section of writing in a larger essay or letter, with its own idea or theme, set off by an indent or a line space.

parentheses – Punctuation marks ( ) that enclose a phrase or sentence as an explanation or afterthought.

participle – A verb ending in *-ing*, differing from the *-ing* of the continuous, which tells time. A participle is timeless, as in *Hoping to pass the test, Fred studied hard*. *Hoping* has no time reference. It also appears with the *-ed* and *-tten* endings, as in *Forgotten by everyone, Fred sank into a deep depression*.

parts of speech – The eight grammatical terms: verb, noun, pronoun, adjective, adverb, preposition, conjunction, and exclamation.

passive voice – Where the subject is acted upon by the object, such as *The crops were damaged by the rain*. This form is used when the doer is unknown or if responsibility is being avoided. See *active voice* and *verb*.

past perfect – Another name for the *past real duo*, such as *had done*. See *duo*.

past tense – A verb tense that indicates that something happened before now. See *verb*.

Grammar Glossary

perfect – Another name for the three *real duos*, present, past, and future.

period – A punctuation mark at the end of a sentence (.). Also used in .com, but it is called *dot*. Used with numbers, such as 10.5, it is called a point or a decimal point.

person – The individual identified by the verb tense, such as *first person plural: we*.

phoneme – The smallest possible sound unit with no actual meaning, such as the P in *pit*. In plain English, it is simply a consonant sound or a vowel sound. Two letters can also form a single phoneme, such as SH or CH because they make a single sound. See *morpheme*.

phrase – A partial sentence. See *sentence* and *clause*.

pitch – The degree of highness or lowness of the voice, used to indicate a stressed syllable or an important word. See *intonation*.

placement – See *test*.

plain form – The base form of the main verb, such as the *go* of *to go*. It is used with helping verbs, such as *He should go*. See *verb* and *main verb*.

pluperfect – Another word for the *past real duo*, such as *had done*.

plural – When there is more than one thing, it's most common to add an S, such as *book / books*. Irregular plural nouns include *children, mice, men*, and *feet*. Plural modifiers include *this/these, that/those*. See *modifier*.

polarity – This term is used to explain how tag questions and tag endings work. To form a tag, change the polarity from positive to negative or negative to positive, as in *He is here, isn't he?*

positive – Expressing affirmation through agreement or permission, using words such as *yes, always, or, either, some, all*. Also known as *affirmative*. See *negative*.

possessive – See *pronoun* and *adjective*.

possibility – Something that may happen, which is important in the selection of the helping verb, such as *will, may, could*. See *helping verb*.

preposition – A word that indicates direction (*to*), location (*in*), possession (*of*).

prescriptive – An approach to teaching grammar and pronunciation based on what *ought to be*, as contrasted with *descriptive*, which is based on what actually *is*. The program in this book is descriptive.

present perfect – Another name for the *present real duo*, such as *has done*. See *duo* or *verb*.

present tense – A verb tense that indicates that something is happening in the general sense of now, such as *is* and *does*. See *verb*.

probability – Something that most likely will happen, which is important in the selection of the

helping verb, such as *will, may, could*. See *helping verb*.

progressive – See *continuous* and *-ing*.

pronoun – A word used to replace a noun, both as a subject (*I, you, he, she, it, we, they*) and the object (*me, you, him, her, it, us, them*). The possessive pronoun is used to indicate that something belongs to someone, such as *his, hers, mine, ours*, etc. The reflexive pronoun refers back to the subject, such as *I taught **myself** how to knit*. The relative pronoun is another name for the linking word in a *reverse modifier*, such as *He is the man **who** danced all night*.

punctuation mark – Any of the symbols, such as the period, comma, or parentheses, used to separate sentences into their elements or to clarify meaning.

question flip – The grammatical structure of reversing the position of the subject and the verb from a statement to a question, such as *He is here* to *Is he here?* This symbol is used to indicate the question flip ↻, and this one to indicate its absence ↺.

question mark – A mark used to indicate that the previous statement is asking a question (?).

reduced sounds – Unstressed vowels that lose their clear pronunciation.

reflexive – See *pronoun*.

relative pronoun – See *pronoun*.

reported speech – See *indirect speech*.

reverse modifer – A group of words that follow the noun that they describe, such as *He is the man **who danced all night***. Also called an adjective clause or relative clause.

rhythm – The pitch changes of a spoken sentence, creating a noticeable and informative pattern of information. See *intonation* and *word stress*.

schwa – The most common sound in English, the schwa is a neutral vowel sound, pronounced *uh* and represented with the symbol ə. It can be used with any of the vowel sounds: *was, enemy, possible, some, much, syringe*, or even when there is no vowel present, such as *chasm*. Some dictionaries use an upside-down V for stressed neutral sounds, such as *cup*, but this method only uses the schwa.

semi-colon – A punctuation mark (;) used to separate clauses. It's stronger than a comma, but weaker than a colon.

sentence – A complete group of words in a grammatical order. See *clause, phrase, statement, question flip, command*.

simple form – See *plain form*.

singular noun – One thing, such as *a chair*. See *plural noun*.

speech music – The pitch changes in spoken English. See *intonation*.

staircase – The up-and-down pitch changes in spoken English. See *intonation*.

standard – Widely accepted as the correct form. Words such as *ain't* are considered non-standard.

statement – A type of sentence that gives information, as opposed to a question, which requests information. See *sentence*.

stress – The application of pitch change to a syllable or word. See *intonation*.

subject – In plain English, it's the front end of the SVO sentence, such as ***Bob*** *sees Betty*. The subject is always a noun. See *object*.

subject pronoun – See *pronoun*.

subjunctive – See *duo*.

superlative – An adjective used when comparing and determining the highest order, such as *A is the **best** of all*. See *absolute* and *comparative*.

syllable stress – The syllable that carries the emphasis. This can change the meaning of a word, such as ***con**tent* (n) and *con**tent*** (adj). See *word stress* and *intonation*.

symbol – One of the non-alphabet characters used here to explain pronunciation: ǝ ä ü æ ɛ

synonym – Words with similar meanings, such as *teacher* and *instructor*. See *antonym*.

syntax – The arrangement of words and sentences to make well-formed sentences. Syntax is the rules of English, differing from grammar by being just one part of it, along with morphology, phonology, and semantics.

tag ending – A type of statement or question ending, such as *isn't he!* or *isn't he?*

tag question – A type of question ending, such as *isn't he?*

tense (verb) – One of the grammatical markers that indicate what time the action took place, such as *runs, want**ed**, **will** go*. See *verb*.

tense (vowel) – One of the vowels produced with tensed muscles, such as *ee, oh, ooh*. Also called *long vowels*. See *vowel*.

test – There are four types of tests, *aptitude* (to see what a person is naturally good at), *diagnostic* (to show what a person does wrong), *placement* (to determine what level a person should be within a program), and *achievement* (to demonstrate what a person has accomplished so far).

transitive verb – A verb that can have an object, such as *He opened the window*. See *verb*.

uncountable noun – A noun that cannot have a number attached, such as *beauty* or *water*. See *countable noun*.

unvoiced consonant – See *consonant* and *voiced consonant*.

verb – Either an action word such as *to run*, or a state, *to have* or *to be*. See *tense (verb)*, *modal*, *helping verb*, *active*, *passive*, *transitive*, *intransitive*.

voice – A way that a verb acts. If the subject is in charge, it is called the active voice, such as *The rain **damaged** the crops*. If the subject is acted upon, it is called the passive voice, such as *The crops **were damaged** by the rain*.

voiced consonant – See *consonant*.

vowel – A, E, I, O, U are the vowel letters. English has 14 vowel sounds. See *tense, lax, consonant*.

word connection – See *liaison*.

word stress – The word(s) in a sentence that carries the emphasis. The primary form is ***Subject-Verb-Object*** (SVO). Secondary forms include contrast, emphasis, and complex intonation. See *syllable stress* and *intonation*.

Index

Consonant and Vowel Symbols

ä — xiii, 3, 28, 61, 75, 124, 181–182
ā — xiii
æ — xiii, 3, 28, 109, 124
b — xxiii, 166
ch — xxiv, 4, 8
d — xxiii, 61, 181
ə — xiii, 3, 61, 68, 75, 124, 151, 182
ē — xiii, 28, 75, 181–182
ε — xiii, 61, 75, 181–182

f — xxiii, 166
g — xxiii
h — xxiii
i — xiii, 68, 75, 181
ī — xiii
j — xxiii, 4, 8
k — xxiii
l — xxiii, 180–182
m — xxiii, 225
n — xxiii, 181, 225
ng — xxiii, 225
ō — xiii, 181–182
oi — xiii
ow — xiii, 109, 182

p — xxiii, 166
q — xxiii, 4, 32, 109, 210
r — xxiii, 3, 180–182
s — xxiv, 4, 6, 8, 9, 10, 61
sh — xxiv, 8
t — xxiii, 61, 181, 226
th — 3, 82
ü — xiii, 61, 75
ū — xiii
v — xxiii, 166
w — xxiii, 4, 166, see also *Word connections*

x — xxiv, 8, 12, 13, 52, 80, 109, 129
y — xiii, 4, 8, see also *Plurals* and *Word connections*
z — xxiv, 4, 6, 8, 9, 10, 61
zh — 23
-ed — 61
-ied — 61
-ies — 37, 38
-ing — see *Continuous*
5 Ws — 89, 128, 130–134, 156, 157, 177–178, 212

A

A, see *Article*
Ability, 41, 140. See also *Helping verb*
Absolute, 55–56
Acronym, 83, 98
Active voice, xii, 227, 232–234. See also *Passive voice*
Adjective, xiii, 23, 55–58, 70, 97, 98, 99, 101, 107, 135, 150, 152, 153, 167, 183, 185, 187, 188, 202, 216, 227, 247, 248
Adverb, vii, viii, 70, 92, 98, 101, 130, 156, 183
Alveolar ridge, 182, 279
American D, 61, 181
American R, 3, 180–182
American speech music — see *Intonation*
Analysis, xxiv
Answer Key, 251
Antonym, 243
Article, vii, 52, 76, 96, 98, 99, 121, 125, 243. See also *Modifier*
Attitude, 180
Auxiliary verb — see *Helping verb*

B

Base form — see *Unchanging form*
Be, 7, 11, 12, 17–22, 216
Bit or Beet?, 75
Brackets, 35, 151

C

Cadence — see *Intonation*
Capitalize, 221
Cat? Caught? Cut?, 3
Causative, xii, 177, 195, 198–199, 215
Clause, viii, 128, 154, 227, 243
Colloquial, viii, 48, 227
Colon, 279
Comma, 154, 243
Command, 48, 49
Comparative, viii, 55, 56
Complement, viii, 158
Complex Verbs — see *Grammar in a nutshell*
Compound Nouns, 30–31, 97–98, 183–185
Comprehension, 81, 207–210
Conditional, xi, 17, 114, 135, 213. See also *Duo*

Confirmation, 22. See also *Tag*
Conjugate, x, xiii, 17, 37, 61, 128, 135
Conjunction, vii, viii, 30, 35, 49, 51, 73, 96, 97, 99, 100, 121, 125, 128, 130, 216
Consonant, xiii, 4, 55, 61, 225–226
Consonant chart, xxiii
Continuous, xiii, 4, 74, 83–87, 88, 94, 113, 115, 126, 136
Contraction, 19–20, 43, 63–64, 85, 111
Contrast, 3, 30–31, 86, 104, 111, 166, 226
Countable noun, 53, 74, 76–80, 101, 106–109, 186, 201, 243. See also *Uncountable noun*

D

Dangling participle, vi, 280
Dash, 280
Definite article — see *Article*
Demonstrative, 280
Descriptive phrases, xiii, 30–32, 97–99, 153, 183–186. See also *Intonation*

Determiner — see *Modifier*
Diagnostic test, xxiii
Direct object, 2, 11, 91–92, 118, 131–134, 155, 158, 218, 227, 232–233
Direct speech, vii. See also *Reported speech*
Direction preposition, see *Preposition*
Duo, x–xi, xix, 17, 114–115, 128, 135–139, 163–166, 169–170, 174–175, 195–197, 202, 204, 213, 215, 222, 235, 237

E

-ed, 61. See also *Past tense*
-er, 56
-est, 56
Emotions, 88, 180
Empathy, 180
Emphasis — see *Intonation*
Emphatic form, 36, 39, 40, 42–44, 61, 62, 64
Exclamation, 280
Exclamation mark, 47, 280

F

Figurative, 280. See also *Literal*
Four-word phrases, 184–185. See also *Intonation*
Future tense, 110–115. See also *Duo*

G

Get, 68, 88
Gin-Soaked Raisins, 209–210
Give, 220
Grammar in a Nutshell, 115–118, 218–220

H

Had, 215. See also *Duo*
Have, 166. See also *Phrasal verbs* or *Duo*
Held T, 226
Helping verb
   Obligation, 140, 169
   Opinion, 139, 144, 169
   Possibility, 138–139, 169
   Probability, 139, 169
Hope, 137
How, 92, 101–103, 156–158, 186–187

I

If clause, 197, see *Duo*
Indefinite article — see *Article*
Indirect speech — see *Reported speech*
Infinitive, 41, 59, 141, 189, 281
Inflection — see *Intonation*
Interjection — see *Exclamation*
Intonation, 80, 183–186
   Attitude, 180
   Adjective, 183–185
   Complex verbs, 115–118, 218–220
   Compound nouns, 31
   Confirmation, 180
   Contrast, 31
   Descriptive phrase, 30–31, 183–185

Four-word phrase, 183–185
Grammar in a nutshell, 115–118, 218–220
New information, 30
Non-verbal, 180
Noun stress — see *Noun intonation*
Intransitive verb, 281
It has, 166
Invisible R, 182

J, K, L

Lax vowels, 75
Literal, 280
Location preposition — see *Preposition*
Long vowels — See *Tense vowels*

M

Main verb, 31, 36–44, 60–61, 70–71, 89–91, 92, 103, 115, 137, 196
Make, 118, 200. See also *Phrasal verbs*
Manner
   Adverbs of — see *Adverb*
   Prepositions of, 79
   Using *how*, 156
Middle I List, 68
Mnemonic device, 168
Modal, xii. See also *Helping verb*
Modifier, 7, 16, 30, 34, 53–58, 76–78
   Reverse, 152–153
   Multiple, 183–185
Morpheme, 281

N

Nasal consonants, 225–226
Negative, 19–22, 42–43, 61–63, 85, 88, 110–111, 116–117, 158, 162
New information, 4–5, 30, 54. See also *Intonation*
Noun
   Common, 281

Countable, 76, 77, 78, 101, 106–108
Intonation, xiii, 3–6, 8, 12, 13, 14, 15, 18, 20, 23, 24, 28, 30–32, 34, 52, 67, 68, 74, 78, 80, 82, 85, 96–98, 129, 150, 177, 183–186, 204, 218–219, 229
Plural, 7–9, 10, 37, 99, 101
Proper, 281
Reduced sound, 29, 75
Question, 1, 2, 10, 11, 21–22, 43–44, 45, 50, 64, 65, 72, 89, 90, 91, 92, 94, 102, 112, 132–134
Singular, 7, 8, 9, 10
Staircase, 180. See also *Intonation*
Statement, xi, xiii, 10, 11, 19, 21, 26, 39, 40. See also *Question*
Tag endings, 22, 46, 47, 50, 66, 67, 72, 171–172
Three-word phrases, 183. See also *Intonation*
Two-word phrases, 162, 184. See also *Intonation*
Uncountable nouns, 76, 77, 78, 101–102

O

Obama speech, 229–231
Object noun, 2, 11, 17–18, 91–92, 131–134, 218, 227, 233
Object pronoun, 13, 16, 91, 131–134, 158
Obligation, 140, 169. See also *Helping verb*
Old information, 4, 5, 30, 51. See also *Intonation*
Only, 227

Opinion, 139, 144, 169. See also *Helping verb*
Outline, 242

P

Paragraph, 281
Parentheses, 281
Participle, 281
Parts of speech, vii, 281
Passive voice, 232–235. See also *Active voice*
Past perfect tense — see *Duo*
Past tense
   Continuous, 74, 83, 84, 86, 94
   Simple, 60–61, 67, 163–165
   Unreal duo, 169, 195–196. See *Duo*
Period, 282
Person, 12, 13, 18–20, 37, 39–43, 158
   Part of speech — See *Noun*
Personality, 154
Phrasal verbs, 98
   Do, 118, 200
   Get, 68–69, 88
   Give, 220
   Make, 118, 200. See also *Causative*
   Take, 145–146
   Turn, 172
   Stand, 119–120
Phoneme, 282
Phrase, 8, 10, 33, 34, 35, 56, 59, 69, 70, 73, 78, 88, 97, 98, 99, 156. See also *Intonation for 2-, 3-, 4-word phrases.*
Intro phrase, 130, 138
Phrasing, 3–5, 10, 35. See also *Intonation*
Pitch — see *Intonation*
Placement test
   Dictation, vii
   Grammar, xv
Plain form — see *Unchanging form*
Pluperfect, vi

Index

Plural
  Nouns, 7, 8, 9, 10, 25, 99, 101
  Pronouns, 8, 13
  Verbs, 37
Polarity, 22, 46
Positive, 104, 162. See also *Negative*
Possessive, 16, 17
Possibility, 138–139, 169. See also *Helping verb*
Preposition, 189–195
  Of direction, 58–60, 78
  Of location, 33, 49
  Of time, 78, 93
  Of manner, 79, 93
Present perfect — see *Duo*
Present tense, 17–18, 24, 36–48, 113
Probability, 139, 169. See also *Helping verb*
Progressive — see *Continuous*
Pronoun, 11–17, 21, 25–26, 31–32, 45, 49, 56, 63, 65, 72, 85, 112, 117
Pronoun stress, 11–12, 14, 15, 17, 29, 32, 36, 45, 58, 59, 65, 85
Pronunciation — see *chart at beginning of Index*
Punctuation mark, 282

Q

Question, 21–22, 43, 46, 64, 66, 85, 89, 90, 91, 132, 134, 228
Question flip, 21–22, 26, 43–45, 47, 50, 64, 65, 72, 85, 90–92, 103, 116, 227, 228
Question intonation, 10–11, 19

R

R, American, 182, 280
Reduced sounds, 29, 75

Reflexive pronoun, 282
Relative pronoun, 150–152. See also *Reverse modifier*
Reported speech, 128, 130–134, 177–178, 212
Reverse modifier, 152–153, 227
Rhythm, 18, 19, 153. See also *Intonation*

S

Schwa [ə], 6, 29, 68, 75, 82, 180–182
Semi-colon, 282
Sentence
  Clause, viii, 154, 227, 279
  Command, 48
  Phrase — see *Intonation for 2-, 3-, 4-word phrases*
  Question — see *Noun question*
  Statement — see *Noun statement*
Sign language, 81
Simple form — see *Unchanging form*
Singular noun — see *Noun, singular*
Sound/meaning shifts, 97–99. See also *Intonation*
Speech analysis, xxiv
Speech music, 183–186. See also *Intonation*
Squeezed out syllables, 53
Staircase intonation, 5, 7, 29, 180, 181
Stand, 119–120. See also *Phrasal verb*
Statement, indirect, 132–134. See also *Reported speech*
Story, 1–6, 28, 52, 74, 96, 129, 150, 177, 204, 225
Stress, 183–186. See also *Noun intonation* and *Pronoun stress*
Subject noun, 11–12, 40
  Compacting, 154

Subject pronoun — see *Pronoun*
Subjunctive — see *Duo*
Superlative, 55–58
Symbol — see *chart at beginning of Index*
Synonym, 232
Syntax, 283

T

T sounds, 61, 181, 226
Tag, 22, 46–47, 66–67, 115, 171
Tense (verb), 17, 24, 25, 26, 36, 48, 60–62, 65, 67, 94, 212–213, 218–220, 238
Tense (vowel), 75
Test diagnostic, xxiv
Test placement, vii, xv–xxii
That, 151, 152
The — see *Article*
There is, 166–167
Three-word phrases, 184–185. See also *Intonation*
Time words, 23, 159. See also *Modifier*
Transitions of nouns and verbs, 80, 188
Two-word phrases, 183–184. See also *Compound noun* and *Intonation*

U

Unchanging form, 39, 41, 43–44, 48, 59, 60
Uncountable noun — see *Nouns, uncountable*
Unvoiced consonant, 61, 82

V

V sound, 166
Verb
  Active, 227, 232–235
  Helping verb, 39–42, 50, 60, 62, 64, 65, 70, 83, 85, 110
  Obligation, 140, 169
  Opinion, 139, 144, 169

Possibility, 138–139, 169
Probability, 139, 169
Intonation, 80, 85, 218–220. See also *Intonation*
Intransitive, 281
Modal, 281
Passive, 216, 227, 232–235
Perception, 143–145
Tense, 212, 213, 218–220, 238. See *Past tense, Present tense, Duo*
To be, 17–18, 24, 28, 34, 46, 48, 60, 70–71, 83, 89–92, 216–218
Transitive, 283
Verb map, xii
Voice, 283. See also *Active voice* and *Passive voice*
Voiced consonant, 61, 82
Vowel, 4, 6, 7, 29, 61, 75
Vowel Chart, xiii

W

W, xxiii. See also *Word connections*
What, 151
Who, 152
Wish, 137
Word connections, 4–6, 12, 13, 14, 29, 75, 180
Word order, 227–228. See also *Question flip*
Word stress, 82. See *Intonation, Noun intonation,* and *Verb intonation*
Would, 215. See also *Duo*
Writing, 4, 22, 153, 232, 233

X, Y, Z

Y — see *Word connections*
Z or S, xxiv, 4, 6, 8, 9, 10, 61